THE RUSSIAN REFERENCE GRAMMAR

Core Grammar in Functional Context

John L. Watzke
College of Education
University of Iowa
Iowa City, Iowa

James W. Sweigert, Jr.
Price Laboratory School
Northern University High School
University of Northern Iowa
Cedar Falls, Iowa

ACTR
American Council of Teachers of Russian
1776 Massachusetts Ave., NW Washington DC 20036

KENDALL/HUNT PUBLISHING COMPANY
4050 Westmark Drive   Dubuque, Iowa 52002

Quick Reference Table of Contents

Acknowledgments

The Russian Reference Grammar
is dedicated in memory of

Jane Barley and Frederick Johnson

**May We Carry on
Their Tradition of Excellence
in Russian Language Education!**

This reference book would not have been possible without grants from the U.S. Department of Education to the Center of Russian Language and Culture (CORLAC) (Zita Dabars, Director), in cooperation with the American Council of Teachers of Russian (ACTR) (Dan Davidson, Executive Director). Grateful appreciation is extended to Jose L. Martinez of the U.S. Department of Education, International Research and Studies Program. This project was directed by Zita Dabars, Friends School, Baltimore, MD with contributions from George Morris, St. Louis University High School, St. Louis, MO. Their guidance and feedback proved invaluable during the development of this reference text. Thanks is extended to the staff at CORLAC, who facilitated correspondence over the two years of this project and to Patricia Kardash and Helen Meigs for the proofing of late drafts. The authors are grateful to Patricia Kardash for her careful editing of drafts and for her willingness to assist us throughout the entire editing process of this book.

Many colleagues in the Russian teaching community field-tested and made valuable suggestions for *The Russian Reference Grammar*: Helen Meigs (Allderdice High School, Pittsburgh, PA), Alan James (St. Mary's High School, Medford, OR), Jane Shuffelton (Brighton High School, Rochester, NY), Larry Lonard (Topeka High School, Topeka, KS), Guenther Teschauer and Ruth Edelman, (Tenafly High School and Middle School, Tenafly, NJ), Nicholas Toodzio (Eastern High School, Lansing, MI). During the seventh (1995) NEH/CORLAC Institute in Russian Language and Culture at Bryn Mawr College, Bryn Mawr, PA, teachers of Russian who were participants reviewed *The Russian Reference Grammar* materials. Thanks also to Professor Tom Garza (Department of Slavic Languages, University of Texas at Austin) for early feedback and encouragement. Special thanks to Matthew Doyle, зверёк, for help with final page layout of the text. Огромное спасибо for the understanding and support of our multilingual wives: Lisa and Ella.

Text Layout and Design: Matthew Doyle, Jim Sweigert, Jr. and John Watzke
Cover Design: John Watzke
Illustrations: Ivan Bilibin, 1899
Editor: Patricia Kardash

Any errors found in *The Russian Reference Grammar* are solely the responsibility of the authors.

Colleagues interested in appropriate textbooks for use with this reference text may choose to consult *Russian Face to Face*, Level 1 and *Russian Face to Face*, Level 2, published by National Textbook Company, Lincolnwood, IL and *Russian Faces and Voices* and *Мир русских*, published by Kendall/Hunt Publishing Company, Dubuque, IA.

The Russian Reference Grammar
Core Grammar in Functional Context

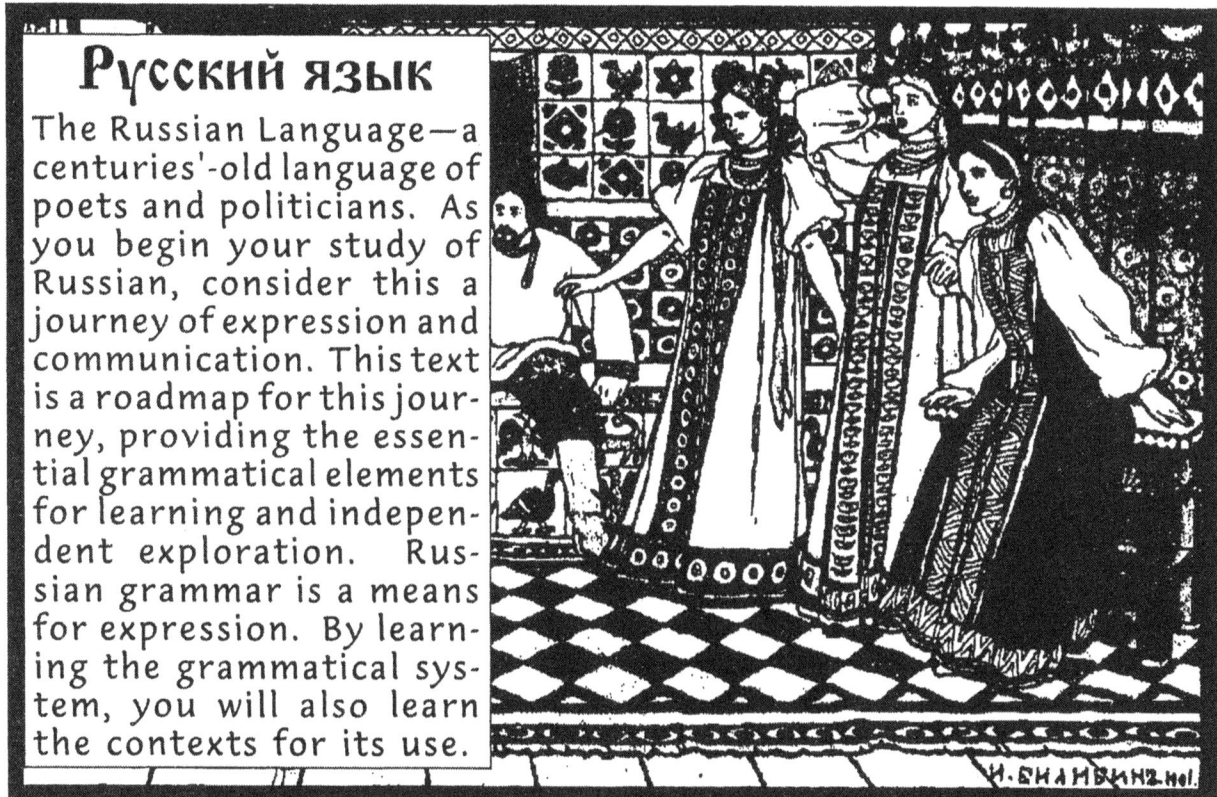

Русский язык

The Russian Language—a centuries'-old language of poets and politicians. As you begin your study of Russian, consider this a journey of expression and communication. This text is a roadmap for this journey, providing the essential grammatical elements for learning and independent exploration. Russian grammar is a means for expression. By learning the grammatical system, you will also learn the contexts for its use.

Purpose of *The Russian Reference Grammar*

This reference text is designed to be a supplemental tool for use with the most current Russian language textbooks. It is a practical guide which will benefit novice through advanced learners with its presentation of a substantial core grammar in an easy-to-use and relevent text. The presentation of grammatical categories and of grammar points follows a descriptive organization, while noting the functional and contextual usage these grammar points facilitate. Students will find *The Russian Reference Grammar* an ideal tool for their study and exploration of the Russian language. Teachers will find the text useful for planning and designing instructional sequences and as a resource text for student remediation.

Organization of the Text

The Russian Reference Grammar includes multiple ways to reference questions of grammatical rules and their functional use. **Chapters** are organized according to parts of speech. Each chapter begins with an **overview**, designed to introduce the learner to grammatical concepts. **Reference tables** have been created to provide short and concise resources for the student. *Grammar points* are presented in descriptive order. Each grammar point is introduced by a *reference header*, designed to aid both student and teacher:

Chapter *Grammar point*   *Grammar point title*

5.16 THE PHRASE ДРУГ ДРУ́ГА **IN DIFFERENT CASES**
    Function: Expressing reciprocal actions (the idea of
    "each other")

> Faces and Voices
> Chapter 1 B
> Pages 12-15

    Related function   *Textbook reference*

Several reference lists help to organize the core grammar. Both a **short** and **expanded table of contents** outline the grammar points in each chapter. A list of all reference tables and *indices* of *functions and topical usage* and the *Russian grammatical system* allow for the quick access of information.

Suggested Uses for *The Russian Reference Grammar*
Many uses for this reference text were employed in practice during its piloting. The following list highlights suggestions made by piloting teachers.

Student copies - By providing that each student receives his or her own copy of the reference text, teachers can encourage the taking of additional notes, the highlighting of important or key elements, and the increase in familiarity with this resource over the course of four to five years of language study.

Comprehensive review - This reference text provides a complete summary of the grammatical concepts presented on a lesson, unit and semester basis. Class review of these grammar points can begin from the earliest levels of instruction.

Practice using the reference grammar - Walk students through using the reference grammar to locate information. With very little practice, students will find this an intuitive text to aid in their study of the language.

A single text for all levels - Some Russian language programs have mixed levels of Russian in the classroom. This reference resource provides a single text for all students and encourages peer teaching in its design.

Individual student help - When students are absent from class, provide students with the grammar points related to classwork to aid in their quick completion of make-up work. Students should be encouraged to consult the reference grammar before seeking individual help or when studying away from the classroom. Students who own their own copy of the reference should be encourage to add additional notes to the text.

Student projects - Encourage students to use the reference text when working on individual and group projects in Russian. Related functions will aid in their coupling of accurate grammatical usage and creative expression.

The authors welcome comments and suggestions for improvement to future editions of *The Russian Reference Grammar*. Teachers with experience using this reference text with students at every level of instruction are encouraged to contact the authors at their addresses listed in the annual American Council of Teachers of Russian (ACTR) membership directory.

List of Abbreviations

The following abbreviations are used throughout the reference grammar and are commonly found in Russian language textbooks.

Abbreviation	Full word/meaning	Abbreviation	Full word/meaning
I	type one conjugation	n.	noun
II	type two conjugation	num.	numeral, number
acc.	accusative (case)	obj.	object
adj.	adjective	pf., perf.	perfective
adv.	adverb	pl.	plural
anim.	animate	poss.	possession/-ive
comp.	comparative	pred.	predicate
conj.	conjunction	prep.	preposition/-al
dat.	dative (case)	pron.	pronoun
demonstr.	demonstrative	refl.	reflexive
det.	determinate	Rus.	Russian
dim., dimin.	diminutive	sent.	sentence
dir. obj.	direct object	sing.	singular
Engl.	English	s.o.	someone
f., fem.	feminine	s.t.	something
gen.	genitive (case)	subj.	subject
impf., imperf.	imperfective	subord.	subordinate
impers.	impersonal	super., superl.	superlative
inan.	inanimate	v.	verb
indet.	indeterminate	v. intrans.	intransitive verb
indir. obj.	indirect object	VOM	verb(s) of motion
instr.	instrumental (case)	v. trans.	transitive verb
interj.	interjection	***textbooks:***	
interr.	interrogative	Face to Face L1	Face to Face Level One
lit.,	literally	Face to Face L2	Face to Face Level Two
m., masc., mas.	masculine	Faces and Voices	Russian Faces and Voices
n., neut.	neuter		
nom.	nominative(case)	Мир русских	Мир русских

The Firebird, **Жар-птица**, is a mythical character in Russian fairy tales. Like the Russian language, it is both beautiful and elusive. We have chosen the Firebird as a symbol of the magic of language learning and of the world which is opened by the study of Russian.

List of Reference Tables

Comprehensive Table of Contents

Chapter 1

ALPHABET and PRONUNCIATION
Алфавит и произношение

1.1   The Russian alphabet: Русский алфавит.   Saint Cyrill is credited with creating what is now known as the Russian or Cyrillic alphabet (кириллица). Borrowing from the Greek alphabet, Slavonic monks devised an early spelling system for their language. The modern Russian alphabet is presented below, with notes on spelling rules and pronunciation in the following section.

REFERENCE TABLE 1A: THE CYRILLIC ALPHABET: HANDWRITTEN, PRINT, [RUSSIAN NAME], APPROXIMATE PRONUNCIATION IN ENGLISH (BOLD LETTERS)

Аа	А а	[a] **ah**, n**o**t	*Кк*	К к	[ка] **c**ar	*Хх*	Х х	[ха] **wh**o
Бб	Б б	[бэ] **b**et	*Лл*	Л л	[эль] fe**ll**	*Цц*	Ц ц	[цэ] Me**ts**
Вв	В в	[вэ] **v**et	*Мм*	М м	[эм] hi**m**	*Чч*	Ч ч	[чэ] **ch**air
Гг	Г г	[гэ] **g**et	*Нн*	Н н	[эн] **h**en	*Шш*	Ш ш	[ша] **sh**ot
Дд	Д д	[дэ] **d**ead	*Оо*	О о	[o] l**ow**	*Щщ*	Щ щ	[ща] **sh**eet
Ее	Е е	[e] **ye**t	*Пп*	П п	[пэ] **p**en	*Ъъ*	Ъ Ъ	[твёрдый знак] hard sign
Ёё	Ё ё	[ё] **yo**-yo	*Рр*	Р р	[эр] **R**ico (rolled)	*Ыы*	Ы ы	[ы] fair**ly**
Жж Ж ж	Ж ж	[ж] plea**s**ure	*Сс*	С с	[эс] re**s**t	*ьь*	Ь ь	[мягкий знак] soft sign
Зз	З з	[зэ] **Z**en	*Тт*	Т т	[тэ] **t**ent	*Ээ*	Э э	[э] b**e**t
Ии	И и	[и] f**ee**t	*Уу*	У у	[у] c**oo**l	*Юю*	Ю ю	[ю] yo**u**th
Йй	Й й	[и краткое] bo**y**	*Фф*	Ф ф	[эф] e**ff**ort	*Яя*	Я я	[я] **ya**rd

REFERENCE TABLE 1B: COMPARISON OF WRITTEN AND PRINTED WORDS IN RUSSIAN

Russian handwriting	Russian print	
Пишите.	Пиши́те.	Write.
Где школа?	Где шко́ла?	Where is the school?
Вот она.	Вот она́.	There it is.
Наша школа	На́ша шко́ла.	Our school.
Хорошо. Плохо.	Хорошо́. Пло́хо.	Good. Bad.
Магазин.	Магази́н.	Store.

Note: When Russians write in their language, they do not place a stress mark above the stressed vowel in a word. In most Russian language textbooks for foreigners, these marks are placed over stressed vowels. Students of Russian are often required to write them to aid in the memorization of pronunciation patterns. However, authentic texts in Russian do not have stress marks and often do not distinguish a e from a ё. As students learn Russian, they gradually acquire an ear for stress. In the mean time, writing the stress of a word will facilitate this process.

1.2   Notes on pronunciation and spelling. Several letters in the Cyrillic alphabet are quite similar to English in both spelling and pronunciation: А а, Е е, К к, М м, О о, Т т. Others look like familiar English letters, but are pronounced differently: В (like "**v**" in **v**et), И (like "**ee**" in f**ee**t), Н н (like "**n**" in he**n**), Р р (like "**r**" in **R**ico), С с (like "**s**" in re**s**t), У у (like "**oo**" in c**oo**l). Still others have spelling which is unfamiliar and may have pronunciation with no English equivalent: Ж ж, Й й, Ы ы, Щ щ, etc..

Most Russian language textbooks include extensive sections and corresponding audiotapes to aid in pronunciation practice. Careful practice of the pronunciation of words and statements should be observed.

<u>Vowels</u>

Russian has ten vowels, which are paired according to whether they occur after soft or hard consonants.

Hard vowels, those which follow hard consonants	а	э	ы	о	у
Soft vowels, those which follow soft consonants	я	е	и	ё	ю

CHAPTER 1: ALPHABET AND PRONUNCIATION

Consonants Russian consonants are either voiced or unvoiced (*when a voiced consonant is pronounced, vibration can generally be felt on one's Adam's apple*). Most of these consonants have both hard and soft counterparts. Hardness and softness is often referred to in terms of palatalization. When a consonant is pronounced hard, it is **unpalatalized**: the middle of the tongue is lowered and drawn back somewhat. The consonants ж and й are always hard. When a consonant is pronounced soft, it is **palatalized**: the middle of the tongue flattens against the upper hard palate of the mouth. The consonants ш, ц, ч and щ are always soft. Soft consonants can be distinguished in spelling as they are followed by a soft sign, ‑ь, or the soft vowels я, е, и, ё and ю: учи́тель, Та́ня.

Voiced consonants	б, в, г, д, з, л, м, н, р	*always hard:* ж, й
Unvoiced consonants	п, ф, к, т, с, х,	*always soft:* ш, ц, ч, щ

Spelling Rules Spelling rules outline specific instances when certain vowels cannot follow certain consonants. The following basic spelling rules should be memorized. The knowledge of spelling rules aids in the correct usage of declension endings and spelling.

REFERENCE TABLE 1C: BASIC SPELLING RULES

Rule 1:	Write и, never ы after:	ж ш ч щ г к х *example:* хоро́ший, кни́ги, ма́рки
Rule 2:	Write а and у, never я or ю after:	ж ш ц ч щ г к х *example:* му́жа, хоро́шую кни́гу
Rule 3:	Write е, never о, when unstressed after:	ж ш ц ч щ *example:* хорошо́, but хоро́шее; большо́й but бо́льше

1.3 Tongue twisters. Russian tongue twisters, **скорогово́рки**, are numerous. The following provide the learner with examples of pronunciation and spelling rules.

REFERENCE TABLE 1D: RUSSIAN TONGUE TWISTERS FOR PRONUNCIATION AND SPELLING RULES

Скорогово́рка	**Tongue twister**
У Са́ши ша́шки.	Sasha has checkers pieces.
Шла Са́ша по шоссе́.	Sasha walked along the highway.
Мака́ра укуси́л кома́р.	Makar was bitten by a mosquito.

Хохла́тые хохоту́шки
   хохота́ли: Ха-ха-ха!
	With their hair sticking up (*lit.*,
	   tufted), the laughers laughed,
	   "ha, ha, ha!"

Ма́ма мы́ла Ми́лу мы́лом.	Mom washed Mila with soap.

На дворе́ — трава́,
   на траве́ — дрова́.
	The yard is covered with grass;
	   there's firewood on the grass.

Chapter 2

NOUNS
Имена́ существи́тельные

2.1   Overview: Nouns in Russian. In Russian, as in English, nouns are words that represent **people, places** and **things.** Russian nouns function and appear very much like their English counterparts, although there are some differences:

No use of articles Russian nouns **are not** set off by articles (*a, an, the*). For example: Мы ви́дели **заво́д.** In this sentence the word **заво́д** can mean either *a factory* or *the factory*, depending on the context.

Use of gender Russian nouns possess grammatical gender, that is, words are masculine, feminine, or neuter. While English has natural gender, determined by the sex of a person (*sister* is feminine, *brother* is masculine), in Russian this applies not only to people, but also to places and things.

REFERENCE TABLE 2A: USE OF GENDER IN NOMINATIVE SINGULAR

Masculine		Feminine		Neuter	
1) Nouns ending in hard consonant: **брат** *brother*		1) Most nouns ending in -а/-я: **сестра́** *sister*		1) Almost all nouns ending in -о/-е/-ё: **окно́** *window,* **кафе́** *café,* **бельё** *linens*	
2) Nouns ending in -й: **воробе́й** *sparrow*		2) Most nouns ending in a soft sign: **мать** *mother,* **дочь** *daughter*			
3) Some nouns ending in -а/-я, especially certain people: **де́душка** *grandpa,* **па́па** *dad*				2) Nouns ending in -мя: **и́мя** *name*	
4) Some nouns ending in a soft sign: **медве́дь** *bear,* **дождь** *rain*					
брат	brother	сестра́	sister	письмо́	letter
парк	park	фа́брика	factory	зда́ние	building
стол	table	ру́чка	pen	окно́	window
музе́й	museum	семья́	family	вре́мя	time
мужчи́на	man	тетра́дь	notebook	кино́	cinema
гусь	goose	дверь	door	метро́	subway

Indeclinable nouns Some borrowed (foreign) words in Russian are indeclinable, that is, they do not change for grammatical case. Most of these words are **neuter.** While the list below is by no means exhaustive, the words given are ones often used:

Borrowed and proper nouns (ending in -о/-е/-и/-ю):

метро́	subway	кака́о	cocoa
кино́	cinema	фойе́	foyer
пиани́но	piano	шоссе́	highway
ра́дио	radio	такси́	taxi
купе́	compartment	меню́	menu
кафе́	café	интервью́	interview
Чика́го	Chicago	Со́чи	Sochi (masc.)

Plural Plural forms indicate the presence of **more than one** of the objects being mentioned. Plural forms do not have gender, and follow different patterns for their formation, regardless of the gender of the noun. Modifying adjectives are same for the plurals of all genders. Below are examples in the **nominative case:**

Singular (gender is used)		Plural (gender not used)	
но́в**ый стол**	*the new table*	но́в**ые** стол**ы́**	*new tables*
но́в**ая ка́рта**	*the new map*	но́в**ые** ка́рт**ы**	*new maps*
но́в**ое окно́**	*the new window*	но́в**ые** о́кн**а**	*new windows*

Formation of the Nominative Plural For most singular nouns that are masculine or feminine, any vowels on the end of the word are dropped, and the ending -ы/-и is added. Remember that after the letters г, ж, к, х, ч, ш, щ only и can be added. **Do not use ы**

REFERENCE TABLE 2B: FORMATION OF THE NOMINATIVE PLURAL FROM MASCULINE AND FEMININE SINGULAR

Singular nouns ending in hard consonant: Add -ы/-и			
стол столы́		парк па́рки	
Singular nouns ending in a vowel -а/-я: Drop -а/-я, add -ы/-и:			
ка́рта	ка́рты	ру́чка ру́чки	
мужчи́на	мужчи́ны	семья́ се́мьи	
Most singular nouns ending in a -ь, й: Drop -ь, й, add -и:			
преподава́тель	преподава́тели	музе́й	музе́и
тетра́дь	тетра́ди	воробе́й	воробе́и

Most neuter nouns form plurals differently. Unless the noun is indeclinable, the -о is dropped and an -а is added, or the -е is dropped and a -я is added:

REFERENCE TABLE 2C: FORMATION OF THE NOMINATIVE PLURAL FROM NEUTER SINGULAR

Drop -о, add -а		Drop -е, add -я	
окно́	о́кн**а**	зда́ние	зда́ни**я**
письмо́	пи́сьм**а**	упражне́ние	упражне́ни**я**

Special plural forms Some plural forms are different from the ones already listed and should be considered exceptions. (The list below is only a partial one.)

REFERENCE TABLE 2D: SPECIAL NOMINATIVE PLURAL FORMS

1) Masculine nouns with plural in -á/-я

бéрег	берегá	shore	**shores**
вéчер	вечерá	evening	**evenings**
глаз	глазá	eye	**eyes**
гóрод	городá	city	**cities**
дирéктор	директорá	director	**directors**
дóктор	докторá	doctor	**doctors**
дом	домá	house	**houses**
лес	лесá	forest	**forests**
нóмер	номерá	number; issue	**numbers; issues**
пáспорт	паспортá	passport	**passports**
пóезд	поездá	train	**trains**
профéссор	профессорá	professor	**professors**
учúтель	учителя́	teacher	**teachers**

2) Masculine nouns with plural in -ья (-ья)

стул	стýлья	chair	**chairs**
брат	брáтья	brother	**brothers**
дéрево	дерéвья	tree	**trees**
муж	мужья́	husband	**husbands**
сын	сыновья́	son	**sons**
друг	друзья́	friend	**friends**

3) Plurals of nouns in -анин/-янин

англичáнин	англичáне	Englishman	**Englishmen**
россия́нин	россия́не	Russian [resident(s) of Russia]	**Russians**
армяни́н	армя́не	Armenian	**Armenians**
граждани́н	граждáне	citizen	**citizens**

4) Plurals of nouns in -ёнок/-онок

котёнок	котя́та	kitten	**kittens**
утёнок	утя́та	duckling	**ducklings**
ребёнок	ребя́та (or) дéти *	child	**kids, guys** (or) **children**
волчóнок	волчáта	wolf cub	**wolf cubs**

5) Plural of the word человéк

человéк	лю́ди **	person	**people**

* Note: Ребёнок has two plurals: ребя́та, which means *kids, guys, young men*, and дéти, which means *children*. Дéти is preferred when a parent is referring to her/his own children, or when an adult is referring to little children, while ребя́та is preferred in direct address: Ребя́та, давáйте сыгрáем в баскетбóл. *Hey, guys, let's play basketball.*

** Note: The plural лю́ди looks nothing like человéк. When used in the genitive plural, especially after numbers (семь человéк), the form is the same as the singular.

Nouns Used in the Plural Only Some nouns, especially those indicating objects found in pairs or comprised of two or more components, are used only in the plural. These nouns are **never** used as singular nouns in Russian, and therefore have no gender. Examples:

брюки, штаны, джинсы	pants, slacks, jeans
ножницы	scissors
трусы/трусики	underpants/panties
очки	(eye)glasses
весы	scale(s)
выборы	election(s)

Nouns Used in the Singular Only Many nouns, especially those denoting foods like vegetables and fruits, are viewed as a collective, whole species, and are thus used only in the singular. A different word will be when speaking about just one item.

Collective singular (whole species)	English	One item (e.g. *one* grape, carrot, etc.)
виноград	grapes	виноградина
капуста	cabbage	кочан капусты (head of...)
картофель (картошка)	potatoes	картофелина, картошка
морковь	carrots	морковка
лук	onions	луковица
изюм	raisins	изюмина
горох	peas	горошина
шоколад	chocolate	шоколадка

Some nouns have plural forms, but are often used in the singular to express the idea of the collective whole—again, a certain type or species. This is especially true of animals and trees:

Sample sentences

Когда мы жили в Сан-Диего, у нас в саду была только **пальма**.	When we lived in San Diego we just had **palm trees** in our yard.
В Курганской области живёт **кабан**.	In the Kurgan region live **wild boars**.

Animacy In Russian, all **animate** masculine nouns (livings beings like people and animals) have the same form for the accusative case as the genitive case. This differs from the declension of inanimate nouns.

Sample sentences

Таня видит **стол**.	Tanya sees the **table**. (inanimate accusative case)
Таня видит **Дейва** и **тигра**.	Tanya sees **Dave** and the **tiger**. (animate accusative case)
Это машина **Дейва** и **тигра**.	This is the car **of Dave** and the **tiger**. (genitive case)

Note that feminine nouns have the same ending in the accusative case, regardless of animacy:

Таня видит **школу**.	Tanya sees the **school**. (inanimate)
Таня видит **Наташу**.	Tanya sees **Natasha**. (animate)

Diminutives Diminutives are formed by adding a suffix to a noun. They are used to denote smallness, as well as emotional nuances such as affection, irony, etc. The emotional nuance used depends on context, much like colloquial speech in any language. Diminutives are used in everyday colloquial speech and are an essential part of the Russian usage of nouns. Whereas English simply says *a small table*, the Russian counterpart **столик** may express a variety of meanings, from *a small table*, or *a nice little table*, to *a restaurant table*.

REFERENCE TABLE 2E: DIMINUTIVE FORMS OF NOUNS

1) Masculine diminutives: formed with suffixes -ец, -ик, -чик, -ок/-ек/-ёк

брат	**брáтец**	brother (affectionate)
дом	**дóмик**	house (smallness, or making fun of)
суп	**сýпчик**	soup (affectionate—*a little bit*)
чай	**чаёк**	tea (affectionate—*a little bit*)
друг	**дружóк**	friend (affectionate, esp. with pets)

2) Feminine diminutives: formed with suffixes -ица, -ичка, -(оч)ка

сестрá	**сестрица, сестрИчка**	sister (affectionate, and **сестрИчка** even more so)
пéсня	**пéсенка**	little song (affectionate)
минýта	**минýточка**	"little" minute/second (smallness)

3) Neuter diminutives: formed with suffixes -(и)ко, -(е)цо/це

лицó	**лИчико**	face (smallness, affection)
óблако	**óблачко**	cloud (smallness)
письмó	**письмецó**	letter (smallness)

Diminutives are also common when forming nicknames from first names. When addressing one another, Russian family members and friends most often use the diminutive form of the first name. While some names have more than one diminutive, the ones listed below are the most frequently used:

REFERENCE TABLE 2F: DIMINUTIVE FORMS OF FIRST NAMES

Boys' Names		Girls' Names	
Full Form	*Diminutive*	*Full Form*	*Diminutive*
Алексáндр	Сáша, Шýра	Алексáндра	Сáша
Алексéй	Алёша	Анна	Аня
Андрéй	Андрюша	ВалентИна	Вáля
БорИс	Бóря	ЕкатерИна	Кáтя
ВИктор	ВИтя	Елéна	Лéна
ВладИмир	Волóдя	ИрИна	Ира
Лев	Лёва	МарИя	Мáша
МихаИл	МИша	Натáлья	Натáша
Николáй	Кóля	НИна	НИна
Олéг	Алик	Оксáна	Ксéня
Пётр	Пéтя	Ольга	Оля
Ромáн	Рóма	Светлáна	Свéта
Сергéй	Серёжа	Татьяна	Тáня

Use of Adjectives as Nouns

An adjectival noun is one that looks like an adjective but functions as a noun. Usually the "missing" noun is understood, and instead of saying a longer phrase (adjective + noun), Russians use only the adjective part:

столо́вая	cafeteria	(ко́мната—room is understood)
ру́сский	Russian	(челове́к—person is understood)

Adjectival nouns are often found in:

1) **Names of rooms or establishments** (understood noun is ко́мната)

ва́нная	bathroom	пра́чечная	laundry
столо́вая	dining room	убо́рная	janitor's closet
спа́льня	bedroom	учи́тельская	teacher's lounge
гости́ная	living room	пельме́нная	dumpling bar

2) **Names of grammatical terms** (understood noun is и́мя *name*)

прилага́тельное	adjective
существи́тельное	noun
числи́тельное	numeral

3) **Names of time terms** (understood noun is вре́мя *time*)

про́шлое	the past
настоя́щее	the present
бу́дущее	the future

Note: Adjectival nouns decline like other adjectives (в гости́н**ой** *in the living room*).

Russian Names Russians have both first (и́мя) and last (фами́лия) names. They also have patronymics (о́тчество), a name formed from the father's first name placed between the first and last names. For example, Tatyana and Mikhail Petrov (Татья́на и Михаи́л Петро́вы) have a father whose name is Ivan (Ива́н):

First name	Patronymic	Last name
Татья́на	Ива́новна	Петро́ва*
Михаи́л	Ива́нович	Петро́в

*****Note:** Last names, like patronymics, also follow rules of gender. In most cases a Russian woman's last name ends in **-a** .

Note that feminine patronymics end in **-овна** (**-евна**), and masculine patronymics end in **-ович** (**-евич**). Below are some common patronymics:

REFERENCE TABLE 2G: MASCULINE AND FEMININE PATRONYMICS

Father's first name	Masculine patronymic	Feminine patronymic
Алекса́ндр	Алекса́ндрович	Алекса́ндровна
Алексе́й	Алексе́евич	Алексе́евна
Андре́й	Андре́евич	Андре́евна
Анто́н	Анто́нович	Анто́новна
Бори́с	Бори́сович	Бори́совна
Валенти́н	Валенти́нович	Валенти́новна
Ви́ктор	Ви́кторович	Ви́кторовна
Влади́мир	Влади́мирович	Влади́мировна
Ива́н	Ива́нович	Ива́новна
Игорь	Игорьевич	Игорьевна
Михаил	Миха́йлович	Миха́йловна
Никола́й	Никола́евич	Никола́евна
Оле́г	Оле́гович	Оле́говна
Пётр	Петро́вич	Петро́вна
Рома́н	Рома́нович	Рома́новна
Серге́й	Серге́евич	Серге́евна

Though somewhat like a middle name, a patronymic has more importance because it is a sign of respect, especially toward adults older than you or ones you don't know very well. The closest English equivalent is *Miss, Mrs., Mr.* Russians addressing foreigners would rarely form a patronymic out of their name, and might address an adult using **господи́н** (Mr.) or **госпожа́** (Mrs.):

До́брое у́тро, **господи́н Джоунс**!	Good morning, **Mr. Jones**!
До́брый день, **госпожа́ Ро́бинсон**!	Good afternoon, **Mrs. Robinson**!

REFERENCE TABLES 2H: DECLENSION OF RUSSIAN AND NON-RUSSIAN PROPER NAMES

Russian Male Names

nom.	Андре́й Буля́нов	Игорь Бу́нин	Вита́лий Ту́льский
gen.	(у) Андре́я Буля́нова	Игоря Бу́нина	Вита́лия Ту́льского
dat.	(к) Андре́ю Буля́нову	Игорю Бу́нину	Вита́лию Ту́льскому
acc.	Андре́я Буля́нова	Игоря Бу́нина	Вита́лия Ту́льского
instr.	(с) Андре́ем Буля́новым	Игорем Бу́ниным	Вита́лием Ту́льским
prep.	(об) Андре́е Буля́нове	Игоре Бу́нине	Вита́лии Ту́льском

Russian Female Names

nom.	Ка́тя Бога́това	Све́та Рае́вская	Ната́лья Во́лгина
gen.	(у) Ка́ти Бога́товой	Све́ты Рае́вской	Ната́льи Во́лгиной
dat.	(к) Ка́ти Бога́товой	Све́те Рае́вской	Ната́лье Во́лгиной
acc.	Ка́тю Бога́тову	Све́ту Рае́вскую	Ната́лью Во́лгину
instr.	(с) Ка́тей Бога́товой	Све́той Рае́вской	Ната́льей Во́лгиной
prep.	(о) Ка́те Бога́товой	Све́те Рае́вской	Ната́лье Во́лгиной

Non-Russian Male Names

nom.	Джон Смит	Хью Ба́рли
gen.	(у) Джо́на Сми́та	(у) Хью Ба́рли
dat.	(к) Джо́ну Сми́ту	(к) Хью Ба́рли
acc.	Джо́на Сми́та	Хью Ба́рли
instr.	(с) Джо́ном Сми́том	(с) Хью Ба́рли
prep.	(о) Джо́не Сми́те	(о) Хью Ба́рли

Non-Russian Female Names

nom.	Джейн Смит	Са́ра Фо́нда
gen.	(у) Джейн Смит	(у) Са́ры Фо́нды
dat.	(к) Джейн Смит	(к) Са́ре Фо́нде
acc.	Джейн Смит	Са́ру Фо́нду
instr.	(с) Джейн Смит	(с) Са́рой Фо́ндой
prep.	(о) Джейн Смит	(о) Са́ре Фо́нде

2.2	**GENDER OF NOUNS**	Face to Face L1
	Function: Finding out where someone or something is	Chapter 2C Pages 67-69

Nouns in Russian can be one of **three genders**: **masculine**, **feminine**, or **neuter**. Determining the gender of a noun is important because the speaker can then substitute the appropriate gender of the pronoun and can also determine the appropriate endings for the noun. For example:

Где **соба́ка**? Вот **соба́ка**.　　　Where is the **dog**? There's the **dog**.
may be written or spoken...
Где **она́**? Вот **она́**.　　　Where is **it/she**? There **she/it is**.

The **gender** of a noun can generally be determined by its **ending**. The few exceptions to the general rules should simply be memorized when they are encountered.

Gender of Russian Nouns

Masculine:	**Examples**
•Nouns ending in a hard consonant	стол, дневни́к, уче́бник
•Nouns that refer to males	Ва́ня, Джон, Ми́ша, де́душка
•Some nouns ending in a soft sign	слова́рь, портфе́ль, ла́герь
•Nouns ending in a soft sign and　denoting a profession	учи́тель, писа́тель
•Nouns ending in - **й**	музе́й, воробе́й, мавзоле́й
Feminine:	
•Nouns ending in - **а** or - **я**	Москва́, шко́ла, семья́
•Nouns that refer to females	Ма́ша, А́нна, Мэ́ри
•Some nouns that end in a soft sign	тетра́дь, пло́щадь, о́сень
•Nouns ending in - **ия**	аудито́рия, геогра́фия
Neuter:	
•Nouns ending in - **о** or -**е**	письмо́, мя́со, мо́ре, упражне́ние
•Nouns ending in - **мя**	и́мя, вре́мя, зна́мя

2.3 PLURAL NOUNS
Function: Expressing plurality, making objects plural

Face to Face L1
Chapter 4B
Pages 102-103

Basic plural endings for nouns in Russian are formed by adding or replacing the final vowel of **masculine** and **feminine** nouns with -ы or -и and by adding -а or -я to **neuter** nouns.

Spelling rules often require the use of -и in place of -ы to form the plural of masculine and feminine nouns. After the letters ж, ш, ч, щ (hushings), г, к, х (gutturals), and whenever the noun ends in -й or -ь, -и is used to form the plural. Examples are given in the chart below:

Plural nouns		Чей, Чья, Чьё?	Чьи?
Masculine noun endings		*Singular*	*Plural*
-consonant	-ы	журна́л	журна́л**ы**
		телеви́зор	телеви́зор**ы**
		америка́нец*	америка́н**цы**
-ь *becomes*	-и	слова́рь	словар**и́**
-й	-и	музе́й	музе́**и**
spelling rule	-и	каранда́ш	карандаш**и́**
Feminine noun endings		*Singular*	*Plural*
-а *becomes*	-ы	газе́т**а**	газе́т**ы**
-я	-и	семь**я́**	семь**и́**
-ия	-ии	фами́ли**я**	фами́ли**и**
-ь	-и	тетра́д**ь**	тетра́д**и**
spelling rule	-и	кни́г**а**	кни́г**и**
Neuter noun endings		*Singular*	*Plural*
-о *becomes*	-а	письм**о́**	письм**а́**
		окн**о́**	окн**а́**
-е	-я	мо́р**е**	мор**я́**
-ие	-ия	упражне́н**ие**	упражне́н**ия**

* **Note**: Some masculine nouns like this and **пода́рок** (**пода́рки** pl.) have "filler" or "fleeting" vowels in thei nominative singular form. Whenever a vowel is added at the end of these nouns, such as in forming the plural, the filler or fleeting vowel is dropped.

Chapter 3

ADJECTIVES
Имена прилагательные

3.1 Overview: An introduction to Russian adjectives. The two basic functions of adjectives are:

1) to describe nouns:

Какая у неё машина?	**What kind** of car does she have?
У неё **новая** машина.	She has a **red** car.
Какой он человек?	**What kind** of person is he?
Он **добрый** человек.	He is a **good** person.
Какого цвета ваш рюкзак?	**What** color is your backpack?
Синего цвета.	Dark **blue**.
Ваша школа **большая**.	Your school is **large**.
Вчера он был **болен**.	Yesterday he was **sick**.

2) to compare and contrast nouns:

Этот цветок **красивее**.	This flower is **prettier**.
Кто **старше**, твой брат или сестра?	Who is **older**, your brother or sister?
Это его **самая хорошая** песня.	That is his **best** song.
Она **самая умная** ученица.	She is the **smartest** student.

Adjectives in Russian agree in *gender*, *number* and *case* with the words they modify. Note the examples below.

gender, number and case agreement

В Москве **высокие** здания.
In Moscow there are **tall** buildings.

высокие — *neuter, plural, nominative case agreeing with* здания

Конечно, Москва **большой** город.
Of course, Moscow is a **large** city.

большой — *masculine, singular, nominative case agreeing with* город

В Москве мы видели **Красную** площадь.
In Moscow we visited **Red** Square.

Красную — *feminine, singular, accusative case agreeing with* площадь

Long-form adjectival declension follows three basic patterns: hard-stem, soft-stem, mixed-stem. Mixed-stem patterns contain elements of both hard- and soft-stem adjectival endings. The following reference tables present these three adjectival declension patterns with nouns for each of the six cases in Russian by the animacy of the nouns (whether a noun is animate [living] or inanimate [non-living]).

REFERENCE TABLE 3A: MASCULINE ADJECTIVES AND NOUNS (INANIMATE) BY CASE

case	hard-stem	soft-stem	mixed-stem
NOMINATIVE ИМЕНИТЕЛЬНЫЙ	пе́рв**ый** класс	после́дн**ий** кора́бль	*ру́сск**ий** музе́й
GENITIVE РОДИТЕЛЬНЫЙ	пе́рв**ого** кла́сс**а**	после́дн**его** корабл**я́**	ру́сск**ого** музе́**я**
DATIVE ДАТЕЛЬНЫЙ	пе́рв**ому** кла́сс**у**	после́дн**ему** корабл**ю́**	ру́сск**ому** музе́**ю**
ACCUSATIVE ВИНИТЕЛЬНЫЙ	пе́рв**ый** класс	после́дн**ий** кора́бль	ру́сск**ий** музе́й
INSTRUMENTAL ТВОРИТЕЛЬНЫЙ	пе́рв**ым** кла́сс**ом**	после́дн**им** корабл**ём**	ру́сск**им** музе́**ем**
PREPOSITIONAL ПРЕДЛОЖНЫЙ	(о) пе́рв**ом** кла́сс**е**	(о) после́дн**ем** корабл**е́**	(о) ру́сск**ом** музе́**е**

*Note: Spelling rule — after **к** the letter **и** must be written, never **ы**.

REFERENCE TABLE 3B: MASCULINE ADJECTIVES AND NOUNS (ANIMATE) BY CASE

case	hard-stem	soft-stem	mixed-stem
NOMINATIVE ИМЕНИТЕЛЬНЫЙ	пе́рв**ый** журнали́ст	после́дн**ий** секрета́рь	ру́сск**ий** свяще́нник
GENITIVE РОДИТЕЛЬНЫЙ	пе́рв**ого** журнали́ст**а**	после́дн**его** секретар**я́**	ру́сск**ого** свяще́нник**а**
DATIVE ДАТЕЛЬНЫЙ	пе́рв**ому** журнали́ст**у**	после́дн**ему** секретар**ю́**	ру́сск**ому** свяще́нник**у**
ACCUSATIVE ВИНИТЕЛЬНЫЙ	пе́рв**ого** журнали́ст**а**	после́дн**его** секретар**я́**	ру́сск**ого** свяще́нник**а**
INSTRUMENTAL ТВОРИТЕЛЬНЫЙ	пе́рв**ым** журнали́ст**ом**	после́дн**им** секретар**ём**	ру́сск**им** свяще́нник**ом**
PREPOSITIONAL ПРЕДЛОЖНЫЙ	(о) пе́рв**ом** журнали́ст**е**	(о) после́дн**ем** секретар**е́**	(о) ру́сско**м** свяще́нник**е**

REFERENCE TABLE 3C: FEMININE ADJECTIVES AND NOUNS (INANIMATE/ANIMATE) BY CASE

case	hard-stem	soft-stem	mixed-stem	mixed-stem
NOMINATIVE ИМЕНИТЕЛЬНЫЙ	пе́рв**ая** балери́на	после́дн**яя** неде́л**я**	ру́сск**ая** исто́ри**я**	хоро́ш**ая** стать**я́**
GENITIVE РОДИТЕЛЬНЫЙ	пе́рв**ой** балери́н**ы**	после́дн**ей** неде́л**и**	ру́сск**ой** исто́ри**и**	хоро́ш**ей** стать**и́**
DATIVE ДАТЕЛЬНЫЙ	пе́рв**ой** балери́н**е**	после́дн**ей** неде́л**е**	ру́сск**ой** исто́ри**и**	хоро́ш**ей** стать**е́**
ACCUSATIVE ВИНИТЕЛЬНЫЙ	пе́рв**ую** балери́н**у**	после́дн**юю** неде́л**ю**	ру́сск**ую** исто́ри**ю**	хоро́ш**ую** стать**ю́**
INSTRUMENTAL ТВОРИТЕЛЬНЫЙ	пе́рв**ой** балери́н**ой**	после́дн**ей** неде́л**ей**	ру́сск**ой** исто́ри**ей**	хоро́ш**ей** стать**ёй**
PREPOSITIONAL ПРЕДЛОЖНЫЙ	(о) пе́рв**ой** балери́н**е**	(о) после́дн**ей** неде́л**е**	(о) ру́сско**й** исто́ри**и**	(о) хоро́ш**ей** стать**е́**

REFERENCE TABLE 3D: NEUTER ADJECTIVES AND NOUNS BY CASE

case	hard-stem	soft-stem	mixed-stem
NOMINATIVE ИМЕНИТЕЛЬНЫЙ	*втор **ó**е письм**ó**	сѝн **ее** мóр**е**	хорóш**ее** увлечéни**е**
GENITIVE РОДИТЕЛЬНЫЙ	втор **ó**го письм**á**	сѝн**его** мóр**я**	хорóш**его** увлечéни**я**
DATIVE ДАТЕЛЬНЫЙ	втор **ó**му письм**ý**	сѝн**ему** мóр**ю**	хорóш**ему** увлечéни**ю**
ACCUSATIVE ВИНИТЕЛЬНЫЙ	втор **ó**е письм**ó**	сѝн **ее** мóр**е**	хорóш**ее** увлечéни**е**
INSTRUMENTAL ТВОРИТЕЛЬНЫЙ	втор **ы́**м письм**óм**	сѝн**им** мóр**ем**	хорóш**им** увлечéни**ем**
PREPOSITIONAL ПРЕДЛОЖНЫЙ	(о) втор**ó**м письм**é**	(о) сѝн**ем** мóр**е**	хорóш**ем** увлечéни**и**

*Note: Adjectives with stressed endings have the ending -**ó**й in the masculine nominative singular and inanimate accusative singular: больш**ó**й, плох**ó**й.

REFERENCE TABLE 3E: PLURAL ADJECTIVES AND NOUNS (ANIMATE) BY CASE

case	hard-stem	soft-stem	mixed-stem
NOMINATIVE ИМЕНИТЕЛЬНЫЙ	пéрв**ые** журналѝст**ы**	послéдн**ие** секретар**ѝ**	рýсск**ие** балерѝн**ы**
GENITIVE РОДИТЕЛЬНЫЙ	пéрв**ых** журналѝст**ов**	послéдн**их** секретар**éй**	рýсск**их** балерѝн
DATIVE ДАТЕЛЬНЫЙ	пéрв**ым** журналѝст**ам**	послéдн**им** секретар**ям**	рýсск**им** балерѝн**ам**
ACCUSATIVE ВИНИТЕЛЬНЫЙ	пéрв**ых** журналѝст**ов**	послéдн**их** секретар**éй**	рýсск**их** балерѝн
INSTRUMENTAL ТВОРИТЕЛЬНЫЙ	пéрв**ыми** журналѝст**ами**	послéдн**ими** секретар**ями**	рýсск**ими** балерѝн**ами**
PREPOSITIONAL ПРЕДЛОЖНЫЙ	(о) пéрв**ых** журналѝст**ах**	(о) послéдн**их** секретар**ях**	(о) рýсских балерѝн**ах**

REFERENCE TABLE 3F: PLURAL ADJECTIVES AND NOUNS (INANIMATE) BY CASE

case	hard-stem	soft-stem	mixed-stem	mixed-stem
NOMINATIVE ИМЕНИТЕЛЬНЫЙ	пéрв **ые** клáссы	послéдн**ие** недéл**и**	втор **ы́е** пѝсьм**а**	хорóш**ие** увлечéни**я**
GENITIVE РОДИТЕЛЬНЫЙ	пéрв **ых** клáсс**ов**	послéдн**их** недéль	втор **ó**го пѝсьм**á**	хорóш**их** увлечéни**й**
DATIVE ДАТЕЛЬНЫЙ	пéрв **ым** клáсс**ам**	послéдн**им** недéл**ям**	втор **ы́**м пѝсьм**ам**	хорóш**им** увлечéни**ям**
ACCUSATIVE ВИНИТЕЛЬНЫЙ	пéрв **ые** клáссы	послéдн**ие** недéл**и**	втор **ы́е** пѝсьм**а**	хорóш**ие** увлечéни**я**
INSTRUMENTAL ТВОРИТЕЛЬНЫЙ	пéрв **ыми** клáсс**ами**	послéдн**ими** недéл**ями**	втор **ы́ми** пѝсьм**ами**	хорóш**ими** увлечéни**ями**
PREPOSITIONAL ПРЕДЛОЖНЫЙ	(о) пéрв**ых** клáсс**ах**	(о) послéдн**их** недéл**ях**	(о) втор**ы́х** пѝсьм**ах**	(о) хорóш**их** увлечéни**ях**

Short-form adjectives and comparatives formed from adjectives have endings based on spelling rules and consonant mutations. The tables below provide a brief overview of these endings. Individual sections detailing the various forms and functions of adjectives in Russian follow.

REFERENCE TABLE 3G: SHORT-FORM, SIMPLE AND COMPOUND COMPARATIVE AND SUPERLATIVE ADJECTIVAL ENDINGS

long-form adjective (declines)	short-form adjective (does not decline)*	simple comparative (does not decline)**	compound comparative (declines)	compound superlative (declines)
красивый, -ая, -ое, -ые	красив, -а, -о, -ы	красивее	более (менее) красивый	самый красивый
добрый, -ая, -ое, -ые	добр, -а, -о, -ы	добрее	более (менее) добрый	самый добрый
дорогой, -ая, -ое, -ые	дорог, -а, -о, -и	дороже	более (менее) дорогой	самый дорогой

*Note: Short forms change for gender and number, but not for case and are always used as predicates in sentences. The masculine form is normally equal to the adjective stem (-ø), the feminine adds **-a**, the neuter adds **-o**, and the plural adds **-ы** (**-и**).

Note: Simple comparative adjectives are formed by adding the suffixes **-ee or **-e**. Some final stem consonants undergo mutation (see grammar point 3.14 in this chapter).

Long-Form Adjectives

3.2	ADJECTIVES IN THE NOMINATIVE SINGULAR AND PLURAL	Face to Face L1
	Function: Pointing out and describing objects	Chapter 9 A Pages 187-190

Adjectives describe nouns, and therefore, have the function of describing objects such as people, places, and things. Russian adjectives must agree with their nouns in **gender**, **number**, and **case**. The basic long-form adjectival endings are as follows: (See point 3.1 for a comparison of long-form and short-form adjectives.)

Adjective	masculine* -ый,-ой/-ий	feminine -ая/-яя	neuter -ое/-ее	plural -ые/-ие
Which? What kind of..?	Какой дом? house	Какая школа? school	Какое здание? building	Какие цветы? flowers
beautiful	красивый	красивая	красивое	красивые
big	большой	большая	большое	большие
small	маленький	маленькая	маленькое	маленькие
good	хороший	хорошая	хорошее	хорошие

*Note: Adjectives are generally listed in dictionaries and references in their masculine form.

Sample sentences

Какóй большóй стадиóн!	What a **big** stadium!
Какóй это стадиóн?	**What** is the stadium **like**?
Это большóй стадиóн.	This is a **large** stadium.
Это мáленькая собáка.	This is a **small** dog.
Это красúвое здáние.	This is a **beautiful** building.

3.3 ADJECTIVES THAT NAME COLORS; THE PREPOSITION У WITH ANIMATE NOUNS
Function: Talking about color and naming colors

Face to Face L1
Chapters 11 B
Pages 231-233

The names for colors in Russian are expressed as **adjectives**. As with all long-form adjectives, colors decline according to **gender**, **number**, and **case**.

цветá		colors
крáсный	(**-ая, -ое, -ые**)	red
орáнжевый		orange
рóзовый		pink
фиолéтовый		purple
бéлый		white
жёлтый		yellow
корúчневый		brown
чёрный		black
зелёный		green
голубóй		light blue
сúний	(**-яя, -ее, -ие**)	(dark) blue

Sample sentences

— Какáя у тебя́ (у вас) машúна?*

— У меня́ нóвая крáсная машúна. У пáпы бéлый «бьюик», у мáмы чёрная «хонда», а у сестры́ и брáта нет машúны.

What kind of car do you have?

I have a new **red** car. Dad has a **white** Buick, Mom has a **black** Honda, but my sister and brother don't have a car.

*Note: The genitive case is commonly used to ask the color of objects;

Это какóго цвéта?	What color is this? (*lit.*, *This is of what color?*)
Это крáсного цвéта.	This is red. (*lit.* : *This is of the red color.*)

3.4 THE ADJECTIVE ЦÉЛЫЙ AND THE PRONOUN ВЕСЬ
Function: Describing objects—*a/the whole, entire*

Мир рýсских
Lesson 4
Pages 131-132

Цéлый refers to an amount which the speaker considers to be very large, or even excessively large. Весь is used for the whole, all, full amount of something or somebody, without exception.

In English, this distinction is often expressed by the use of the articles *a* or *the*. Цéлый corresponds to *a whole, an entire*, while весь corresponds to *the whole, the entire*.

Sample sentences

целый , целое, целая, целые

Он взял с собо́й **це́лый** чемода́н книг.

He took **a whole** suitcase of books with him. (*as if the amount was too much or surprisingly large*)

Шко́льница прочита́ла **це́лую** кни́гу, а ей всего́ семь лет.

The schoolgirl read **an entire** book, and she's only seven years old.

Ко́шка вы́пила **це́лую** таре́лку молока́.

The cat drank **a whole** saucer of milk.

весь, всё , вся, все

Весь чемода́н был по́лон книг.

The entire suitcase was full of books.

Студе́нт прочита́л **все** кни́ги э́того писа́теля.

The student has read **all of the** books by this author. (all—each and every one)

Ко́шка вы́пила **всё** молоко́.

The cat drank **all the** milk.

Sometimes these words can be synonymous:

Его́ не́ было до́ма **це́лый/весь** день.

He wasn't home **a/the whole** day. (*Regardless of the connotation, the person was away from home for the given time period.*)

Short-Form Adjectives

3.5   An overview of short-form adjectives. Recall that short-form adjectives have a predicative function; they follow the noun and are linked by a verb in the sentence, thus forming the predicate of the sentence. Note the subject and predicate in each sentence below.

[Subject   predicate.]

Я	ра́да.	I **am glad**.
Она́	больна́	She **is sick**.
Мы	знако́мы.	We **are acquainted**.

Whereas long-form adjectives typically denote more permanent qualities or characteristics of a noun, **short-form adjectives are often used to denote temporary states or conditions**:

Я **рад**, что вы пришли́!

I **am glad** you arrived (are here). (*At this particular moment, the person is glad/happy.*)

Сего́дня, на́ша учи́тельница **больна́**.

Our teacher **is ill** today. (*However, she is not chronically sick.*)

Short-form adjectives agree in **gender** and **number** with the person or object to which they refer. The four basic endings according to gender are presented below.

рад	glad	**Masculine**
знако́м	acquainted	**-ø (zero ending)**
ра́д**а**		**Feminine**
знако́м**а**		**-а/-я**
ну́жн**о**	needed, necessary	**Neuter**
похо́ж**е**	similar	**-о/-е**
нужн**ы́**		**Plural**
похо́ж**и**		**-ы/-и**

<table>
<tr><td>

3.6 РАД + **INFINITIVE**; РАД + ЧТО
    Function: Expressing gladness

</td><td>

Face to Face L2
Chapter 2 A, B, D
Pages 39, 41; 44;
53

</td></tr>
</table>

To express gladness use the constructions **рад + verb infinitive** or **рад + что**.
Рад is a short-form adjective and declines for gender and number. Past and future
tense is expressed by conjugating the verb **быть** (to be).

Present tense

Я, ты, он рад.	I, you, he am/are/is glad. (*masc.*)
Я, ты, она́ ра́да.	I, you, she am/are/is glad. (*fem.*)
Мы, вы они́ ра́ды.	We, you, they are glad. (*plural*)

Past tense

Я, ты, он был рад.	I, you, he was/were glad. (*masc.*)
Я, ты, она была́ ра́да.	I, you, she was/were glad. (*fem.*)
Мы, вы, они́ бы́ли ра́ды.	We, you, they were glad. (*plural*)

Future tense

Я бу́ду рад(а).	I will be glad (*masc./fem.*)
Ты бу́дешь рад(а).	You will be glad (*masc./fem.*)
Он(а́) бу́дет рад(а).	He/She will be glad (*masc./fem.*)
Мы бу́дем ра́ды.	We will be glad (*plural*)
Вы бу́дете ра́ды.	You will be glad (*plural*)
Они́ бу́дут ра́ды.	They will be glad (*plural*)

To express satisfaction that something has been, is being, or will be done, use either of
the two constructions:

рад + infinitive	**рад + что**
Я рад ви́деть тебя́.	Я рад, что ви́жу тебя́.
I am glad to see you.	I am glad to see you.
Я ра́да узна́ть это.	Я ра́да, что узна́тла это.
I am happy to find that out.	I am glad that I found that out.
Мы ра́ды познако́миться с вами.	Мы ра́ды, что познако́мились с вами.
We are glad to meet you.	We are glad to make your acquaintance.

Note that the construction **рад + infinitive** is not used in complex sentences in
which two different subjects are implied, such as, "**I'm** glad that **you** came." In such
cases, the construction **рад + что** should be used.

3.7 ПОХÓЖ НА + ACCUSATIVE CASE
Function: Asking and expressing opinions, similarity

Face to Face L2
Lesson 3 B, D
Pages 64-66; 71

To express the similarity of one object or person with another, use the construction **похóж (-а/-е/-и) на + the accusative case**. The short form **похóж** agrees in gender and number with the subject of the sentence. Nouns following the preposition **на** are declined in the accusative case. **Похóж на** may be translated as *similar to* or *looks like*.

Sample sentences

masc.	Он **похóж на** мáму.	He **looks like** his mother.
fem.	Онá **похóжа на** отцá.	She **looks like** her father.
neut.	Это слóво не **похóже на** английское слóво.	This word is **not similar** to the English word.
pl.	Эти словá немнóго **похóжи**.	These words are somewhat **similar**.

3.8 SHORT-FORM ЗНАКÓМ
Function: Expressing acquaintance, familiarity

Face to Face L2
Chapter 4 A, D
Pages 78-82; 90

The short form **знакóм (-а/-о/-ы)** may be used to express familiarity with someone or some topic of information. This short form is often followed by the preposition **с + the instrumental case**, conveying the meaning *with someone or something*.

Sample sentences
with c + instrumental

Он **знакóм с** Мáшей.	He is **acquainted** with (knows) Masha.
Онá **знакóма с** Ивáном.	She is **acquainted** with Ivan.
Мы **знакóмы** друг **с** дрýгом.	They are **acquainted** with each other.

without preposition

Это слóво мне не **знакóмо**.	This word is not **familiar** to me.
Они́ **знакóмы** ужé пять лет.	They have been **acquainted** (have known each other) for five years.

3.9 ДОЛЖЕН **WITH THE INFINITIVE** *Function:* Expressing an obligation	Faces and Voices Chapter 5 A Page 121

The construction **дóлжен/должнá/должны́ + a verb in the infinitive** expresses an "obligation to do something." This is a stronger connotation than the use of **нáдо** or **нýжно** constructions. **Дóлжен** expresses that one *must, and is obligated to, perform the action.* Note below that the masculine, feminine, or plural forms of **дóлжен** agree with the gender or number of the subject.

Sample sentences

Он дóлжен (был, бýдет) рабóтать на компью́тере.	**He must** (had to, will have to) work on the computer.
Онá должнá (былá, бýдет) изучáть англи́йский язы́к.	**She must** (had to, will have to) study English.
Они́ должны́ (бы́ли, бýдут) учи́ться печáтать на маши́нке.	**They must** (had to, will have to) learn to use the typewriter.
— Что **вы должны́** дéлать на рабóте в музéе?	What **do you have to do** (at work) at the museum?
— Я должнá отвечáть на телефóнные звонки́, должнá принимáть посети́телей, отвечáть на пи́сьма.	**I have to/must** answer phone calls, receive visitors, and answer letters.

3.10 **THE SHORT-FORM ADJECTIVE** НÝЖНО *Function:* Stating a need for something	Faces and Voices Chapter 9 A Pages 238

The word **нýжно**, used with an **infinitive verb form**, means the same as **нáдо**. Compare:

Мне **нáдо купи́ть** что-нибудь мóдное. Мне **нýжно купи́ть** что-нибудь мóдное.	*both convey:* I **need to buy** something stylish.

When talking about a need for something, the short-form adjective **нýжен, нужнá, нужнó, нужны́** is used. The form of the adjective depends on the gender of the object that is needed, **not** on the gender of the person needing it. As with **нáдо**, the person who needs the object is in **the dative case**:

masc.	Мне **нýжен** *э́тот журнáл.*	I **need** *this magazine.*
fem.	Емý **нужнá** *э́та кни́га.*	He **needs** *this book.*
neut.	Ей **нýжно** *крáсное плáтье.*	She **needs** *a red dress.*
pl.	Тебé **нужны́** *чёрные тýфли.*	You **need** *black shoes.*

To express **нýжен** in the past and future tenses, use the verb **быть** in its past and future conjugations. Note the the conjugated forms of **быть** agree in gender and number with the same noun as **нýжен**:

	present	past	future	
Мне **I**	нýжен *m.* **need**	был *m.* **needed**	бýдет *sing.* **will need**	костю́м. *m.* **a suit.**
Тебé **You**	нужнá *f.* **need**	былá *f.* **needed**	бýдет *sing.* **will need**	кýртка. *f.* **a jacket.**
Ей **She**	нýжно *n.* **needs**	бы́ло *n.* **needed**	бýдет *sing.* **will need**	плáтье. *n.* **a dress**
Нам **We**	нужны́ *pl.* **need**	бы́ли *pl.* **needed**	бýдут *pl.* **will need**	боти́нки. *pl.* **boots.**

Word order in the past and future tenses may follow two patterns:

Нам **нужнá былá** кýртка. or Нам **былá нужнá** кýртка.
Ивáну **нужны́ бýдут** боти́нки. or Ивáну **бýдут нужны́** боти́нки.

Sample sentences

Тебé **нýжен** хорóший журнáл мóды. You need a good fashion magazine.

Мне **нýжен** был большóй рýсско- I needed a large Russian-English
английский словáрь. dictionary.

Мне **нýжно** бýдет плáтье? Will I need a dress?

Мне **нужны́** очки́. I need my glasses.

3.11 IMPERSONAL CONSTRUCTIONS (LOGICAL SUBJECT IN THE DATIVE); SHORT-FORM ADJECTIVES AND VERBS THAT TAKE THE DATIVE

Function: Talking about clothing that is too big, small, long, short

Faces and Voices Chapter 9 Б Pages 244-247

Some verbs require that the logical subject appear in the **dative case.** The same is true of the verb идти́ when it is used to tell whether clothing fits well or is flattering or suitable. The short-form adjectives **вели́к, мал, дли́нен,** and **кóроток** are also commonly used with the dative case as well as with constructions describing a mental or physical state.

Sample sentences (logical subjects in the dative)

Эта шля́па **мне нрáвится**, но, по-мóему, **I like** this hat, but I don't think it's **right**
мне не идёт. **for me.**

Этот плащ **вели́к Антóну, мал Макси́му,** This raincoat to **too big for Anton, too**
но **как раз Ви́ктору.** **small for Maxim,** but **just right for Victor.**

Антóн болéл, у негó былá высóкая Anton was sick, he had a high
температýра, **емý бы́ло плóхо.** temperature, and **he felt bad.**

На ýлице морóз, пургá, **мне** óчень Outside it's freezing, there's a blizzard,
хóлодно. and **I am cold.**

Хорошó, когдá мы мóжем сказáть себé: It's good when we can say to ourselves,
«**Мне хорошó!** У меня́ всё хорошó в **"I'm doing great!** Everything in my
жи́зни!» life is good!"

Sample sentences (verbs that require the dative)

Модельéры **помогáют лю́дям** найти́
свой стиль.

Models **help people** find their style.

Оди́н му́дрый человéк **посовéтовал
Ири́не** кáждый день **говори́ть себé**,
что всё хорошó в жи́зни.

One wise man **advised Irina** to **tell
herself** every day that all in life is
good.

Натáша **позвони́ла Ири́не**.

Natasha **phoned Irina**.

Муж Ири́ны **связáл дéтям** мóдные
сви́теры.

Irina's husband **knitted the children**
stylish sweaters.

Ири́на сегóдня óчень счастли́вая, **ей
хóчется улыбáться всем лю́дям**.

Irina is very happy today. **She feels like
smiling at everyone.** (*lit.*, *at all
people*)

3.12 SHORT-FORM ADJECTIVES USED AS PREDICATES
   Function: Describing objects

Мир ру́сских
Lesson 3
Pages 89-92

Formation The short form of an adjective has the endings **Ø** (краси́в — masculine), **-а**
(краси́ва — feminine), and **-о** (краси́во — neuter). The plural ending is **-ы** (краси́вы). If
difficult-to-pronounce consonant clusters result when the masculine short-form adjective
is formed (у́зкий — узк, больнóй — больн), then a "fill" vowel (**о** or **е**) is inserted between
the final two consonants.

Before final **к** insert **о**:		Before final **н** insert **е**:	
у́зкий —у́з**ок**	narrow	тру́дный — тру́д**ен**	difficult
корóткий — кóрот**ок**	short	си́льный — си́л**ен**	strong
я́ркий — я́р**ок**	bright	больнóй — бóл**ен**	sick, ill

Short forms вели́к, мал The adjectives **большóй** and **мáленький** do not form
their own short forms. Instead, the short forms of **вели́кий** (вели́к, великá, великó,
велики́) and **мáлый** (мал, малá, малó, малы́) are used. When used in their short
forms, **вели́кий, мáлый** carry the meaning *too....* Compare:

Эта маши́на **большáя**.

This car is **big.**

Эта маши́на **великá**.

This car is **too big.**

Sample sentences

Нóвая шáпка мне **малá**.

The new hat is **too small** for me.

К сожалéнию, этот нóмер **вели́к**.

Unfortunately, this (hotel) room is **too
large.**

Кроссóвки **малы́** Адáму.

The athletic shoes are **too small** for
Adam.

Short and Long Forms in the Predicate
   Both the long forms and the short forms of adjectives are used as predicates.
(Long-form examples are given below in parentheses):

Sample sentences

Рýсская кýхня **простá и разнообрáзна**.
   (простáя и разнообрáзная)

Russian cuisine is **simple and diverse.**

Óвощи вмéсте с холóдным квáсом
   осóбенно **приятны** в лéтний день.
   (приятные)

Vegetables with cold kvass are
especially **pleasant** on a summer
day.

Егó расскáзы всегдá **интерéсны**.
   (интерéсные)

His stories are always **interesting**.

Use with verb быть in the past and future   The past and future forms of the
verb **быть** are used with both short-form and long-form adjectives. The main
difference is that short-form adjectives **do not** decline for case:

Long form (in instrumental case):

Егó расскáзы **бы́ли** интерéсн**ыми**
   (**бýдут** интерéсн**ыми**).

Short form (no change of ending):

Егó расскáзы **бы́ли** интерéсн**ы** (**бýдут**
интерéсн**ы**).

Short Form Denoting a Temporary State If the adjective names an absolute or
permanent condition or state, then the long-form adjective is used. If the condition or
state is temporary or transitory, the short-form is used. Compare:

Long-form adjective (permanent):

Мой брат — человéк **здорóвый и
си́льный**.

My brother is a **healthy, strong** person.

В э́том мóре водá всегдá **холóдная**.

The water in this sea is always **cold**.

Молодáя пáра всегдá **весёлая**.

The young couple always are **cheerful.**

Short-form adjective (temporary):

Мой брат сейчáс **бóлен** и óчень **слаб**.

My brother is **sick** now and very **weak**.

Как сегóдня **хóлодно**!
How **cold** it is today!

В день свáдьбы пáра былá осóбенно
веселá.
On their wedding day the couple was
especially **cheerful.**

Comparative Degree

3.13 What is the comparative degree? The comparative degree of adjectives and
adverbs is used whenever qualities, traits, amounts, or actions are compared, either
within the same sentence or in a broader context. If an adjective or an adverb denotes
a quality which can be compared in its strength, intensity, etc., with other qualities of
the kind, then it has not only positive degrees—like the adjectives **металли́ческий**
metal, metallic, **англи́йский** *English,* **зи́мний** *winter,* etc. — but also **comparative** and
superlative degrees. They express a **greater** and the **greatest** degree of the compared
qualities. In Russian and in English there are both simple and compound
comparatives.

3.14 THE COMPARATIVE DEGREE OF ADJECTIVES AND ADVERBS: SIMPLE/COMPOUND COMPARATIVES, AND CONSTRUCTIONS USED IN COMPARATIVE SENTENCES
Function: Using the comparative degree

Мир русских
Lesson 1
Pages 13-17

Simple comparatives

Simple comparatives are formed using two suffixes: -**ee** and -**e**, which are added to the stem of the adjective or adverb. These comparatives do not have case forms. The simple comparative forms of adjectives and adverbs are identical.

1) The simple comparative is most frequently formed using the suffix -**ee**.

adjective	adverb	comparative	
у́мный	у́мно	**умне́е**	smarter
глу́пый	глу́по	**глупе́е**	more stupid

If an adjective or an adverb has fewer than three or four syllables, the stress frequently moves to -**е́е**.*

adjective	adverb	comparative	
кра́сный	кра́сно	**красне́е**	redder
горя́чий	горячо́	**горяче́е**	hotter

If the adjective contains **ё** in the initial form, the **ё** usually becomes an unstressed **е** in the comparative form.

adjective	adverb	comparative	
тёмный	темно́	**темне́е**	darker
весёлый	ве́село	**веселе́е**	more joyful

If the adjective or adverb has three or more syllables, the stress usually does not move.

adjective	adverb	comparative	
интере́сный	интере́сно	**интере́снее**	more interesting
аккура́тный	аккура́тно	**аккура́тнее**	more thorough
краси́вый	краси́во	**краси́вее**	more beautiful

Exceptions:

adjective	adverb	comparative	
ра́нний	ра́но	**ра́ньше**	earlier
по́здний	по́здно	**по́зже, поздне́е**	later
ста́рый	————	**ста́рше**	older
большо́й	————	**бо́льше**	bigger, larger

*Note: The suffix -**ee** has the variant -**ей** (краси́в/ый - краси́в/ей) which is used primarily in colloquial Russian and sometimes in poetry (for purposes of rhyme).

2) The suffix -**e** is usually used when the stem of the adjective or adverb ends in **г, к, х, д, ст,** and sometimes **в**. Before the suffix an alternation of stem consonants takes place:

REFERENCE TABLE 3H: COMPARATIVES WITH A CONSONANT MUTATION

грóмче	грóм**к**-ий грóм**к**-о	**к → ч**	louder	ча́ще	ча́**ст**-ый ча́**ст**-о	**ст → щ**	more frequently
лéгче	лёг**к**-ий лег**к**-ó	**к → ч**	lighter	прóще	про**ст**-óй прó**ст**-о	**ст → щ**	simpler
я́рче	я́р**к**-ий я́р**к**-о	**к → ч**	brighter	тóлще	тóл**ст**-ый тóл**ст**-о	**ст → щ**	fatter
корóче	корóт**к**-ий корóт**к**-о	**к → ч**	shorter	богáче	богá**т**-ый	**т → ч**	richer
блúже	блú**зк**-ий блú**зк**-о	**зк → ж**	closer	дорóже	доро**г**-óй дóро**г**-о	**г → ж**	more expensive
слáще	слá**дк**-ий слá**дк**-о	**дк → щ**	sweeter	тúше	тú**х**-ий тú**х**-о	**х → ш**	quieter
чúще	чú**ст**-ый чú**ст**-о	**ст → щ**	cleaner	молóже	моло**д**-óй	**д → ж**	younger
дешéвле	дешё**в**-ый дёше**в**-о	**в → вл**	cheaper	твéрже	твёр**д**-ий твёр**д**-о	**д → ж**	harder

Other common comparatives include:

жáркий > **жáрче**	hot > **hotter**	высóкий > **вы́ше**	tall > **taller**
сухóй > **сýше**	dry > **drier**	нúзкий > **нúже**	low > **lower**

Exception: худóй → худéе   *thinner*

Sometimes certain other irregularities take place before the suffix:

adjective, adverb	comparative	
высóк-ий, высок-ó	**вы́ше**	taller, higher
тóнк-ий, тóнк-о	**тóньше**	thinner
глубóк-ий, глубок-ó	**глýбже**	deeper
далёк-ий, далек-ó	**дáльше**	farther
дóлг-ий, дóлг-о	**дóльше**	longer
широ́к-ий, широк-ó	**шúре**	wider

3)   When comparing ages, the words **стáрше, млáдше,** and **молóже** are used. **Млáдше** is normally used when comparing relatives' ages. For example:

Дéдушка **стáрше бáбушки**.	Grandfather is **older than grandmother**.
Брат **млáдше меня́**.	My brother is **younger than me**.
Этот человéк **молóже меня́**.	This person is **younger than me**.

The comparative forms of the following words are derived from other stems (roots):

adjective	adverb	comparative	
хорóший	хорошó	**лýчше**	better
плохóй	плóхо	**хýже**	worse
мáленький	мáло	**мéньше**	smaller
большóй	мнóго	**бóльше**	more

Compound comparatives Compound comparatives are formed by the addition of the indeclinable words бóлее (more) or мéнее (less) immediately preceding the adjective or adverb.

Adjective:	холóдный	бóлее холóдный *more cold*	мéнее холóдный *less cold*
Adverb:	хóлодно	бóлее хóлодно *more coldly*	мéнее хóлодно *less coldly*

In theory, either a suffix or the words бóлее or мéнее can be used to form comparatives, e.g., холоднéе or бóлее холóдный. However, simple comparatives are usually preferred in conversation. Russians more frequently say интерéснее (*more interesting*), красúвее (*more beautiful, handsome, prettier*), блúже (*closer*), вы́ше (*higher, taller*), etc., than бóлее интерéсный, бóлее красúвый, etc.

Some adjectives and adverbs have only simple comparatives. Бóлее and мéнее cannot be used with большóй, мáленький, хорóший, and плохóй.

Use of the comparative in sentences

Two constructions can be used to name the person or thing being compared:

1) The simple comparative with the **genitive case**:

Эта кнúга **интерéснее пéрвой**. This book is **more interesting than the first** (book).

2) The simple or compound comparative form with the conjunction чем and the **nominative case**. A comma is required before чем:

Эта кнúга **интерéснее, чем пéрвая**. This book is **more interesting than the first** (book).

Эта кнúга **бóлее интерéсная, чем пéрвая**.

The words намнóго (much), немнóго (a little), в два (три) рáза (two, three times), на два (три) процéнта (two, three percent) and others are often used when comparisons are made:

Эта машúна **намнóго лýчше и дорóже**. This car is **much better and more expensive**.

Эта машúна **немнóго лýчше и дорóже** той. This car is a **bit better and more expensive than that** (one).

Эта машúна **в два рáза лýчше и бóлее дорогáя, чем** та. This car is **two times better and more expensive than that** (car).

3)   The word **ещё** + the simple comparative.

Та машина дорогая, а эта **ещё дороже.**   That car is expensive, but this one is
                                             even more expensive.

Эта машина **ещё дороже**, чем та.   This car is **even more expensive** than
                                      that (car).

<table>
<tr><td></td><td rowspan="4">Face to Face L2
Chapter 18 B, D
Pages 394-396;
399-400</td></tr>
</table>

3.15 COMPARATIVES OF ADJECTIVES AND ADVERBS
Function: Making comparisons

The forms of comparative adjectives and their corresponding adverbs are the same. Below are some of the most frequently used comparatives:

adjective	adverb	comparative	
большой	много	**больше**	more, bigger
маленький	мало	**меньше**	less, smaller
хороший	хорошо	**лучше**	better
плохой	плохо	**хуже**	worse
дорогой	дорого	**дороже**	more expensive
дешёвый	дёшево	**дешевле**	cheaper
красивый	красиво	**красивее**	more beautiful
интересный	интересно	**интереснее**	more interesting

Comparisons is often expressed using a comparative adjective or adverb in the first clause of a sentence, and then beginning the second clause with the conjunction **чем** *than*. Words following **чем** are in the nominative case or are declined after a preposition.

Sample sentences

В Измайлово **больше** художников, **чем**   In Izmailovo there are **more** artists **than**
на Арбате.   on the Arbat.

У художников сувениры **красивее**, **чем**   Artists have **more beautiful** souvenirs
в магазинах.   **than** stores do.

<table>
<tr><td></td><td>Face to Face L2
Chapter 6 A, D
Pages 115-118;
137</td></tr>
</table>

3.16 THE ADVERB ЛУЧШЕ + VERB
Function: Stating a preference

Note that the comparative degree of the adverb **хорошо** is **лучше** (better), which is often used to express a preference:

До Большого театра **лучше** ехать на   The best way to get to the Bolshoi Theater
метро.   is by subway.
    (note that in Russian one says, "the
    better way")

Наве́рное, мне **лу́чше** пое́хать на такси́.	The best way for me to go is probably by taxi.
	(the dative pronoun **мне** expresses the logical subject *me*)

3.17 COMPARATIVES БО́ЛЬШЕ, МЕ́НЬШЕ
Function: Making comparisons

Face to Face L2
Chapter 12 A, D
Pages 249; 265

The comparatives **бо́льше** (more, larger), **ме́ньше** (less, smaller) **+ the genitive case** express and compare amounts of objects.

Sample sentences

У меня́ мно́го ру́сских ма́рок, а у друга́ **ме́ньше ру́сских ма́рок**.	I have many Russian stamps, but my friend has **fewer Russian stamps**.
В Сиби́ри обы́чно быва́ет **бо́льше сне́га**, чем в Москве́.	Siberia usually has **more snow** than Moscow does.*

*****Note:** The word **чем** (than) is often used in comparative expressions and is followed by the nominative of nouns or by prepositional phrases:

Он чита́ет бо́льше, **чем** я.	He reads more **than** I (**чем + nom.**).
У нас бо́льше сне́га, **чем** на ю́ге.	We have/get more snow **than** in the South (**чем + prepositional phrase**).

Superlative Degree

3.18 What is the superlative degree?
While the comparative degree stresses more or less of a quality, the superlative degree expresses the utmost degree of a quality possible (most/least).

3.19 THE SUPERLATIVE DEGREE OF ADJECTIVES: SIMPLE AND COMPOUND SUPERLATIVES
Function: Using the superlative degree

Мир ру́сских
Lesson 1
Pages 17-18

Compound superlative forms Compound superlatives are formed by adding the word **са́мый** (**са́мая, са́мое, са́мые**) *(the) most* immediately preceding the adjective. The word **са́мый** agrees with its corresponding adjective in gender, case, and number.

са́мый краси́вый ма́льчик	the most handsome boy
са́мая краси́вая де́вушка	the most beautiful girl
са́мое краси́вое де́рево	the most beautiful tree
са́мые краси́вые се́рьги	the most beautiful earrings

Sample sentences

Профéссия врачá — престúжная, но профéссия адвокáта **сáмая престúжная.**	To be a doctor is prestigious, but the legal profession is **the most prestigious.**
Сáмое высóкое здáние в США — Сирс Тáуэр (Sears Tower) в Чикáго.	**The tallest** building in the U.S. is the Sears Tower in Chicago.
Все знáют, что **сáмый большóй** штат по плóщади — Аля́ска.	Everyone knows that **the biggest** state in area is Alaska.
Сáмый лýчший спортсмéн в истóрии мúра — э́то баскетболúст Майкл Джóрдан.	**The best** athlete in the history of the world is the basketball player Michael Jordan.

Simple superlative form

The simple form of the superlative degree is formed with the help of suffixes:

1) **-айший** if the positive form of the adjective ends in **г, к, х**:

высóкий	высоч**áйший**	(к → ч)	the tallest, highest
стрóгий	строж**áйший**	(г → ж)	the strictest
тúхий	тиш**áйший**	(х → ш)	the quietest

2) **-ейший** for all other adjectival endings:

ýмный	умн**éйший**	the smartest
красúвый	красúв**ейший**	the prettiest

The compound superlative is used more frequently than the simple superlative, although both forms are equally correct.

3.20 СÁМЫЙ + QUALIFYING ADJECTIVE
Function: Using the superlative degree

Face to Face L2
Chapter 13, A, D
Pages 274-278; 284

The word **сáмый/сáмая/сáмое/сáмые** is used with an adjective to state that a person or thing possesses the superlative (most) degree of a characteristic (*the most...*, *the biggest...*, etc.). Superlative endings are adjectival and decline based on gender, number, and case. Below are **nominative** examples.

Sample sentences

Э́то мой **сáмый любúмый** прáздник.	It's my **favorite** holiday.
Э́то **сáмая хорóшая** пéсня.	It's the **best** song.
Э́то **сáмое удóбное** мéсто.	It's the **most comfortable** place.
Э́то **сáмые интерéсные** вéщи.	These are the **most interesting** things.

Chapter 4

DECLENSION
of NOUNS and ADJECTIVES
Склонéния имён сушествùтельных и прилагáтельных

4.0.1 Overview: What is declension? In Russian, the endings of words change to indicate their function in a sentence. **Declension** is the changing of the forms of nouns, adjectives and pronouns because word order alone will not signify the subject, direct object, etc. in a Russian sentence.

Declension patterns in Russian are organized into six cases. Each **case** can be associated with several functions in sentences. Verbs, prepositions, numbers and impersonal structures, such those with **нрáвитсься** (to like), require the use of a specific case with words that follow them or to which they refer.

Finally, words decline according to their gender (masc., fem., neut.), number (singular, plural) and whether a noun is animate (living) or inanimate (non-living). Refer to Chapter 2, Nouns, and Chapter 3, Adjectives, for review of these characteristics of nouns and adjectives.

The sentences below exemplify declension and case meaning. In each sentence, the feminine noun **Мáша** declines.

Sample Sentences

1. Мáша хóдит в шкóлу.
   Masha attends school.

2. Это учùтель Мáши.
   This is **Masha's** teacher.

3. Он читáет скáзку Мáше.
   He reads a fairytale **to Masha.**

4. Он слýшает Мáшу, когдá онá отвечáет на вопрóс.
   He listens to **Masha** when she answers a question.

5. Он гордùтся Мáшей. Онá ýмница!
   He is proud of **Masha**. She is an intelligent girl!

6. Все говоря́т о Мáше. Говоря́т, что онá стáнет президéнтом!
   Everyone talks **about Masha**. They say she will become president!

Case *Example Function*
Nominative - the subject of a sentence.
Genitive - signifies possession.
Dative - signifies the indirect object.
Accusative - signifies the direct object.
Instrumental - signifies the person/object used to perform/accomplish an action, state, or activity.
Prepositional - only used with specific prepositions. Often denotes location of people/objects and conversation "about".

REFERENCE TABLE 4.0A: CASE NAMES IN RUSSIAN

Именительный падеж	—	Кто/Что?	Nominative Case
Родительный падеж	—	Кого/Чего?	Genitive Case
Дательный падеж	—	Кому/Чему?	Dative Case
Винительный падеж	—	Кого/Что?	Accusative Case
Творительный падеж	—	Кем/Чем?	Instrumental Case
Предложный падеж	—	о Ком/о Чём?	Prepositional Case or Locative Case

REFERENCE TABLE 4.0B: OVERVIEW OF BASIC CASE USAGE AND ENDINGS

Case	Usage	Verbs	Prepositions		m.	n.	f.
Nom. кто что	•Subject, doer (predicate noun/adj.)			Sing. nouns	-ø -й -ь	-о -е -ие	-а -я -ь -ия
				adj.	-ый/-ий	-ое/-ее	-ая/-яя
				Pl. nouns	-ы -и -и	-а -я -ия	-ы -и -и -ии
				adj.		-ые/-ие	
Gen. кого чего	•Possession •Negation: нет, не́ было, не бу́дет •Numerals: **2-4, 22-24,** **etc.** (sing.) **5-20, 25-30,** **etc.** (plural) •Quantity words: мно́го, ма́ло (plural)	желать бояться	у о́коло по́сле для из до от с — from без	Sing. nouns	-а -я -я	-а -я -ия	-ы -и -и -ии
				adj.	-ого/-его		-ой/-ей
				Pl. nouns	-ов -ев -ей	-ø -ей -ий	-ø -ø -ей -ий
				adj.		-ых/-их	
Dat. кому́ чему́	•Indirect object, to or for whom •Impersonal expressions: мо́жно, нельзя́, на́до	показа́ть жела́ть подари́ть сове́товать нра́виться каза́ться (ка́жется)	к по	Sing. nouns	-у -ю	-у -ю	-е -и
				adj.	-ому/-ему		-ой/-ей
				Pl. nouns adj.		-ам/-ям -ым/-им	
Acc. кого́ что	•Direct object •Destination w/motion verbs: куда́ •Time expressions	Action Verbs: ви́деть люби́ть чита́ть писа́ть учи́ть знать	в, на — to *after:* идти́/ходи́ть е́хать/е́здить лете́ть/лета́ть похо́ж(а) на кого́ че́рез	Sing. nouns			-у -ю
				adj.	*anim.* see gen.	neuter nouns and	-ую/-юю
				Pl. nouns	*inanim.* see nom.	adjs. see nom.	*anim.* see gen.
				adj.			*inanim.* see nom.

REFERENCE TABLE 4.0B: OVERVIEW OF CASE USAGE AND ENDINGS (cont.)

Case	Usage	Verbs	Prepositions		m.	n.	f.
Instr. кем чем	•Agent of Action, "by means of" •Change of state (future, past) •Some time expressions	быть: был будет быть кем? будь(те) заниматься познакомиться	с — with над под перед за между рядом с	Sing. nouns adj. Pl. nouns adj.	-ом -ем -ым/-им	-ом -ем -ами/-ями -ыми/-ими	-ой -ей -ой/-ей
Prep. о ком о чём	•Prepositional phrases: где	играть на ездить/ ехать на	в — in на — at, on о (об)	Sing. nouns adj. Pl. nouns adj.	-е -и -ом/-ем	-е -и -ах/-ях -ых/-их	-е -и -ой/-ей

Nominative Case

Кто? Что?
Именительный падёж

4.1.2 Overview: What are the functions of the nominative case? The nominative case is the basic unchanged or undeclined form of a noun or adjective. This is often called its "dictionary form" because words are generally listed in Russian language dictionaries this way. The basic function of the nominative case in Russian sentences is to denote the subject of a sentence and answers the questions Who? *Кто?* or What? *Что?*. Note the subject in bold in the sentences below.

— **Маша** читает и слушает музыку.

— Кто? **Маша**.

Что это? Это **Пушкинский музей**.

Masha is reading and listening to music.

Who? Masha.

What is that? That's the **Pushkin Museum**.

Nominative case usage is further described throughout the reference grammar. The tables below outline basic usage and endings. Refer to the chapters on nouns, adjectives and sentence structure for additional references.

REFERENCE TABLE 4.1A: TYPICAL USES OF THE NOMINATIVE CASE

•The subject of sentences and the "doer" of actions.
•The predicate of a sentence in the form of a noun introduced by **Это**... (Это *Анна*.— This is *Anna*.) or **Вот**... (Вот *она*.—Here *she* is.) or introduced by an adjective (Я *должен*. —I *should*.)
•The undeclined form of nouns, as found in English-Russian dictionaries, are presented in the nominative case (usually in their masculine form).

REFERENCE TABLE 4.1B: BASIC NOMINATIVE CASE ENDINGS BY GENDER

Singular	Masculine	Neuter	Feminine
nouns	-cons. -й -ь	-о -е -ие	-а -я -ия -ь
adjectives	-ый/-ий	-ое/-ее	-ая/-яя
Plural			
nouns	-ы/-и	-а/-я	-ы/-и
adjectives	<—————	-ые/-ие	—————>

REFERENCE TABLE 4.1C: EXAMPLE NOUNS IN THE NOMINATIVE CASE BY GENDER IN THEIR SINGULAR AND PLURAL FORMS

Masculine	-consonant	-й	several in -я	several in -ь
sing.	стол (table, desk) ученик (student m.)	музе́й (museum)	дя́дя (uncle)	слова́рь (dictionary)
pl.	столы́ ученики́*	музе́и	дя́ди	словари́

Neuter	-о	-е	-ие	several in -мя
sing.	письмо́ (letter)	мо́ре (sea)	зда́ние (building)	и́мя (first name)
pl.	пи́сьма	моря́	зда́ния	имена́

Feminine	-а	-я	-ия	-ь
sing.	шко́ла (school) кни́га (book)	дере́вня (countryside)	лаборато́рия (laboratory)	пло́щадь (square)
pl.	шко́лы кни́ги*	дере́вни	лаборато́рии	пло́щади

*Spelling rule: и follows the consonants к/г/х, not ы.

REFERENCE TABLE 4.1D: SPECIAL NOUN CATEGORIES IN THE NOMINATIVE CASE

Noun Type		Singular	Plural
•Feminine nouns	дочь (daughter) and мать (mother)	дочь мать	до́чери (-ер-) ма́тери
•Feminine nouns	любо́вь (love) and це́рковь (church)	любо́вь це́рковь	no plural form церкви́
•Masculine nouns in -анин/-янин		граждани́н (citizen)	гра́ждане
•Masculine nouns in -онок/-ёнок		котёнок (kitten)	котя́та
•Neuter nouns in -мя: и́мя		и́мя (first name)	имена́ (-мен-)
•Neuter nouns	не́бо (sky, heaven) and чу́до (miracle)	не́бо чу́до	небеса́ чудеса́

Accusative Case

Кого? Что?
Вини́тельный паде́ж

4.2.3 Overview: What are the functions of the accusative case? This case typically denotes the direct object in a sentence (Masha wrote *a letter* to her brother). Several prepositions, particularly with verbs of motion and many other verbs, govern this case.

REFERENCE TABLE 4.2A: TYPICAL USES OFTHE ACCUSATIVE CASE

•Answers the questions Кого? (Who?)/Что? (What?).
•Identifies the direct object of a sentence with a transitive verb (a verb which performs an action on another person or thing).
•Used after prepositions в and на when denoting motion to a place; Answers the question Куда? (To where?).
•With the preposition в in telling time "*at*" a particular hour, and with the prepositions похо́ж на (similar to) and че́рез (across).

REFERENCE TABLE 4.2B: BASIC ACCUSATIVE CASE ENDINGS

Singular	Masc. animate	Masc. inanimate & Neuter	Feminine
nouns	-а/-я *like genitive*	no change	-у/-ю
adjectives	-ого/-его	no change	-ую/-юю
Plural *nouns*	*like gen. pl.*	no change	*like gen. pl.*
adjectives	-ых/-их	no change	-ых/-их

REFERENCE TABLE 4.2C: EXAMPLE NOUNS IN THE ACCUSATIVE CASE BY GENDER IN THEIR SINGULAR AND PLURAL FORMS

Masculine	-consonant	-й	several in -а/-я	several in -ь
sing.	стóл (table, desk) ученикá (student anim.)	музéй (museum)	дéдушку (grandfather)	словáрь (dictionary) учи́теля (teacher anim.)
pl.	столы́ ученикóв	музéи	дéдушек	словари́ учителéй

Neuter	-о	-е	-ие	several in -мя
sing.	письмó (letter)	мóре (sea)	здáние (building)	и́мя (first name)
pl.	пи́сьма	моря́	здáния	именá

Feminine	-а	-я	-ия	-ь
sing.	шкóлу (school) кни́гу (book)	дерéвню (country-side)	лаборатóрию (laboratory)	плóщадь (square)
pl.	шкóлы кни́ги*	дерéвни	лаборатóрии	плóщади

*Spelling rule: и follows the consonants к/г/х, not ы.

REFERENCE TABLE 4.2D: SPECIAL NOUN CATEGORIES IN THE ACCUSATIVE CASE

Noun Type		Singular	Plural
•Feminine nouns	дочь and мать	дочь мать	дочерéй (-ер-) матерéй
•Feminine nouns	любóвь and цéрковь	любóвь цéрковь	no plural form церкви́
•Masculine nouns in -анин/-янин		граждани́на	грáждан
•Masculine nouns in -онок/-ёнок		котёнка	котя́т
•Neuter nouns in -мя: и́мя		и́мя	именá (-мен-)
•Neuter nouns	нéбо and чýдо	нéбо чýдо	небесá чудесá

4.2.4   THE ACCUSATIVE CASE OF INANIMATE NOUNS
Function: Expressing the objects of actions

| Face to Face L1 Chapter 6 C Pages 158-161 |

When nouns are used as direct objects in sentences they require accusative case endings. The accusative case answers the question Что? (What?) or Когó? (Who?). These noun endings change according to gender and to whether the noun is animate (living) or inanimate (non-living). ***Inanimate*** noun endings for masculine, neuter, and feminine nouns are given in the reference table below.

REFERENCE TABLE 4.2E: INANIMATE ACCUSATIVE NOUN ENDINGS

	Кто? Что?	Кого? Что?
Masculine noun endings	*Nominative*	*Accusative*
	журнáл	журнáл
ø zero ending	телевíзор	телевíзор
does not change	словáрь	словáрь
	музéй	музéй
Neuter noun endings	*Nominative*	*Accusative*
	письмó	письмó
-о -е endings	окнó	окнó
do not change	мóре	мóре
	упражнéние	упражнéние
Feminine noun endings	*Nominative*	*Accusative*
-а *becomes* -у	кнíга	кнíгу
	газéта	газéту
-я -ю	семья́	семью́
-ия -ию	фамíлия	фамíлию
(-ь does not change)	тетрáдь	тетрáдь

Sample sentences

Что вы читáете? — **What** are you reading?

Онá читáет **кнíгу**, а он читáет **газéту**. — She is reading **a book** and he is reading **the newspaper**.

Я читáю **журнáл**. — I am reading **a magazine**.

Мáма пúшет **письмó**. — Mom is writing **a letter**.

Мы слýшаем **рáдио**. — We are listening to **the radio**.

4.2.5	USING ЛЮБИТЬ WITH INFINITIVES AND NOUNS IN THE ACCUSATIVE, ANIMATE NOUNS *Function:* Talking about knowing, understanding, studying	Face to Face L1 Chapter 7 C Page158-161

Masculine animate nouns (people, animals, etc.) take different endings in the accusative case. These endings are like the genitive case endings for masculine nouns **ø** (zero ending) and become **-а** or **-я**:

Я не знáю егó брáт**а**.	**ø > -а**
Марúна не любит Андрé**я**.	**-й > -я**

Note that if a man's name (especially a diminutive or nickname) ends in a vowel such as **-а** or **-я**, the ending will change like a feminine name:

Я не знáю егó дéдушк**у**.	**-а > -у**
Марúна не любит Тóл**ю**.	**-я > -ю**

Feminine animate *singular* nouns keep their regular accusative case endings presented in the section above. Plural feminine animate nouns are declined like the genitive plural (See reference table 4.3B and C for genitive case endings).

Sample sentences

masculine animate singular		feminine animate singular	
Я люблю...	брáт**а**		сестр**ý**
	Борúс**а**		Мáш**у**
Ты лю́бишь...	учúтел**я**		учúтельниц**у**
	пáп**у**		мáм**у**
Онú лю́бят...	дéдушк**у**		бáбушк**у**
	Андрé**я**		Марú**ю**
	Мúш**у**		Вéр**у**

4.2.6	**USING THE ACCUSATIVE CASE WITH DESTINATIONS** (КУДА?)	Face to Face 1 Chapter 12 C Pages 248-251
	Function: Talking about destinations	

When specifying a destination with verbs of motion, the the prepositions **в** and **на + the accusative case** are used to answer the question Кудá? (To where?):

Кудá ты идёшь?	Where are you going?
Я идý **в** шкóлу.	I am going **to school**.
Онá éдет **на** концéрт.	She is going **to the concert**.

Compare the use of Кудá with verbs of motion to denote destination and Где to denote location below.

Кудá?		**Где?**	
Кудá ты идёшь?	Where are you going?	Где ты?	Where are you?
Кудá онá éдет?	Where is she going?	Где онá?	Where is she?

REFERENCE TABLE 4.2F: USE OF В OR НА, IN SPECIFYING DESTINATION

В + Accusative - As a general rule, в is used to denote destination to an enclosed area or building. However there are exceptions and the places requiring the preposition **в** should be memorized:		**На + Accusative** - As a general rule, на is used to denote destination towards an event or performance. However, there are exceptions and the places requiring the preposition **на** should be memorized:	
в шкóлу	to school	на концéрт	to the concert
в инститýт	to the institute	на экскýрсию	to the excursion
в цирк	to the circus	на урóк	to the lesson
в теáтр	to the theater	на стадиóн	to the stadium
в парк	to the park	на óзеро	to the lake
в музéй	to the museum	на завóд	to the plant/factory
в класс	to the classroom	на фáбрику	to the factory
в кинó	to the movie theater	на пóчту	to the post office

Exception: To express the idea of motion towards home (дом) a special form домóй is used:

Что?	Кудá?	Где?
дом (home/house)	домóй (to home/house)	дóма (at home)

4.2.7 PERSONAL PRONOUNS IN THE ACCUSATIVE CASE TO EXPRESS THE DIRECT OBJECT OF AN ACTION
Function: Discussing sports

Face to Face L1
Chapter 13 C
Pages 270-273

When the direct object in a sentence is a personal pronoun, accusative forms must be used. These accusative forms are like the genitive forms.

The difference between я and меня, for example, is the same as the difference between "I" and "me" in English:

— Ната́ша, ты ви́дишь **меня́**?   Natasha, do you see **me**?
— Да, я ви́жу **тебя́**.   Yes, I see **you**.

nominative	accusative *(like genitive)*
я	меня́
ты	тебя́
он	его́
она́	её
оно	его́
мы	нас
вы	вас
они́	их

Note that just as with pronouns in the nominative case, these pronouns can still replace common and proper nouns or objects of the same gender or number. Because they now perform as direct objects, the pronouns change to their accusative forms.

Sample sentences

— Ты понима́ешь э́ту кни́гу?   Do you understand the book?
— Нет, я не понима́ю **её**.   No, I don't understand **it**.

— Где журна́л «Огонёк?»   Where is the magazine, "Ogonyok?"
— Па́па и ма́ма чита́ют **его́**.   Dad and mom are reading **it**.
— Ва́ня! Где твои́ кни́ги? Я не ви́жу **их**.   Vanya, where are your books? I don't see **them**.

4.2.8 THE QUESTION КОГДА? USING THE PREPOSITION В WITH THE ACCUSATIVE CASE TO TELL WHEN AN EVENT OCCURRED
Function: Using expressions of time: at a certain time, days of the week, on a day

Face to Face L1
Chapter 14 B
Pages 287-291

Когда́? (When?) is a general question which can be answered with either a clock time expression or day of the week. (See Chapter 6, grammar points 6.5-6, for an overview of telling time in Russian.)

Expressing time at a specific hour Both Во ско́лько? (At what time?) and Когда́? (When) can be used to ask at what time an event will take place. In responding to this question, the preposition **в + the accusative case** is used.

Sample sentences

— Во ско́лько?	At what time?
— В час дня.	At 1:00 P.M.
— Когда́?	When?
— В три часа́.	At three.
— В семь часо́в ве́чера.	At seven in the evening.
— В двена́дцать часо́в.	At 12:00 o'clock.

Expressing an event on a specific day of the week Both В како́й день? (On what day?) and Когда́? (When?) can be used to express the days on which an event takes place. The preposition **в + the accusative case** is used to respond to these questions. (Note the accusative endings for days of the week change in the feminine -a> -y and the use of **во** with consonant cluster in **вто́рник**)

Sample sentences

— В како́й день?	On which day?
— В понеде́льник.	On Monday.
— Когда́?	When?
— Во вто́рник.	On Tuesday.
— В сре́ду.	On Wednesday.
— В четве́рг.	On Thursday.
— В пя́тницу.	On Friday.
— В суббо́ту.	On Saturday.
— В воскресе́нье.	On Sunday.

Expressing days of the week: present, past, future To express the day of the week in answering the question Како́й сего́дня день? (What day is it today?), the word **сего́дня** (today) is followed by the day of the week in the nominative case.

Sample sentences

— Како́й сего́дня день?	What day is it today?
— **Сего́дня** понеде́льник.	**Today is** Monday
вто́рник	Tuesday
среда́	Wednesday
четве́рг	Thursday
пя́тница	Friday
суббо́та	Saturday
воскресе́нье	Sunday

Today, Yesterday, Tomorrow — The words *today* (сего́дня), *yesterday* (вчера́), and *tomorrow* (за́втра) are used to name the days of the week in the present, past, and future. Note agreement of the past tense form of the verb *to be* (был, была́, бы́ло) and the gender of the day of the week in the examples below.

Сего́дня - today

Сего́дня понеде́льник/вто́рник/четве́рг.	Today is Monday/Tuesday, etc.
Сего́дня среда́/пя́тница/суббо́та.	
Сего́дня воскресе́нье.	

Вчера - yesterday

Вчера́ был понеде́льник/вто́рник/четве́рг.	Yesterday was Monday, etc.
Вчера́ была́ среда́/пя́тница/суббо́та.	
Вчера́ бы́ло воскресе́нье.	

За́втра - tomorrow

За́втра бу́дет понеде́льник/вто́рник/четве́рг.	Tomorrow will be Monday, etc.
За́втра среда́/пя́тница/суббо́та.	
За́втра воскресе́нье.	

4.2.9	**VERBS THAT REQUIRE THE PREPOSITION** В **+ THE ACCUSATIVE CASE** *Function:* Review	Faces and Voices Chapter 10 Г Page 279

Below is a short list of commonly used verbs which require the preposition **в** + **the accusative case**.

ве́рить (II)/пове́рить (II)		to believe in...
влюбля́ться (I)/влюби́ться (II)	**в кого́/что**	to fall in love with...
вкла́дывать (I)/вложи́ть (II) ду́шу		to put one's heart and soul into...

Sample sentences
phrases

Ве́рить	в Бо́га	To believe	**in God**
	в нау́ку		**in science**
	в челове́ка		**in man/womankind**
	в добро́		**in good**
Влюби́ться	в де́вушку	To fall in love with	**a girl**
	в па́рня		**a guy**
	в го́род		**a city**
	в профе́ссию		**a profession**
Вкла́дывать ду́шу	в учёбу	to put one's heart into	**one's studies**
	в рабо́ту		**one's work**

Genitive Case

Кого́? Чего́?
Роди́тельный паде́ж

4.3.10 Overview: What are the functions of the genitive case? This case generally denotes possession and relationships (This is *Masha's* home.). Several prepositions, verbs and constructions govern the genitive case.

REFERENCE TABLE 4.3A: TYPICAL USES OF THE GENITIVE CASE

- Answers the questions Кого? (Who?), Чего? (Of what?), and Чей? (Whose?).
- Denotes possesion in two ways:

1) Это дом Máши. (This is *Masha's* house.) Here word order is reversed as the person possessing follows the objected possessed.

2) У Мáши есть дом. (*Masha has* a house.)

- Denotes relationships; Онá дирéктор *нáшей шкóлы*. (She is the principal *of our school.*)
- Denotes negation after нет, нé было, не бýдет.
- Governed by several verbs and prepositions including: у (near), óколо (nearby), пóсле (after), для (for), из (from), до (up to), от (from), с (from), без (without).
- Adjectives and nouns are declined in the genitive case after the numerals 2, 3, 4, 22, 23, 24, etc. (genitive singular) and 5-20, 25-30, etc. (genitive plural).

REFERENCE TABLE 4.3B: BASIC GENITIVE CASE ENDINGS

Singular	Masculine	Neuter	Feminine
nouns	-а/-я	-а/-я	-ы/-и
adjectives	<—— -ого/-его ——>		-ой/-ей
Plural			
nouns	-ов/-ев/-ей	-ø/-ей/-ий	-ø/-ь/-ий
adjectives	<————— -ых/-их —————>		

REFERENCE TABLE 4.3C: EXAMPLE NOUNS IN THE GENITIVE CASE BY GENDER IN THEIR SINGULAR AND PLURAL FORMS

Masculine	-consonant	-й	several in -а/-я	several in -ь
sing.	столá (table, desk) ученикá (student m.)	музéя (museum)	дéдушки (grandfather)	словаря (dictionary)
pl.	столóв ученикóв	музéев	дéдушек	словарéй
Neuter	-о	-е	-ие	several in -мя
sing.	письмá (letter)	мóря (sea)	здáния (building)	ймени (first name)
pl.	пúсем	морéй	здáний	имён
Feminine	-а	-я	-ия	-ь
sing.	шкóлы (school) кнúги* (book)	дерéвни (countryside)	лаборатóрии (laboratory)	плóщади (square)
pl.	шкóл кнúг	дерéвень	лаборатóрий	площадéй

*Spelling rule: и follows the consonants к/г/х, not ы.

REFERENCE TABLE 4.3D: SPECIAL NOUN CATEGORIES IN THE GENITIVE CASE

Noun Type		Singular	Plural
•Feminine nouns	дочь and	дóчери (-ер-)	дочерéй (-ер-)
	мать	мáтери	матерéй
•Feminine nouns	любóвь and	любви́	no plural form
	цéрковь	цéркви́	церквéй
•Masculine nouns in -анин/-янин		граждани́на	грáждан
•Masculine nouns in -онок/-ёнок		котёнка	котя́т
•Neuter nouns in -мя: и́мя		и́мени (-мен-)	имён (-мен-)
•Neuter nouns	нéбо and	нéба	небéс
	чу́до	чу́да	чудéс

4.3.11 GENITIVE OF PERSONAL PRONOUNS (У + THE GENITIVE CASE), USE OF ЕСТЬ

Function: Talking about possessions and relations

Face to Face L1
Chapter 8 A
Pages 169- 174

One common construction to express possession (*I have, He has, She has*) is **у + the genitive case.** Personal pronouns (I, he, she, etc.) may be used with this construction to express possession.

У меня́ (есть) + nominative *I have...*

Sample sentences

У меня́ есть собака.	**I have** a dog.	*меня́ is the genitive of* **я**
У негó есть ручка.	**He has** a pen.	*егó is the genitive of* **он**
У неё два брáта.	**She has** two brothers.	*её is the genitive of* **онá**

REFERENCE TABLE 4.3E: GENITIVE OF PERSONAL PRONOUNS

Nominative	Genitive	
КТО	когó	У когó
Я	меня́	У меня́
ТЫ	тебя́	У тебя́
ОН	егó	У негó *
ОНá	её	У неё *
МЫ	нас	У нас
ВЫ	вас	У вас
ОНИ́	их	У них *

*Note: When **егó, её**, and **их** follow prepositions the letter **н-** is added to these declined pronouns: У негó, У неё, У них.

Use of есть with the у + genitive construction Есть (literally an archaic present tense form of the verb "to be") is used when expressing possession in the **у + genitive** construction *when there is a question of existence or possession of an object* (Do you, or do you not have it?).

Sample sentences

У меня **есть** подруга в Москве́.	I have a friend in Moscow. (*The person with whom you are speaking may not know this fact. The speaker may simply be telling about him/herself.*)
У тебя́ **есть** каранда́ш?	Do you have a pencil? (*You are being asked whether you have one that might be borrowed or if you are prepared to write some information down.*)
У меня́ **есть** соба́ка.	I have a dog. (*This may not be known to others.*)

Есть is *not used* with the **у + genitive** construction when *describing objects or emphasizing a thought other than existence.*

Sample sentences

У меня́ све́тлые во́лосы.	I have light hair. (*The emphasis is simply on physical description.*)
У него́ две сестры́.	He has two sisters. (*Here the number of sisters is of most importance.*)
У меня́ соба́ка.	I have the dog. (*This statement emphasizes a subject/object that has been previously discussed. Note the use of the word "the" in the English translation.*)

4.3.12 GENITIVE SINGULAR OF NOUNS WITH NEGATION (У МЕНЯ́ НЕТ + GENITIVE)
Function: Talking about possessions and relations

> Face to Face L1
> Chapter 8 A
> Pages 169-174

The construction **У меня́ нет + genitive (I don't have...)** expresses lack of possession. The nouns following нет must be in the genitive case.

> **У меня́ нет + genitive *I don't have...***

Sample sentences

У меня́ **нет журна́ла**.	I don't have the/a magazine.
У неё **нет словаря́**.	She does not have the/a dictionary.
У нас **нет сестры́**.	We don't have a sister.
У них **нет бра́та**.	They do not have a brother.

REFERENCE TABLE 4.3F: SINGULAR NOUNS IN THE GENITIVE CASE

		Кто? Что?	Кого? Чего?
Masculine nouns endings		*Nominative*	*Genitive*
-consonant	**-а**	журна́л	журна́л**а**
		телеви́зор	телеви́зор**а**
-ь *becomes*	**-я**	слов́арь	словар**я́**
-й	**-я**	музе́й	музе́**я**
Neuter nouns endings		*Nominative*	*Genitive*
-о *becomes*	**-а**	письм**о́**	письм**а́**
		окн**о́**	окн**а́**
-е	**-я**	мо́р**е**	мо́р**я**
-ие	**-ия**	упражне́н**ие**	упражне́н**ия**
Feminine nouns endings		*Nominative*	*Genitive*
-а *becomes*	**-ы**	газе́т**а**	газе́т**ы**
-я	**-и**	семь**я́**	семь**и́**
-ия	**-ии**	фами́ли**я**	фами́ли**и**
-ь	**-и**	тетра́д**ь**	тетра́д**и**
spelling rule	**-и**	кни́г**а**	кни́г**и**

4.3.13 THE PREPOSITION У + GENITIVE CASE
   Function: Naming a person as a location

Face to Face L2
Chapter 2 A, D
Pages 38-41, 52

The preposition **y** + **the genitive case** of a noun or a pronoun can express the meaning *at someone's house, at someone's place.*

Sample sentences

—Вчера́ **у меня́** бы́ли друзья́.   Yesterday, friends were at my place.

—Мы за́втра ве́чером бу́дем **у Ни́ны**.   Tomorrow evening we will be at Nina's.

                                         In summer Tom lives at his
—Ле́том Том живёт **у ба́бушки**.   grandmother's place.

Note: This construction can also express location *near someone or something:*
Она́ сиди́т **у меня́**.   She is sitting **near me**.

4.3.14 DEFINING ONE NOUN WITH ANOTHER, POSSESSION
   Function: Responding to introductions, showing possession

Face to Face L2
Chapter 1 B, D
Pages 25, 31

The genitive case can be used to express that something *belongs to, is possessed by, or is part of something or someone.* This often corresponds to the English *'s* as in *Ivan's brother.* Note that in this construction, the noun *possessing* or *belonging to* is in the genitive case:

Sample sentences
phrases

учи́тель **ру́сского языка́**   teacher of **Russian language**
брат **Ива́на**   the brother **of Ivan/Ivan's...**
шко́льники **Москвы́**   the students **of Moscow**
столи́ца **страны́**   the capital **of the country/country's...**
исто́рия **го́рода**   the history **of the city/city's...**

4.3.15 THE GENITIVE PLURAL WITH МНОГО, МАЛО, СКОЛЬКО
Function: Expressing quantity, talking about choosing professions

Face to Face L1
Chapter 18 A
Pages 359-365

The **genitive plural** is used after много (much, many), мáло (few, little), скóлько (how much, how many) to express quantity in Russian:

Sample sentences

— Скóлько у вас в шкóле учени́к**óв**?

How many students do you have in (your) school?

— У нас в шкóле **мнóго** учени́кóв.

We have **many students** in (our) school.

— А у нас **мáло** учени́к**óв**.

We have **few students**.

The genitive plural noun endings can be quite complex. Many of the phrases used when expressing quantity can be memorized initially together with the genitive case endings.

REFERENCE TABLE 4.3G: BASIC GENITIVE PLURAL NOUN ENDINGS

Скóлько?, мнóго, мáло...

Masculine noun endings		*Nominative*	*Genitive*
-consonant	-ОВ	институ́т	институ́т**ов**
		учени́к	учени́к**óв**
-й	-ев	музéй	музé**ев**
-ь *becomes*	-ей	учи́тель	учи́тел**ей**
		словáрь	словар**éй**
-ж,-ч,-ш,-щ	-ей	карандáш	карандаш**éй**
Neuter noun endings		*Nominative*	*Genitive*
-о *becomes*	- ø	письмó	пи́сем
		окнó	óкон
-е	-ей	мóр**е**	мóр**ей**
-ие	-ий	упражнéн**ие**	упражнéн**ий**
Feminine noun endings		*Nominative*	*Genitive*
-а *becomes*	- ø	газéт**а**	газéт
		кни́г**а**	кни́г
-я	-ь/ ø	недéл**я**	недéл**ь**
		пéсн**я**	пéсен
-ья	-ей	семь**я́**	семь**éй**
-ия	-ий	фами́л**ия**	фами́л**ий**
-ь	-ей	тетрáд**ь**	тетрáд**ей**

Note: Several nouns have genitive plural forms which are identical to the nominative singular when used with скóлько (how much, how many): человéк, солдáт. For example, Скóлько человéк? (How many people?), Скóлько солдáт? (How many soldiers?), *but*, Мнóго/Мáло людéй/солдáтов. (Many/Few people/soldiers.)

4.3.16 GENITIVE PLURAL OF ADJECTIVES AND PRONOUNS
Function: Expressing genitive case of adjectives in plural form

Face to Face L2
Chapter 14 A, D
Pages 298, 312

The plural forms of adjectives and some pronouns (эти, мои, твои, наши, ваши, свои, какие, такие, другие) end in **-ых/-их** in the genitive case. These endings are similar for the adjectival prepositional and the accusative masculine animate plurals.

Sample sentences
Genitive

У нас нет так**их** маскара́дн**ых**
  нового́дн**их** костю́мов.

We (in our country) don't have such
  New Year's Eve costumes.

Prepositional

Кто у вас хо́дит в так**их**
  маскара́дн**ых** нового́дн**ых**
  костю́мах?

Who in your country wears such New
  Year's Eve costumes?

4.3.17 COMPARATIVES БОЛЬШЕ, МЕНЬШЕ
Function: Making comparisons

Face to Face L2
Chapter 12 A, D
Pages 249, 265

The comparatives **бо́льше** (more, larger), **ме́ньше** (less, smaller) **+ the genitive case** express and compare amounts of objects.

Sample sentences

У меня́ мно́го ру́сских ма́рок, а у друга́
  ме́ньше ру́сских ма́рок.

I have many Russian stamps, but my
  friend has **fewer Russian stamps**.

В Сиби́ри обы́чно быва́ет **бо́льше сне́га**,
  чем в Москве́.

Siberia usually has **more snow** than in
  Moscow.*

*Note: The word **чем** (than) is often used in comparative expressions and is followed by the nominative of nouns or by prepositional phrases:

Он чита́ет бо́льше, чем я.

He reads more than I (**чем + nom.**).

У нас бо́льше сне́га, чем на ю́ге.

We have/get more snow than in the South (**чем + prepositional phrase**).

4.3.18 THE PREPOSITION ДЛЯ + GENITIVE
Function: The idea of *for someone or something*

Face to Face L2
Chapter 14 A, D
Pages 295, 311

The preposition **для + the genitive case** expresses *for* and *intended for*.

Sample sentences

У меня́ есть **для вас** пода́рок.

I have a present **for you**.

Эти цветы́—**для учи́тельницы**.

These flowers are **for the teacher**.

Это помидо́ры **для сала́та**.

Here are some tomatoes **for the salad**.

Это шкату́лка **для пи́сем**.

This is a lacquer box **for letters**.

4.3.19 THE PREPOSITION ПОСЛЕ (AFTER) WITH THE GENITIVE CASE | Face to Face L1
Chapter 18 C
Pages 373-377

Function: Talking about decisions and intensions

The preposition **после** (after) may be used to express the decision or intention to do something *after* an event has taken place.

Sample sentences

После шко́лы все ребя́та реши́ли поступи́ть в университе́т. | **After completing school**, all the kids decided to enroll in the univeristy.

Что вы хоти́те де́лать **по́сле уро́ка**? | What do you want to do **after class**?

По́сле кани́кул мы бу́дем в шко́ле. | **After vacation** we will be in school.

4.3.20 THE PREPOSITIONS ИЗ AND С WITH THE GENITIVE CASE | Face to Face L2
Chapter 1 A, D
Pages 20-23, 31

Function: Asking and telling where one is from

The prepositions **из** and **с + the genitive case** are used to express the places from where people come or have arrived. These expressions answer the question **Откуда?** (Where from?). Note the pairing of **из** and **с** with the prepositions **в** and **на** which express motion to a place.

Sample sentences

Отку́да? | Куда́?

Са́ша прие́дет **из Вашингто́на**. | Са́ша пое́дет **в Вашингто́н**.
Sasha is arriving **from Washington**. | Sasha is going **to Washington**.

Она́ придёт **с трениро́вки**. | Ла́ура пойдёт **на трениро́вку**.
Laura will come **from practice**. | Laura will go **to practice**.

Often the question **отку́да?** is used to ask where people are from (denoting their country of origin), as in the question **Отку́да вы?**

| —Отку́да вы? | **Where are you from?** |
| — Я **из** Аме́рики/Кана́ды/ Росси́и/Герма́нии. | I'm **from** America/Canada/ Russia/Germany. |

Some foreign borrowed nouns ending in **-о** (**метро́**, **кино́**) and proper names ending in **-о**, and **-и** (**Чика́го**, **Со́чи**) do *not* decline: **из кино́**, **в метро́**, **в Со́чи**, **из Со́чи**.

4.3.21 THE PREPOSITION ИЗ + THE GENITIVE CASE | Faces and Voices
Chapter 6 Б
Pages 167-168

Function: Indicating what something is made of

To indicate *what something is made of/from*, the preposition **из + the genitive case** is used:

Sample sentences

Она́ вяза́ла ко́фту **из ше́рсти**. | She knitted a sweater **from wool**.

Э́то пла́тье **из ше́рсти**. | The dress is made **of wool**.

Они пьют сок **из виногра́да**.

The are drinking grape juice (*lit., made from grapes*).

Они пьют сок **из я́блок**.

The are drinking juice **from apples**.

4.3.22 THE PREPOSITION ОТ + GENITIVE CASE
Function: Special occasions—giving gifts

Face to Face L2
Chapter 9 A, D
Pages 187-88, 201

The preposition **от + genitive** can express *from someone* in the case someone: 1) sends you mail, 2) gives you presents, or 3) is a source of information:

Sample sentences

Мне пришло́ письмо́ **от дру́га**.	A letter **from a friend** arrived for me.
От кого́ э́тот пода́рок?	**From whom** is this present?
От кого́ ты узна́л об э́том?	**From whom** did you find out about this?
От учи́теля.	**From the teacher**.

If a *place* is a source, then **из + genitive** is used:

Га́ля получи́ла письмо́ **из Нью-Йо́рка**.	Galya got a letter **from New York**.
Майкл получи́л но́вости **от дру́га из Росси́и**.	Michael received news **from a friend in (from) Russia**.

4.3.23 THE PREPOSITIONS ОТ AND ДО + GENITIVE CASE
Function: Suggesting going somewhere, getting around town

Face to Face L2
Chapter 6 A,D
Pages 115, 120-121, 135-136

When indicating relative locations the prepositions **от** (from), **до** (up to, as far as) are often used with verbs of motion. These prepositions take the genitive case.

недалеко́ **от** + genitive case	*not far from...*
идти́ **от** + gen. **до** + gen.	*to go from...to...*

Sample sentences

—Где нахо́дится Кра́сная пло́щадь?	Where is Red Square located?
—Недалеко́ **от но́вой гости́ницы**.	Not far **from the new hotel**.
—Недалеко́ **от но́вого теа́тра**.	Not far **from the new theater**.
Они́ иду́т **от шко́лы до до́ма**,	They are going **from the school to the house**,
и пото́м **от до́ма до пло́щади**.	and then **from the house up to the square**.

The preposition **до** is also used with the prefixed verbs of motion **дойти́/ дое́хать** when asking for directions. In this sense, the verb and preposition express *to reach or go as far as a destination*. (For more on this consult Chapter 7, grammar point 7.69.)

Sample sentences

—Извините, как мне **дойти до** Исторического театра/Красной площади?

Excuse me, how do I **get to/reach** the Historical Museum/Red Square?

—Нам надо **доехать до вокзала** или **до гостиницы**?

—Do we need **to get to the train station** or **to the hotel**?

4.3.24	**THE PREPOSITION БЕЗ + THE GENITIVE CASE** **Function:** Talking about the absence of an object or a person	Faces and Voices Chapter 7 A Pages 191

The preposition **без + the genitive case** (without) refers to the exclusion or the absence of something or someone.

Sample sentences

Мы пошли в театр **без Наташи**, потому что она заболела.

We went to the theater **without Natasha** because she got sick.

Конечно, **без машины** в деревне трудно.

Of course, it's difficult (to get by) in the countryside **without a car**.

Без классики жить нельзя.

It's impossible to live **without the classics**.

Трудно переводить статьи **без хорошего словаря**.

It's difficult to translate articles **without a good dictionary**.

4.3.25	**THE PREPOSITION ПРОТИВ + THE GENITIVE CASE** **Function:** Expressing opposition or objection	Faces and Voices Chapter 9 Б Pages 242-243

The preposition **против** (opposed, against, opposite) may be used in three ways: 1) by itself in the meaning *against* or *opposed*, 2) with pronouns, adjectives, and nouns in **the genitive case** in the meaning *against something/someone* or *contrary to something/someone*.

Sample sentences

Я очень люблю длинные волосы, а моя мама **против**.

I really like long hair, but my mom **is opposed to it**.

Я не могу идти **против моды**.

I can't go **against fashion**.

Finally, 3) the opposite of **против** is **за** (for). It can also be used either by itself, or can be followed by **the accusative case**.

Sample sentences

Я всегда был против хардрока, а мой брат — **за**.

I was always against hard rock, and my brother was **for it**.

Я **за миниюбки**. Но маме они совсем не нравятся.

I am **for miniskirts**. But mom doesn't like them at all.

4.3.26 **МНÓГО AND МНÓГИЕ AND THEIR USAGE WITH PRONOUNS**
Function: Expressing large quantities (many, much, a lot, etc.)

Мир русских
Lesson 2
Pages 55-57

Both **мнóго** and **мнóгие** are translated from Russian as *many, much, a lot*, etc., but they differ in their meaning and usage in Russian.

Мнóго (many, a lot, much) The adverb **мнóго** denotes a large number of people or a large amount of something. **Мнóго** is used as an antonym to **мáло** (few) , **немнóго** (some), and **нескóлько** (several, a few).

У негó **мнóго** книг.	He has **a lot** of books.
У негó **немнóго** книг.	He has **some** books.
У негó **мáло** книг.	He has **few** books.
У негó тóлько **нéсколько** книг.	He has only **a few** books.

In sentences with **мнóго** as the subject, the verb is usually used in the neuter singular.

Мнóго + noun (gen. pl. with countable nouns) + Verb (neuter singular)

Приéхало /Приéдет **мнóго** турѝстов.	**Many tourists** came/will come.

Мнóго + noun (gen. sing. with abstract/singular nouns)

Он купѝл мнóго книг, потрáтил **мнóго** врéмени и дéнег.	He bought many books, and spent **a lot of time** and money.

Мнóгие and Мнóгие из + the Genitive Case (many of, many, much, a lot) Мнóгие translates as *many* or *a lot* and denotes part or a large number of a certain whole:

Мнóгие ученики...	Many students (in a class or in a school)
Мнóгие лю́ди...	Many people (on the street or living in a town)
Мнóгие сéмьи...	Many families (in this town or living on this street)

The certain whole to which **мнóгие** refers may be either named or implied. **Мнóгие** (not **мнóго**) usually stands before the plural subject beginning a sentence. In sentences with **мнóгие** as the subject, the verb is used in the plural form.

мнóгие + plural noun (belonging to a whole) + verb in the plural

Мнóгие дéвушки занимáются спóртом.	**Many** girls are involved in sports. (*Many girls* out of all in a school or of girls in general.)
Мнóгие лю́ди так дýмают.	**Many** people think so. (*Many people* who hold opinions on a certain topic.)
Мнóгие молоды́е сéмьи снимáют квартѝру.	**Many** young families rent apartments. (*Many young families* out of families in general.)

Мно́гие ребя́та в кла́ссе игра́ют на гита́ре.	**Many** guys in the class play the guitar. (*Many of the guys* in class).
Мно́гие дома́ на э́той у́лице ста́рые.	**Many** houses on this street are old. (*Many houses* particularly of those on this street.

Мно́гие may also be used with the preposition из + **the genitive case** to name the group or whole. This translates as "Many of..."

```
┌─────────────────────────────────────────────────────────────┐
│ МНО́ГИЕ + ИЗ + a noun or a pronoun in the genitive case      │
└─────────────────────────────────────────────────────────────┘
```

У него́ мно́го друзе́й. **Мно́гие из них** у́чатся в на́шей шко́ле.	He has many friends. **Many of them** study in our school.
Я зна́ю мно́гих его́ друзе́й. Я знако́м со **мно́гими из его́ друзе́й***.	I know many of his friends. I am acquainted **with many of his friends**.

***Note:** Мно́гие declines like plural adjectives: мно́гие, мно́гих, мно́гим, мно́гими, мно́гих.

The opposite of **мно́гие** is expressed by **немно́гие** (a few, not many) and **не все** (not all). As with **мно́гие**, these constructions modify a plural noun or pronoun:

Мно́гие дере́вья уже́ жёлтые.	**Many** trees are already yellow.
То́лько **немно́гие** дере́вья уже́ жёлтые.	Only **a few** trees are already yellow.
Не все, но **мно́гие** дере́вья жёлтые.	**Not all,** but **many** trees are yellow.

4.3.27 НЕСКОЛЬКО, НЕКОТОРЫЙ, НЕКОТОРЫЕ AND THEIR USAGE WITH NOUNS OR PRONOUNS

Function: Expressing "a few", "several", "some", "a couple of"

Мир ру́сских Lesson 2 Pages 58-59

Не́сколько **(several)** Не́сколько denotes a small number of persons or things and is usually translated from Russian as *several, a couple of, a few* or *some*. As with мно́го (much, many, a lot), не́сколько is generally used in the predicate of a sentence.

```
┌─────────────────────────────────────────────────────────────┐
│ не́сколько + genitive plural of a concrete/countable noun     │
└─────────────────────────────────────────────────────────────┘
```

Он купи́л **не́сколько** книг.   He bought **a few/some** books.

Recall that the special genitive plural forms челове́к (people) and раз (times) are used with **не́сколько, ско́лько** (how much, how many) and **сто́лько** (so much, so many). These special forms are the same as their nominative singular forms.

не́сколько челове́к	several people
не́сколько раз	several times

Не́который, Не́которые **(some)** Не́который, and its plural form Не́которые, is usually translated in English as *some*. They can be used in two ways.

1)   With abstract nouns (time, doubt, etc.) to denote a small number or amount. Не́который agrees in number and gender with its referent noun.

некоторый agreeing in number and gender + abstract noun

не́которое вре́мя (вре́мя n.)   **some** time
не́которая стра́нность(стра́нность f.)   **some** irregularity/strangeness
не́которые сомне́ния (doubts pl.)   **some** doubts

2)   **Не́который** and **не́которые** are used to express a small, imprecise number of persons or things as a part a stated or implied whole. This usage is similar to that of **мно́гие** (many) and **мно́гие из** (many of). **Не́который** can modify the plural subject of a sentence.

не́которые agreeing in number/gender + a countable noun
or
не́которые + из + genitive case of a countable noun or a pronoun

Не́которые его́ друзья́ счита́ют, что я был прав.

Я зна́ю то́лько **не́которых из его́ друзе́й.**

Он чита́л мно́гие его́ стихи́. **Не́которые из них** он зна́ет наизу́сть.

Some of his friends consider me to be correct.

I know only **some of his friends.**

He read many of his poems. **Some of them** he memorized (knew by heart).

Sample Sentences
Не́сколько (several)

Я зна́ю **не́сколько** ру́сских наро́дных пе́сен.

— Ты ви́дел все фи́льмы на э́том фестива́ле?

— Нет, я ви́дел то́лько **не́сколько.**

В це́нтре го́рода есть **не́сколько** ма́леньких магази́нов.

В э́том году́ из на́шего кла́сса в Москву́ е́дут **не́сколько** ребя́т.

I know **several** Russian folk songs.

Did you see all of the films at the festival?

No, I saw only **several.**

Downtown (*lit., in the center of the city*) there are **several** small stores.

This year **several** kids from our grade are going to Moscow.

Не́который, Не́которые (some)

— Все фи́льмы понра́вились?

—Не́которые понра́вились, а **не́которые** нет.

— Ты зна́ешь все э́ти пе́сни?

— Не́которые я услы́шал в де́тстве.

— Ты до́лго занима́ешься джо́гингом?

— Не́которое вре́мя.

Did you like all off the films?

Some I liked, and some I didn't.

Do you know all of these songs?

Some I heard when I was little (*lit., in childhood*).

Have you been jogging long?

For **some** time.

4.3.28 THE VERBS ХВАТА́ТЬ/ХВАТИ́ТЬ AND THE GENITIVE *Function:* Expressing the idea of "enough"	Faces and Voices Chapter 7 Б Page 197

To express the idea of *enough*, use the construction **хвата́ть/хвати́ть + the genitive case**. These verbs are used only in the third-person singular or plural. The logical subject is either in the dative case or the genitive case with the preposition **у**.

Of what don't/didn't they have enough?

Чего́	*им*	(не) хвата́ет/(не) хвати́ло?	*logical subject in the dative case*
Чего́	*у них*	(не) хвата́ет/(не) хвати́ло?	*logical subject in the genitive case*

Dative Мне *or* Genitive with у... У меня́	don't have enough не хвата́ет didn't have enough не хвати́ло	+ Genitive Чего́

Sample sentences

Я хоте́л бы бо́льше занима́ться спо́ртом, но **у меня́** никогда́ **не хвата́ет вре́мени**.

I would like to play sports more but I never have **enough time**.

Мне не хвати́ло де́нег, что́бы купи́ть большу́ю ва́зу, поэ́тому я купи́л ма́ленькую.

I didn't have **enough money** to buy a large vase, therefore I bought a small one.

Моему́ бра́ту всегда́ **хвата́ет эне́ргии**, что́бы всё сде́лать краси́во и хорошо́.

My brother always has **enough energy** to do everything beautifully and well.

Dative Case

КомУ́? ЧемУ́?
Да́тельный паде́ж

4.4.29 Overview: What are the functions of the dative case? This case generally denotes the indirect object in sentences and phrases marking the recipient of the action (She sent a letter to her *brother*.). Several prepositions and verbal contructions govern the dative case.

REFERENCE TABLE 4.4A: TYPICAL USES OF THE DATIVE CASE

•Answers the questions **КомУ́?** (To whom?) **ЧемУ́?** (To what?). Denotes the indirect object in a sentence.

•Expresses the logical subject in impersonal expressions with **мо́жно** (possibility), **нельзя́** (not allowed, not permitted), and **на́до/ну́жно** (necessary, need to) and when stating one's age.

•Typically used with the prepositions **к** (to, toward) and **по** (on, along, by).

•Governed by several verbs including **нра́виться** (to be pleasing, to like) and **каза́ться** (to seem).

REFERENCE TABLE 4.4B: BASIC DATIVE CASE ENDINGS

Singular	Masculine	Neuter	Feminine
nouns	-у/-ю	-у/-ю	-е/-и
adjectives	<—— -ому/-ему ——>		-ой/-ей
Plural			
nouns	<——— -ам/-ям ———>		
adjectives	<——— -ым/-им ———>		

REFERENCE TABLE 4.4C: EXAMPLE NOUNS IN THE DATIVE CASE BY GENDER IN THEIR SINGULAR AND PLURAL FORMS

Masculine	-consonant	-й	several in -а/-я	several in -ь
sing.	столу́ (table, desk) ученику́ (student m.)	музе́ю (museum)	де́душке (grandfather)	словарю́ (dictionary)
pl.	стола́м ученика́м	музе́ям	де́душкам	словаря́м

Neuter	-о	-е	-ие	several in -мя
sing.	письму́ (letter)	мо́рю (sea)	зда́нию (building)	и́мени (first name)
pl.	пи́сьмам	моря́м	зда́ниям	имена́м

Feminine	-а	-я	-ия	-ь
sing.	шко́ле (school) кни́ге (book)	дере́вне (countryside)	лаборато́рии (laboratory)	пло́щади (square)
pl.	шко́лам кни́гам	дере́вням	лаборато́риям	площадя́м

REFERENCE TABLE 4.4D: SPECIAL NOUN CATEGORIES IN THE DATIVE CASE

Noun Type	*Singular*	*Plural*
•Feminine nouns дочь and мать	до́чери (-ер-) ма́тери	дочеря́м (-ер-) матеря́м
•Feminine nouns любо́вь and це́рковь	любви́ це́ркви	no plural form церква́м
•Masculine nouns in -анин/-янин	граждани́ну	гра́жданам
•Masculine nouns in -онок/-ёнок	котёнку	котя́там
•Neuter nouns in -мя: и́мя	и́мени (-мен-)	имена́м (-мен-)
•Neuter nouns не́бо and чу́до	не́бу чу́ду	небеса́м чудеса́м

4.4.30	**USING THE DATIVE CASE TO NAME THE INDIRECT OBJECT** *Function:* Naming the recipient of an action	Face to Face L1 Chapter 19 B Pages 391-393

Indirect objects are the objects or people in sentences which indirectly receive the action of the verb. They are expressed by the dative case and answer the questions **Кому?** (*to* whom?) and **Чему?** (*to* what?).

— **Кому** ты написа́ла это письмо́?   **To whom** did you write this letter?
— Я написа́ла письмо́ **ба́бушке**.   I wrote the letter **to grandma**.

In the above example **кому** and **ба́бушке** are indirect objects which receive the direct object, the letter (письмо́).

REFERENCE TABLE 4.4E: SINGULAR NOUNS IN THE DATIVE CASE

		Кто? Что?	Кому? Чему?
Masculine nouns endings		*Nominative*	*Dative*
-consonant	-у	Ива́н	Ива́н**у**
-й	-ю	Андре́й	Андре́**ю**
-ель	-елю	учи́тель	учи́тел**ю**
-ь *becomes*	-ю	И́горь	Иго́р**ю**
Neuter nouns endings		*Nominative*	*Dative*
-о *becomes*	-у	окно́	окн**у́**
-е	-ю	мо́ре	мо́р**ю**
-ие	-ию	зда́ние	зда́н**ию**
Feminine nouns endings		*Nominative*	*Dative*
-а *becomes*	-е	Ма́рта	Ма́рт**е**
-я	-е	Та́ня	Та́н**е**
-ия	-ии	Мари́я	Мари́**и**
-ь	-и	ло́щадь	ло́щад**и**

Sample sentences

Я показа́ла **учи́тельнице** мою́ тетра́дь.   I showed **the teacher** my notebook.

Кто написа́л письмо́ **Анто́ну**?   Who wrote the letter to **Anton**?

Я купи́л слова́рь **моему́ дру́гу**.   I bought a dictionary **for my friend**.

Мо**я** ма́ма чита́ла кни́гу **мне**.   My mom was reading the book **to me**.

4.4.31	**USING THE VERB** НРА́ВИТЬСЯ **WITH DATIVE PRONOUNS** *Function:* Expressing likes and dislikes	Face to Face L1 Chapter 9 C Pages 195-198

While the verb **люби́ть** (to like, to love) generally refers to a feeling that is long-term and to something or someone always liked, **нра́виться** (*lit., it is pleasing to me*) describes liking something upon first encounter as an initial impression. Compare the use of these two verbs below:

любить

Я **люблю** Москву́. Это о́чень краси́вый го́род!
I like/love Moscow. It's a very beautiful city!

(Positive feeling developed over years of living there or many visits there.)

нра́виться

Мне **нра́вится** Москва́. Это о́чень краси́вый го́род!
I like Moscow. It's a very beautiful city!

(Positive feeling expressed by someone who doesn't know Moscow well or is stating their impression from a visit — therefore the avoidance of using **люби́ть**.)

The verb **нра́виться** conjugates according to the number (singular or plural) of the object of affection in the statement. The person who is expressing pleasure or displeasure is in the dative case.

	Dative		**Singular object**	I/You/etc. like...
я	Мне		э́тот го́род.	this city.
ты	Тебе́		э́та у́лица.	this street.
он	Ему́	**нра́вится**	это зда́ние.	this building.
она́	Ей		шко́ла.	the school.
мы	Нам		хокке́й.	hockey.
вы	Вам		ваш дом.	your house.
они́	Им		э́тот фильм.	this film.
			Plural object	I/You/etc. like...
	Мне		ша́хматы.	chess.
	Ей	**нра́вятся**	э́ти значки́.	these badges.
	Им		э́ти цветы́.	these flowers.
			э́ти цвета́.	these colors.

To express not liking or *displeasure* as an impression, negate the verb: **не нра́виться**.

Мне **не нра́вится** борщ.   I **don't like** the borsht.
Мне **не нра́вятся** конфе́ты.   I **don't like** the candy.

4.4.32 USE OF THE DATIVE CASE OF PERSONAL PRONOUNS WHEN INDICATING AGE
Function: Talking about age

Face to Face LI
Chapter 17 B
Pages 346-347

When talking about age, the person, pronoun, or name of the person whose age is stated is declined in **the dative case**.

Sample sentences
— Ско́лько **тебе́** лет?   How old are **you**?
— **Мне** 14 лет.   **I'm** 14 years old.
Ива́ну 14 лет.   **Ivan** is 14 years old.
Ма́ше 21 год.   **Masha** is 21 years old.
Ему́ 15 лет.   **He's** 15 years old.

Ей 20 лет.	**She's** 20 years old.
Ма́ме 42 го́да.	**Mom** is 42 years old.
Бра́ту 34 го́да.	**My brother** is 34 years old.
Сестре́ 17 лет.	**Sister** is 17 years old.

When stating one's age, the word for year (год), declines depending on the number preceding it. Refer to Chapter 6, Numbers, and its overview section, grammar point 6.1 for complete listing of numbers and usage with statements of one's age.

numerals	form of год (year)	case
1 (21, 31, 41...)	год	Nominative case
2 (22, 32, 42...)	го́да	Genitive singular
3, 4 (23, 34, 43, 54...)	го́да	Genitive singular
5-20, 25-30 (35-40)	лет	Genitive plural

4.4.33 THE DATIVE PLURAL OF NOUNS AND POSSESSIVE PRONOUNS *Function:* Naming the recipient of a gift	Face to Face L2 Chapter 18 A, D Pages 386-391, 399

The dative case can express *for whom something is intended*, as in a gift or a purchase:

Я покупа́ю пода́рки сво**и́м** роди́тел**ям** и сво**и́м** шко́льн**ым** друзь**я́м**.	I buy presents **for my parents** and **my friends from school**.

The **plural forms** of the dative case are the same for all genders: -ым/-им for adjectives and some pronouns, and -ам/-ям for nouns.

— Кому́ ты покупа́ешь пода́рки?	**For whom** are you buying presents?
— Я покупа́ю пода́рки...	I am buying presents...

possessive adjectives	*adjectives*	*nouns*	
мо**и́м**	но́в**ым**	подру́г**ам**	for my new girlfriends
тво**и́м**	ста́р**ым**	друзь**я́м**	for your old friends
его́/её	мла́дш**им**	бра́ть**ям**	for his/her younger brothers
на́ш**им**	хоро́ш**им**	учител**я́м**	for our good teachers
ва́ш**им**	ста́рш**им**	сёстр**ам**	for your older sisters
их	у́мн**ым**	учени́к**ам**	for their smart students

4.4.34 ПАМЯТНИК + THE DATIVE CASE *Function:* Mentioning "to whom" monuments and memorials are dedicated	Face to Face L2 Chapter 6 B,D Pages 124-126, 138

The dative case expresses the name of the person *to whom* a statue or monument is dedicated. Note that all feminine last names, as well as masculine last names ending in -ий, have adjectival endings:

Sample sentences

Вот здесь памятник Пушкин**у**	*masc., noun ending*	Here is a statue to Pushkin.
...Маяковск**ому**	*masc., adjectival ending*	..(dedicated) to Mayakovsky.
...Ахматов**ой**	*fem. (all like adjectives)*	..(in memory of) Akhmatova.

First names decline like regular nouns:

памятник	Юри**ю** Долгорук**ому**	A statue to Yuri Dolgoruki.
	Александр**у** Пушкин**у**	Alexander Pushkin.
	Анн**е** Ахматов**ой**	Anna Akhmatova.
	Натальe Баранск**ой**	Natalya Baranskaya.
	Екатерин**е** Втор**ой**	Catherine the Great.

4.4.35 THE PREPOSITION ПО WITH THE DATIVE CASE
Function: Giving directions or instructions; getting around town

> Face to Face L2
> Chapter 7 A, D
> Pages 145-147, 158

The preposition **по + dative case** has numerous translations. It is frequently used with a noun to relate where the action occurs. Compare:

> Я иду в парк (destination). —
> Я иду в парк **по бульвару** (location).

Sample sentences

Мы шли **по улице** и разговаривали.	We were walking **along the street** and talking.
Я люблю кататься на велосипеде **по нашему парку**.	I like to ride my bike **around our park**.

4.4.36 THE PREPOSITION К + THE DATIVE CASE
Function: Naming people's homes as destinations

> Face to Face L2
> Chapter 8 B, D
> Pages 171-174, 179

The construction **к + the dative case** with verbs of motion expresses movement *towards* a person or person's place or home.

Sample sentences

Давай пойдём **к другу/ подруге/друзьям**.	Let's go see **(our) friend/female friend/friends**.
Сегодня придут **к Борису/Наташе** Джон и Мэри.	Today John and Mary are coming over **to Boris's/Natasha's**.
Гости вчера пришли **к Джону Смиту и Саре Смит**.*	The guests arrived yesterday **to John Smith's and Sarah Smith's**.
Гости вчера пришли **к Марии Смит**.*	The guests arrived yesterday **to Maria Smith's**.

*****Note:** When using foreign (non-Russian) names, if a woman's first and last names do not end in a vowel, they will not decline. Refer to Chapter 2, Nouns, for an overview on declension of foreign names.

4.4.37 **THE PREPOSITION К + THE DATIVE CASE IN THE EXPRESSION** ГОТОВИТЬСЯ/ПОДГОТОВИТЬСЯ; СПОСОБНОСТЬ К ЧЕМУ?
Function: Preparing for an event; Talking about peoples' abilities and talents

Faces and Voices
Chapter 2 A; 2 Б
Pages 34-35; 41

Events The reflexive verbs **готовиться /подготовиться** (to prepare for) are intransitive and take the preposition **к + the dative case**: **готовиться /подготовиться к чему?** The event towards which one is preparing follows the preposition **к** and is declined in the dative case.

Sample sentences

ГОТОВИТЬСЯ	*к чему?*	
Я готов**люсь**	к экза́мен**у**.	I am preparing for an exam.
Ты гото́вишься	к пра́здник**у**.	You're preparing for a holiday.
Они гото́вятся	к Но́в**ому** го́д**у**.	They are preparing for New Year's.
	к соревнова́ни**ю**.	for the competition.
	к интервь**ю**.	for an interview.

Abilities To talk about the abilities and talent of someone, the construction **спосо́бности к + the dative case** is used:

спосо́бности (нет спосо́бностей) *a talent for (no talent for)...*	к чему?	
У Татья́ны есть спосо́бности . . .	к му́зык**е**.	music
	к спо́рт**у**.	sports
У Ви́ктора нет спосо́бностей . . .	к матема́тик**е**.	math
	к рисова́ни**ю**.	drawing
	к язык**а́м**.	languages
	к поэ́з**ии**.	poetry

Another common way to speak about general talents and abilities is to use the adjectival form of the talent to modify the plural noun **спосо́бности**.

спосо́бности к му́зыке   or   **музыка́льные** спосо́бности
спосо́бности к рисова́нию   or   **худо́жественные** спосо́бности.

У Ви́ктора есть	музыка́льные спорти́вные матема́тические	спосо́бности.
У Татья́ны нет	музыка́льных спорти́вных матема́тических	спосо́бностей.

Sample sentences

— А у Илю́ши есть **спосо́бности к му́зыке**?

Is Ilyusha **talented musically**? (*lit., Does he have talents towards music?*)

— Да, у него **большие музыкальные способности**. Я считаю, что он очень талантливый музыкант.

Yes. He he has **great musical talents**. I consider him a very talented musician.

4.4.38 THE VERB ОТНОСИТЬСЯ WITH THE PREPOSITION К AND THE DATIVE CASE
Function: Talking about how one relates to something or someone

| Faces and Voices |
| Chapter 2 A |
| Page 36 |

The verb and preposition **относиться к + the dative case** is used to express an *opinion, feelings, or how one relates to someone or something*. Note in the examples below, that a literal translation is not possible, but the general feelings or opinions about someone or something are defined by an adverb (e.g., **плохо**, **хорошо**, etc.).

Sample sentences

Как ты **относишься к кому/чему**?

How do you **feel/relate to someone/ something**?

Я **отношусь к моде** нормально.

I'm not really a slave **to fashion**.

Я знаю, что ты плохо **относишься к року**.

I know that you don't really like **rock music**.

Он плохо **относится к классике**.

He doesn't like **the classics** (music, literature, etc.).

Мы с интересом **относимся к группе «ДДТ»**.

We're always interested in what **the group DDT** is doing.

Не понимаю, почему вы плохо **относитесь к Эрику Клаптону**.

I don't understand why you don't like **Eric Clapton**.

Американцы хорошо **относятся к Горбачёву**.

Americans are very fond of **Gorbachev**.

Как ты **относишься к русской церкви**?

What do you think of the **Russian Orthodox Church**?

Школьники хорошо **относятся к новому учителю**.

The students get along really well with their **new teacher**.

Instrumental Case

Кем? Чем?
Творительный падеж

4.5.39 Overview: What are the functions of the instrumental case? This case typically denotes the agent or instrument with which an action is done (e.g., to write *with a pen*). It also may be used in describing how or the manner with which an action is done (to go *by foot* - **пешком**). Several prepositions, verbs, and constructions require the use of the instrumental case.

REFERENCE TABLE 4.5A: TYPICAL USES OF THE INSTRUMENTAL CASE

•Answers the questions Кем? (By whom?)/С кем? (With whom?) and Чем? (By means of what?)/С чем? (With what?).

•Denotes the agent or instrument of an action by answering the question Чем? (By means of what?): Она́ пи́шет ру́чкой. (She is writing *with a pen*.).

•Used to denote the location of things with the prepositions: с (with), над (above), под (below), пе́ред (in front of), за (behind), ме́жду (between), ря́дом с (next to).

•Expressed "in" or "at" with parts of the day and seasons of the year: у́тром (in the morning), ле́том (during the summer).

•Several verbs govern this case including быть in the past and future tense.

REFERENCE TABLE 4.5B: BASIC INSTRUMENTAL CASE ENDINGS

Singular	Masculine	Neuter	Feminine
nouns	-ом/-ем	-ом/-ем	-ой/-ей
adjectives	<—— -ым/-им ——>		-ой/-ей

Plural	
nouns	<———— -ами/-ями ————>
adjectives	<———— -ыми/-ими ————>

REFERENCE TABLE 4.5C: EXAMPLE NOUNS IN THE INSTRUMENTAL CASE BY GENDER IN THEIR SINGULAR AND PLURAL FORMS

Masculine	-consonant	-й	several in -a/-я	several in -ь
sing.	столо́м (table, desk) учени́ко́м (student m.)	музе́ем (museum)	де́душкой (grandfather)	словарём (dictionary)
pl.	стола́ми учени́ка́ми	музе́ями	де́душками	словаря́ми

Neuter	-o	-e	-ие	several in -мя
sing.	письмо́м (letter)	мо́рем (sea)	зда́нием (building)	и́менем (first name)
pl.	пи́сьмами	моря́ми	зда́ниями	имена́ми

Feminine	-a	-я	-ия	-ь
sing.	шко́лой (school) кни́гой (book)	дере́вней (country-side)	лаборато́рией (laboratory)	пло́щадью (square)
pl.	шко́лами кни́гами	дере́внями	лаборато́риями	площадя́ми

REFERENCE TABLE 4.5D: SPECIAL NOUN CATEGORIES IN THE INSTRUMENTAL CASE

Noun Type		Singular	Plural
•Feminine nouns	дочь and мать	дóчерью (-ер-) мáтерью	дочерьмú (-ер-) матерями
•Feminine nouns	любóвь and цéрковь	любóвью цéрковью	no plural form церквáми
•Masculine nouns in -анин/-янин		гражданúном	грáжданами
•Masculine nouns in -онок/-ёнок		котёнком	котятами
•Neuter nouns in -мя: úмя		úменем (-мен-)	именáми (-мен-)
•Neuter nouns	нéбо and чýдо	нéбом чýдом	небесáми чудесáми

4.5.40 USING THE PREPOSITION C WITH THE INSTRUMENTAL CASE

***Function:* Explaining with whom or with what**

Face to Face L1
Chapter 14 C
Pages 292-295

The preposition **c + the instrumental case** is used to answer the questions С кем? (With whom?) and С чем? (With what?). This prepositional phrase describes *with whom/what* or *in the company of whom/what* an action takes place.

Basic singular instrumental case endings for nouns are formed by the following rules:

REFERENCE TABLE 4.5E: SINGULAR NOUNS IN THE INSTRUMENTAL CASE

		Кто? Что?	Кем? Чем?
Masculine nouns endings		*Nominative*	*Instrumental*
-consonant	-ОМ	журнáл	журнáл**ом**
-й	-ем	Андрéй	Андрé**ем**
-ель	-елем	учúтель	учúтел**ем**
-ь (-ь)	-ем (-ём)	словáрь	словар**ём**
Neuter nouns endings		*Nominative*	*Instrumental*
-о *becomes*	-ом	письмó окнó	письм**óм** окн**óм**
-е	-ем	мóр**е**	мóр**ем**
-ие	-ием	упражнéн**ие**	упражнéн**ием**
Feminine nouns endings		*Nominative*	*Instrumental*
-а *becomes*	-ой	газéт**а**	газéт**ой**
-я	-ей	Тáн**я**	Тáн**ей**
-ия	-ией	фамúли**я**	фамúли**ей**
-ь	-ю	тетрáд**ь**	тетрáд**ью**

Sample sentences

Мы идём в цирк **с Тамáрой**.

С кем? С Тамáрой.

Я игрáю **с Ивáном**.

We are going to the circus **with Tamara**.

With whom? **With Tamara**.

I am playing **with Ivan**.

Я люблю́ пить чай **с са́харом**.	I like to drink tea **with sugar**.
С чем? С са́харом.	**With what**? **With sugar**.
*Мы с сестро́й е́дем в кино́.	**My sister and I** are going to the movies.

*Note: The construction Мы с + **the instrumental case** is used to express *whomever and I*. For example:

Мы с бра́том идём в кино́.	**My brother and I** are going to the movies.
Мы с Ма́шей игра́ем в ша́хматы.	**Masha and I** are playing chess.

4.5.41   THE VERB БЫТЬ + ADJECTIVES IN THE INSTRUMENTAL CASE, SINGULAR AND PLURAL
Function: Expressing opinions

> Face to Face L2
> Chapter 4 B, D
> Pages 85-86, 89

The verb **быть** is frequently used with the instrumental case of adjectives to express qualities people would like to possess. Adjectival endings for the instrumental singular are -**ой**/-**ей** in the case of an adjective modifying a feminine noun and -**ым**/-**им** for adjectives modifying masculine and neuter nouns. Plural adjectives modifying plural nouns (regardless of gender) end in -**ыми**/-**ими**:

Masculine/Neuter	-**ым**/-**им**	
Он хоте́л бы быть...	до́бр**ым**	*kind*
He would like to be	хоро́ш**им**	*good*
	си́льн**ым**	*strong*
	спорти́вн**ым**	*athletic*
	высо́к**им**	*tall*

Feminine	-**ой**/-**ей**	
Она́ хоте́ла бы быть...	до́бр**ой**	*kind*
She would like to be	хоро́ш**ей**	*good*
	си́льн**ой**	*strong*
	спорти́вн**ой**	*athletic*
	высо́к**ой**	*tall*

Plural	-**ыми**/-**ими**	
Они́ хоте́ли бы быть...	до́бр**ыми**	*kind*
They would like to be	хоро́ш**ими**	*good*
	си́льн**ыми**	*strong*
	спорти́вн**ыми**	*athletic*
	высо́к**ими**	*tall*

Note the **conditional** phrase, *(S)he would like to be...* Он(а) хоте́л(а) бы...,) and its use to express a wish, desire or opinion. The conditional may be replaced by the indicative:

Она́ хоте́ла бы быть...	**+ instrumental**	*conditional mood*
Она́ хочет быть...	**+ instrumental**	*indicative mood*

Sample sentences

Máша хотéла бы быть **спорти́вной**, потому́ что она́ хо́чет быть (хотéла бы быть) гимна́сткой или тенниси́сткой.

Masha would like to be **athletic**, because she wants to be (would like to be) a gymnast or a tennis player.

Ми́ша хотéл бы быть **высо́ким**, потому́ что он хо́чет быть (хотéл бы быть) баскетболи́стом.

Misha would like to be **tall**, because he wants to be (would like to be) a basketball player.

Ви́тя и Мари́я хотéли бы быть **у́мными**, поэ́тому они́ у́чат ру́сский язы́к.

Vitya and Maria would like to be **intelligent**, therefore they study Russian.

4.5.42	**THE PREPOSITION C WITH INSTRUMENTAL FORMS OF PLURAL NOUNS AND ADJECTIVES** *Function:* Describing a person's appearance	Face to Face L2 Chapter 3 A, D Pages 60-63, 70

The instrumental case with the preposition **c(o)** (*with*) is frequently used to describe physical characteristics. The endings of nouns and adjectives in the instrumental plural are the same for all genders: **-ыми/-ими** for adjectives and **-ами/-ями** for nouns:

Вот дéвушка с голубы́ми глаза́ми, со свéтлыми волоса́ми.

Here's the girl with **light blue eyes** and **light hair**.

Вот молодо́й человéк с бородо́й, с уса́ми, с дли́нными волоса́ми.

Here's the young man with the beard, **mustache** and **long hair**.

Note: The word **борода́** (beard) is singular, but **усы́** (mustache) is plural.

4.5.43	**THE VERBS ПОЗНАКО́МИТЬ, ПОЗНАКО́МИТЬСЯ C + PRONOUNS IN THE INSTRUMENTAL CASE** *Function:* Getting acquainted with people	Face to Face L2 Chapter 3 A, D Pages 60, 70-71

The verb **знако́мить/познако́мить** is a second conjugation verb and is used when one speaks about *introducing someone to someone else*. The verb **(по)знако́миться**, adding the reflexive particle **-ся**, is used when a person wants to acquaint him/herself directly. Note the use of pronouns in the instrumental case below.

познако́мить кого? (acc.) с кем? (instrumental)
Я хочу́ познако́мить тебя́ **с ним**.
Познако́мить тебя́ **с ней**?

I want to introduce you **to him**.
Should I introduce you **to her**?

познако́миться с кем? (instrumental)
Я рад, что познако́мился **с тобо́й**.
Вы ужé познако́мились?

I'm glad to have met **you**.
Did you have a chance to meet each other?

Завтра познако́мимся **с ни́ми**.

Tomorrow we'll meet **them**.

Conjugation: **познако́млю(сь), познако́мишь(ся), познако́мят(ся)**

Pronouns with the preposition **с + the intrumental case**:

познакомиться с кем?

со мной (с собой)	я (себя)
с тобой	ты
с ним	он
с ней	она
с нами	мы
с вами	вы
с ними	они

4.5.44   USING THE NOUNS AND ADVERBS FOR SEASONS:
ЛЕТО—ЛЫОМ, ЗИМА—ЗИМОЙ, ВЕСНА—ВЕСНОЙ,
ОСЕНЬ/ОСЕНЬЮ
Function: Talking about the seasons

> Face to Face L1
> Chapter 16 C
> Pages 328-334

The instrumental forms of the names for seasons are used to form the adverbial expressions *during/in a season*. These expressions answer the question **Когда?** (When?). Note the following expressions and their related questions:

Времена года - Seasons (literally: times of the year)

		Когда?	When?
зима	winter	зимой	during the winter
весна	spring	весной	during the spring
лето	summer	летом	during the summer
осень	fall/autumn	осенью	during the fall/autumn

Sample sentences

Летом у нас очень жарко, а зимой холодно.	**During the summer** here it's hot, and **during the winter** it's cold.
Я люблю весну. Весной тепло, красиво.	I like spring. **During spring** it's warm and beautiful.
Какая погода у вас осенью?	What kind of weather do you have **in the fall**?

4.5.45   USING THE VERB ЗАНИМАТЬСЯ WITH NOUNS IN THE INSTRUMENTAL CASE
Function: Talking about activities

> Face to Face L1
> Chapter 17 A
> Pages 341-345

The verb **заниматься** can be translated in a number of ways. It means *to be occupied with* or *to be involved with*, and in some cases, *to study*. This verb governs **the instrumental case**:

занима́ться	Чем?	
я занима́юсь	спо́ртом	sports
ты занима́ешься	гимна́стикой	gymnastics
он занима́ется	литерату́рой	literature
она́ занима́ется	бе́гом	running

мы занима́емся	пла́вани **ем**	swimming
вы занима́етесь	рисова́ни **ем**	drawing
они́ занима́ются	му́зык **ой**	music

Sample sentences

Чем ты занима́ешься?

What are you doing/like to do/occupying yourself with?

Ва́ня **занима́ется** му́зыкой.

Vanya's **involved in** music.

Мы **занима́емся** футбо́лом.

We **play** soccer.

Я **занима́юсь** бе́гом.

I am **involved in** running

Они́ **занима́ются** рисова́нием.

They **like to** draw.

Ма́ша **занима́ется** фи́зикой.

Masha **has an interest in** physics.

Шéри и Ви́ка **занима́ются** баскетбо́лом.

Sheri and Vicky **play** basketball.

4.5.46 **THE INSTRUMENTAL CASE IN DISCUSSING A PROFESSION** *Function:* Talking about choosing professions	Face to Face L1 Chapter 18 A Pages 359-365

When the verb **быть** (to be) is used in its infinitive, future, or present tense forms in a sentence, the noun which forms the predicate of the sentence takes the instrumental case. When talking about professions, the instrumental case form of the name for the profession is used whenever the verb **быть** is present.

Sample sentences
future tense — быть + instrumental

Кем ты бу́дешь?

Who/What will you be?

Я бу́ду **врачо́м**.

I will be **a doctor**.

Она́ бу́дет **дипло́матом**.

She will be **a diplomat**.

Он бу́дет **учи́телем**.

He will be **a teacher**.

past tense — быть + instrumental

Моя́ ма́ма была́ **врачо́м**.

My mom was **a doctor**.

Она́ была́ **учи́тельницей**.

She was **a teacher**.

Он был **учи́телем**.

He was **a teacher**.

infinitive — быть + instrumental

Я хочу́ быть **дипло́матом**.

I want to be **a diplomat**.

Она́ хо́чет быть **врачо́м**.

She wants to be **a doctor**.

Он хо́чет быть **учи́телем**.

He wants to be **a teacher**.

no verb — быть + nominative

Я врач.

I am a doctor.

Она́ учи́тельница.

She is a teacher.

Он дипло́мат.

He is a diplomat.

*Она́ дипло́мат.

She is a diplomat.

*Note: Many names for professions in Russian have only one, masculine form: **врач**, **инжене́р**, **дипло́мат**, **адвока́т**. These nouns may be used with both men and women and take the masculine instrumental and case endings.

REFERENCE TABLE 4.5F: PROFESSIONS IN THE INSTRUMENTAL AND NOMINATIVE CASES

Instrumental case Я буду...	*Nominative case*	
бизнесме́ном	бизнесме́н	businessperson
врачо́м	врач	doctor
инжене́ром	инжене́р	engineer
учи́телем	учи́тель	teacher (m)
учи́тельницей	учи́тельница	teacher (f)
медсестро́й	медсестра́	nurse
диплома́том	диплома́т	diplomat
адвока́том	адвока́т	lawyer
фе́рмером	фе́рмер	farmer
хи́миком	хи́мик	chemist
ме́неджером	ме́неджер	manager
секретарём	секрета́рь	secretary
машини́сткой	машини́стка	typist
программи́стом	программи́ст	programmer
сле́сарем	сле́сарь	locksmith
шахтёром	шахтёр	miner
то́карем	то́карь	lathe operator
продавцо́м	продаве́ц	salesman
продавщи́цей	продавщи́ца	saleswoman
рабо́чим	рабо́чий	worker
поли́тиком	поли́тик	politician
шофёром	шофёр	chauffeur, driver
матема́тиком	матема́тик	mathematician
экономи́стом	экономи́ст	economist
строи́телем	строи́тель	builder/construction worker

4.5.47	THE PHRASE РЯ́ДОМ С + INSTRUMENTAL CASE *Function:* Suggesting going somewhere and stating locations	Face to Face L2 Chapter 6 A,D Pages 115, 136

The phrase **ря́дом с + instrumental case** (near, next to, alongside) may be used to express the location of places or people.

Sample sentences

—Где музе́й Пу́шкина?	Where is the Pushkin museum?
—**Ря́дом с** э́тим больши́м до́мом.	**Next to** this big house.
—Где Покро́вский собо́р?	Where is St. Basil's Cathedral?
—**Ря́дом с** э́той но́вой гости́ницей.	**Next to** this new hotel.

4.5.48	THE VERBS УВЛЕКА́ТЬСЯ/ИНТЕРЕСОВА́ТЬСЯ WITH THE INSTRUMENTAL CASE *Function:* Talking about hobbies and interests	Faces and Voices Chapter 1 A Page 8-9

The verbs **увлека́ться (кем?/чем?)** and **интересова́ться (кем?/чем?)** (to be interested in, to enjoy) may be used to express interests or hobbies. They require the instrumental case. Grammar point 4.5.49 below lists additional verbs of emotion and attachment requiring the instrumental case.

Sample sentences
Hobby (хо́бби) увлека́ться/интересова́ться

Эрик Кла́птон (Eric Clapton)	**Я**	Я увлека́юсь/интересу́юсь Эри́к**ом** Кла́птон**ом**.
хокке́й (hockey)	**Ты**	А ты чем увлека́ешься/интересу́ешься? Хокке́**ем**?
му́зыка (music)	**Он/Она́**	На́дя увлека́ется/интересу́ется му́зык**ой**.
фотогра́фия (photography)	**Мы**	Мы увлека́емся/интересу́емся фотогра́фи**ей**.
пла́вание (swimming)	**Вы**	А вы увлека́етесь/интересу́етесь пла́вани**ем**?
ма́рки (stamps)	**Они́**	Ребя́та в кла́ссе увлека́ются/интересу́ются ма́рк**ами**.

Note: The conjugations of these two verbs with the reflexive particle **-ся**. Consult the subsection on Reflexive Verbs in Chapter 7, grammar points 7.30-37, for more information on conjugating reflexive verbs.

4.5.49   OVERVIEW OF USES OF THE INSTRUMENTAL CASE: EMOTIONAL REACTION/EVALUATION, LOCATION, MEANS

Function: Expressing an emotional reaction or evaluation; Expressing the location of objects; Expressing the means or agent by which an action is done

Мир ру́сских Lesson 3 Pages 92-94

The instrumental case may be used in expressions of emotion or evaluation, describing the location of objects, and indicating the means by which an action is done.

Emotional reaction or evaluation   Several verbs that name an emotional state require a noun phrase in the instrumental case:

восхища́ться		to be captivated (by)
горди́ться		to be proud of
сла́виться	**+ noun, noun phrase or**	to be famous for
любова́ться	**pronoun**	to admire
наслажда́ться	**in the instrumental case**	to enjoy, take pleasure in
интересова́ться		to be interested in
увлека́ться		to be captivated by, to be involved in, to be interested in

Sample Sentences

Купе́ческий клуб **сла́вился** ква́сами и фрукто́выми во́дами.	The Merchant's Club was **famous for** its kvass and fruit drinks.
Мы до́лго стоя́ли на горе́ и **любова́лись** го́родом.	We stood on the mountain for a long time and **admired** the city.
Москвичи́ **гордя́тся** свои́ми теа́трами.	Moscovites are **proud of** their theaters.
Де́ти **наслажда́лись** моро́женым.	The children **enjoyed** the ice-cream.
Зри́тели **восхища́лись** го́лосом певи́цы.	The audience was **captivated by** the singer's voice.
Мно́гие ученики́ **интересу́ются** компью́терами.	Many students are **interested in** computers.
Мари́я **увлека́ется** америка́нской рок-му́зыкой.	Maria is **interested in** American rock music.

Location   Noun phrases in the instrumental case with the prepositions над (above, over), под (under, beneath), пе́ред (before, in front of), and за (beyond, behind) name a place and answer the question Где? (Where?).

Sample Sentences

Над столо́м виси́т ла́мпа.	A lamp is hanging **over the table**.
Ко́шка сиди́т **под столо́м**.	The cat is sitting **under the table**.
Пе́ред магази́ном стоя́ло мно́го люде́й.	Many people were standing **in front of the store**.
За столо́м сиди́т вся семья́.	The whole family is sitting **at the table**.

Means or agent of an action   Nouns in the instrumental case are used to name the instrument, means or agent by which an action is accomplished. This answers the question Чем? (By what? With what?).

Sample Sentences

Я пишу́ **ру́чкой**.	I am writing **with a pen**.
Же́нщина ре́жет хлеб **ножо́м**.	A woman is cutting bread **with a knife**.
Я ре́жу бума́гу **но́жницами**.	I am cutting paper **with scissors**.
Ру́сские едя́т сла́дкое **ло́жкой**.	Russians eat dessert **with a spoon**.

4.5.50 VERBS THAT TAKE THE INSTRUMENTAL CASE *Function:* Review	Faces and Voices Chapter 11 Г Page 314

Below is a short list of frequently encountered verbs which govern the instrumental case. Nouns, pronouns, and adjectives appear in **the instrumental case** following these verbs:

горди́ться (II)	кем/чем	to be proud of
интересова́ться (I)	кем/чем	to be interested in
увлека́ться (I)	кем/чем	to enjoy
занима́ться (I)	кем/чем	to be occupied with

стать (ста́н -у, -нешь, -нут) (I)	кем/чем	to become
рабо́тать (I)	кем	to work as
лечи́ться (II)	чем	to be cured by
боле́ть (I)	чем	to be sick with

Sample sentences

— Когда́ ты упа́ла на гимна́стике, ты до́лго лежа́ла?

When you fell in gymnastics were you laid up long?

— Нет, я лечи́лась **движе́нием, спо́ртом**.

No. I got well by **exercising** and doing **sports**.

— Посмотри́, кака́я ху́денькая де́вочка! **Чем** она́ боле́ет?

Look, what a thin girl! **What kind of illness** does she have? (*lit.*, **with what is she sick?**)

— Она́ не боле́ет, она́ же занима́ется **бале́том**.

She is not ill. She studies **ballet**.

— Ты не зна́ешь, ско́лько лет бы́ло На́де Па́вловой, когда́ она́ ста́ла **изве́стной балери́ной**?

You wouldn't know how old Nadya Pavlova was when she became a **famous ballerina**?

— Вы горди́тесь **Ле́ной**, когда́ ви́дите её на сце́не, в спекта́клях?

Are you proud of **Lena** when you see her on the stage in shows?

— Коне́чно, мы о́чень горди́мся **ей**.

Of course. We are very proud of **her**.

— Ле́на, а чем вы увлека́етесь: **му́зыкой, бале́том, теа́тром**?

Lena, what do you enjoy: **music, ballet, theater**?

— Осо́бенно интересу́юсь **исто́рией** ру́сского бале́тного теа́тра.

I am especially interested in the **history** of Russian ballet theater.

Prepositional Case

О ком? О чём?
Предло́жный паде́ж

4.6.51 Overview: What are the functions of the prepositional case? The prepositional case, sometimes called the locative case, is always used with prepositions. This case commonly expresses the location and position of objects and other specific relationships.

REFERENCE TABLE 4.6A: TYPICAL USES OF THE PREPOSITIONAL CASE

•Prepositional phrases answering the question Где? (Where?), О ком? (About whom?) and О чём? (About what?).
•With the prepositions: в (in/at), на (on/at), о (об/о) (about).
•The prepositional case is the only case that is never used without a preposition.

Although the prepositional case is always used with a preposition, not all prepositions take this case. Refer to Chapter 9, Prepositions, reference table 9A, for a list of common prepositions and the cases they govern.

REFERENCE TABLE 4.6B: BASIC PREPOSITIONAL CASE ENDINGS

Singular	Masculine	Neuter	Feminine
nouns	-е	-е/-ии	-е/-и
adjectives	<—— -ом/-ем ——>		-ой/-ей

Plural		
nouns	<————— -ах/-ях —————>	
adjectives	<———— -ых/-их —————>	

REFERENCE TABLE 4.6C: EXAMPLE NOUNS IN THE PREPOSITIONAL CASE BY GENDER IN THEIR SINGULAR AND PLURAL FORMS

Masculine	-consonant	-й	several in -а/-я	several in -ь
sing.	о столе́ (table, desk) об ученике́ (student m.)	о музе́е (museum)	о де́душке (grandfather)	о словаре́ (dictionary)
pl.	о стола́х об ученика́х	о музе́ях	о де́душках	о словаря́х

Neuter	-о	-е	-ие	several in -мя
sing.	о письме́ (letter)	о мо́ре (sea)	о зда́нии (building)	об и́мени (first name)
pl.	о пи́сьмах	о моря́х	о зда́ниях	об имена́х

Feminine	-а	-я	-ия	-ь
sing.	о шко́ле (school) кни́ге (book)	о дере́вне (countryside)	о лаборато́рии (laboratory)	о пло́щади (square)
pl.	о шко́лах о кни́гах	о дере́внях	о лаборато́риях	о площадя́х

REFERENCE TABLE 4.6D: SPECIAL NOUN CATEGORIES IN THE PRESPOSITIONAL CASE

Noun Type		Singular	Plural
•Feminine nouns	дочь and мать	о до́чери (-ер-) о ма́тери	о дочеря́х(-ер-) о матера́х
•Feminine nouns	любо́вь and це́рковь	о любви́ о це́ркови	no plural form о церква́х
•Masculine nouns in -анин/-янин		о граждани́не	о гра́жданах
•Masculine nouns in -онок/-ёнок		о котёнке	о котя́тах
•Neuter nouns in -мя: и́мя (-мен-)		об и́мени	об имена́х
•Neuter nouns	не́бо and чу́до	о не́бе о чу́де	о небеса́х о чудеса́х

| 4.6.52 | NOUNS IN PREPOSITIONAL CASE WITH В AND НА TO TELL LOCATION
Function: asking and telling locations | Face to Face L1
Chapter 3 B
Pages 83-86 |

The prepositional case is most often used to express the location of people and objects:

Это шко́ла. Я сейча́с **в шко́ле**.	This is a school. I am now **at school**.
Она́ **в библиоте́ке**.	She is **in the library**.
Это заво́д. Па́па сейча́с **на заво́де**.	This is a factory. Dad is now **at the factory**.
Он **на по́чте**.	He is **at the post office**.

The prepositions **в** (in, at) and **на** (on, at) are both used to express being located *at* a place. Some locations take the preposition **в** and other places take the preposition **на**. This requires memorization, although there is a general rule that exists:

в — small enclosed spaces (theaters, stores, schools) and some large unenclosed spaces (cities and countries almost always take **в**); places with finite boundaries

на — larger enclosed spaces (factories, post offices, etc.) and some larger unenclosed spaces (streets, stadiums, farms), especially when boundaries seem infinite or relatively undefined

REFERENCE TABLE 4.6E: PLACES REQUIRING USE OF THE PREPOSITION В

	Prepositional Phrase	
магази́н	в магази́не	store
апте́ка	в апте́ке	pharmacy; drug store
поликли́ника	в поликли́нике	clinic
больни́ца	в больни́це	hospital
клуб	в клу́бе	club
теа́тр	в теа́тре	theatre
музе́й	в музе́е	museum
о́фис	в о́фисе	office
шко́ла	в шко́ле	school
институ́т	в институ́те	institute
университе́т	в университе́те	university
го́род	в го́роде	city
Аме́рика	в Аме́рике	America
парк	в па́рке	park
класс	в кла́ссе	classroom

REFERENCE TABLE 4.6F: PLACES REQUIRING USE OF THE RUSSIAN PREPOSITION на

Place	**Prepositional phrase + на**	
бале́т	на бале́те	at the ballet
бульва́р	на бульва́ре	on the boulevard
ве́чер	на ве́чере	at a party
война́	на войне́	in, at a war
вокза́л	на вокза́ле	at the train station
восто́к	на восто́ке	in the east
встре́ча	на встре́че	at a meeting

REFERENCE TABLE 4.6F: PLACES REQUIRING USE OF THE PREPOSITION на (cont.)

дискотéка	на дискотéке	at a dance club
завóд	на завóде	at a factory
зáпад	на зáпаде	in the west
именúны	на именúнах	at a name-day party
канúкулы	на канúкулах	on vacation
концéрт	на концéрте	at a concert
лéкция	на лéкции	at a lecture
матч	на мáтче	at a game, match
набережная	на набережной	on an embankment
олимпиáда	на олимпиáде	at the Olympics
óпера	на óпере	at the opera
óстров	на óстрове	on an island
перехóд	на перехóде	on a crosswalk
пикнúк	на пикникé	on a picnic
платфóрма	на платфóрме	on a platform
плóщадь	на плóщади	on a square
пóчта	на пóчте	at the post office
проспéкт	на проспéкте	on an avenue
рабóта	на рабóте	at work
рок-концéрт	на рок-концéрте	at a rock concert
рýнок	на рýнке	at an open-air market
свáдьба	на свáдьбе	at a wedding
сéвер	на сéвере	in the north
собрáние	на собрáнии	at a meeting
сóлнце	на сóлнце	on the sun
соревновáние	на соревновáнии	at a competition
спектáкль	на спектáкле	at a play (theatre)
стадиóн	на стадиóне	at a stadium
стоя́нка	на стоя́нке	in a parking lot
территóрия	на территóрии	in, on the territory (of)...
тренирóвка	на тренирóвке	at practice (sports)
ýлица	на ýлице	in, on a street; outside
урóк	на урóке	in class
фáбрика	на фáбрике	at a factory
факультéт	на факультéте	in a (acad.) department
фúрма	на фúрме	in a (business) firm
эквáтор	на эквáторе	at the Equator
экскýрсия	на экскýрсии	on an excursion, tour
этáж	на этажé	on (...) floor (of building)
юг	на юге	in the south

Geographical place names that take на:

Some mountain ranges, most lakes and seas:

на... Кавкáзе, Памúре, Урáле, Алтáе — **in** the Causasus, Pamirs, Urals, Altai

на...Байкáле, Мичигáнском óзере — **on/at**...Lake Baikal, Lake Michigan

Most islands, archipelagoes, peninsulas:

на...Аля́ске, Гавáйях, Кúпре, Кóрсике, Мáльте, Яве, Чукóтке, Крúте — **in**...Alaska, Hawaii, Cyprus, Corsica, Malta, Java, Chukotka, **on**... Crete

Some parts of Moscow and other cities:

на..Арбáте, Сóколе, Брáйтоне — on the Arbat, in Sokol, in Brighton Beach (New York City)

| 4.6.53 | USING THE PREPOSITIONAL CASE WITH НА WITH MEANS OF TRANSPORTATION *Function:* Means of transportation | Face to Face L1 Chapter 12 C Pages 252-258 |

One common way to express the means of transportation is to use the preposition **на + the prepositional** case of the vehicle name. This answers the question На чём? (*lit., on what?*).

Sample sentences

На чём éдете в шкóлу?

How (*lit.,* ***on what***) are you going to school?

Мы éдем в шкóлу **на автóбусе**.

We are going to school **on the bus**.

На чём он éдет в теáтр?

How is he going to the theater?

Он éдет в теáтр **на машúне**.

He is **taking the car** to the theater.

REFERENCE TABLE 4.6G: EXPRESSIONS OF MEANS OF TRANSPORTATION

	Prepositional Phrase	
автóбус	на автóбусе	on/take the **bus**
машúна	на машúне	on/take the **car**
велоспéд	на велосипéде	on/take the **bicycle**
трамвáй	на трамвáе	on/take the **tram**
троллéйбус	на троллéйбусе	on/take the **trolleybus**
мотоцúкл	на мотоцúкле	on/take the **motorcycle**
пóезд	на пóезде	on/take the **train**
*метрó	на метрó	on/take the **subway**
*таксú	на таксú	on/take the **taxi**

*Note: Both метрó and таксú are indeclinable nouns.

| 4.6.54 | PREPOSITION О WITH THE PREPOSITIONAL CASE *Function:* Talking about what or about whom | Face to Face L1 Chapter 18 B Pages 366-372 |

The preposition **о** + the prepositional case expresses *about something or someone* and answers the questions О чём?, О ком? There are many verb combinations which can be used with this construction: дýмать о + prep., говорúть о + prep., etc. Below is a list of verbs which may be used with this construction.

о + the prepositional	**О чём? (About what?)**	**О ком? (About whom?)**	
говорúть (to talk)	об институ́те*	*обо мне	*about me*
читáть (to read)	о рабóте	о тебé	*about you*
спрáшивать (to ask)	о профéссии	о нём (о ней)	" *him (her)*
дýмать (to think)	об ýлице*	о нас	" *us*
расскáзывать (to tell, relate)	об Ивáне*	о вас	" *you*
спóрить (to argue)	о мáтче	о них	" *them*

*Note: The preposition о takes the form of об or обо before certain words:

1) об : Use об when the proceeding word begins with a vowel. For example, об институ́те, об ýлице, об Ивáне.

2) обо : Use обо when the proceeding word begins with a consonant cluster. For example, обо мне, обо всём (about everything).

Sample sentences

— О чём вы говорите?
— Мы говорим о шко́ле.

What are you talking **about**?
We are talking **about school**.

— О чём ты чита́ешь?
— Я чита́ю об исто́рии.

What are you reading **about**?
I am reading **about history**.

— О ком он спра́шивает?
— Он спра́шивает о Лари́се.

Whom is he asking **about**?
He is asking **about Larisa**.

— О ком вы ду́маете?
— Я ду́маю о дру́ге в Москве́.

Whom are you thinking **about**?
I am thinking **about a friend** in Moscow.

4.6.55	**В/НА WITH THE PREPOSITIONAL CASE: ADJECTIVE AND NOUN FORMS IN THE SINGULAR** *Function:* Asking and giving directions	Face to Face L2 Chapter 6 B Pages 122-123, 137

Those adjectives which modify nouns in the prepositional must also change according to case, gender and number.   Note the singular endings for adjectives and nouns in the phrases below.

<u>Gender</u>	<u>Nominative case</u>	<u>Prepositional case</u>
masculine	ста́рый цирк	в ста́р**ом** ци́рк**е**
(nouns: -е)	хоро́ший дом	в хоро́ш**ем** до́м**е**
(adjs: -ом/-ем)	Куту́зовский проспе́кт	на Куту́зовск**ом** проспе́кт**е**
	э́тот университе́т	в э́т**ом** университе́т**е**
neuter	ру́сское сло́во	в ру́сск**ом** сло́в**е**
(nouns: -е/-и)	хоро́шее зда́ние	в хоро́ш**ем** зда́н**ии**
(adjs: -ом/-ем)	э́то письмо́	в э́том письме́
feminine	Кра́сная пло́щадь	на Кра́сн**ой** пло́щад**и**
(nouns: -е/-и)	хоро́шая кварти́ра	в хоро́ш**ей** кварти́р**е**
(adjs: -ой/-ей)	э́та шко́ла	в э́т**ой** шко́л**е**

4.6.56	**THE PREPOSITIONAL CASE OF ADJECTIVES, PRONOUNS AND NOUNS IN THE PLURAL** *Function:* Talking about location at more than one setting	Face to Face L2 Chapter 14 A Pages 312

The prepositional plural of adjectives/pronouns **-ых/-их** and nouns **-ах/-ях** can be memorized by remembering the common letter **х**. Note that because the plural is used, there are only two basic ending for adjectives and nouns:

	<u>**Nominative plural**</u>	<u>**Prepositional plural**</u>
adjectives	ста́рые у́лицы	на ста́р**ых** у́лиц**ах**
	хоро́шие дома́	в хоро́ш**их** дом**а́х**
pronouns	каки́е лю́ди	о как**и́х** люд**я́х**
	свой дома́	в сво**и́х** дом**а́х**

| **nouns** | но́вые шко́лы | (в) но́в**ых** шко́л**ах** |
| | плохи́е словари́ | (в) плохи́х словар**я́х** |

Sample sentences

— Где нахо́дятся бы́вшие дома́ Пу́шкина?	Where are Pushkin's former homes located?
—На э́т**их** ста́р**ых** у́лиц**ах**.	On these old streets.
— Где жил Пу́шкин?	Where did Pushkin live?
— В э́т**их** ста́р**ых** дом**а́х**.	In these old houses.

4.6.57 MASCULINE NOUNS WHICH END IN -У WHEN NAMING LOCATION
Function: Expressing location with certain masculine nouns

> Мир ру́сских
> Lesson 6
> Pages 187-189

Nouns in the prepositional case most often have the ending **-е** (о ком?, о чём? — о дру́ге, о кни́ге, где? — в го́роде, на у́лице). Several masculine nouns, however, take the ending **-у** after the prepositions **в** and **на** when indicating location. Note the stress shift to the final vowel **-у́** in these declined forms. These nouns must be memorized.

REFERENCE TABLE 4.6H: MASCULINE NOUNS WHICH TAKE -У IN THE PREPOSITIONAL

год - в году́ *year*	в э́том году́, в про́шлом году́, в бу́дущем году́	**this year, last year, next year**
шкаф - в шкафу́ *wardrobe*	Ве́щи вися́т **в шкафу́**.	Things are hanging **in the wardrobe.**
мост - на мосту́ *bridge*	Мы стои́м **на мосту́**.	We are standing **on the bridge.**
бе́рег - **на берегу́** *shore*	Де́ти сидя́т **на берегу́** реки́.	The children are sitting **on the bank** of the river.
сад - в саду́ *garden*	Де́душка рабо́тает **в саду́**.	Grandfather is working **in the garden**.
пол - на полу́ *floor*	Не при́нято сиде́ть **на полу́**!	Sitting **on the floor** isn't done!
ряд - в ряду́ *row*	Мы сиди́м **во второ́м ряду́**.	We are sitting **in the second row**.
лес - в лесу́ *forest*	Они́ лю́бят собира́ть грибы́ **в лесу́**.	They like to gather mushrooms **in the forest.**
снег - в снегу́ *snow*	Он потеря́л ключи́ **в снегу́**.	He lost his keys **in the snow.**
рот - во рту́ *mouth*	Соба́ка де́ржит кость **во рту́**.	The dog is holding a bone **in its mouth**.
аэропо́рт - в аэропорту́ *airport*	Мы втре́тились **в аэропорту́**.	We met **in/at the airport.**
у́гол - в углу́, на углу́ *corner*	Телеви́зор стои́т **в углу́** ко́мнаты.	The television is **in the corner** of the room.
	Магази́н нахо́дится **на углу́** у́лицы Пу́шкина и у́лицы Чайко́вского.	The store is located **on the corner** of Pushkin Street and Tchaikovsky Street.

4.6.58 **THE PREPOSITIONAL CASE IN TIME EXPRESSIONS WITH YEARS AND WEEKS**

Function: Telling the year something happened: this/last/next year, in a certain year; In a particular week: this/last/next week

Faces and Voices
Chapter 3 Б
Pages 75-77

The preposition **в + the prepositional case** is used to express *in a year (this/last/next year)* and *in a certain or specific year*:

в э́том году́	**this year**
в про́шлом году́	**last year**
в бу́дущем году́	**next year**

The preposition **на + the prepositional case** is used to express *this/last/next week*:

на э́той неде́ле	**this week**
на про́шлой неде́ле	**last week**
на бу́дущей неде́ле	**next week**

Expressing the year in which an event occured, as in *It happened in 1993* (Это случи́лось в ты́сяча девятьсо́т девяно́сто тре́тьем году́) is expressed in Russian by using the preposition **в + the prepositional case** and a combination of cardinal and ordinal numbers (their noun and/or adjective forms). All but the last word are cardinal numbers. The last word is an ordinal number, which is declined like an adjective.

Note also that years in this century in Russian are given using **ты́сяча девятьсо́т** (*lit., one thousand nine hundred*) and **not** the way it can be done in English, *nineteen hundred.*

— Како́й сейча́с год? (nom. case)   — В како́м году́ э́то бы́ло? (prep. case)
— What is this year?   — In what year *was this*?

REFERENCE TABLE 4.6I: YEARS IN THE PREPOSITIONAL CASE

In 1211	В ты́сяча две́сти **оди́ннадцатом** году́
In 1970	В ты́сяча девятьсо́т семидеся́т**ом** году́
In 1971	В " " се́мьдесят **пе́рвом** году́
In 1972	В " " се́мьдесят **второ́м** году́
In 1973	В " " се́мьдесят **тре́тьем** году́
In 1984	В ты́сяча девятьсо́т во́семьдесят **четвёртом** году́
In 1985	В " " во́семьдесят **пя́том** году́
In 1996	В ты́сяча девятьсо́т **шесто́м** году́
In 1997	В " " девяно́сто **седьмо́м** году́
In 1998	В " " девяно́сто **восьмо́м** году́
In 1999	В " " девяно́сто **девя́том** году́
In 2000	В **двухты́сячном** году́
In 2001	В две ты́сячи **пе́рвом** году́

| 4.6.59 | THE VERBS РАБОТАТЬ AND ИГРАТЬ WITH THE PREPOSITION НА
Function: Talking about the equipment people use at work; Playing an instrument | Faces and Voices
Chapter 5 A
Page 122 |

Working on office equipment To express using equipment, such as a computer or typewriter, to perform office work, use the construction **рабо́тать на + the prepositional case**. Note the examples below using typical office and school equipment.

На чём работаешь?

рабо́тать на	чём?	
to work on...	компью́тер**е**	computer
	ксе́рокс**е**	photocopier
	телефа́кс**е**	(tele)fax
	пи́шущей маши́нк**е**	typewriter

Playing an instrument Students may be familiar with the construction used to express *playing an instrument*: the verb **игра́ть** (I) with the preposition **на + the prepositional case**. Below are examples of this construction used with various names of instruments.

игра́ть на + prepositional	to play an instrument

Sample sentences

На чём **вы игра́ете**?	What do **you play**?
Я **игра́ю** на гита́ре.	**I play** the guitar.
Ты **игра́ешь** на спри́пке.	**You play** the violin.
Они́ **игра́ют** на пиани́но*.	**They play** the piano.

Note: пиани́но is an indeclinable noun.

Chapter 5

PRONOUNS
Местоиме́ния

5.1 Overview: What are pronouns? Pronouns are words which can replace nouns that have been mentioned or implied in previous statements or questions. Pronouns can replace animate (living), inanimate (non-living), singular and plural nouns in sentences.

REFERENCE TABLE 5A: BASIC RUSSIAN PRONOUNS

Я	I
Ты	you (singular/familiar)
Он	he, it (masculine)
Она́	she, it (feminine)
Оно́	it (neuter)
Мы	we
Вы	you (plural/polite)
Они́	they (plural)
Кто?	Who ?
Что?	What ?

In Russian, one must pay particular attention to the fact that the pronouns **он, она́, они́** can replace both objects and people.

Где Ива́н?	Where is Ivan?
Где **он**? (*masculine, animate, singular*)	Where is **he**?
Вот кни́га.	Here is the book.
Вот **она́**. (*feminine, inanimate, singular*)	Here **it** is.
Где Ната́ша и Ма́ша?	Where is Natasha and Masha?
Вот **они́**. (*animate, plural*)	Here **they** are.
Где каранда́ш и ру́чка?	Where is the pencil and pen?
Вот **они́**. (*inanimate, plural*)	Here **they** are.

There are many different types of pronouns depending on their function in a statement or question: personal pronouns, demonstrative pronouns, possessive pronouns, interrogative pronouns, relative pronouns, reflexive pronouns, negative pronouns. Pronouns and their related functions are presented in the sections below.

REFERENCE TABLE 5B: DECLENSION OF PERSONAL PRONOUNS

NOMINATIVE ИМЕНИ́ТЕЛЬНЫЙ	Я I	ТЫ you	ОН he/it	ОНО́ it	ОНА́ she/it	МЫ we	ВЫ you	ОНИ́ they	КТО who	ЧТО what
GENITIVE РОДИ́ТЕЛЬНЫЙ	меня́	тебя́	*(н)его́	*(н)её	нас	вас	*(н)их	кого́	чего́
DATIVE ДА́ТЕЛЬНЫЙ	мне	тебе́	(н)ему́	(н)ей	нам	вам	(н)им	кому́	чему́
ACCUSATIVE ВИНИ́ТЕЛЬНЫЙ	меня́	тебя́	(н)его́	(н)её	нас	вас	(н)их	кого́	что
INSTRUMENTAL ТВОРИ́ТЕЛЬНЫЙ	мной	тобо́й	(н)им·	(н)ей	на́ми	ва́ми	(н)и́ми	кем	чем
PREPOSITIONAL ПРЕДЛО́ЖНЫЙ	мне	тебе́	нём	(н)ней	нас	вас	них	ком	чём

*Note: The third person pronouns (он, оно́, она́, они́) add an initial н- when functioning as the objects of prepositions.

Себя́ has no nominative form; otherwise, it is declined like the personal pronouns **ты** and **я** in all other cases—see grammar point 5.16:

	себя́ itself, myself, etc.
GENITIVE РОДИ́ТЕЛЬНЫЙ	себя́
DATIVE ДА́ТЕЛЬНЫЙ	себе́
ACCUSATIVE ВИНИ́ТЕЛЬНЫЙ	себя́
INSTRUMENTAL ТВОРИ́ТЕЛЬНЫЙ	собо́й
PREPOSITIONAL ПРЕДЛО́ЖНЫЙ	себе́

REFERENCE TABLE 5C: POSSESSIVE PRONOUN (POSSESSIVE ADJECTIVES) МОЙ (MY) IN THE NOMINATIVE CASE FORMS

Person		Singular		Plural
	Masculine	**Feminine**	**Neuter**	
Я	мой	моя́	моё	мои́
ТЫ	твой	твоя́	твоё	твои́
ОН	его́	(Same for all genders and plural)		
ОНА́	её	(Same for all genders and plural)		
МЫ	наш	на́ша	на́ше	на́ши
ВЫ	ваш	ва́ша	ва́ше	ва́ши
ОНИ́	их	(Same for all genders and plural)		

Note: Like all adjectives, the possessive adjectives must agree with the noun modified in case. number, and gender.

REFERENCE TABLE 5D: DECLENSION OF THE POSSESSIVE PRONOUNS (POSSESSIVE ADJECTIVES) МОЙ (ТВОЙ, СВОЙ) AND НАШ (ВАШ)

Case	Singular						Plural	
	Masculine		**Feminine**		**Neuter**			
Nom.	мой	наш	мо**я**	наш**а**	мо**ё**	наш**е**	мо**и́**	на́ш**и**
Gen.	мо**его́**	на́ш**его**	мо**е́й**	на́ш**ей**	мо**его́**	наш**его**	мо**и́х**	на́ш**их**
Dat.	мо**ему́**	на́ш**ему**	мо**е́й**	на́ш**ей**	мо**ему́**	наш**ему**	мо**и́м**	на́ш**им**
Acc. (inan.)	мой	наш	мо**ю́**	на́ш**у**	мо**ё**	наш**е**	мо**и́**	на́ш**и**
Acc. (an.)	мо**его́**	на́ш**его**	мо**ю́**	на́ш**у**	—	—	мо**и́х**	на́ш**их**
Instr.	мо**и́м**	на́ш**им**	мо**е́й**	на́ш**ей**	мо**и́м**	на́ш**им**	мо**и́ми**	на́ш**ими**
Prep.	мо**ём**	на́ш**ем**	мо**е́й**	на́ш**ей**	мо**ём**	на́ш**ем**	мо**и́х**	на́ш**их**

Note: твой and свой have the same endings in all cases as мой. Ваш has the same endings as наш in all cases.

REFERENCE TABLE 5E: DECLENSION OF THE INTERROGATIVE PRONOUN ЧЕЙ (WHOSE)

case	masculine	neuter	feminine	plural
NOMINATIVE ИМЕНИ́ТЕЛЬНЫЙ	чей	чь**ё**	чь**я**	чь**и**
GENITIVE РОДИ́ТЕЛЬНЫЙ	чь**его́**		чь**ей**	чь**их**
DATIVE ДА́ТЕЛЬНЫ	чь**ему́**		чь**ей**	чь**им**
ACCUSATIVE ВИНИ́ТЕЛЬНЫЙ	чей / чь**его́**	чь**ё**	чь**ю**	чь**и** / чь**их**
INSTRUMENTAL ТВОРИ́ТЕЛЬНЫЙ	чь**ем**		чь**ей**	чь**и́ми**
PREPOSITIONAL ПРЕДЛО́ЖНЫЙ	(обо) чь**ём**		(обо) чь**ей**	(обо) чь**их**

REFERENCE TABLE 5F: DECLENSION OF THE DEFINITE PRONOUN ВЕСЬ (ALL)

case	masculine	neuter	feminine	plural
NOMINATIVE ИМЕНИ́ТЕЛЬНЫЙ	весь	всё	вся	все
GENITIVE РОДИ́ТЕЛЬНЫЙ	всего́		всей	всех
DATIVE ДА́ТЕЛЬНЫЙ	всему́		всей	всем
ACCUSATIVE ВИНИ́ТЕЛЬНЫЙ	весь / всего́	всё	всю	все / всех
INSTRUMENTAL ТВОРИ́ТЕЛЬНЫЙ	всем		всей	все́ми
PREPOSITIONAL ПРЕДЛО́ЖНЫЙ	(обо) всём		(обо) всей	(обо) всех

REFERENCE TABLE 5G: DECLENSION OF THE DEMONSTRATIVE PRONOUNS ЭТОТ (THIS) AND ТОТ (THAT)

case	masculine	neuter	feminine	plural
NOMINATIVE ИМЕНИ́ТЕЛЬНЫЙ	э́тот тот	э́то то	э́та та	э́ти те
GENITIVE РОДИ́ТЕЛЬНЫЙ	эт**о́го** то**го́**		эт**о́й** то**й**	э́т**их** тех
DATIVE ДА́ТЕЛЬНЫЙ	эт**о́му** то**му́**		эт**о́й** то**й**	э́т**им** тем
ACCUSATIVE ВИНИ́ТЕЛЬНЫЙ	э́тот тот эт**о́го** то**го́**	э́то то	э́т**у** т**у**	э́т**и** те э́т**их** тех
INSTRUMENTAL ТВОРИ́ТЕЛЬНЫЙ	э́т**им** те**м**		эт**о́й** то**й**	э́т**ими** те́**ми**
PREPOSITIONAL ПРЕДЛО́ЖНЫЙ	(об) э́т**ом** (о) то**м**		(об) эт**о́й** (о) то**й**	(об) э́т**их** (о) тех

REFERENCE TABLE 5H: DECLENSION OF THE INTERROGATIVE PRONOUN (ADJECTIVE) КАКО́Й (WHAT KIND/SORT) AND THE DEMONSTRATIVE PRONOUN (ADJECTIVE) ТАКО́Й (SUCH)

case	masculine	neuter	feminine	plural
NOMINATIVE ИМЕНИ́ТЕЛЬНЫЙ	како́й тако́й	како́е тако́й	кака́я така́я	каки́е таки́е
GENITIVE РОДИ́ТЕЛЬНЫЙ	како́го тако́го		како́й тако́й	каки́х таки́х
DATIVE ДА́ТЕЛЬНЫЙ	како́му тако́му		како́й тако́й	каки́м таки́м
ACCUSATIVE ВИНИ́ТЕЛЬНЫЙ	како́го /како́й тако́го/ тако́й	како́е тако́й	каку́ю таку́ю	каки́х /каки́е таки́х /таки́е
INSTRUMENTAL ТВОРИ́ТЕЛЬНЫЙ	каки́м таки́м		како́й тако́й	каки́ми таки́ми
PREPOSITIONAL ПРЕДЛО́ЖНЫЙ	о како́м о тако́м		о как**о́й** о так**о́й**	о каки́х о таки́х

5.2 ТЫ/ВЫ — **FAMILIAR/POLITE AND SINGULAR/PLURAL FORMS OF ADDRESS** *Function:* greeting people, saying goodbye	Face to Face L1 Chapter 1 A Pages 36-44

Russian uses both formal and informal forms of "You" and distinguishes between singular and plural when addressing people.

Ты - **Informal, familiar and singular**   Use **ты** when speaking with someone your own age and who you know well, such as a classmate. If you are on a first-name basis or use the person's diminutive or shortened nickname form (Аня for Анна or Ваня for Ива́н), use **ты** in conversation as well. See Chapter 12, Word-Building, for more information on diminutive forms of first names.

Вы - Formal, respectful and plural Use **вы** when speaking with more than one person, regardless of how well you know this group of people. When addressing adults, such as a student to teacher or conversation between adult colleagues at the workplace, use **вы** to show respect and to reflect more formal settings. If you address a person using their patronymic (**Пётр Иванович** or **Анна Николаевна**), use **вы** in conversation as well. See Chapter 12, Word-Building, for more information on the formation of patronymics.

Greeting people and saying goodbye In Russian, many of the forms used to express "hello" or "goodbye" depend on differences between informal/formal and singular/plural usage. Note these differences below.

Expression	Ты form: first name or diminutive	Вы form: to group of people, patronymic
Hello!	Здравствуй!	Здравствуйте!
Hi!	Привет!	— — — —
Goodbye!	Пока! (See 'ya!)	До свидания!
Good morning!	Доброе утро!	Доброе утро!
Good afternoon!	Добрый день!	Добрый день!
Good evening!	Добрый вечер!	Добрый вечер!

Sample sentences
Between a young girl /boy and an adult:

— Здравствуйте, Пётр Николаевич! Hello, Pyotr Nikolaevich!
— Здравствуй, Нина!   Hello, Nina!

Between two adult colleagues:

— Доброе утро, Анна Ивановна! Good morning, Anna Ivanovna!
— Здравствуйте, Нина Петровна! Hello, Nina Petrovna!

Between one young boy and a group of kids:

— Здравствуйте, ребята!   Hi, guys!
— Привет, Саша!   Hi, Sasha!

Usage of ты and вы:

— Извините, **вы** Нина Михайловна? — Excuse me. Are **you** Nina Mikhalovna?
— Да.   — Yes.
— Я Майкл из Америки.   — I'm Michael from the U.S.
— Майкл! **Ты** только что приехал? — Michael! Have **you** just arrived? Come
  Входи!   in!

5.3   PERSONAL PRONOUNS ОН, ОНА́, ОНО́, ОНИ́
    Function: Finding out where someone or something
        is located

Face to Face L1
Chapter 2 C
Pages 67-69

The pronouns **он** (he/it), **она́** (she/it), **оно́** (it), **они́** replace masculine, feminine, neuter, and plural nouns and may replace both animate and inanimate objects in sentences. These pronouns are often used to answer questions pertaining to the location of objects. Note their agreement in gender and number with their referent noun below.

Sample sentences
Animate objects

Где Ива́н? Вот **он**.	Where is Ivan? There/Here **he** is.
Где Мари́я? Вот **она́**.	Where is Maria? There/Here **she** is.
Где волк? Вот **он**.	Where is the wolf? There/Here **it** is.
Где Ива́н и соба́ка? Вот **они́**.	Where is Ivan and the dog? There/Here **they** are.

Inanimate objects

Где журна́л? Вот **он**.	Where is the magazine? There **it** is.
Где ру́чка? Вот **она́**.	Where is the pen? Here **it** is.
Где письмо́? Вот **оно́**.	Where is the letter? There **it** is.
Где ру́чка и бума́га? Вот **они́**.	Where is the pen and paper? Here **they** are.

Note: The word **вот** can mean either *here* or *there*.

5.4   INTERROGATIVE PRONOUNS КТО AND ЧТО
    Function: Finding out about people and animals,
        Finding out about things

Face to Face L1
Chapter 2 A, B
Pages 59-63, 64-66

The pronouns **кто** (who) and **что** (what) are called interrogative because they may be used to ask questions about nouns.   Note, in the sentences below, that in Russian both animals and people are **animate**; that is, an animal is a "who" or a **«кто»**. The interrogative pronoun **что** can be used to ask about the identity of objects and to ask about the character or type of an action.

Sample sentences
About people and animals

Кто э́то?	**Who** is this?
Это Ната́ша.	This is Natasha.
Это волк.	This is a wolf.

About objects

Что э́то? Это тетра́дь.	**What** is this? This is a notebook.

About actions

Что Мари́я де́лает?	**What** is Maria doing?
Она́ игра́ет.	She is playing.

5.5 **INTERROGATIVE PRONOUNS** чей, чья, чьё, чьи
(**POSSESSIVE ADJECTIVES**)
Function: Talking about possessions ("Whose?")

Face to Face L1
Chapter 11 A
Pages 225-227

The interrogative pronouns **чей**, **чья**, **чьё**, **чьи** express the question "whose?" and must agree in gender, number, and case of the noun they modify.

Sample sentences

Чей это дом? Это мой дом.	**Whose** house is it? It's my house.
Чья это машина? Это моя машина.	**Whose** car is it? It's my car.
Чьё это письмо? Это моё письмо.	**Whose** letter is it? It's my letter.
Чьи это книги? Это мой книги.	**Whose** books are these? They're my books.

5.6 **POSSESSIVE PRONOUNS (ADJECTIVES)** мой, твой, наш, ваш
Function: Talking about the family ("My, Your, ...")

Face to Face L1
Chapter 3 A
Pages 75-82

Possessive pronouns indicate possession. With the exception of the third-person pronouns (his/her/their), Russian possessive pronouns must agree with the word they modify in gender, number and case. In the table below, note gender and number agreement of each possessive pronoun (adjective) with the sample noun.

possessive pronoun	masculine	feminine	neuter	plural
My	мой брат	моя сестра	моё окно	мой мама и папа
Your (fam.)	твой (brother)	твоя (sister)	твоё (window)	твой (Mom and Dad)
His	его	его	его	его
Her	её	её	её	её
Our	наш	наша	наше	наши
Your (formal)	ваш	ваша	ваше	ваши
Their	их	их	их	их
Whose?	чей	чья	чьё	чьи

Sample sentences

Это **мой** карандаш.	This is **my** pencil.	
Это **моя** ручка.	This is **my** pen.	
— Это **твоя** книга? — Да, **моя**.	Is this **your** book?	Yes, it's **mine**.
— Это **ваша** книга? — Да, **моя**.	Is this **your** book?	Yes, it's **mine**.
— Да, **наша**.		Yes, it's **ours**.

Only the possessive pronouns **мой/твой** and **наш/ваш** decline. These pronouns must agree in case, in addition to number and gender, with the noun they modify. The charts below provide an overview of their declensions.

мой/твой decline according to the same pattern:

case	masculine	neuter	feminine	plural
NOMINATIVE ИМЕНИ́ТЕЛЬНЫЙ	МОЙ ТВО-Й	МОЁ ТВО-Ё	МОЯ́ ТВО-Я́	МОИ́ ТВО-Й
GENITIVE РОДИ́ТЕЛЬНЫЙ	МО его́ ТВО его́		МО е́й ТВО е́й	МО и́х ТВО и́х
DATIVE ДА́ТЕЛЬНЫЙ	МО ему́ ТВО ему́		МО е́й ТВО е́й	МО и́м ТВО и́м
ACCUSATIVE ВИНИ́ТЕЛЬНЫЙ	мой / тво й мо его́ / тво его́	МО ё ТВО е́	МО ю́ ТВО ю́	мо и́ / тво и́ мо и́х / тво и́х
INSTRUMENTAL ТВОРИ́ТЕЛЬНЫЙ	МО и́м ТВО и́м		МО е́й ТВО е́й	МО и́ми ТВО и́ми
PREPOSITIONAL ПРЕДЛО́ЖНЫЙ	(О) МОём (О) ТВОём		(О) МО е́й (О) ТВО е́й	(О) МО и́х (О) ТВО и́х

*Note: The possessive pronoun (adjective) **свой** also follows this declension pattern. See grammar point 5.8 below.

наш/ваш decline according to the same pattern:

case	masculine	neuter	feminine	plural
NOMINATIVE ИМЕНИ́ТЕЛЬНЫЙ	наш ваш-	на́ше ва́ш-е	на́ша ва́ш-а	на́ши ва́ш-и
GENITIVE РОДИ́ТЕЛЬНЫЙ	на́ш его ваш его		на́ш ей ваш ей	на́ш их ваш их
DATIVE ДА́ТЕЛЬНЫЙ	на́ш ему ваш ему		на́ш ей ваш ей	на́ш им ваш им
ACCUSATIVE ВИНИ́ТЕЛЬНЫЙ	наш / ваш на́ш его/ваш его	на́ш е ваш е	на́ш у ваш у	на́ш и/ваш и на́ш их/ваш их
INSTRUMENTAL ТВОРИ́ТЕЛЬНЫЙ	на́ш им ваш им		на́ш ей ваш ей	на́ш ими ваш ими
PREPOSITIONAL ПРЕДЛО́ЖНЫЙ	(О) на́шем (О) ваш ем		(О) на́шей (О) ваш ей	(О) на́ших (О) ваш их

5.7 THE INTERROGATIVE PRONOUN (ADJECTIVE) КАКО́Й, КАКО́Е, КАКА́Я, КАКИ́Е (WHICH/WHAT KIND/SORT)
Function: Pointing out/describing objects; Expressing surprise/exclamation

| Face to Face L1 |
| Lesson 9 A |
| Pages 187-191 |

Using како́й to gather descriptive information Како́й translates as *which/what*, *what kind* and *what sort*. . It can be used to pose questions as to the description of objects or to clarify "which" object a speaker has in mind. **Како́й** must agree in gender, number and case with the noun it modifies.

Sample sentences

— **Кака́я** у тебя́/у вас маши́на?　　　What kind of car do you have?
— У меня́ но́вая чёрная «хо́нда.»　　　I have a new black Honda.

— Я люблю́ э́ту пе́сню!　　　I love that song!
— **Каку́ю** пе́сню (ты лю́бишь)?　　　Which song?
— Вот э́та пе́сня по ра́дио.　　　This one on the radio.

Using какóй to express surprise and exclamation Какóй can be used to express both positive and negative exclamation. In this usage, it is very similar to the English *What (a)...!* Gender, number and case agreement must be observed.

Sample sentences

Какóй у вас красúвый дом!	**What** a beautiful home you have!
Какúе высóкие здáния!	**What** tall buildings!
Какáя у нас холóдная погóда!	**What** cold weather we are having!
Какóй/-áя ты молодéц!	**What** a good boy/girl!

5.8   THE POSSESSIVE PRONOUN СВОЙ
Function: Expressing refusal and confirmation

> Face to Face L2
> Chapter 12 B, D
> Pages 256-259,
> 267

The possessive pronoun (adjective) **свой** refers to the logical subject of a sentence and stresses the meaning *one's own*. It must agree in gender, number and case with the noun it modifies. **Свой** commonly replaces the possessive pronouns **мой**, **твой**, **наш** and **ваш**. The use of **свой** is preferred in these cases. **Свой** cannot be used to begin a sentence: **Мой** брат ýчится в университéте. ***Not свой !***

Sample sentences

Принесú **свои**/твой дúски на вечерúнку!	Bring **your** CDs to the party!
Не вúдели **свои** тýфли?	You haven't seen (found) **your** shoes?
Рýсские ученикú показáли нам **свою** шкóлу.	The Russian high school students showed us **their** school.

Remember that **свой** refers back to the original subject, even if the subject is only implied (принесú **свои** дúски—implied subject is **ты**), and cannot refer to another subject when the meaning desired is 'one's own':

Принесú **свои** дúски на вечерúнку! Bring your (own) CDs to the party!	Я принесý **твои** дúски на вечерúнку. I'll bring **your** CDs to the party.
Не вúдели **свой** тýфли? You haven't seen your (own) shoes?	Я не вúдел **вáши** тýфли. I haven't seen **your** shoes.
Рýсские ученикú показáли нам **свою** шкóлу. The Russian high school students showed us their (own) school.	Потóм онú посетúли **нáшу** шкóлу. Then they came to visit **our** school.

Свой is also used to replace the third person possessive pronouns **егó** (his), **её** (her) and **их** (their) in clauses. In this usage, **свой** makes clear any ambiguity as to whom the object belongs or refers. Gender, number and case must be observed. Compare the sample sentences below with and without **свой**.

Sample sentences

Она́ написа́ла письмо́ **своему́** бра́ту.	She wrote a letter to **her** (own) brother. *(Her own brother, not someone else's!)*
Она́ написа́ла письмо́ **её** бра́ту.	She wrote a letter to **her** (not her own) brother. *(Whose brother? To a girlfriend's? A Russian may assume the letter was sent to someone else's brother.)*
—Дать тебе́ ру́чку?	Should I give you a pen?
—Спаси́бо, у меня́ есть **своя́**.	Thanks, but I have **my own**. (Here **свой** refers to the logical subject "I" or «у меня́».
У меня́ есть...	I have...
...**свой** фотоаппара́т.	my (own) camera.
...**своё** ме́сто.	my (own) place.
...**свои́** карти́ны.	my (own) pictures.

*Note: It may help to think of the **свой** as adding the connotation "**...own...**" to the possession: **своя́ сестра́** (her *own* sister) versus **её сестра́** (her sister).

5.9 DEMONSTRATIVE PRONOUNS ЭТОТ, ЭТА, ЭТО, ЭТИ (THIS/THESE) IN THE NOMINATIVE AND THE ACCUSATIVE CASES

Function: Specifying or being specific

Face to Face L1 Chapter 9 B Pages 192-193

Demonstrative pronouns point out specific items or people. They point out which things we are talking about-- *this* vs. *that*, for example, and clearly "demonstrate" this relationship. The demonstrative pronouns **этот** must agree in gender, number and case with the nouns they modify. In this respect they are very similar to adjectives and most possessive pronouns.

Sample sentences

Этот значо́к краси́вый.	**This** pin is beautiful.
Да́йте мне **этот** значо́к.	Give me **this** pin.
Эта кни́га неплоха́я.	**This** book is not bad.
Да́йте мне **эту** кни́гу.	Give me **this** book.
Это письмо́ о́чень ста́рое.	**This** letter is very old.
Да́йте мне **это** письмо́.	Give me **this** letter.
Эти газе́ты но́вые.	**These** newspapers are new.
Да́йте мне **эти** газе́ты.	Give me **these** newspapers.

While the **Этот** points ou "this object" or "these things", it should not be confused with the short-form subject **Это** used to convey the meaning *this is* and *these are*. Compare:

Demonstrative Pronoun Этот Како́й...? **Which...?**	**Short-Form Subject** Это Что э́то? **What is this?**
Этот значо́к краси́вый. **This** pin is beautiful.	**Это** значо́к. **This is** a pin.
Эта кни́га неплоха́я. **This** book is not bad.	**Это** кни́га. **This is** a book.
Это письмо́ о́чень ста́рое. **This** letter is very old.	**Это** ста́рое письмо́. **This is** an old letter.
Эти газе́ты но́вые. **These** newspapers are new.	**Это** но́вые газе́ты. **These are** new newspapers.

5.10 DEMONSTRATIVE PRONOUNS тот, та, то, те
Function: Pointing out objects, people ("that, those")

Face to Face L2
Chapter 3 A,D
Pages 60, 71

The demonstrative pronouns тот, та, то, те (that, those) are used to point out someone or something farther away. **Тот** agrees in gender, number and case with the noun is modifies. These pronouns are often combined with the word **вон**, especially when pointing out something or someone at a distance:

—Кто Ира? —Вон **та** де́вушка, с дли́нными волоса́ми.	Who is Ira? **That** girl over there with the long hair.

Sample sentences
phrases:

вон **тот** челове́к	**that** person over there
вон **та** де́вушка	**that** girl over there
вон **то** зда́ние	**that** building over there
вон **те** кни́ги	**those** books over there

5.11 DEMONSTRATIVE PRONOUNS весь, всё, вся, все
Function: Describing objects, people ("whole, all, every")

Face to Face L2
Chapter 11 D
Page 241

The demonstrative pronouns (adjectives) весь, всё, вся, все (all, every, whole) agree with the nouns they modify in gender, number and case.

Sample sentences

На конце́рте был **весь** класс.	The **whole** class was at the concert.
Вся гру́ппа была́ на экску́рсии.	The **whole** group was at the tour.
Мы прочита́ли **всё** письмо́.	We read the **whole** letter.
Аня реши́ла **все** зада́чи.	Anya solved **all** the problems.

When used without a noun, **все** means *everybody* or *everyone*, and **всё** means *everything*.

Все встретились у входа в телецентр.　**Everyone** met at the entrance to the TV station.

Я хотела бы **всё** здесь попробовать.　I would like to try **everything** here.

5.12　SUBORDINATE CLAUSES WITH такой *Function:* Talking about the weather	Face to Face L1 Chapter 16 A Pages 319-322

The demonstrative pronoun **такой, такая, такое, такие** (such, like that) may be used to form a subordinate clause of the type: **Когда у нас такая погода,**... (When we have *such* weather,...). Note that this phrase is translated in several ways.

Sample sentences

Когда у нас **такая** температура, маленькие дети не учатся в школе.　When we have a temperature **like that**, children don't go (study) to school. (or **such a temperature...**)

Когда у нас **такая** погода, мы играем в бейсбол.　When we have **such** weather, we play baseball.

Когда на улице **такая** тёплая погода, мы любим играть в теннис.　When there is **such** warm weather outside, we like to play tennis.

5.13　THE RELATIVE PRONOUN который FUNCTIONING AS A CONJUNCTION *Function:* Relating information about a person or thing	Face to Face L2 Chapters 18 A, 19 B, Pages 400- 401, 425

The relative pronoun **который** *who..., which..., that...* refers to the subject or direct object in the preceding clause in a sentence.

> Это Виктор, **который** играет на гитаре.
> This is Victor, **who** is playing the guitar.

Который can function as both the subject of its own clause and further define or clarify the subject of the preceding clause.

> Это Виктор, | **который** играет на гитаре.
> This is Victor, **who** is playing the guitar.
> (In this clause, **который** is the subject of its clause and further describes or defines **Виктор**, the subject of the preceding clause.)

Который agrees in gender and number with its referent noun in the main clause. It may be appear in another case (declined) depending on its use in its own clause.

Это Ви́ктор, с кото́рым мы познако́мились вчера́.
This is Victor, **whom** we met yesterday.
(In this clause, кото́рый agrees in gender and number with Ви́ктор (masculine and singular) but is declined in the instrumental case with the construction познако́миться с.

For additional information about кото́рый, refer to grammar point 5.14 below.

Sample sentences

Вот челове́к, **кото́рый** рабо́тает на заво́де.	Here's the person **who** works at the factory. (кото́рый refers back to челове́к, the subject of the sentence; it agrees in gender and number).
Вот челове́к, **о кото́ром** вы говори́ли.	Here's the man **about whom** you were talking.

*__Note:__ In the second example above, кото́рый is used in a case other than the nominative and refers back to the original subject. In this example it is not the subject of its own clause.

Declension of кото́рый

case	masculine	neuter	feminine	plural
NOMINATIVE ИМЕНИ́ТЕЛЬНЫЙ	кото́рый	кото́рое	кото́рая	кото́рые
GENITIVE РОДИ́ТЕЛЬНЫЙ	кото́р**ого**		кото́р**ой**	кото́р**ых**
DATIVE ДА́ТЕЛЬНЫЙ	кото́р**ому**		кото́р**ой**	кото́р**ым**
ACCUSATIVE ВИНИ́ТЕЛЬНЫЙ	кото́р**ого** кото́р**ый**	кото́р**ое**	кото́р**ую**	кото́р**ые** кото́р**ых**
INSTRUMENTAL ТВОРИ́ТЕЛЬНЫЙ	кото́р**ым**		кото́р**ой**	кото́р**ыми**
PREPOSITIONAL ПРЕДЛО́ЖНЫЙ	о кото́р**ых**		о кото́р**ой**	о кото́р**ых**

5.14 THE USE OF КОТО́РЫЙ (IN THE PLURAL) **_Function:_** Identifying something by its price	Face to Face L2 Chapter 19 B, D Pages 416, 425

Кото́рый translates as _who..., which..., that..._ in a compound sentence. The rules for using кото́рый are the same as with its usage in the singular. This relative pronoun agrees in number and gender with the noun preceding it and to which it refers (its noun antecedent). The case that it takes depends on its use in the sentence.

Sample sentences

main clause	clause with который
Вот браслёты, Here are the bracelets	**котóрые** стóят óчень дóрого. **which** cost a lot (are very expensive).

Котóрые in this sentence refers to **браслёты**. Because this noun is in the **plural**, котóрые must also be in the plural.

Мой друзья, My friends	**котóрых** ты вѝдела, придýт в гóсти. **which** you saw, are going to visit.

Котóрых in this sentence refers to **друзья**. Because this noun is **plural**, and котóрые is the accusative complement in its own clause, it is in the **accusative plural case**.

Ученикѝ, The students	**котóрых** не бѝло на урóке, не познакóмились с рýсскими шкóльниками. **who** were not at the lesson did not meet the Russian students.

Котóрых in this sentence refers to **Ученикѝ**. Because this noun is **plural**, and не бѝло expresses negation in the second clause, котóрых is the **genitive plural case**.

Браслёты, The bracelets	**котóрым** мнóго лет, стóят óчень дóрого. **which** are many years old cost a lot.

Котóрым is in the **dative case** here, as it now functions as the indirect object in its clause, speaking of the age of the bracelets: ...*which are many years old...* (котóрым мнóго лет). **Браслёты** is the subject of the sentence.

Пёсни, The songs	**котóрыми** вы интересýетесь, тóже популя́рные в Россѝи. in **which** you are interested are also popular in Russia.

Котóрыми in this sentence refers to пёсни. Because this noun is **plural**, and интересовáтся requires an instrumental complement in the second clause, котóрыми is the **instrumental plural case**.

Ребя́та, The kids	**о котóрых** я говорѝл, ужé приéхали. **about which** you were speaking have already arrived.

Котóрых in this sentence refers to ребя́та. Because this noun is **plural**, and the preposition **о** requires use of the prepositional case in the second clause, котóрых is the **prepositional plural case**.

5.15 THE PRONOUN сам/á/и
Function: Expressing actions performed by oneself ("myself, himself, herself, themselves", etc.)

Face to Face L2
Chapter 9 B,D
Pages 192-193, 201

The pronoun **сам** (**самá, сáми**) is used after a noun or pronoun that names a person and corresponds to the English *myself, himself, herself and themselves*. It stresses that an action was performed by that person alone and adds emphasis to these statements. **Сам** is formed like a short form adjective and declines for gender and number.

Sample sentences

Брат обещáл всё принестú **сам**.	(My) brother promised to bring everything over **himself**.
Онá **самá** тебя́ пригласúла?	Did she **herself** invite you?
Мы всё **сáми** приготóвили.	We made everything **ourselves**.

5.16 THE REFLEXIVE PRONOUN себя́
Function: Doing things for oneself

Face to Face L2
Chapter 19 A, D
Pages 408-409, 423

This reflexive pronoun **себя́** indicates that the subject is performing an action *on or for itself*. **Себя́** is used for both genders and for both the singular and the plural — it corresponds to all of the English reflexive pronouns: *oneself, myself, ourselves*, etc. **Себя́** has no nominative form; otherwise, it is declined like the personal pronouns **ты** in all other cases (for example, **себя́—тебя́, себé—тебé**).

Sample sentences

Gen.	Этот словáрь я купúл **для себя́**.	I bought this dictionary **for myself**.
Dat.	Этот словáрь я купúл **себé**.	I bought this dictionary **for myself**.
Acc.	Ты узнáл **себя́** на фотогрáфии?	Did you recognize **yourself** in the photo?
Instr.	Что мóжно взять **с собóй** в самолёт?	What can you take **with yourself** on a plane?
Prep.	Расскажúте нам **о себé**.	Tell us **about yourself**.

5.17 THE PHRASE друг друга IN DIFFERENT CASES
Function: Expressing reciprocal actions (the idea of "each other")

Faces and Voices
Chapter 1 Б
Pages 14-15

To express *each other* in Russian the construction **друг друга** is used. The first word of this phrase does not change, but the *second word* declines when:

1)   it is used in a sentence with a verb governing a specific case:

любить **кого**?   любить друг друг**а**   *to love one another/each other*

помогать **кому**?   помогать друг друг**у**   *to help one another/each other*

2)   when it is used in a prepositional phrase. When a preposition is used, the preposition is inserted *between* the two parts:

думать **о** ком?   друг **о** друге   *to think about each other*
разговаривать **с** кем?   друг **с** другом   *to talk with each other*

Sample sentences

	Genitive case
Они получили письма **друг от друга**.	They received letters **from each other**.
	Dative case
Они пишут **друг другу**.	They write **to each other**.
	Accusative case
Они любят **друг друга**.	They love **each other**.
	Instrumental case
Они часто разговаривают **друг с другом** по телефону.	They often talk **with each other** on the phone.
	Prepositional case
Они думают **друг о друге**.	They think **about each other**.

5.18 THE NEGATIVE PRONOUNS НИКТО, НИЧЕГО IN CASES AND CONSTRUCTIONS
Function: Expressing absence of people and objects as subjects and direct and indirect objects; Expressing double negatives in Russian

Мир русских
Lesson 1
Pages 20-21

Negative pronouns are formed from the interrogatives **кто** and **что** with the help of the particle **ни**: **никто** (no one, nobody) and **ничто** (nothing). Note, however, that nominative case form, **ничто**, is seldom used; **ничего** (nothing) is usually substituted for it. These negative pronouns denote the absence of someone or something. They decline in the same way as **кто** and **что**.

Никто **не** пришёл.   **Nobody** came.
Он **никого** здесь **не** знает.   He knows **nobody** here.
Он **никому** **не** говорил об этом.   He told **no one** about it.

Notice in the examples above that the negative pronoun usually stands before the verb in a sentence. Russian requires the particle **не** before the verb despite the presence of the negative pronouns **никто́**, **ничто́** (this expresses a double negative).

Никто́ **не** зна́ет об э́том.	**No one** knows about this.
Он **никого́ не** зна́ет.	He doesn't know **anyone**.

In constructions with prepositions, the preposition falls between the particle **ни** and the pronoun.

С кем ты говори́л об э́том?	With whom did you speak about this?
Ни с кем.	**With no one.**
Я **ни с кем** не говори́л об э́том.	I did not speak about it **with anybody**.

The antonym of **никто́** is **все** (everybody, all) and the opposite to **ничто́** (**ничего́**) is **всё** (everything). **Никто/ничего́** and **всё** are third-person singular pronouns and are used with third-person singular verb forms (**никто́ не зна́ет**) while **все** is a third-person plural pronoun (**все зна́ют об э́том**).

Никто́ **не** зна́ет об э́том.	**No one** knows about this.
Все зна́ют об э́том.	Everyone knows about this.
Он всё понима́ет.	He knows everything.
Он **ничего́ не** понима́ет.	He **doesn't** understand **anything.**

5.19 INDEFINITE PRONOUNS WITH THE PARTICLES - ТО AND -НИБУ́ДЬ

Function: Expressing an indefinite or undetermined person or object (someone, something)

Мир ру́сских
Lesson 4
Pages 117-119

Indefinite pronouns with the particles -**то** and -**нибу́дь** are used when speaking about an indefinite, undetermined object:

кто-**то**	someone
что-**то**	something
како́й-**то** (кака́я-**то**,	some kind, sort
како́е-**то**, каки́е-**то**)	

кто-**нибу́дь**	anyone
что-**нибу́дь**	anything
како́й-**нибу́дь** (кака́я-**нибу́дь**,	any kind, sort
како́е-**нибу́дь**, каки́е-**нибу́дь**).	

Usage of pronouns with -то and -нибу́дь As a rule, indefinite pronouns with the particle -**нибу́дь** are used when speaking about an indefinite, undetermined object. Pronouns with the particle -**то** are used when speaking of a definite object whose name is unknown to the speaker.

Sample sentences

Пусть **кто́-нибу́дь** из друзе́й позвони́т ему́ домо́й.

Have **one of** his friends call him at home (**any of** his friends, it doesn't matter who).

Когда́ тебя́ не́ было до́ма, **кто́-то** звони́л тебе́, но я не зна́ю, кто э́то был.

While you were away, **someone** called you, but I don't know who it was (the person is unknown to the speaker).

Купи́ мне, пожа́луйста, **како́й-нибу́дь** сок.

Please buy me **some kind of** juice (it doesn't matter what kind, **any kind**).

Я ви́дел, что он брал **како́й-то** сок.

I saw him take **some kind of** juice (the speaker doesn't know what kind it was).

Additional usage of pronouns with -нибу́дь Indefinite pronouns with the particle -нибу́дь are generally used in expressing:

1) Questions: **Кто́-нибу́дь** был у вас?
Was **anyone** at your place?

2) Inducements and wishes: Спой нам **каку́ю-нибу́дь** пе́сню.
Sing us a (**some, any**) song.

Declension of pronouns with -то and -нибу́дь Indefinite pronouns decline in the same way as the pronoun without the suffix -то **or** -нибу́дь.

Sample sentences
Nominative
Никто́ не хо́чет пое́хать с на́ми.

No one wants to go with us.

Accusative
По телефо́ну:
— Ми́ша до́ма?
— Его́ нет. Ему́ **что́-нибу́дь** переда́ть?

On the phone:
Is Misha home?
He's not here. Should I tell him **anything** (Can I take a message?)

Genitive
Она́ **никого́** не бои́тся.

She is not afraid of **anyone**.

Dative
Мы ходи́ли по **како́й-то** у́лице, разгова́ривая и смея́сь.

We walked along **some** street, talking and laughing.

Instrumental
Она́ прие́хала на конце́рт с **каки́м-то** челове́ком.

She came to the concert with **some** guy.

Prepositional
Учи́тель говори́л о **чём-то**, но никто́ не слу́шал.

The teacher was talking about **something**, but no one was listening.

Chapter 6

NUMERALS
Имена числительные

6.1 Overview: An introduction to the numeral system in Russian.

Numbers in Russian govern specific cases and decline like nouns. In addition, constructions requiring the use of numbers (telling time, stating one's age, etc.) follow very specific rules. Below, a series of reference tables reviews the numeral system, case usage, and common constructions. Students may benefit by initially learning expressions, such as stating their age or time on the hour, as lexical items.

	Grammar points:
Overview of Numbers and Reference Tables	6.1
Numbers and their Usage	6.2-6.4
Telling Time and Time constructions	6.5-6.9

REFERENCE TABLE 6A: CARDINAL AND ORDINAL NUMBERS

Cardinal	Case		Ordinal	
ноль (scores, tel. numbers, conversational) нуль (weather, math, technical)	+ gen. sing. and pl.	zero	------	------
один, одна, одно, одни	+ nom.	one	пе́рвый	first
два,. две	+ gen. sing.	two	второ́й	second
три	" "	three	тре́тий	third
четы́ре	" "	four	четвёртый	fourth
пять	+ gen. pl.	five	пя́тый	fifth
шесть	" "	six	шесто́й	sixth
семь	" "	seven	седьмо́й	seventh
во́семь	" "	eight	восьмо́й	eighth
де́вять	" "	nine	девя́тый	ninth
де́сять	" "	ten	деся́тый	tenth

REFERENCE TABLE 6A (cont.): CARDINAL AND ORDINAL NUMBERS

одиннадцать	+ gen. pl.	eleven	одиннадцатый	eleventh
двенадцать	" "	twelve	двенадцатый	twelfth
тринадцать	" "	thirteen	тринадцатый	thirteenth
четырнадцать	" "	fourteen	четырнадцатый	fourteenth
пятнадцать	" "	fifteen	пятнадцатый	fifteenth
шестнадцать	" "	sixteen	шестнадцатый	sixteenth
семнадцать	" "	seventeen	семнадцатый	seventeenth
восемнадцать	" "	eighteen	восемнадцатый	eighteenth
девятнадцать	" "	nineteen	девятнадцатый	nineteenth
двадцать	" "	twenty	двадцатый	twentieth
тридцать	" "	thirty	тридцатый	thirtieth
сорок	" "	forty	сороковой	fortieth
пятьдесят	" "	fifty	пятидесятый	fiftieth
шестьдесят	" "	sixty	шестидесятый	sixtieth
семьдесят	" "	seventy	семидесятый	seventieth
восемьдесят	" "	eighty	восьмидесятый	eightieth
девяносто	" "	ninety	девяностый	ninetieth
сто	" "	hundred	сотый	hundredth
двести	" "	two hundred	двухсотый	two-hundredth
триста	" "	three hundred	трёхсотый	three-hundredth
четыреста	" "	four hundred	четырёхсотый	four-hundredth
пятьсот	" "	five hundred	пятисотый	five-hundredth
шестьсот	" "	six hundred	шестисотый	six-hundredth
семьсот	" "	seven hundred	семисотый	seven-hundredth
восемьсот	" "	eight hundred	восьмисотый	eight- hundredth
девятьсот	" "	nine hundred	девятисотый	nine- hundredth
тысяча	" "	thousand	тысячный	thousandth
две тысячи	" "	two thousand	двухтысячный	two-thousandth
пять тысяч	" "	five thousand	пятитысячный	five-thousandth
миллион	" "	million	миллионный	millionth
два миллиона	" "	two million	двухмиллионный	two-millionth
миллиард	" "	billion	миллиардный	billionth

Ordinal numbers (first, second, third, etc.) have the same case, number, and gender endings as other adjectives. All are hard and have hard adjectival endings, except for **третий** (declined in *reference table 6H* below).

Тысяча is a feminine noun; numbers ending in the word одна take тысяча (e.g., 21.000=двадцать одна тысяча), numbers ending in the word две, три, or четыре take тысячи (e.g., 22.000=двадцать две тысячи), numbers ending in the word пять or higher take тысяч (e.g., 25.000=двадцать пять тысяч).

Миллион is a masculine noun: With 2, 3, 4 use миллиона, with numbers ending in a number higher than 4, use миллионов.

REFERENCE TABLE 6B: USAGE OF NUMBERS—OVERVIEW

Construction	Usage / Example
1. Numbers and Case Usage: (1) agrees with noun in gender, number and case: оди́н, одна́, одно́ singular одни́ plural (like short-form adj.)	оди́н учени́к одна́ учини́ца one student one student одно́ пла́тье одни́ часы́ one dress one watch/clock
(21, 31, 101, 241, etc.) + **nominative case**, agrees with noun	два́дцать оди́н учени́к twenty-one students
Adjectives Agree in number and case with the noun.	одна́ но́вая учени́ца one new student
(2, 3, 4) + **genitive singular** два (for masc./neuter nouns) две (for feminine nouns)	два ученика́ two students
(22, 43, 364, etc.) + **genitive singular**	два́дцать три ученика́ twenty-three students две́сти три́дцать четы́ре ученика́ two hundred and thirty-four students
Adjectives **Genitive plural** form with masc./neuter nouns. **Nominative plural** form with feminine nouns. [Note—the nom. pl. form is preferred when the gen. sing. and nom. pl. form of the noun are the same (e.g., кни́ги). The genitive plural adjectival form is preferred when the gen. sing. and nom. pl. forms are not the same (e.g., сестры́ - сёстры).]	три больши́х магази́на, зда́ния three large stores, buildings две интере́сные кни́ги two interesting books
(5-20) + **genitive plural**	пять ученико́в five students
(25-30, 35-40, etc.) + **genitive plural**	два́дцать шесть ученико́в twenty-six students
(100, 1,000, etc.) + **genitive plural**	сто, ты́сяча ученико́в one hundred, one thousand students
Adjectives **Genitive plural form**	пять хоро́ших ученико́в five good students во́семь дли́нных неде́ль eight long weeks
2. Expressing "about a quantity": Reverse the word order: declined noun + numeral	Мне лет пятна́дцать. I'm **about** 15 years old. Она́ вы́шла мину́т на пять. She stepped out **for about** five minutes.

REFERENCE TABLE 6B (cont.): USAGE OF NUMBERS—OVERVIEW

Construction	Usage / Example
3. Indefinite Numerals: Indefinite numerals generally take the **genitive plural** of nouns that can be counted. ско́лько + gen. pl. (in most cases) сто́лько " " не́сколько " " мно́го " " ма́ло " " немно́го " " доста́точно " "	how much/many (лет, зим, и.т.д.) so much/many (де́нег, вы́боров, и.т.д.) several (слов, учени́ц, и.т.д.) much/many (друзе́й, рубле́й, и.т.д.) few (копе́ек, ученико́в, и.т.д.) a few/a little/not many (зада́ний, и.т.д.) enough (книг, уче́бников)
Substances (food, time) The **genitive singular** form of nouns follows these numerals to denote the quantity of substances, food, time, etc.	Ско́лько вре́мени? What time is it? How much time? Ма́ло еды́. Мно́го воды́. Little food. Much water.
челове́к/люде́й; солда́т/солда́тов Generally, ско́лько, не́сколько, and сто́лько take the forms челове́к and солда́т.	Ско́лько челове́к пришло́? How many people came?
Ма́ло, мно́го, etc. take the plural forms люде́й and солда́тов. To express surprise or emotion, also use the genitive plural forms.	Ма́ло люде́й пришло́. Few people came. Ско́лько люде́й на стадио́не! How many people there are at the stadium!
4. Stating Age: **Dative case** *of person* + years old	Мне шестна́дцать лет. I am 16 years old. Ему́/Ей пятна́дцать лет. He/She is 15 years old.
5. Stating the Date: ***Today's date*** **Neuter ordinal** form of the number + **genitive** of the month + **genitive of the ordinal** of the year	Сего́дня вто́рник, пя́тое (число́) ма́я 1998-ого го́да. Today is Tuesday the fifth of May, 1998.
On a day Genitive ordinal form of the number + genitive of the month and year.	Во вто́рник, пя́того ма́я 1998-ого го́да. On Tuesday, the fifth of May 1998.
6. Stating the temperature: плюс/ми́нус + number + гра́дус *declined* The scale may also be included if it is not clear from the context: по фаренге́йту (Fahrenheit) or по це́льсию (Celsius)	Кака́я температу́ра сего́дня? What is the temperature today? Кака́я сего́дня пого́да? What is the weather like today? Плюс шестьдеся́т оди́н гра́дус. 61° Ми́нус два гра́дуса по фаренге́йту. -2° F. Два́дцать гра́дусов по це́льсию. 20° C. Восемна́дцать гра́дусов. 18°

REFERENCE TABLE 6B (cont.): USAGE OF NUMBERS—OVERVIEW

Construction	Usage - Example
7. Basic Arithmetic:	
Addition	
numeral плюс *numeral* бу́дет *sum*	*пять плюс пять бу́дет де́сять* 5 + 5 + 10
Subtraction	
num. ми́нус *num.* бу́дет *quantity*	*шесть ми́нус три бу́дет три* 6 - 3 = 3
Multiplication	
num. умно́женное на *num.* бу́дет *quantity*	четы́ре умно́женное на два бу́дет во́семь 4 x 2 = 8
Division	
num. делённое на *num.* бу́дет *quantity*	де́вять делённое на три бу́дет три 9 ÷ 3 = 3
8. Decimal Points and Thousands:	
Thousands are expressed using periods: 2.000,00 p.	2.000,00 рубле́й two thousand rubles
Decimal points are expressed using commas: π = 3,14	3,14 three point one four, 3 and 14 hundredths
Time—a period is used in place of a colon: 11.00 = eleven o'clock	2.00 ча́са 8.00 утра́ two o'clock eight in the morning
9. Fractions:	
(1 as numerator) одна́ + the fem. ordinal form	1/2 = одна́ втора́я *(часть -part)* 1/6 = одна́ шеста́я 1/100 = одна́ со́тная
(2-9 as numerator) две + the gen. plural ordinal form	2/5 = две пя́тых 5/6 = пять шесты́х 9/10 = де́вять деся́тых 5/100 = пять со́тных
1/4 = че́тверть 1/3 = треть 1/2 = полови́на пол- *with the gen. sing. of a noun*	3/4 = три че́тверти three fourths 2/3 = две тре́ти two thirds 2,5% = два с полови́ной проце́нта полго́да полчаса́ half a year half an hour
10. Expressing "Both":	
о́ба (masc./neuter nouns) + gen. sing. о́бе (fem. nouns) + gen. sing.	о́ба отве́та, окна́ both answers, windows о́бе кни́ги, статьи́ both books, articles

REFERENCE TABLE 6B (cont.): USAGE OF NUMBERS—OVERVIEW

Construction	Usage - Example
11. Collective Numerals: Collective numeral are used with nouns that have only plural forms and typically with masculine animate nouns. Nouns are declined in the **genitive plural**. (2) двóе + gen. plural (3) трóе " " (4) чéтверо " " (5) пятеро " " (6) шéстеро " " (7) сéмеро " " *Above 7, collective numerals are rarely used.*	***With plural nouns*** У них двóе детéй. They have two children. Здесь тóлько трóе людéй. There are only three people here. Нас бýдет пятеро. There will be seven of us. ***With masculine animate nouns*** чéтверо мáльчиков four boys двóе друзéй two friends

REFERENCE TABLE 6C: TELLING TIME

Both cardinal and ordinals are used to state clock time in Russian. Students may follow the progression presented in the table below by first learning to state time on the hour, then quarters and halves past and before the hour, and, finally, minutes before and after the hour.

Time expression - Construction	Usage - Example
Time on the hour: The word **час** (hour) is declined according to the number used. 1.00 Час. (*одúн* is understood) 2.00 Два часá. 3.00 Три часá. 4.00 Четы́ре часá. 5.00- Пять чаóв. 12.00 Двенáдцать часóв.	Скóлько врéмени? What time is it? *or* Котóрый час? What time is it? Шесть часóв. It is six o'clock.
Time of day: When stating the time, the day is divided into four periods, each according to the following approximate times: утрá — sunrise (5 a.m.) to 11 a.m. дня — 11 a.m. to sunset (6 p.m.) вéчера — sunset (6 p.m.) to midnight (12 a.m.) нóчи — midnight to sunrise пóлдень — noon пóлночь — midnight	Онá встáла в шесть часóв утрá. She got up at six in the morning. Передáча начинáется в семь вéчера. The program begins at seven in the evening. Скóлько врéмени? Пóлдень. What time is it? It is noon.

REFERENCE TABLE 6C (cont.): TELLING TIME

Time expression - Construction	Usage - Example
"At" the hour: "At a time" — use the construction: **в + the accusative**	Во ско́лько? At what time? *or* В кото́ром часу́? At what time? В час. В шесть часо́в. At one. At six o'clock. В по́лдень. В оди́ннадцать часо́в. At noon. At eleven o'clock.
Expressing quarters and halves: 00.15 пятна́дцать мину́т (*15 minutes*) че́тверть (*quarter*) 00.30 три́дцать мину́т (*30 minutes*) полови́на (half) пол- (*half—conversational*)	Без че́тверти два. Quarter 'til two. Полови́на второ́го. Полвторо́го. Half past one.
Time after the hour: *minutes after* + ordinal of the upcoming hour in **the genitive case** 1.05 пять мину́т второ́го 2.10 де́сять мину́т тре́тьего 4.15 че́тверть пя́того 6.20 два́дцать седьмо́го 8.25 два́дцать пять девя́того 12.30 полови́на пе́рвого, по́лпе́рвого	Ско́лько вре́мени? Оди́ннадцать деся́того. It is eleven (minutes) after nine. Во ско́лько? В полови́не восьмо́го. At seven-thirty.
Time before the hour: без + minutes until in **the genitive case** + the cardinal of the upcoming hour 1.55 без пяти́ мину́т два 2.50 без десяти́ мину́т три 4.45 без пятна́дцати/че́тверти пять 6.40 без двадцати́ семь 8.35 без двадцати́ пяти́ де́вять 12.31 без двадцати́ девяти́ час (три́дцать онда́ мину́та пе́рвого is more common)	Ско́лько вре́мени? Без оди́ннадцати де́сять. It is eleven (minutes) until ten. Во ско́лько? *Без шести́ мину́т во́семь. At six (minutes) before eight. *Note: The gen. plural **мину́т** is used after a declined number.
Schedules/24 hour time: Twenty-four hour time, or military time, is used in schedules, on the radio, and in other official contexts. The number of hours are stated followed by the number of minutes. 24.00 два́дцать четы́ре часа́, по́лно́чь 12.00 двена́дцать часо́в; по́лде́нь 17.15 семна́дцать пятнадцать 18.45 восемна́дцать со́рок пять	Переда́ча начина́ется в восемна́дцать часо́в. The program begins at six p.m. midnight noon

REFERENCE TABLE 6D: DECLENSION OF THE NUMBER ONE*

CASE	MASC.	NEUT.	FEM.	PL.
NOMINATIVE	один	одно́	одна́	одни́
GENITIVE	одного́		одно́й	одни́х
DATIVE	одному́		одно́й	одни́м
ACCUSATIVE				
inanimate	один	одно́	одну́	одни́
animate	одного́			одни́х
INSTRUMENTAL	одни́м	одни́м	одно́й	одни́ми
PREPOSITIONAL	(об) одно́м	(об) одно́м	(об) одно́й	(об) одни́х

* Note: Zero — **Нуль** and **ноль** are declined like soft masculine nouns ending in a soft sign with stress on the end: **с нуля** (genitive)—**from zero, from nothing**.

REFERENCE TABLE 6E: DECLENSION OF THE NUMBERS TWO, THREE, FOUR

CASE	MASC.	NEUT.	FEM.		
NOMINATIVE	два		две	три	четы́ре
GENITIVE	двух			трёх	четырёх
DATIVE	двум			трём	четырём
ACCUSATIVE					
inanimate	два	два	две	три	четы́ре
animate	двух		двух	трёх	четырёх
INSTRUMENTAL	двумя́			тремя́	четырьмя́
PREPOSITIONAL	(о) двух			(о) трёх	(о) четырёх

REFERENCE TABLE 6F: DECLENSION OF THE NUMBERS 5, 50, 40, 90, 100

NOMINATIVE	пять	пятьдеся́т	со́рок	девяно́сто	сто
GENITIVE	пяти́	пяти́десяти	сорока́	девяно́ста	ста
DATIVE	пяти́	пяти́десяти	сорока́	девяно́ста	ста
ACCUSATIVE	пять	пятьдеся́т	со́рок	девяно́сто	сто
INSTRUMENTAL	пятью́	пятью́десятью	сорока́	девяно́ста	ста
PREPOSITIONAL	пяти́	пяти́десяти	сорока́	девяно́ста	ста

REFERENCE TABLE 6G: DECLENSION OF THE ORDINAL тре́тий *(THIRD)**

CASE	MASC.	NEUT.	FEM.	PL.
NOMINATIVE	тре́тий	тре́тье	тре́тья	тре́тьи
GENITIVE	тре́тьего		тре́тьей	тре́тьих
DATIVE	тре́тьему		тре́тьей	тре́тьим
ACCUSATIVE			тре́тью	
inanimate	тре́тий	тре́тье		тре́тьи
animate	тре́тьего			тре́тьих
INSTRUMENTAL	тре́тьим		тре́тьей	тре́тьими
PREPOSITIONAL	(обо) тре́тьем		(обо) тре́тьей	(обо) тре́тьих

*Note: All other ordinals decline like hard adjectives.

REFERENCE TABLE 6H: DECLENSION OF о́ба/о́бе AND COLLECTIVE NUMERALS

CASE	о́ба	о́бе	дво́е, тро́е		че́тверо, etc.
NOMINATIVE	о́ба	о́бе	дво́е	тро́е	че́тверо
GENITIVE	обо́их	обе́их	двои́х	трои́х	четверы́х
DATIVE	обо́им	обе́им	двои́м	трои́м	четверы́м
ACCUSATIVE					
inanimate	о́ба	о́бе	дво́е	тро́е	че́тверо
animate	обо́их	обе́их	двои́х	трои́х	четверы́х
INSTRUMENTAL	обо́ими	обе́ими	двои́ми	трои́ми	четверы́ми
PREPOSITIONAL	обо́их	обе́их	двои́х	трои́х	четверы́х

6.2 CARDINAL NUMBERS 1-20, 20-100
Function: Dealing with numbers; scores

Face to Face L1
Chapter 13 A, B
Pages 261-269,
268

The cardinal numbers 1-20 and 20-30 are listed below along with the cases each take. The proper pronunciation and stress of each should be memorized. Sample sentences are presented below in the context of talking about sports scores.

Numeral		Case
1 оди́н m. одно́ n., одна́ f., одни́ pl.		+ nominative, agrees with noun
2 два m./n., две f.		+ genitive singular
3 три		" "
4 четы́ре		" "
5 пять		+ genitive plural
6 шесть		" "
7 семь		" "
8 во́семь		" "
9 де́вять		" "
10 де́сять		" "
11 оди́ннадцать	16 шестна́дцать	+ genitive plural
12 двена́дцать	17 семна́дцать	" "
13 трина́дцать	18 восемна́дцать	" "
14 четы́рнадцать	19 девятна́дцать	" "
15 пятна́дцать	20 два́дцать	" "
20 два́дцать	70 се́мьдесят	+ genitive plural
30 три́дцать	80 во́семьдесят	" "
40 со́рок	90 девяно́сто	" "
50 пятьдеся́т	100 сто	" "
60 шестьдеся́т		" "

Note: When counting off, as in a competition, раз (once) generally replaces оди́н. «Раз, два, три...вперёд!» *"One, two, three...go!"*

The common phrase, "One minute/moment!", is expressed using the feminine accusative: «Одну́ мину́ту!»

Sample sentences
— Како́й сейча́с счёт? What's the score now?
— (6:3) **шесть-три** **Six to three**.
— Ничья́, (5:5) **пять-пять** It's a tie. **Five to five**.
— (0:14) **ноль-четы́рнадцать** **Zero-fourteen**.
— (34:42) **три́дцать четы́ре-со́рок два** **Thirty-four to forty-two**.

6.3 QUANTITIVE NOUNS/ SPECIAL NUMERALS AS NOUNS
Function: Talking about grades

Face to Face L1
Chapter 9 D
Page 202

Nouns may be formed from numerals to denote quantity in specific meanings. Grades in Russian number from 5 (excellent) to 1 (fail). Grades are listed below with their official and slang names.

Grade	Official names	Student slang
5	пятёрка (отлично - *excellent*, очень хорошо - *very good*)	отл, пята́к
4	четвёрка (хорошо́ - *good*)	хор
3	тро́йка (удовлетворительно - *satisfactory*)	уд, троя́к
2	дво́йка (неудовлетвори́тельно - *unsatisfactory*)	па́ра, не́уд
1	едини́ца (*fail*)	кол, бана́н

6.4   COLLECTIVE NUMERALS: ДВОЕ, ТРОЕ, ETC.
ADVERBS DERIVED FROM COLLECTIVE NUMERALS:
ВДВОЁМ, ВТРОЁМ, ВЧЕТВЕРОМ, ВПЯТЕРОМ ... ВДЕСЯТЕРОМ
Function: Naming numbered groups of persons, animals or things

| Мир русских |
| Lesson 1 |
| Pages 25-28 |

Collective numerals The main function of collective numerals is to name numbered groups of persons, animals, or things. They are often used interchangeably with cardinal numerals, but are not used for counting. **Дво́е, тро́е,** and **че́тверо** are the most commonly used. Nouns used with collective numerals take the genitive plural form.

	collective numeral	+ genitive plural	
2	дво́е	дво́е ма́льчиков	two boys
3	тро́е	тро́е дете́й	three children
4	че́тверо	че́тверо ученико́в	four students
5	пя́теро		
6	ше́стеро		
7	се́меро		
8	во́сьмеро		
9	де́вятеро		
10	де́сятеро		

There are five basic rules for the usage of collective numerals:

1)   **Masculine nouns denoting persons and young animals**
Collective numerals may be used instead of cardinal numerals (**два, три, че́тыре, пять,** etc.) with masculine nouns denoting persons:

дво́е ма́льчиков	два ма́льчика	two boys
че́тверо ученико́в*	четы́ре ученика́*	four students

They can also be used with nouns denoting young animals:

У ко́шки **тро́е** котя́т.   У ко́шки три котёнка.

The cat has three kittens.

*Note: In this usage some of the students may be female. The masculine plural is used to express mixed-sex groups.

2)   Use with specific singular, plural and paired nouns
Collective numerals are always used with the words **мужчи́на, де́ти,** and **ребя́та**. They are also used with nouns that have no singular form, such as **но́жницы** (scissors) and collective nouns that imply the word **па́ра** (pair), denoting "paired" objects: **брю́ки,** (pants), and **очки́** (eye glasses), **носки́** (socks), **ту́фли** (shoes), **перча́тки** (gloves).

Там разгова́ривали **дво́е** (**тро́е**) **мужчи́н**.	**Two** (**three**) **men** were conversing there.
У них **дво́е** (**тро́е, че́тверо, пя́теро**...) дете́й.	They have **two** (**three, four, five**) children
Около шко́лы стоя́ли **дво́е** (**тро́е, че́тверо, пя́теро**...) ребя́т.	**Two** (**three, four, five**) kids were standing near the school.
В столе́ **дво́е но́жниц**.	There are **two** pairs of **scissors** in the table.
Там лежи́т **дво́е носко́в** (па́ра носко́в).	A **pair of socks** is lying there.

3)   Representing a group of people and in idiomatic expressions
When collective numerals are used without a noun, they usually denote a number of persons (either male or female) taken as a whole or a group. Thus, **дво́е** means **два челове́ка** (two persons), **тро́е** means **три челове́ка** (three persons), etc.

Пришли́ все **тро́е**.	All **three** of them came.
Их бы́ло **дво́е**.	There were **two** of them.
То́лько э́ти **дво́е** зна́ют об э́том.	Only these **two** know about it.
Нас бу́дет **тро́е**.	There will be **three of us**.

The idiomatic expressions Он рабо́тает за двои́х (He works very much—*lit.*, for two) and Он ест за трои́х (He eats a lot—*lit.*, for three) are also examples of the above usage. Here, за двои́х and за трои́х can be translated as *very much*.

4)   Use with personal pronouns
Collective numerals are used with personal pronouns in combinations such as **мы дво́е** (the two of us), **они́ тро́е** (the three of them), etc., where the collective numeral follows the personal pronoun.

Мы дво́е зна́ем об э́том.   **The two of us** know about it.

5)   Words used in place of челове́к

Collective numerals are normally *not* used with the word **челове́к** denoting a person, either male or female, or with its usual plural, **лю́ди**. Instead, **два** (**три**, **четы́ре**, **пять**...) **челове́к(а)** or **дво́е** (**тро́е**, **че́тверо**, **пя́теро**...) **мужчи́н**, **же́нщин**, **дете́й**, etc. are used.

Sample sentences

Дво́е ма́льчиков пла́вают в бассе́йне.	**Two boys** are swimming in the pool.
but	
Две де́вочки " ".	Two girls " ".
Тро́е котя́т спа́ли в углу́.	The **three kittens** were sleeping in the corner.
but	
У них три кота́.	They have three cats.
Здесь **че́тверо мужчи́н**.	There are **four men** here.
but	
Здесь четы́ре челове́ка.	There are four people here.
В чемода́не **дво́е брю́ки** и две руба́шки.	There are **two pair of pants** and two shirts in the suitcase.
Мы **дво́е** пошли́ в кино́, а други́е оста́лись до́ма.	The **two of us** went to the movies, but the others stayed home.

Adverbs вдвоём, втроём, вчетверо́м, впятеро́м ... вдесятеро́м

These adverbs mean *two (three, etc.) together, as a unit*. They are derived from the collective numerals **дво́е**, **тро́е**, **че́тверо**, etc.). **Вдвоём** and **втроём** are most frequently used.

Recall that adverbs answer the question **Как?** *How?* These adverbs decribe the nature of the action by the number of people, the couple, etc., who perform it.

Sample sentences

Мы живём **втроём**: я и мои́ роди́тели.	**The three of us** live together: my parents and I.
Как они́ живу́т? Втроём.	**How** do they live? The three of them together.
Я́щик был о́чень тяжёлый: они́ **вдвоём** его́ с трудо́м подня́ли.	The box was very heavy, **the two of them** had a difficult time picking it up.
Оди́н я э́того не сде́лаю, мы мо́жем сде́лать э́то то́лько **вдвоём**.	I shall not be able to do it alone, only **the two of us** together can do it.

6.5 **THE USE OF NUMBERS WITH NOUNS OF TIME**
THE QUESTION КОГДА? WITH THE ACCUSATIVE CASE TO
TELL WHEN AN EVENT OCCURRED
Function: Talking about time (telling clock time)
Using expressions of time

Face to Face L1
Chapter 14 A, B
Pages 283-286,
287-291

Telling time in Russian requires the use of numbers with the properly declined nouns **час** (hour) and **минута** (minute):

	Сколько времени?	What time is it?
	Который час?	What time is it?
1.00	Час. (nom. case)	It is one o'clock.
1.01	Час одна минута.	It is one-o-one.
2.00	Два часа. (gen. sing. 2-4)	It is two o'clock.
2.02	Два часа две минуты.	It is two-o-two.
5.00	Пять часов. (gen. pl. 5-20)	It's five o'clock.
5.05	Пять часов пять минут.	It's five-o-five.

Expressing the time of day In general conversation, the twelve-hour clock is used. The time expressions **полдень** (noon) and **полночь** (midnight) are commonly used to denote time of day. To delineate a.m. and p.m. the day is divided into four periods: **утро** (morning), **день** (day), **вечер** (evening), **ночь** (night). The **genitive singular** of these parts of the day are used when stated with the time.

Шесть часов вечера.	Six in the evening (p.m.)
Два часа дня.	Two in the afternoon (p.m.)
Три часа ночи.	Three in the morning (*lit., at night*) (a.m.)
Восемь часов утра.	Eight in the morning (a.m.)

дня	noon (11 a.m.) to sunset (5 p.m.)
вечера	sunset (5 p.m.) to 11 p.m.
ночи	11 p.m. to sunrise (5 a.m.)
утра	sunrise (5 a.m.) to 11 a.m.

Twenty-four hour time The 24-hour clock is often used for schedules and official times such as at train stations, for movie schedules, on radio broadcasts, etc.

00.00	ноль часов.	zero hours, midnight
24.00	24 часов.	24 hundred hours, midnight
12.00	12 часов.	12 o'clock, noon
18.00	18 часов.	6 p.m.

Expressing "time at" with days and clock time Both expressions *at a specific time* and *on a specific day* use the construction **в + the accusative case**. This construction answers the questions **Когда?** (When?) and **Во сколько?** (At what time?).

Какой сегодня день?		Когда?	В какой день?
Which day is it today?		When?	On which day? *On...*
Сегодня...			
понедельник	Monday		в понедельник
вторник	Tuesday		*во вторник
среда	Wednesday		в среду
четверг	Thursday		в четверг
пятница	Friday		в пятницу
суббота	Saturday		в субботу
воскресенье	Sunday		в воскресенье

Сколько времени? **or**	Когда?	*Во сколько? **or**
Который час?		В котором часу?
What time is it?	When?	At what time?
Час.		В час.
Два часа.		В два часа.
Шесть часов.		В шесть часов.
Двадцать четыре часа.		В двадцать четыре часа.

*Note: an -o is added to the preposition **в** before the consonant cluster **вт-** (во вторник) and **ск-** (во сколько).

Sample sentences

Когда будет концерт?
Во вторник в восемь часов вечера.

When is the concert?
On Tuesday at 8 p.m.

6.6 TELLING TIME DURING THE FIRST HALF OF THE HOUR
TELLING TIME DURING THE SECOND HALF OF THE HOUR
USING БЕЗ + THE GENITIVE

Function: Asking and telling when something begins and ends. Telling time conversationally	Face to Face L2 Chapter 16 B,D Pages 346-352, 357-358

Expressing beginning and ending times Several verbs and expressions are used with time to state when an event begins and ends. Note the use of the reflexive verbs начинаться (to begin) and кончаться (to end). These verbs are only used in the third-person (он, она, оно, они) conjugations.

начинаться **to begin**
Когда **начинается** фильм? — When does the film **begin**?
Фильм **начинается** в семь. — The film **begins** at seven.
Уроки **начинаются** в 8.10. — School (*lit.*, classes) **begins** at 8:10.
кончаться **to end**
Когда **кончается** фильм? — When does the film **end**?
Фильм **кончается** в девять. — The film **ends** at nine.
Уроки **кончаются** в три. — School (*lit.*, classes) **ends** at three.

The nouns начало (beginning) and конец (end) with the event in the genitive case can also be used in time expressions.

нача́ло + gen. "beginning of..."
Нача́ло пе́рвого уро́ка в 8.10.   The **beginning of** first period is at 8:10.
Нача́ло фи́льма в семь.   The **beginning of** the film is at seven.

коне́ц + gen. "end of..."
Коне́ц седьмо́го уро́ка в три.   The **end of** the seventh period is at three.
Коне́ц фи́льма в де́вять.   The **end of** the film is at nine.

The plural часы́ (clock, watch) with time expressions The word for *watch/clock*, часы́, is plural. All verbs and modifiers must agree with this plurality. Note the use of the construction **на + accusative** to express *by how many minutes*.

Мой **часы́** иду́т то́чно.   My **watch** is running on time (*lit., exactly*).

Ва́ши **часы́** остаю́т на одну́ мину́ту.   Your **watch** is behind by a minute.
Часы́ в кла́ссе спеша́т на пять мину́т. The **clock** in the classroom is fast by five minutes.

На́ши **часы́** совсе́м стоя́т.   Our **clock** has stopped entirely .

Time before and after the hour In official, 24-hour time, time before and after the hour is expressed by reading off the hour followed by the number of minutes.

13.05	трина́дцать часо́в пять мину́т.	1:05 p.m.
18.30	восемна́дцать часо́в три́дцать мину́т.	6:30 p.m.

In conversation (colloquially), the number of minutes before and after the hour are expressed by constructions dividing the clock into halves: number of minutes until the next hour, number of minutes after and of the next hour.

Time 'til the Hour	Time After the Hour
Без + gen. of minutes 'til + nom. of next hour	Minutes after + gen. of ordinal (adj.) of upcoming hour

'before' 'after'
без

'til		After	
12.59	без одно́й мину́ты час	одна́ мину́та пе́рвого	12.01
1.58	без двух два	две мину́ты второ́го	1.02
2.57	без трёх три	три мину́ты тре́тьего	2.03
3.56	без четырёх четы́ре	четы́ре мину́ты четвёртого	3.04
4.55	без пяти́ пять	пять мину́т пя́того	4.05
5.54	без шести́ шесть	шесть мину́т шесто́го	5.06
6.53	без семи́ семь	де́сять мину́т седьмо́го	6.10
7.52	без восьми́ во́семь	пятна́дцать мину́т восьмо́го	7.15
8.51	без девяти́ де́вять	че́тверть девя́того	8.15
9.50	без десяти́ де́сять	два́дцать мину́т деся́того	9.20
10.49	без оди́ннадцати оди́ннадцать	три́дцать мину́т оди́ннадцатого	10.30
11.48	без двена́дцати двена́дцать	полови́на двена́дцатого	11.30
12.40	без двадцати́ час	полпе́рвого	12.30
1.35	без двадцати́ пяти́ два	*30 minutes after the hour is*	
3.45	без че́тверти четы́ре	*expressed as time after/past*	

Note: In conversation, **час** and **мину́та** may be omitted (**без двух два**—1.58). The genitive plural forms **часо́в** and **мину́т**, when used, are used after declined numbers (**без двух мину́т два**—1.58).

6.7 THE PREPOSITIONS «С — ДО», «ОТ — ДО», AND «С — ПО» WITH NUMERALS

Function: Expressing time *from-until, from-through* with numbers

Мир русских
Lesson 5
Page 162

Prepositions с and до + genitive: "from...until..." After the prepositions с (from) and до (until), numerals are declined in **the genitive case.**

| Магазин работает с 8 (восьми) до 5 (пяти). | The store is open **from eight until five.** |
| Занятия в классе с 9 (девяти) до 2 (двух). | Classes in this classroom are **from nine until two.** |

Prepositions от and до + genitive: "from...until..." The preposition от (from) + **the genitive case** is frequently used instead of с in phrases with numerals.

| Мы ждали вас от 12 (двенадцати) до 3 (трёх). | We waited for you **from twelve until three.** |

Prepositions с + the genitive case and по + the accusative case with ordinal numerals: "from...through..." The prepositions с + **the genitive case** and по (**up to and including**) + **the accusative case** are used with **ordinal** numerals (first, second, etc.) to express inclusive dates or numbers of pages or editions.

| Мы должны были прочитать с 17 (семнадцатой) по 20 (двадцатую) страницу. | We were supposed to read **from the seventeenth through the twentieth** page. |
| Мы будем в Петербурге с двадцатого по двадцать третье июля. | We will be in (St.) Petersburg **from the twentieth through the twenty-third** of July. |

Sample sentences

Надпись на окне:	Sign in a window:
Магазин работает **с девяти до восемнадцати**.	The store is open **from nine a.m. to six p.m.**
После школы я работаю **с четырёх до девяти**.	After school I work **from four until nine.**
На уроке:	In class:
Прочитайте на завтра **с тридцатого по сорок пятую** страницу.	Read pages **32 to 45** for tomorrow.
Меня не будет дома **с третьего по седьмое**.	I won't be home **from the third through the seventh.**

6.8 THE PREPOSITION К WITH THE DATIVE CASE IN TIME CONSTRUCTIONS
Function: Expressing toward or by a certain time

Мир русских
Lesson 7
Page 229

The preposition **к + the dative case** has the meaning of *towards* or *by* a named time. This construction can be used with numerals, parts of the day and seasons of the year:

Sample sentences

Я зайду́ **к оди́ннадцати**.	I'll drop in **towards eleven**.
Дождь пошёл **к но́чи**.	It began to rain **towards night**.
Она́ обы́чно прихо́дит домо́й **к семи́**.	She usually gets home **by seven.**
Сего́дня я приду́ домо́й то́лько к **ве́черу**.	I'll arrive home only **towards evening** today.
Я верну́сь **к трём**.	I'll return **by three**.
Муж прие́дет из командиро́вки **к ле́ту**.	My husband will come back from his business trip **by summer**.

6.9 TIME CONSTRUCTIONS: THE PREPOSITIONS ПО + DAT., НА + ACC., ЗА + ACC., ACCUSATIVE CASE, ВО́ ВРЕМЯ AND ВОВРЕ́МЯ
Function: Expressing repeated times/occasions, in an amount of time, for how long, on time and during

Мир русских
Lesson 6
Page 189

The following time constructions are frequently encountered in Russian. Each denotes a specific connotation of time:

Repeated segments of time To express action performed *repeatedly on the same day of the week*, two constructions can be used:

По + the dative plural case *meaning* **"on..."**

по суббо́там	on Saturdays
по воскресе́ньям	on Sundays

Ка́ждый modifying the day in the accusative case meaning "every..."

ка́ждую суббо́ту	every Saturday
ка́ждое воскресе́нье	every Sunday

The expression **вре́мя от вре́мени** means *from time to time, sometimes,* and can also express repeated segments of time:

Sample sentences

Лётом **по суббóтам и воскресéньям** мы обязáтельно éдем на дáчу.	**On Saturdays and Sundays** in the summer we go to our country house no matter what (*lit.*, *without fail*).
Кáждую суббóту и воскресéнье (кáждые выходны́е) мы обязáтельно éдем на дáчу.	**Every Saturday and Sunday** (every weekend)...
Егó родители жи́ли в другóм гóроде, и он éздил к ним **врéмя от врéмени** (иногдá).	His parents lived in another city, and he went to see them **from time to time** (sometimes).

<u>**"During" and "On time"**</u> The two-word prepositional phrase **во врéмя + the genitive case** means *during*. **Во врéмя** is **not** used with specific time words or phrases (such as **лéто** or **год**). Its usage is more general and relates to an activity or event (such as **концéрт** — *the concert* or **перерыв** — *the break*)*.

The one-word adverb **вóвремя** means *on time, in time, opportunely*. This adverb answers the questions **Как?** How? and describes the action being performed.

Sample sentences

Во врéмя болéзни онá не выходи́ла из дóма.	**During her illness** she didn't leave the house.
Мы пришли́ в теáтр **вóвремя**. (Мы не опоздáли.)	We reached the theater **on time**. (We were not late.)

*Note: The expression **в течéние+ the genitive case** (during the course of) can be used when naming a time-associated word or phrase, such as **лéто** or **год**:
Он был там **в течéние лéт а**. He was there **during the course of the whole summer**.

<u>**Approximation of time**</u> The following constructions denote an approximation of time:

1)   **Numeral + the phrase с ли́шним лет**

Онá рабóтает в э́том институ́те **двáдцать с ли́шним лет**. (бóлее двадцати́ лет)	She has been working in this institute **for some twenty years**. (more than twenty years)

2)   **Ordinal number modifying час**

Сейчáс **трéтий час**.	It's **after 2:00** now. (*lit.*, Now is the third hour. — meaning any time between 2:00 and 3:00)

3)   **Скóро + the stated time**

Скóро шесть.	It'll **soon be six**.

4)   **В начáле (at the beginning of) or в концé (at the end of) + time in the genitive case**

Он пришёл **в начáле вторóго**.	He arrived **just after one** (at the beginning of the second hour).

5)   Preposition о́коло + the genitive case of the time

Он пришёл о́коло двух.   He arrived **at about two**.

6)   Inverted order: declined noun preceding the number

Я позвоню́ тебе́ часа́ в два.   I'll call you **at about two o'clock**.

Он рабо́тает в плодопито́мнике лет   He has been working in the fruit tree
два́дцать.   nursery **for about twenty years**.

Мы прие́дем неде́ли че́рез две.   We'll come **in about two weeks**.

Time expressions in the accusative case: Expressing "for" and "in" a period of time Three basic constructions in Russian express the idea of performing an action *for* or *in* a period of time. Each construction denotes a different connotation and can only be used in specific contexts. The following chart and subsequent explanations outline this usage.

Imperfective verb + accusative case:

TIME LINE	⤳⟶
	Она́ чита́ла **два часа́**.
	She read **for two hours**.
	[the action occurs for this duration]

Perfective verb + за + accusative case:

TIME LINE	⊢———⊣
	Она́ прочита́ла кни́гу **за два часа́**.
	She read the book **in two hours**.
	[the action was completed in this amount of time]

на + accusative case:

TIME LINE	⤳⟶
	Она́ пойдёт в кино́ **на два часа́**.
	She is going to the movies **for two hours**.
	[the intended duration of time begins once the action is completed]

1)   Time expressions in the accusative case without prepositions: Stressing how long a particular actions lasts

To stress the length of time an action lasts, such as Я чита́ла **два часа́**. (I read **for two hours**.), the length of time is expressed in the accusative case without a preposition and always with an imperfective verb.

Ива́н не люби́л рыба́лку. Сиде́ть   Ivan didn't like to go fishing. To sit
це́лый день без дел — как ску́чно!   **all day** with nothing to do — how
                                            boring!

сиде́ть (imperfective verb; intransitive) це́лый день (accusative of time)

По суббо́там, Ива́н е́здил на | On Saturdays, Ivan rode the train **for**
электри́чке **два часа́** до (свое́й) | **two hours** to his dacha.
да́чи. |

| е́здил (imperfective verb; intransitive) **два часа́** (accusative of time) |

Sentences with **быть** and a time expression also have the time expression in the accusative case without a preposition.

Он был там **всю неде́лю**. | He was there **all week**.

| был (imperfective verb; intransitive) **всю неде́лю** (accusative of time) |

This time construction is usually used with intransitive verbs. Recall that intransitive verbs are those which do not take a direct object (the action is not performed on another noun: **сиде́ть, е́здить, быть**). However, transitive verbs may be used while still stressing that the action took place during the stated time:

Я чита́ла кни́гу **два часа́**. | I read *the book* (direct object) **for two hours**.

Мы смотре́ли телеви́зор **всю ночь**. | We watched *TV* (direct object) **all night**.

2)   Preposition за + the accusative case: stating the completion of an action in an amount of time

To express the completion of a task *in a specific amount of time*, the preposition **за + the accusative case** with a perfective verb is used. The construction denotes that the action was accomplished more quickly than one might have expected under normal circumstances.

Он писа́л бы́стро и успе́л написа́ть | He wrote quickly and managed to
письмо́ **за пятна́дцать мину́т**. | write a letter **in fifteen minutes**.

Я хочу́ в кино́ ве́чером, поэ́тому мне | I want to go to the movies this
ну́жно сде́лать уро́ки по́сле | evening, so I need to do and finish
заня́тий **за два часа́**. | my lessons after class **in two hours**.

Compare the use of the perfective and the preposition **за** + the accusative case to stress completion, with the imperfective and accusative to stress duration:

Неде́лю я чита́л э́ту кни́гу. | I read this book **all week**.

| (accusative case without a preposition, usually with an imperfective verb)

За неде́лю я прочита́л э́ту кни́гу, несмотря́ на то, что она́ така́я дли́нная. | I read this book **in a week**, despite the fact that it was so long.
| (**за** + accusative case, always with a perfective verb)

3)   **Preposition** на **+ the accusative case: Stating the intention to perform an action "for" an amount of time**

Time constructions with на + the accusative case state the intended segment of time an action will or did occupy.

Что вы бу́дете де́лать **на кани́кулы**?	What will you do **for the holidays**?
Мы пое́дем в Москву́ **на неде́лю**.	We are going to Moscow **for a week**.
	(We **intend** to be there a week, once we get there.)
Мы пое́дем на да́чу **на три дня**.	We are going to our dacha **for three days**.
	(We **intend** to be there three days.)
Мы пое́дем в го́сти **на ме́сяц**.	We will visit friends **for a month**.
	(We **intend** to to stay with them for a month.)

To remember this construction, it is helpful to learn the associated questions frequently encountered in Russian:

Что вы бу́дете де́лать **на кани́кулы**? **на выходны́е**?	What will you do **for the holidays**? **for the weekend**?
Куда́ вы е́дете **на ле́то**? **на Но́вый год**?	Where are you going **for the summer**? **for New Year's**?
Что ты бу́дешь де́лать **на твой день рожде́ния**?	What will you do **for your birthday**?
Мы е́дем в рестора́н **на ве́чер**.	We are going to the restaurant **for the evening**.
Мы е́дем в Со́чи на **две неде́ли**.	We are going to Sochi **for two weeks**.
Мы е́дем в музе́й **на не́сколько часо́в**.	We are going to a museum **for a few hours**.

Sample sentences

Подожди́ его́, он вы́шел **на мину́ту**.	Wait for him. He stepped out **a minute**.
Мы дошли́ до институ́та **за 15 мину́т**.	We reached the institute **in fifteen minutes**.
Де́ти уе́хали за́ город **на всё ле́то**.	The children left for the countryside **for the entire summer**.
Де́ти отдыха́ли за го́родом **ле́то**.	The children relaxed in the countryside **for a summer**.
За ле́то де́ти хорошо́ отдохну́ли.	**By the end of the summer** the children were well-rested.
Шко́льник гото́вил уро́ки **час**.	The student did his homework (*lit.* prepared his lessons) **for an hour**.
Шко́льник пригото́вил уро́ки **за два часа́**.	The student completed his homework **in two hours**.
Инжене́р уе́хал в командиро́вку **на ме́сяц**.	The engineer left **for a month** on a business trip.
Э́тот дом постро́или **за три ме́сяца**.	They built this house **in three months**.
Шко́лу стро́или **три ме́сяца**.	**For three months** they built this school.
Библиоте́ку закры́ли **на ме́сяц**, что́бы сде́лать ремо́нт.	They closed the library **for a month** to do renovations.

Chapter 7

VERBS
Глаго́лы

7.1 Overview: What are verbs? Verbs express action in sentences, such as *to write* and *to run*. The **infinitive** form of a verb is its dictionary, or unconjugated, form. In English the infinitive is expressed using "to": to read, to write. Most Russian infinitives end in the letters -ть and drop this ending when they are conjugated. **Conjugation** refers to the pattern endings verbs take according to the subject to which they refer.

Infinitive form	чита́ть	to read
Conjugated form	Я чита́ю.	I read.
	Ты чита́ешь.	You read.
	Они́ чита́ют.	They are reading.

The first person singular (**я**), second person singular (**ты**), and third person plural (**они́**) forms of verbs are listed throughout this text. These three forms refer to the two basic conjugation patterns in Russian and provide information on additional changes such as consonant mutations. The section on verbal conjugation (beginning with grammar point 7.2) provides a more comprehensive overview of the use of the **я**, **ты**, and **они́** forms to aid in verbal conjugation.

The following topics are covered extensively in this chapter on Russian verbs:

	Grammar points:
Verbal Conjugation	7.3-7.23
Imperatives and Command Constructions	7.24-7.29
Reflexive Verb Forms	7.30-7.37
Verbal Aspect	7.38-7.50
Obligation, Possibility, Potential, Necessity, and Permission	7.51-7.58
Verbs of Motion	7.59-7.72
Impersonal Constructions	7.73-7.74
Subjunctive and Conditional Moods	7.75-7.78
Participles	7.79-7.81
Verbal Adverbs (Gerunds)	7.82-7.83
Special Verb Groups	7.84-7.96
Comprehensive List of Verb Pairs	Table 7U

Verbal Conjugation

7.2 Overview: How do verbs conjugate in Russian? Russian verbs conjugate according to two basic patterns—**Type I** first conjugation pattern and **Type II** second conjugation pattern. The infinitive form of verbs may be followed by a Roman numeral **I** or **II** to denote to which conjugation pattern it belongs. The basic procedures for conjugating verbs are outlined in the tables below.

Sections covering specific aspects of conjugation:

	Grammar points:
Overview of Verbal Conjugation	7.2
Type I, First Conjugation Pattern	7.3-7.13
Type II, Second Conjugation Pattern	7.14-7.20
Formation of the Past Tense	7.21
Irregular Verbs	7.22-7.23

REFERENCE TABLE 7A: BASIC CONJUGATION PATTERNS FOR TYPES I AND II VERBS IN PRESENT, PAST, AND FUTURE TENSES

First conjugation—Type I			Second conjugation—Type II		
Present tense			**Present tense**		
1) Drop the -т from the 3rd person (они) form* to form verb stem.			1) Drop the -т from the 3rd person (они) form to form the verb stem.		
они **чита́**-ют		*they read*	они **говор**-я́т		*they speak*
они **пи́ш**-ут**		*they write*	они **у́ч**-ат**		*they study*
они **гуля́**-ют		*they walk*	они **смо́тр**-ят		*they watch*
они **ид**-у́т		*they go*	они **ве́р**-ят		*they believe*
они **целу́**-ют		*they kiss*	они **сид**-я́т		*they sit*
они **жив**-у́т		*they live*	они **лю́б**-ят		*they love*
2) Add the following endings to the verb stem:			2) Add the following endings to the verb stem:		
Я	чита́ю	-ю	Я	говорю́	-ю
	(пишу́)	(-у)		учу́	(-у)
Ты	чита́ешь	-ешь	Ты	говори́шь	-ишь
Он/а́	чита́ет	-ет	Он/а́	говори́т	-ит
Мы	чита́ем	-ем	Мы	говори́м	-им
Вы	чита́ете	-ете	Вы	говори́те	-ите
Они	чита́ют	-ют	Они	говоря́т	-ят
	(пи́шут)	(-ут)		(у́чат)	(-ат)

*Note: With many Type I verbs ending in **-ать**, the **-ть** can be dropped from the infinitive form to conjugate them in the present tense. This method, however, *should be avoided* because many common verbs, such as **писа́ть**, require stem changes when conjugated (**я пишу́, он пи́шет**, etc.)

Note: Many first conjugation verbs have **consonant stem changes in the present tense conjugation: **жить (я живу́, он живёт, они живу́т), писа́ть (я пишу́, она́ пи́шет, они пи́шут)**. When the present or future stem of a verb ends in a **consonant**, especially one which involves a **spelling rule**, **-у** is used for the first person singular (**я**) form and **-ут** is used for the third person plural (**они**) form. Spelling rules dictate that **-у** and **-а** are written after **ч, ж, ш, щ, ц, к, г, х**. The letters **-ю** and **-я** cannot be written after these consonants.

REFERENCE TABLE 7A: BASIC CONJUGATION PATTERNS FOR TYPE I AND II VERBS IN PRESENT, PAST, AND FUTURE TENSES (cont.)

Past tense		

1) Drop the -ть from the infinitive form to form the stem.
2) Add the following endings to form the past tense according to the **gender** and **number** of the subject:

	писа́-ть	говори́-ть	
Он	писа́л	говори́л	-л
Она́	писа́ла	говори́ла	-ла
Оно́	писа́ло	говори́ло	-ло
Они́	писа́ли	говори́ли	-ли

Future tense

1) Form the **compound future** of **imperfective verbs** by conjugating the verb **быть** (to be) followed by the infinitive of the intended verb:

Я бу́ду чита́ть	I will be reading/I will read
Ты бу́дешь чита́ть	You will be reading
Они́ бу́дут чита́ть	They will be reading

2) For **perfective verbs** form the **perfective future** by conjugating the verb:

ку́пить (II)	to buy
Я куплю́	I will buy
Ты ку́пишь	You will buy
Они́ ку́пят	They will buy

REFERENCE TABLE 7B: FORMATION OF IRREGULAR VERBS

The irregular verbs below are neither Type I nor Type II verbs. Their endings do not completely belong to either conjugation pattern, and therefore they are listed as irregular. These verbs must be memorized. Note that all of the verbs below are imperfective, **except дать,** which is perfective (its imperfective partner is **дава́ть.)**

	хоте́ть to want	есть to eat	дать to give	мочь to be able
Present tense				
я	хочу́	ем	дам	могу́
ты	хо́чешь	ешь	дашь	мо́жешь
он/а́	хо́чет	ест	даст	мо́жет
мы	хоти́м	еди́м	дади́м	мо́жем
вы	хоти́те	еди́те	дади́те	мо́жете
они	хотя́т	едя́т	даду́т	мо́гут
Past tense				
я, ты, он	хоте́л	ел	дал	мог
я, ты, она́	хоте́ла	е́ла	дала́	могла́
оно́	хоте́ло	е́ло	да́ло	могло́
мы, вы, они́	хоте́ли	е́ли	да́ли	могли́

REFERENCE TABLE 7C: CONJUGATION OF TYPE I VERBS ENDING IN -ЕТЬ: SUFFIX -Е- RETAINED

уме́ть	to know how (to)	боле́ть*	to be sick (ill)
я уме́ю	мы уме́ем	я боле́ю	мы боле́ем
ты уме́ешь	вы уме́ете	ты боле́ешь	вы боле́ете
он/а́ уме́ет	они́ уме́ют	он/а́ боле́ет	они́ боле́ют

*Note: the verb **боле́ть** can be conjugated in two different ways, depending on meaning. In the above form, it indicates that someone is sick. However, to express that a certain body part aches or is causing pain (to ache/hurt), the verb follows the Type II pattern.

Я боле́ю.	*I am sick.*
У меня́ боли́т нога́.	*My leg hurts.*

These types of verbs have regular past tense endings.

REFERENCE TABLE 7D: TYPE I VERBS ENDING IN -ОВАТЬ/-ЕВАТЬ: SUFFIX -ОВА-/ -ЕВА- REPLACED WITH -У-

рисова́ть to draw		танцева́ть to dance	
я рису́ю	мы рису́ем	я танцу́ю	мы танцу́ем
ты рису́ешь	вы рису́ете	ты танцу́ешь	вы танцу́ете
он/а́ рису́ет	они́ рису́ют	он/а́ танцу́ет	они́ танцу́ют
Past tense (regular conjugation)			
я, ты, он рисова́л		я, ты, он танцева́л	
я, ты, она́ рисова́ла		я, ты она́ танцева́ла	
оно́ рисова́ло		оно́ танцева́ло	
мы, вы, они́ рисова́ли		мы, вы. они́ танцева́ли	

Verbal Conjugation

First conjugation—Type I: 7.3-7.13

7.3 PRESENT TENSE OF VERB CONJUGATION I: THE VERB ЗНАТЬ (TO KNOW)

Function: Asking whether someone knows something, expressing actions

Face to Face L1
Chapter 3 C
Pages 87-89

The verb **знать** (to know) follows the type I conjugational pattern. This verb may be used to express knowing or not knowing something or someone.

		знать	**to know**
я	(не)	зна́ю	I (don't) know.
ты	(не)	зна́ешь	You (don't) know.
он/а́	(не)	зна́ет	They (don't) know.
мы	(не)	зна́ем	We (don't) know.
вы	(не)	зна́ете	You (don't) know.
они́	(не)	зна́ют	They (don't) know.

Sample sentences

— Ты зна́ешь, где па́па?

Do **you know** where Dad is?

— Да, зна́ю. Он в о́фисе.

Yes, **I know**. He's at the office.

— Вы. не зна́ете, где мой слова́рь?

You don't know where my dictionary is, do you?

— Нет, я не зна́ю.

No, **I don't know**.

— Она́ зна́ет, где Ива́н?

Does **she know** where Ivan is?

— Да, она́ зна́ет.

Yes. **She knows**.

7.4 **THE FIRST CONJUGATION PATTERN (TYPE I): THE VERBS ЧИТАТЬ, ДЕЛАТЬ, СЛУШАТЬ, ПИСАТЬ IN THE PRESENT TENSE**
Function: Talking about activities

Face to Face L1
Chapter 6 A
Pages 133-137

Several examples of verbs of the first conjugation pattern are provided below. Note that throughout the text, the **я, ты,** and **они** forms are provided to indicate the conjugation pattern and any changes in stem or stress. Consult the reference tables at the beginning of this chapter or in the preceding sections for additional information on verbal conjugation.

	to do **де́лать**	to listen **слу́шать**	to write **писать**	to answer **отвеча́ть**	to ask **спра́шивать**
я	де́лаю	слу́шаю	пишу́	отвеча́ю	спра́шиваю
ты	де́лаешь	слу́шаешь	пи́шешь	отвеча́ешь	спра́шиваешь
они	де́лают	слу́шают	пи́шут	отвеча́ют	спра́шивают

7.5 **THE VERB ИГРАТЬ WITH В (+ ACCUSATIVE CASE) AND НА (+ PREPOSITIONAL CASE)**
Functions: Using the verb **игра́ть** (to play); expressing to play a game or sport and to play an instrument

Face to Face L 1
Chapter 8 B
Pages 175-177

Playing sports and games

To express playing a sport or game, use the verb **игра́ть** (I) with the preposition **в + the accusative case.** Below are examples of this construction used with various sports and games.

игра́ть в + accusative	to play a sport or game

Sample sentences

Во что **вы игра́ете**?	What are **you playing**?
Я **игра́ю** в футбо́л.	**I am playing** soccer/football.
Вы игра́ете в бейсбо́л?	**Do you play** baseball?
Нет, **мы игра́ем** в те́ннис.	No. **We play** tennis.

Playing an instrument

To express playing an instrument, use the verb **игра́ть** (I) with the preposition **на + the prepositional case.** Below are examples of this construction used with various names of instruments.

игра́ть на + prepositional	to play an instrument

Sample sentences

На чём **вы игра́ете**?	What do **you play**?
Я **игра́ю** на гита́ре.	**I play** the guitar.
Ты **игра́ешь** на скри́пке.	**You play** the violin.
Они́ **игра́ют** на пиани́но.*	**They play** the piano.

*Note:** пиани́но is an indeclinable noun.

7.6 **THE VERB** понимать **IN SIMPLE AND COMPLEX SENTENCES**
Function: Saying that you understand or do not understand

Face to Face L 1
Chapter 6 B
Pages 138-139

Sentences in Russian can be simple or complex. A **simple sentence** stands alone as one complete idea and does not contain other clauses providing additional information.

Sample sentences

— Я понимаю. Я не понимаю.   I understand. I don't understand.

— Я понимаю русский язык.   I understand Russian.

Complex sentences can be formed using the explanatory conjunction что (that/what) and когда (when) with verbs of understanding, thinking, and saying.

Sample sentences

Я не понимаю, что ты читаешь.   **I don't understand what** you are reading.

Я не понимаю, что она говорит.   **I don't understand what** she is saying.

Как это будет по-английски? **Я не понимаю когда** он говорит по-французски.   How is that (will it be) in English? **I don't understand when** he speaks French.

7.7 **COMPOUND SENTENCES WITH THE VERB** считать
Function: Expressing an opinion

Faces and Voices
Chapter 2 Б
Pages 37-40

The verb считать (I) expresses a carefully-thought-out opinion. It is used in the construction считать, что... (to consider that..., to think that...). Questions are formed by the construction Как вы считаете...? (What do you think...?). Compare the use of считать below with other expressions of opinion.

Моя мама **считает, что**...   А как твоя мама считает?
My mom **thinks that**...   What does your mom think?

Я **думаю, что**...   А что (как) ты думаешь?
I think that...   What do you think?

Мне **кажется, что**...   А тебе что (как) кажется?
It seems to me that...   How does it seem to you?

Sample sentences

Я не считаю, что трудно выбрать профессию.

I don't think it is difficult to choose a profession.

Я считаю, что людям надо учить иностранные языки.

I think that people should study foreign languages.

Я считаю, что хороший читатель — это человек, который много думает, а не много читает.

I consider that a good reader is a person who thinks a lot, but doesn't necessarily read a lot.

7.8   THE VERB БЫВАТЬ
Function: Discussing actions that occur more than once

> Face to Face L 2
> Chapter 13 A, D
> Pages 278, 284

The verb **бывать** (to be, occur) refers to events that occur with some frequency or occur more than once. As such, this verb is often used with frequency words:

В Миннесоте **часто бывает** снег.
В Миссури иногда **бывает снег**.
В Сан Диего **никогда не бывает** снег.

It **often** snows in Minnesota.
It **sometimes** snows in Missouri.
It **never** snows in San Diego.

Бывать can also be used with people, especially if someone happens to be somewhere on a regular basis or more than once:

Я **часто бываю** в Москве.
Ты **редко бываешь** у нас в Сиэтле.
Они **каждый день бывают** в магазине.

I am often in Moscow.
You rarely visit us in Seattle.
They are in the store **every day**.

Бывать can also be used with the verbs **любить** and **нравиться** to denote places where people like to be.

Я люблю **бывать** на Арбате.
Мне нравится **бывать** в гостях.

I like to spend time on the Arbat.
I like to visit people.

7.9   VERBS—PRODUCTIVE SUFFIXES -А-/-Я- SUCH AS ЧИТАТЬ, ГУЛЯТЬ
Function: Review

> Faces and Voices
> Chapter 1 Г
> Page 20

Verbs can be organized into two large groups: verbs with productive suffixes (new verbs in russian are formed with these suffixes) and those with non-productive suffixes (which do not "produce" new verbs). The conjugation of verbs with *non-productive* suffixes must be memorized (many very important verbs such as **быть, есть, идти, ехать, жить, мочь,** and **пить** belong to this group). **Productive** verbs can be organized into several classes according to their suffixes. One such class are verbs with the suffix **-а-** [**-я-**], exemplified by the verb **читать** and **гулять**:

чит - **а́** - ть	гул - **я́** - ть
чит - **а́** - ю	гул - **я́** - ю
чит - **а́** - ешь	гул - **я́** - ешь
чит - **а́** - ют	гул - **я́** - ют

The verbs **де́лать**, **ду́мать**, **игра́ть**, **отвеча́ть**, **покупа́ть**, **понима́ть**, **рабо́тать**, **слу́шать**, **собира́ть**, and many others conjugate in the same way. These verbs can be recognized by the form of their second person imperative, which is always formed with **й** [чита́й, де́лай, ду́май, игра́й, etc.].

Note, however, that there are some first conjugation verbs with non-productive suffix **-а-** (**писа́ть**) and an entire class of second conjugation verbs (**лежа́ть**, **слы́шать**) which do not retain the **-а-** in their present tense forms.

Consult reference tables 7A-D for a complete listing of verbs with information on conjugation type and stem changes.

7.10 THE PRESENT TENSE OF THE VERB ЖИТЬ (TO LIVE) *Function:* Asking where someone lives	Face to Face L1 Chapter 4 C Pages 106-109

The verb **жить** (to live) may be used to ask and describe where someone lives. This is a **Type I** verb with a consonant stem in **-в-** in the present tense conjugation.

Infinitive		жить (I) to live
Present tense	я	живу́
	ты	живёшь
	он/а́	живёт
	мы	живём
	вы	живёте
	они́	живу́т

Note: When Type I verb endings are stressed, a **-е-** becomes **-ё-**.

Sample sentences

— Где ты **живёшь**, Катя?	Where do you **live**, Katya?
— Я **живу́** на у́лице Дру́жбы.	I **live** on Friendship Street.
Ива́н **живёт** в Росси́и, а Джон живёт в Аме́рике.	Ivan **lives** in Russia, and John lives in America.

7.11 VERBS WITH SUFFIX -ОВА- (ВОЛНОВАТЬСЯ, СОВЕТОВАТЬ) *Function:* Expressing concern or worry, reassuring someone	Face to Face L 2 Chapter 11 A, D Pages 228-231, 240

These Type I verbs belong to the same group as verbs such as **фотографи́ровать** (to photograph) and **рисова́ть** (to draw). In the present tense, the suffix **-ова-** becomes **-у-**. The suffix **-ова-** is retained in the past tense.

волнова́ться (to worry)		сове́товать *кому́* (to advise *someone*)	
я	волну́юсь	я	сове́тую
ты	волну́ешься	ты	сове́туешь
они	волну́ются	они	сове́туют

я, ты, он	волнова́лся	я, ты. он	сове́товал
я, ты, она	волнова́лась	я, ты, она	сове́товала
мы, вы, они	волнова́лись	мы, вы, оны́	сове́товали

Sample sentences

To express anxiety:

Джек, где ты был? Я так. волнова́лась.

Jack, where were you? I **was** so **worried**.

To reassure someone:

Мэ́ри, **не волну́йся***, пожа́луйста.

Mary, please **don't worry**.

To report advice:

Я сове́тую вам сходи́ть в теа́тр и́ли кино́.

I **advise** you to go to the theater or the movies.

*Note: This is the imperative or command form: Не волну́йся/волну́йтесь.. The imperative form of сове́товать is сове́туй(те).

7.12 VERBS IN -ВА- AFTER THE STEMS ДА-, ЗНА-, СТА- **(ДАВАТЬ, ПРОДАВАТЬ, УЗНАВАТЬ, ВСТАВАТЬ)** ***Function:*** Review	Faces and Voices Chapter 6 Г Pages 171-172

Verbs with the suffix **-ва-** after the stems **да-, зна-, ста-** lose the suffix **-ва-** in the **present tense** conjugation. They belong to the first conjugation (Type I) pattern.

The imperfective verbs:

to give	to find out	to get up	to sell
да -ва́- ть	**узна -ва́- ть**	**вста -ва́- ть**	**прода -ва́- ть**
да -ю	узна -ю	вста -ю	прода -ю
да -ёшь	узна -ёшь	вста -ёшь	прода -ёшь
да -ю́т	узна -ю́т	вста -ю́т	прода -ю́т

Sample sentences

— Анна Афана́сьевна, вы ра́но **встаёте**?

Do you **get up** early, Anna Afanasievna?

— Обы́чно в 4-5 утра́, но зимо́й **встаю́** в 6-7 часо́в.

Usually at 4 or 5 in the morning, but in winter I **get up** at 6 or 7 a.m.

— Анна Афана́сьевна, а вы до́рого **продаёте** я́йца, смета́ну, молоко́?

Anna Afanasievna, do you **sell** eggs, sour cream and milk at a high price?

— Я **продаю́** как все в дере́вне, не о́чень до́рого, поэ́тому лю́ди покупа́ют хорошо́. И молоко́ у мое́й коро́вы вку́сное.

Like everyone in the village, I **sell** them at a reasonable price, and therefore people get a good deal. Also my cow's milk is very good.

— Анна Афанáсьевна, а как вы **узнаёте**, скóлько стóит молокó или скóлько стóят яйца?

Anna Afanasievna, how do you **find out** what the prices on milk and eggs are?

— В гóрод éздим, люди говорят.

We often go into the city and people tell us.

7.13 VERBS ENDING IN -ЕТЬ, WHERE THE SUFFIX -E- IS RETAINED
Function: Review

| Faces and Voices |
| Chapter 7 Г |
| Pages 205-206 |

A small group of first conjugation verbs ending in **-еть** retain the suffix **-е-** in the conjugated forms of the present and future tenses. All other verbs with the suffix **-еть** belong to the second conjugation.

бол -é- ть (I) бол -é- ю бол -é- ешь бол -é- ют	to be ill, sick, ailing	Когдá люди **болéют**, они принимáют лекáрство. When people **are ill,** they take medicine.
успéть (I) perf. успéю успéешь успéют	to be on time, have time	Вы **успéете** пойти сегóдня в магазин? Will you **have time** to go to the store today?
жалéть (I) жалéю жалéешь жалéют	to pity, regret	Я **жалéю**, что не стáла врачóм. I **regret** not becoming a doctor.
умéть (I) умéю умéешь умéют	to be able, know how (to)	Вы **умéете** водить машину? **Can** you/**Do** you know how to drive a car?

Second conjugation - Type II: 7.14-7.20

7.14 THE SECOND CONJUGATION PATTERN (TYPE II): VERB УЧИТЬ (TO STUDY)
Function: Talking about studying

| Face to Face L 1 |
| Chapter 7 A |
| Pages 149-153 |

The verb **учить** (to study) is an example of a verb of the second conjugation pattern or Type II conjugation. This verb has a very specific connotation and refers to *studying a particular subject in school* or *studying a particular concept or assignment* (words, a text, a foreign language, math, etc.).

	учи́ть	to study	**Type II conjugation pattern**
Я	учу́		-ю/-у
Ты	у́чишь		-ишь
Он/а́	у́чит		-ит
Мы	у́чим		-им
Вы	у́чите		-ите
Они́	у́чат		-ют/-ат

Sample sentences

Я учу́ ру́сский язы́к.	**I study** Russian.
Ты у́чишь э́тот текст?	**Are you studying** this text?
Она́ у́чит а́лгебру и геоме́трию.	**She studies** algebra and geometry.
Он у́чит хи́мию и исто́рию.	**He studies** chemistry and history.
Мы у́чим уро́к.	**We are studying** the lesson.
Вы у́чите япо́нский язы́к.	**You study** Japanese.
Они́ у́чат биоло́гию и физкульту́ру.	**They study** biology and P.E.

7.15 VERBS УЧИ́ТЬСЯ, УЧИ́ТЬ

Functions: Expressing alternatives, to study

Face to Face L 1
Chapter 8 C
Pages 179-181

The verbs **учи́ть** (to study a subject/specific material) and **учи́ться** (to study at an institution/how one studies) are second conjugation verbs. The verb **учи́ть** takes a direct object and is used to answer the question Что? (What?).

The verb **учи́ться** is a reflexive verb and does not take a direct object. This verb answers the questions Где? (Where?) to describe the location or institution at which one studies or attends and Как? (How?) to describe how well, poorly, etc., one studies. Note the conjugation of this verb with the reflexive particle -ся. For more on reflexive verbs consult the subsection on reflexive verbs in this chapter [7.30-7.37].

Sample sentences

Где ты у́чишься?		**Where do you study/attend school?**
	учи́ться to study (reflexive)	
Я	учу́сь в шко́ле.	**I study** at school. I attend school.
Ты	у́чишься в ко́лледже.	**You study at/attend** college.
Он/а́	у́чится в университе́те.	**He/She studies at/attends** the university.
Мы	у́чимся в институ́те.	**We study at/attend** the institute.
Вы	у́читесь в библиоте́ке.	**You study** at the library.
Они́	у́чатся до́ма.	**They study** at home.
Как она́ у́чится?		**What kind of student is she?** (*lit.,* How does she **study**?)
Она́	у́чится хорошо́.	**She studies** well. (She is a good student.)
Он	у́чится пло́хо.	**He studies** poorly. (He is a poor student.)
Мы	у́чимся вме́сте.	**We are studying** together. (We are in the same grade/class.) (We attend the same school.)
Я	учу́сь удовлетвори́тельно.	**I study** satisfactorily. (I am an average (C) student.)

7.16 USING THE VERB ЛЮБИТЬ WITH INFINITIVES AND
NOUNS IN THE ACCUSATIVE CASE
Functions: Expressing likes and dislikes

Face to Face L 1
Chapter 7 C
Pages 158-161

The verb **любить** (to love/like) is a second conjugation verb which has a consonant mutation or alteration: the letter -л- is added to the first person singular (я) form of the verb in the present tense. A review of Type II verbs with stem alterations can be found in point 7.19 below.

Я люблю	I love
Ты любишь	You love
Они любят	They love

The verb **любить** can be used with nouns in the accusative case and with infinitive forms of verbs to express liking or loving people, things, and engaging in hobbies, recreation, and other actions.

Sample sentences

Я люблю **читать** книги по-русски.	**I like to read** books in Russian.
Ты любишь **отдыхать**.	**You like to rest.**
Он любит Машу.	**He likes/loves** Masha.
Она любит Ваню.	**She likes/loves** Vanya.
Мы любим **смотреть** телевизор дома.	**We like to watch** TV at home.
Вы любите **слушать** рок-н-рол.	**You like to listen** to rock 'n roll.
Они любят **танцевать**.	**They like to dance.**

7.17 USING THE VERB РЕШИТЬ (TO DECIDE, TO SOLVE) WITH
INFINITIVES
Function: Talking about decisions and
intentions

Face to Face L 1
Chapter 18 C
Pages 373-377

In Russian, just as in English, the infinitive form of the verb (the dictionary or unconjugated form) is often used when two verbs are grouped together to express a thought or idea. For example, after the verb **решить** (II) (to decide) the infinitive form of a (perfective) verb is used to express the intention to complete an action.

решить + infinitive of a perfective verb
to decide to do/complete an action

Sample sentences

Маша **решила поступить** в медицинский институт.	Masha **decided to enroll** in the medical institute.
После школы все ребята **решили поступить** в университет.	After completing school, all the kids **decided to enroll** in the university.
Борис **решил быть** историком.	Boris **decided to be** an historian.
Она **решила стать** учительницей.	She **decided to become** a teacher.
Он **решил написать** письмо.	He **decided to write** a letter.

7.18 THE VERBS НАЧИНАТЬ, НАЧАТЬ, КОНЧАТЬ, КОНЧИТЬ
Function: Talking about beginning or ending
an action

Faces and Voices
Chapter 1 A
Page 6

The verbs **начинáть/начáть** (to begin) and **кончáть/кóнчить** (to end, finish) are used to speak about beginning and ending actions or things (nouns). If either of these verbs is followed by another verb, that verb is always in the imperfective form.

	что дéлать?	что?
to begin		
начинáть I (impf.) (начинáю, -ешь, -ют)	рабóтать	рабóту
начáть II (pf.) (начнý, начнёшь, начнýт)	брать	интервью
to end/finish		
кончáть I (impf.) (кончáю, -ешь, -ют)	стрóить	урóк
кóнчить II (pf.) (кóнчу, -ишь, -ат)	игрáть	письмó

Sample sentences

Зáвтра **Натáша кóнчит** интервью в 5 часóв и потóм пойдёт в теáтр.

Натáша с мýжем мóжет пойти в ресторáн во втóрник, потомý что **онá начнёт** встрéчу с артистами балéта в 18 часóв и, навéрное, кóнчит в 19 часóв.

— Во скóлько **вы кóнчите** игрáть в баскетбóл?
— **Мы кóнчим** игрáть в 14 часóв и потóм начнём дéлать урóки.

Tomorrow **Natasha will finish** the interview at five and then go to the theater.

Natasha can go with her husband to the restaurant on Tuesday because **she will begin** the meeting with the ballet dancers at six p.m. and probably finish at seven.

At what time **will you finish playing** basketball?
We'll finish at two, and then we will begin doing our homework.

7.19 PRODUCTIVE VERBS IN -ИТЬ, STEM CHANGES IN CONJUGATION
Function: Review

Faces and Voices
Chapter 2 Г
Page 47

A very large group of Type II productive verbs consists of those verbs that end in the suffix **-ить** such as **говорить**, **дарить**, and **учить**.

говор - и́ть   уч - и́ть
говор - ю́   уч - у́
говор - и́шь   у́ч - ишь
говор - я́т   у́ч - ат

Verbs of this group all belong to the **second conjugation pattern** (Type II). Many have a characteristic mutation in the first person singular (**я**) form of present or perfective future tenses. This mutation occurs when the stem ends in certain consonants and **only** in the first person singular form. The table below lists possible mutations. Examples are given.

с › щ	просить	прощ - ý, прóсишь, прóсят	to ask (a favor)
в › вл	готóвить	готóвл - ю, готóвишь, готóвят	to prepare
б › бл	любить	любл - ю, любишь, лю́бят	to love
м › мл	познакóмить	познакóмл - ю, познакóмишь, познакóмят	to acquaint
ст › ш	простить	прош - ý, простишь, простят	to forgive
з › ж	тормозить	тормож - ý, тормóзишь, тормозят	to brake
т › ч	встрéтить	встрéч - у, встрéтишь, встрéтят	to meet
д › ж	ходить	хож - ý, хóдишь, хóдят	to walk (*indet.*)
п › пл	купить	купл - ю, ку́пишь, ку́пят	to buy
ф › фл	графить	графл - ю, графишь, графя́т	to rule (*paper*)

<table>
<tr><td>

7.20 CONJUGATION OF VERBS ENDING IN -ЕТЬ, STEM CHANGES IN CONJUGATION
Function: Review

</td><td>

Faces and Voices
Chapter 3 Г
Page 82

</td></tr>
</table>

The verb **летéть** and all its prefixed verbs (**прилетéть**, for example) conjugate like the verbs **видеть/увидеть** and **сидéть/посидéть**. These are second conjugation (Type II) verbs with a consonant mutation in the first person singular (**я**), present tense form.

вид -е- ть	виж -у
	вид -ишь
	вид -ят

сид -é- ть	сиж -ý
	сид -йшь
	сид -я́т

лет -é- ть	леч -ý
	лет -йшь
	лет -я́т

In the conjugation of this class of verbs in the present tense:

1) The suffix -e- disappears.
2) A consonant mutation occurs in the first person : д>ж, т>ч, с>ш, and others (see point 7.19 above).
3) The second conjugation endings, -ишь, -ит, -им, -ите, -ат (-ят) are added to the stem.

Past-tense Regular and Irregular verbs: 7.21-7.23

7.21 PAST TENSE OF VERBS БЫТЬ, ИГРАТЬ, ПОБЕДИТЬ *Function:* Talking about past actions	Face to Face L 1 Chapter 13 B Pages 266-269

Note that the basic procedures for forming the past tense of regular verbs is the same for Type I and II verbs. The verbs **играть** and **быть** are Type I, while **победить** is Type II.

To form the past tense of regular verbs:
1) Find the infinitive form of the verb:
    играть (to play)
2) Drop -**ть** from the infinitive:
    игра-
2) Add endings according to gender/number:
-**л** (masculine singular):
    он играл (he played)
-**ла** (feminine singular):
    она играла (she played)
-**ло** (neuter singular):
    оно играло (it played)
-**ли** (all plural):
    мы, вы, они играли (we, you, they played)

	играть to play	**быть** to be	**победить** to win
Masculine			
я, ты, он, кто	играл	был	победил
Feminine			
я, ты, она	играла	была	победила
Neuter			
оно	играло	было	победило
Plural			
мы, вы, они	играли	были	победили

7.22 THE IRREGULAR VERBS ЕСТЬ, ПИТЬ *Function:* Accepting, declining, or complimenting food	Face to Face L 2 Chapter 9 B, D Pages 192-199, 201

The irregular imperfective verbs **есть** (to eat) and **пить** (to drink) govern the accusative case. The stem of the verb **пить** (I) remains soft by adding a -**ь**- to its stem ending.

Пить что?

Я	пью	чай.	I drink	tea.
Ты	пьёшь	кофе.	You drink	coffee.
Он/á	пьёт	воду.	He/she drinks	water.
Мы	пьём	молоко.	We drink	milk.
Вы	пьёте	фанту.	You drink	Fanta.
Они	пьют	пепси.	They drink	Pepsi.

Я, ты, он	пил.	I, you, he	drank.
Я, ты, она	пила́.	I, you, she	drank.
Мы, вы, они	пили.	We, you, they	drank.

Пей(те)!   Drink!

Note that **есть** is an irregular verb and its conjugation must be memorized.

Есть что?

Я	ем	сыр.	I eat	cheese.
Ты	ешь	бутерброд	You eat	a sandwich.
Он/á	ест	колбасу.	He/she eats	sausage
Мы	едим	ветчину.	We eat	ham.
Вы	едите	масло.	You eat	butter.
Они	едят	яблоко.	They eat	the apple.

Я, ты, он	ел.	I, you, he	ate.
Я, ты, она	ела.	I, you, she	ate.
Мы, вы, они	ели.	We, you, they	ate.

Ешь(те)!   Eat!

7.23 CONJUGATION AND USE OF THE VERB ХОТЕТЬ (TO WANT) *Function:* Expressing the desire to do something	Face to Face L 1 Chapter 16 B Pages 323-327

The verb **хотеть** (to want) is considered irregular because it includes elements of both the first (I) and second (II) conjugational patterns. The present tense singular forms (**я, ты, он/á**) follow the first conjugation pattern and the spelling rule after a consonant stem change. The plural forms (**мы, вы, они**) follow the second conjugation pattern.

Я	хочу́	I want	first conjugation
Ты	хо́чешь	You want	" "
Он/á	хо́чет	He/She wants	" "
Мы	хотим	We want	second conjugation
Вы	хотите	You want	" "
Они	хотят	They want	" "

Past tense: хотел/а/о/и

The verb **хотеть** can be used with an infinitive verb to express the desire to do something.

Sample sentences

Погóда хорóшая. **Я хочý** игрáть на ýлице.	The weather is nice. **I want** to play outside.
На ýлице хóлодно. **Я хочý** смотрéть телевúзор дóма.	It's cold outside. **I want** to watch TV at home.
Онú хотя́т слýшать мýзыку, а мы хотúм пойтú в кинó.	**They want** to listen to music, but we want to go to the movies.

Imperatives and Command Constructions

7.24   Overview: What are imperatives? Imperatives are verb forms that indicate that a *direct command* or *request* is being made. They are used informally (to address a person with the **ты** form), or formally/plural (to address a person or a group of people with the **вы** form).

7.25 USING IMPERATIVES
Function: Saying you don't understand something; asking for repetition; giving instructions/directions and making requests

> Face to Face L 2
> Chapter 7 A, D
> Pages 145-147,
> 157

Imperative verb forms are used in the following ways:

1)   Saying you don't understand something:

Простúте, я не всё пóнял/á.   **Excuse me**, I didn't quite understand everything (you said).

2)   Asking for repetition:

Повторúте, пожáлуйста.   Please **repeat** (what you said).

3)   Giving instructions or directions:

Идúте пря́мо, потóм повернúте налéво.   **Go (walk)** straight, and then turn left.

4)   Making requests (general):

Дáйте мне, пожáлуйста, э́ту кнúгу.   Please **give** me that book.

Note that each imperative above ends in **-те**. This is the **вы** form of the request denoting politeness or plurality. The **ты** form (informal) is written without **-те**.

Мáша, **идú** сюдá!   Masha, **come** here!

REFERENCE TABLE 7E: FORMATION OF THE BASIC IMPERATIVE VERB FORM

1) Drop the **-ю/-у** ending from the conjugated first person
   singular (**я**) form of the verb:

   слу́ша—ю   повторя́—ю   говор—ю́   пиш—у́

2) Add the following imperative endings:
   -й singular, **-йте** plural for most Type I verbs

   слу́шай(те)   повторя́й(те)

   -и singular, **-ите** plural for most Type II verbs

   говори́(те)

   Note that many **Type I** verbs with a consonant mutation have endings in **-и(те)**:

   пиши́(те)   иди́(те)   живи́(те)

3) Some verbs have irregular imperative forms. These should be memorized:

   есть—ешь(те)   пить—пей(те)

REFERENCE TABLE 7F: LIST OF COMMON IMPERATIVES

In the reference list below, note that some verbs are imperfective (impf.) and others are perfective (pf.). Note that when a perfective is formed by adding a prefix to the imperfective verb, the formation of the imperative is the same for both verbs.

Чита́й(те) э́ту кни́гу.   **Read** this book.
Прочита́й(те) э́ту кни́гу.   **Read** this book (finish it).

Infinitive	Imperative - ты	Imperative - вы	
смотре́ть (impf.)	смотри́	смотри́те	Look/Watch!
чита́ть (impf.)	чита́й	чита́йте	Read!
писа́ть (impf.)	пиши́	пиши́те	Write!
сказа́ть (pf.)	скажи́	скажи́те	Say/Tell!
рассказа́ть (pf.)	расскажи́	расскажи́те	Tell!
говори́ть (impf.)	говори́	говори́те	Speak/Say!
вы́учить (perf.)	вы́учи	вы́учите	Learn!
повторя́ть (impf.)	повторя́й	повторя́йте	Repeat!
повтори́ть (pf.)	повтори́	повтори́те	Repeat (once)!
идти́ (impf.)	иди́	иди́те	Come/Go/Walk!
спроси́ть (pf.)	спроси́	спроси́те	Ask!
принести́ (pf.)	принеси́	принеси́те	Bring (to)....!
дать (pf.)	дай	да́йте	Give (to)....!
переда́ть (pf.)	переда́й	переда́йте	Pass (give to)....!
откры́ть (pf.)	откро́й	откро́йте	Open!
закры́ть (pf.)	закро́й	закро́йте	Close!
забы́ть (pf.)	(не) забу́дь	(не) забу́дьте	(Don't) forget!
попро́бовать (pf.)	попро́буй	попро́буйте	Try (it)!

7.26 ДАВА́Й(ТЕ) **WITH PERFECTIVE FUTURE TENSE OR IMPERFECTIVE INFINITIVE**
Function: Making suggestions, expressing agreement or refusal

| Face to Face L 2 |
| Chapter 2 A, D |
| Pages 38-39, 53 |

To express the suggestion *Let's...* with the construction Дава́й(те) **+ a verb**, perfective or imperfective verbs are used to express different connotations. This expression is commonly used in everyday speech. Note that this verb form is an **imperative** one, as it makes a suggestion to one or more people.

Дава́й(те) (Let's...) + perfective verb in first person plural (мы form) Дава́й(те) is used most commonly with a perfective verb conjugated in the first person plural (мы) form to suggest some sort of joint action in the near future:

| Ва́ня, **дава́й пое́дем** в Чика́го. | Vanya, **let's go** to Chicago. |
| Ребя́та, **дава́йте пойдём** в кино́! | Hey guys, **let's go** to the movies! |

Дава́й(те) (Let's...) + imperfective verb in infinitive form If a planned action is to take place over a longer period of time, then Дава́й(те) plus an imperfective infinitive may be used:

| **Дава́й говори́ть** то́лько по-ру́сски. | **Let's speak** only Russian. |
| **Дава́йте игра́ть** в футбо́л. | **Let's play** soccer. |

When used with imperfective verbs, the suggested action is assumed to take place for a longer period of time. For example, the suggestion, **Дава́й говори́ть то́лько по-ру́сски**, might be taken to mean, *Let's speak only Russian,* ***from now on.***

It's also possible to suggest not doing something (**Дава́й/те не бу́дем...**):

| **Дава́йте не бу́дем** об э́том говори́ть. | **Let's not** talk about this. |
| **Дава́й не бу́дем** игра́ть в те́ннис. | **Let's not** play tennis. |

The phrase, **дава́й не бу́дем**, literally translates as *let's not be (doing this).*

7.27 **VERBAL ASPECT IN THE IMPERATIVE**
Function: Expressing various connotations in stating commands, requests and negative commands — *Don't...!*

| Мир ру́сских |
| Lesson 9 |
| Pages 297-300 |

Commands using perfective and imperfective verbs have different connotations:

Usage with perfective verbs: Single, completed actions The perfective aspect of a verb pair is typically used to make a request, particularly when someone is to perform a single and complete action:

A student is talking to his classmate, who is sitting near a window:

Откро́й, пожа́луйста, окно́. В кла́ссе о́чень жа́рко.

Please **open** the window. It's really hot in this classroom.

A student is speaking to his teacher:

Я не по́нял э́то пра́вило. **Объясни́те**, пожа́луйста, ещё раз.

I didn't understand this rule. Please **explain** it (to me) again.

Usage with imperfective verbs: Repeated or prolonged actions

The imperfective aspect of a verb pair is used to make a request that an action be performed frequently or repetitively over time:

Ка́ждый ве́чер пе́ред сном **открыва́йте** окно́, что́бы в ко́мнате был све́жий во́здух.

Open the window every evening before you go to bed to get some fresh air in the room.

A doctor is speaking to a patient:

Ча́ще **гуля́йте**, **ку́шайте** бо́льше овоще́й и фру́ктов, **принима́йте** лека́рство три ра́за в день.

Walk more, **eat** more vegetables and fruits, and **take** (the) medicine three times a day.

Directives (perfective) vs. Invitations (imperfective) The imperfective aspect is used to extend invitations and when encouraging an action:

*Company has arrived; the hostess is speaking: a social invitation to begin an action (usually **imperfective** aspect):*

Входи́те, раздева́йтесь, проходи́те в ко́мнату.

Come in, take your coats off, go on into the room.

A telephone operator is speaking: a conventional inducement—use **imperfective**:

Вы хоти́те разгово́р с Москво́й? Мину́точку!...**Говори́те**!

You want a line to Moscow? Just a minute...okay....**Go ahead** (and talk).

Generally, if a request or invitation must be repeated, the imperative may use an imperfective verb to convey annoyance:

Откро́йте окно́ пожа́луйста. **Открыва́йте** окно́!

Open the window please. **Open** the window!

The perfective aspect is used to stress the completion of a single action — as a directive to perform and complete an action:

A teacher is talking to a student: an invitation to complete a single action— **perfective:**

Войди́! Почему́ ты опозда́л?

Come in! Why are you late?

Negated Imperatives: _Don't...!_ The imperfective aspect is usually used for an imperative in negation:

A _teacher says to the students:_
Не разговáривайте!

Don't talk!

Приходи зáвтра в 7 часóв, **не опáздывай**, мы не смóжем тебя ждать.

Come tomorrow at 7:00, and **don't be late.** We won't be able to wait for you.

A perfective verb is used in negation if the speaker is afraid that someone will perform an _undesired action_ and is _giving a warning:_

A _mother is warning her daughter, who is climbing high in a tree:_
Мáша, **не упади!**

Masha, look out, **don't fall!**

At the train station parents seeing off their son say:
До отхóда пóезда остаётся тóлько дéсять минýт, **не опоздáй.**

You only have ten minutes before the train leaves; **don't be late.**

Indirect Commands and Command Constructions

7.28 THE CONJUNCTION ЧТОБЫ AND THE PERFECTIVE PAST TENSE AFTER THE VERB ХОТЕТЬ _Function:_ Saying what is desired of another person	Faces and Voices Chapter 3 A Pages 63-64

To express a wish that _someone else perform an action_, use the constructions:

хотéть _to want_ желáть _to wish_	,чтóбы (_in order to_)	**+ perfective verb in the past tense**

While this is not a true imperative form, it is used as a form of indirect command. Compare the direct command (imperative) and an indirect command:

Direct command (imperative) form:
Амáя, **послýшай** этот компáкт-диск.

Amaya, **listen** to this CD.

Indirect command (чтóбы + past tense) form:
Амáя, я хочý, чтóбы ты послýшала этот компáкт-диск.

Amaya, **I want you to listen to** this CD.

Contrast the use of **хотéть** with an infinitive and **хотéть, чтóбы + the perfective past tense** in the table below.

хотéть + infinitive Subject of the sentence desires something for him-/herself or themselves.	хотéть, чтóбы + perfective verb in the past tense Subject of the sentence wishes that *someone else* perform an action.
Я хочý стать лётчиком. (Я хочý, и я стáну.) **I want to become** a pilot. (I want, and I will become.)	Я хочý, чтóбы мой брат стал лётчиком. (Я хочý, но брат стáнет.) **I want my brother to become** a pilot. (I want, but *my brother* will become.)
Я хочý прочитáть э́тот ромáн. (Я хочý, и я прочитáю.) **I want to finish** (reading) the novel. (I want, and I will read.)	Учи́тель хóчет, чтóбы мы прочитáли э́тот ромáн. (Учи́тель хóчет, но мы прочитáем.) **The teacher wants us to finish** (reading) the novel. (The teacher wants, but *we* will read.)

Note: The construction чтóбы + the past tense expresses the subjunctive mood. For more on the subjunctive mood consult the section "Subjunctive and Conditional Moods" in this chapter [7.75-7.78].

Sample sentences

Владими́р Николáевич, мы хоти́м, чтóбы вы рассказáли нам о сéвере.

Vladimir Nikolaevich, **we want you to tell** us about the North.

Михаи́л, я хочý, чтóбы ты помóг мне с домáшним задáнием.

Mikhail, **I want you to help me** with my homework.

Онá хóчет, чтóбы вы познакóмили её с трéнером клýба моржéй.

She **wants you to introduce** her to the coach of the "Walrus" club.

Я хочý, чтóбы ты сфотографи́ровала меня́ с дрýгом.

I want you to take a picture of me with my friend.

7.29 THE VERB ТРЕБОВАТЬ **+THE GENITIVE CASE**
Function: Expressing requirements

Faces and Voices Chapter 7 Б Page 198

The verbs трéбовать/потрéбовать (I) express a strong directive, order, or command. An infinitive, a noun in the genitive case, or a clause beginning with the conjunction чтóбы is normally used with this verb.

Sample sentences

В нáшей шкóле трéбуют не надевáть на урóки джи́нсы. (infinitive)

In our school **it is required that** jeans **not be worn** in class.

Профéссия врачá трéбует терпéния, любви́, и профессионали́зма. (noun in the genitive)

Being a doctor **demands patience, love, and professionalism.** (*lit., The profession of doctor...*)

Моя́ мáма трéбует, чтóбы я звони́л ей, éсли я не идý домóй пóсле шкóлы. (**чтóбы** clause)

My mom **requires me to phone** her if I do not go home after school.

Reflexive Verb Forms

7.30 What are reflexive verbs? Reflexive verbs reflect the action of the verb back onto the subject of the sentence. Compare the usage of the verbs **одевáть кого́** (to dress someone) and **одевáться** (to get dressed).

Он одевáет млáдшего брáта.
He is dressing his younger brother.
[This is a **transitive verb**; the action is performed upon another person/object.]

Он одевáется.
He is getting dressed.
[This is a **reflexive verb**; the action is performed upon the subject.]

Reflexive verbs do not take a direct object in the accusative case. (The only exception to this rule are verbs that take the reflexive pronoun **себя́**.) For example, The verb **учи́ть** (to study) is a transitive verb and normally takes a direct object in the accusative case, such as a school subject: **áлгебру** (algebra), **фи́зику** (physics). The reflexive verb **учи́ться** (to study, to attend, be enrolled as a student) takes no direct object and usually answers the questions of *How?* (**Как?**) and *Where?* (**Где?**).

Как ты **у́чишься**?	What kind of student are you? (*lit., How do you **study**?*)
Я **учу́сь** хорошо́.	I am a good student. (*lit., I **study** well.*)
Где ты **у́чишься**?	Where do you **study**?
Я **учу́сь** в шко́ле.	I go to school. (*lit., I **study** in a school.*)

7.31 Formation of Reflexive Verbs. Reflexive verbs are formed by adding the reflexive suffix **-ся** to the infinitive of the verb or by using the verb with the reflexive pronoun **себя́** (for example, **чу́вствовать себя́** *to feel*, as in how a person feels in terms of his/her health). (See grammar points **5.16** and **7.36** for notes on the reflexive pronoun **себя́**.)

Verbs with the suffix **-ся** conjugate like normal verbs, adding the suffix **-сь** when the conjugation ends in a *vowel* and **-ся** when the conjugation ends in a *consonant*.

REFERENCE TABLE 7G: CONJUGATION OF VERBS WITH THE REFLEXIVE SUFFIX -СЯ IN PRESENT AND PAST TENSE FORMS

Use -сь when conjugated verb ends in a vowel.
Use -ся when conjugated verb ends in a consonant.

Present tense	учи́ться to study; to be enrolled as a student	занима́ться to be involved in; to practice	нра́виться to like; to be pleasing to
я	учу́сь	занима́юсь	нра́влюсь
ты	у́чишься	занима́ешься	нра́вишься
он/á	у́чится	занима́ется	нра́вится
мы	у́чимся	занима́емся	нра́вимся
вы	у́читесь	занима́етесь	нра́витесь
они́	у́чатся	занима́ются	нра́вятся
Past tense			
я, ты, он	учи́лся	занима́лся	нра́вился
я, ты, она́	учи́лась	занима́лась	нра́вилась
оно́	учи́лось	занима́лось	нра́вилось
мы, вы, они́	учи́лись	занима́лись	нра́вились

Several reflexive verbs, such as **находи́ться** (to be located) and **нра́виться** (to like), are generally used only in third person singular (**он, она́, оно́**) and plural (**они́**) forms.

Магази́н **нахо́дится** в це́нтре го́рода.	The store **is located** downtown.
Они́ **нахо́дятся** на второ́м этаже́.	They **are located** on the second floor.
Мне **нра́вится** ваш го́род!	I **like** your city!
Мне **нра́вятся** ва́ши часы́!	I **like** your watch!

7.32 REFLEXIVE VERBS (VERBS WITH THE SUFFIX -СЯ)

Function: Expressing actions reflected back onto the subject: actions performed on oneself and reciprocal actions

Мир русских Lesson 1 Pages 21-24

Historically, **-ся** was an abbreviation of **себя́** (oneself) which became attached to the verb. In modern Russian the particle **-ся** does not have a single specific meaning, and there are no strict rules that prescribe the use of the verb suffix **-ся**. Reflexive verbs should be learned in the same way as verbs without the suffix **-ся**.

Verbs with **-ся** are always intransitive. They are not used with nouns or pronouns in the accusative case. A few groups of **-ся** verbs are united by a common concept (of grammar or meaning).

Personal reflexives

For example:

одева́ться, оде́ться	to dress (oneself)
умыва́ться, умы́ться	to wash (oneself)
причёсываться, причеса́ться	to comb one's hair
лечи́ться, вы́лечиться	to cure (oneself)

In this group of verbs, the action of each verb is directed back upon the performer of the action. Thus, **одеваться** means *to dress oneself*, and **причёсываться** means *to comb one's hair*. Verbs of this type usually have a transitive counterpart without **-ся**.

Она́ одева́ется.	She is dressing (herself).
Она́ одева́ет дочь.	She dresses/is dressing her daughter.

In many other cases, an action directed upon oneself is expressed by the reflexive pronoun **себя**.

Он лю́бит себя́.	He loves himself.
Он уважа́ет себя́.	He respects himself.

Reciprocal reflexives These verbs denote an action performed by more than one subject directed back upon each of them. (Each person is both performing the action and being acted upon.) The -ся here conveys the idea of *each other* or *one another*.

Они́ познако́мились в Москве́.	They **met** (got acquainted) in Moscow.
Они́ ча́сто **ссо́рятся**.	They often **quarrel** (with each other).

These verbs are used with plural subjects. The words **друг с дру́гом** may also be used.

Они́ с Ни́ной **познако́мились** в Москве́.	(S)he and Nina **met** in Moscow.
Ко́ля с Ма́шей **познако́мились** в Москве́.	Kolya and Masha **met** in Moscow.
Мы с Ни́ной **познако́мились друг с дру́гом** в Москве́.	Nina and I **met each other** in Moscow.

These verbs are also used with singular subjects, followed by the preposition **c** and the name of another person(s) or thing(s).

Он **познако́мился с ней** в Москве́.	He **met her** in Moscow.

Such verbs have a non-reflexive counterpart, a transitive verb that names an action and takes a direct object.

Он **познако́мился с ней**.	He **became acquainted with her**.
Он **познако́мил её** с бра́том.	He **introduced her** to his brother.

Not all verbs which name a reciprocal action have the reflexive suffix -ся, for example, **бесе́довать** (to chat), **дружи́ть** (to be friends), etc.

Passive reflexives Passive reflexives (also called passive verbs) name an action performed upon the subject. Verbs in the passive voice require a phrase in the instrumental case (without a preposition) which denotes the person who performed the action on the subject.

Дом **стро́ится рабо́чими**.	The house **is being built by the workers**.

Inanimate reflexives Usually, verbs of this type have counterparts without -ся (with similar, but not necessarily identical, meanings) that name an action performed by an animate subject (a person or an animal).

Я начинáю рабóту в 10.00.	I begin work at 10:00.
Моя рабóта **начинáется** в 10.00.	My work **begins** at 10:00.
Он открывáет дверь.	He is opening the door.
Дверь **открывáется**.	The door **is opening**.

Some other verbs of this type are:

продолжáться	to continue
кончáться	to end
менáться	to change
поднимáться	to go up; rise
увелúчиваться	to increase

Verbs of this type are used only in the third person singular and plural:

Магазúн **закрывáется** в 5.00	The store **closes** at 5:00.
Спектáкли **начинáются** в 7 часóв.	The performance **starts** at 7 o'clock.

General reflexives There are many reflexive verbs that do not form distinctive or large groups, but which tend to denote an emotional or intellectual state.

беспокóиться	to worry, be anxious about
волновáться	to be worried (about), be agitated
забóтиться	to take care (of something/someone)
тревóжиться	to be anxious, uneasy (about)
интересовáться	to be interested
увлекáться	to be fascinated (by something)
удивлáться	to be surprised
сомневáться	to hesitate, to doubt
пугáться	to be scared
боáться	to be afraid (of)
смеáться	to laugh
улыбáться	to smile

Verbs of this type usually have counterparts without -ся. The verbs **боáться, улыбáться, смеáться** exist only in the reflexive form.

7.33 THE VERB НАХОДИТЬСЯ (TO BE LOCATED) IN THE THIRD PERSON SINGULAR AND PLURAL *Function:* Asking the location of something	Face to Face L1 Chapter 4 A Pages 97-101

The reflexive verb **находúться** (to be located) may be used to describe the location of a place or person. With singular subjects the third person singular (**он, онá, онó**) form is used.

Sample sentences

— Где **нахо́дится** магазин
   «Москви́чка»?

Where is the "Moscovite" store **located**?

— Магази́н «Москви́чка» **нахо́дится**
   на Но́вом Арба́те.

The "Moscovite" store **is (located)** on the
New Arbat.

— Где **нахо́дится** Большо́й теа́тр?

Where is the Bolshoi Theater **(located)**?

— Он **нахо́дится** на Театра́льной
   пло́щади.

It is **(located)** on Theater Square.

If more than one object or person is located somewhere, the third person
plural (**они́**) is used.

> Singular: Магази́н нахо́дится на Но́вом Арба́те.
> Plural: Магази́ны нахо́дятся на Но́вом Арба́те.

7.34 THE VERB ГОТО́ВИТЬСЯ/ПОДГОТО́ВИТЬСЯ WITH THE PREPOSITION К AND DATIVE CASE *Function:* Preparing for an event	Faces and Voices Chapter 2 A Pages 34-35

The reflexive verbs **гото́виться/подгото́виться** (to prepare [for]) are
intransitive and take the preposition **к + the dative case**: гото́виться
/подгото́виться к чему́? The event for which one is preparing follows the
preposition **к** and is declined in the dative case.

Sample sentences

гото́виться	*к чему?*	
Я гото́влюсь	к экза́мену.	I am preparing for an exam.
Ты гото́вишься	к пра́зднику.	You're preparing for a holiday.
Они́ гото́вятся	к Но́вому го́ду, соревнова́ниям, интервью́.	They're preparing for New Year's, the competitions, an interview.

7.35 THE VERB ЛОЖИ́ТЬСЯ/ЛЕЧЬ WITH THE INFINITIVE *Function:* Describing daily activities	Faces and Voices Chapter 2 A Pages 31-33

The reflexive verb **ложи́ться** has a perfective partner **лечь*,** which does not
look reflexive but acts the same way as **ложи́ться.** Both verbs are normally used
with the verb **спать,** and describe the activity of going to bed (*lit., to lie down to
sleep*).

Sample sentences
Present/Future tenses:

Я ложу́сь/ля́гу спать в 21.00.

I go/will go to bed at 9 p.m.

Ты ложи́шься/ля́жешь спать ра́но.

You go/will go to bed early.

Они́ ложа́тся/ля́гут спать по́здно.

They go/will go to bed late.

*Note : Лечь, like **мочь**, is an irregular verb with consonant mutation. See reference table 7B.

Past tense:

Я, Ты, Он *ложился/лёг спать.* | I/You/He **was/were going/went to bed.**

Я, Ты, Она *ложилась/легла спать.* | I/You/She **was/were going/went to bed.**

Мы, Вы, Они *ложились/легли спать* | We/You/They **was/were going/went to bed.**

7.36 THE VERBS ЧУВСТВОВАТЬ СЕБЯ, БОЛЕТЬ, ЛЕЧИТЬСЯ | Faces and Voices
Function: Talking about health | Chapter 7 A
| Pages 185-191

The verbs **чувствовать себя** (to feel), **болеть** (to be ill/sick, to ache/hurt), and **лечиться** (to get well, become cured) are commonly used when talking about health.

чувствовать себя—to feel The verb **чувствовать** in this meaning is used with the reflexive **себя**. Its conjugation follows the Type I pattern for verbs with the suffix -ова-/-ева- (see grammar point 7.11).

Sample sentences

— Как вы **себя чувствуете**? | How do **you feel**?
— Я **чувствую себя**...плохо. | I **feel**... bad.
не очень хорошо. | ...not very well.
хорошо/нормально/прекрасно. | ...good/fine/wonderful.

болеть to be ill/sick (Type I), to ache, hurt (Type II) The verb **болеть** follows the Type I pattern for verbs with the suffix -e- (see grammar point 7.13 and Table 7C) in the meaning *to be ill* or *to be sick*. Unlike the other health-related verbs in this section, it is **not** a reflexive verb but is often used in conjunction with health-related reflexives.

Sample sentences

— Почему Нина не была в театре? | Why wasn't Nina at the theater?
— Она плохо **себя чувствует**. Она **болеет**. | She **feels bad. She is sick.**
— Сколько времени **она болеет**? | How long has **she been sick**?
— Она **болеет** уже неделю. | **She has been** sick for a week.

When used in the meaning *to hurt* or *to ache,* **болеть** is a second conjugation verb. Note the agreement with the gender of the body part which aches in the past tense:

Sample sentences

— А что у вас **болит**? | What **ails** you? (What **hurts**?)
— У меня **болят** уши и **болит** голова. | My ears and head **hurt/ache**.

Вчера у Виктора **болел** глаз. | Yesterday Victor's eye **hurt**.

Вчера́ у Гали́ны **боле́ла голова́**.

Yesterday Galina had **a headache**.

Вчера́ у Ри́ты **боле́ло го́рло**.

Yesterday Rita's throat **hurt** (She had a sore throat).

Вчера́ у Анто́на **боле́ли зу́бы**.

Yesterday Anton had a **toothache** (His teeth hurt).

лечи́ться—to get well, become cured When using this verb, the means by which someone is getting well (aspirin, herbs, vitamins, etc.) is in the **instrumental case**. This expresses the idea *to get well/be cured by means of...*

Sample sentences

— Чем ты **ле́чишься**?

What do you take? (*lit., With what do you cure yourself?*)

— Я **лечу́сь** лека́рством.

I **take medicine**.

Он **ле́чится** тра́вами.

He **is taking herbal medicine**.

Я обы́чно **лечу́сь** витами́нами.

I usually **get well by taking vitamins**.

Когда́ у меня́ температу́ра, **я лечу́сь** аспири́ном.

When I have a temperature, **I take aspirin**.

7.37 **THE VERBS** НАДЕВА́ТЬ, ОДЕВА́ТЬ, ОДЕВА́ТЬСЯ
Function: Talking about wearing clothes and dressing

Faces and Voices
Chapter 9 Б
Page 245

The verbs **надева́ть** (to put on), **одева́ть** (to dress), and **одева́ться** (to get dressed) are used to talk about wearing clothes, getting dressed, and dressing someone else. Only **одева́ться** is reflexive. The other verbs are transitive and take direct objects. Note the differences in meaning in the examples below.

To dress/get dressed	How?	
одева́ться (impf.) (I)	как?	Муж Ири́ны всегда́ **одева́ется** со вку́сом. Irina's husband always **dresses** in good taste.
одéться (pf.) (оде́нусь; оде́нешься; оде́нутся)	хорошо́ плóхо мóдно (stylishly) бы́стро со вку́сом (with taste)	
To dress	**Whom?**	
одева́ть (impf.) (I)	кого́?	Утром Ири́на **оде́ла** сы́на и пошла́ с ним в шко́лу. In the morning, Irina **dressed** her son and went with him to school.
одéть (pf.) (оде́ну; оде́нешь; оде́нут)	бра́та сестру́ дете́й	
To put on	**What?**	
надева́ть (impf.) (I)	что?	За́втра Ири́на **наде́нет** зелёное пла́тье. Tomorrow Irina **will put on** a green dress.
наде́ть (pf.) (наде́ну; наде́нешь; наде́нут)	костю́м ку́ртку пла́тье боти́нки	

To take off/undress	What?	Whom?	Вечером Ирина **раздёнет** своих детей к сну.
раздева́ть (impf.) (I)	что?	кого́?	
разде́ть (pf.)	костю́м	бра́та	In the evening Irina **will**
(раздéну, раздéнешь, раздéнут)	ку́ртку ботинки	сестру́ детéй	**undress** her kids (so that they can be ready) for bed.
To get undressed			*Раздева́йтесь,
раздева́ться (impf.) (I)			пожа́луйста. Проходи́те в ко́мнату.
разде́ться (pf.)			**Take off** your things, and go
(раздéнусь, раздéнешься, раздéнутся)			on into the room.

*Note: The verbs **раздева́ться/разде́ться** are used most commonly in the imperative form (**Раздева́йся, Раздева́йтесь/Разде́нься, Разде́ньтесь**) and are used when someone enters a Russian home. The speaker asks the other person to take off her/his outerwear, such as boots, coat, hat, etc. Because Russians almost never walk around their homes in street shoes, this command will be heard even when the weather is warm.

Verbal Aspect

7.38 What is verbal aspect? Verbs in Russian generally are expressed in aspectual pairs. One verb is **imperfective** and the other is **perfective**. Each verb describes different connotations of the action according to its aspect. Below are some of the main differences in meaning between imperfective and perfective verbs.

REFERENCE TABLE 7H: BASIC MEANINGS OF IMPERFECTIVE/PERFECTIVE VERBS

Imperfective verb	Perfective verb
1) **NAMES THE ACTION THAT IS/WAS/WILL BE OCCURRING; STATES THAT THE ACTION TOOK PLACE** — Что ты вчера́ **де́лала**? What were you **doing** yesterday? — Я писа́ла письмо́. I **was writing** a letter.	1) **EMPHASIZES THE RESULT OR COMPLETENESS OF AN ACTION** Вчера́ я **написа́ла** письма. Yesterday I **wrote** (finished writing) the letters. Я **написа́ла** письмо́ за час. Yesterday I wrote (finished writing) the letter in an hour.
2) **VIEWS OR DESCRIBES THE ACTION AS A PROCESS** Я **писа́ла** письмо́ два часа́. I **was writing** the letter for two hours. Когда́ я **писа́ла** письмо́, я ду́мала о до́ме. While **writing** the letter, I thought of home.	2) **DESCRIBES A SERIES OF COMPLETED ACTIONS (EACH IS COMPLETED BEFORE THE NEXT BEGINS)** Ната́ша **написа́ла** письмо́ и пото́м **позвони́ла** домо́й. Natasha **wrote** (finished writing) the letter and then **called** home.

REFERENCE TABLE 7H: BASIC MEANINGS OF IMPF./PF. VERBS (cont.)

3) CONJUGATED IMPERFECTIVE VERBS FORM THE PRESENT AND PAST TENSES	3) CONJUGATED PERFECTIVE VERBS FORM THE FUTURE AND PAST TENSES
Она́ пи́шет. She **is writing**. Она́ писа́ла. She **was writing**. 4) **DESCRIBES A RECURRING ACTION** Ната́ша вчера́ и сего́дня писа́ла пи́сьма. Natasha **wrote/was writin** letters yesterday and today.	Она́ напи́шет письмо́. She **will write** a letter. Она́ написа́ла письмо́. She **wrote** a letter.

Some imperfective/perfective verb pairs are very similar in appearance. The perfective partner is often formed by adding a prefix to the imperfective form (на-, по-, с-, etc.). Other verb pairs are distinguished by different suffixes: imperfective **реша́ть** and perfective **реши́ть**. And still others have "false prefixes," which can trick us into thinking that a verb is perfective when it is actually imperfective: imperfective **покупа́ть** and perfective **купи́ть**. Whenever possible, this chapter will list the imperfective partner first when it is presented with its perfective counterpart.

REFERENCE TABLE 7I: EXAMPLES OF IMPERFECTIVE AND PERFECTIVE VERB PARTNERS

Imperfective	Perfective	
де́лать (что)	сде́лать	to do; to make
писа́ть (что)	написа́ть	to write
чита́ть (что)	прочита́ть	to read
учи́ть (что)	вы́учить	to study
покупа́ть (что)	купи́ть	to buy
реша́ть (что)	реши́ть	to decide; solve
ви́деть (что, кого́)	уви́деть	to see
говори́ть (что, о чём, кому́)	сказа́ть	to speak/say
дари́ть (что кому́)	подари́ть	to give (as a gift)
дава́ть (что кому́)	дать	to give
рисова́ть (что)	нарисова́ть	to draw
приглаша́ть (кого́)	пригласи́ть	to invite
приноси́ть (что, кому́, куда́)	принести́	to bring
гото́вить (что)	пригото́вить	to prepare
спра́шивать (кого́)	спроси́ть	to ask
проси́ть (что, у кого́)	попроси́ть	to request
встреча́ть(ся) (кого́, с кем)	встре́тить(ся)	to meet
е́хать (куда́)	пое́хать	to go (by vehicle)
идти́ (куда́)	пойти́	to go (on foot)
понима́ть (что, кого́)	поня́ть	to understand
помога́ть (кому́)	помо́чь	to help
мочь	смочь	to be able to
брать (что, у кого́)	взять	to take
переводи́ть (что)	перевести́	to translate

7.39 **VERBAL ASPECTS (BASIC PAST TENSE USAGE)**
    Function: Expressing the completion or result of an action

| Face to Face L 1 |
| Chapter 19 A |
| Pages 387-390 |

The six imperfective/perfective aspectual verb pairs below illustrate the basic formation of verb pairs.

1)   A prefix forms the perfective of the pair:

        читáть/**про**-читáть   to read
        писáть/**на**-писáть   to write
        дéлать/**с**-дéлать   to do
        учúть/**вы́**-учить   to study

2)   A different suffix distinguishes each verb in the pair:

        реш-**á**-ть/реш-**и́**-ть to solve/decide

3)   Aspectual verb pairs may be formed by different verbs, or it may appear that the imperfective has a prefix:

        покупáть/купить to buy

Note that in the sample sentences below, the **perfective past tense** *stresses the completion and/or result of a completed action.* Reference Table 7H summarizes the basic differences in meaning between imperfective and perfective verbs.

Sample sentences
читáть/прочитáть

Аня вчерá дóлго **читáла** все кнúги в библиотéке.
Аня вчерá **прочитáла** все кнúги.

Anya spent a lot of time yesterday **reading** all the books in the library.
Anya **read** all of the books.

учúть/вы́учить

Мы **у́чим** литератýру в шкóле.
В суббóту мой брат **вы́учил** стихотворéние.

We **study** literature in school.
On Saturday my brother **studied** (and **memorized**) the poem.

дéлать/сдéлать

Онú всегдá **дéлали** упражнéния.
Онá **сдéлала** э́то упражнéние.

They always **did** the exercises.
She **completed** this exercise.

писáть/написáть

Я **писáл** письмó и слýшал рáдио.

Мáма **написáла** мне интерéсное письмó.

I **was writing** a letter and listening to the radio.
My mom **wrote** me an interesting letter. [She wrote it, and I have it in my possession.]

реша́ть/реши́ть

Когда́ он **реша́л** зада́чу, все ученики́ говори́ли.

Ты вчера́ **не реши́л** э́ту зада́чу?

While he **was solving** the problem, all of the students were talking.

Did you manage **to solve** this problem yesterday?

покупа́ть/купи́ть

Когда́ я в Москве́ я **покупа́ю** краси́вые ма́рки.

Мы бы́ли на Но́вом Арба́те и Ада́м **купи́л** краси́вые ма́рки.

When I'm in Moscow, I **buy** beautiful stamps.

We were on the New Arbat, and Adam **bought** some beautiful stamps.

	Face to Face L 2
7.40 IMPERFECTIVE AND PERFECTIVE FUTURE TENSES *Function:* Describing future actions and events	Chapter 2 B Pages 51-52

Imperfective verb in the future tense An imperfective action in the future refers to an action viewed as a process (occurring over time), or one that will be repeated and thus is viewed as recurring.

За́втра мы **бу́дем чита́ть**.

Мы **бу́дем чита́ть** э́ту статью́ мно́го раз.

Tomorrow we **will be reading**.

We **will read** this article many times.

Perfective verb in the future tense A perfective action, however, stresses the completeness or result of some action in the future.

Мы за́втра **прочита́ем** рома́н «Коро́ль Лир». Это дома́шнее зада́ние.

Tomorrow we **will read** the novel "King Lear." It's a homework assignment.

In this perfective example, the novel to be read will be completely read, meaning from start to finish. Whether or not it is actually read is yet to be determined, but the need is there; it is homework, and the intention is to finish the novel.

Formation of the future tense To form the future tense of imperfective and perfective verbs, follow these basic rules:

Imperfective verbs		Perfective verbs	
Conjugate the verb **быть** (to be) + **the infinitive form** of the impf. verb.		Conjugate the perfective verb.	
быть + imperfective infinitive		**Perfective conjugated**	
Я бу́ду чита́ть	I will read	Я прочита́ю	I will read
Ты бу́дешь чита́ть	You will "	Ты прочита́ешь	You will "
Он/а́ бу́дет чита́ть	S/he will "	Он/а́ прочита́ет	S/he will "
Мы бу́дем чита́ть	We will "	Мы прочита́ем	We will "
Вы бу́дете чита́ть	You will "	Вы прочита́ете	You will "
Они́ бу́дут чита́ть	They will "	Они́ прочита́ют	They will "

7.41 THE PERFECTIVE VERBS ПРИНЕСТИ, ПРИЙТИ
Function: Conveying another person's promise;
saying someone has arrived

Face to Face L 2
Chapter 8 A, d
Pages 167-8, 178-9

The perfective verbs прийти (to arrive on foot) and принести (to bring) are both examples of motion verbs. The verb прийти describes motion to or arrival at a destination, while принести has the meaning *to carry/bring*. Both verbs are commonly used with **the dative case.**

Где Та́ня? Она обеща́ла **прийти́ к нам** сего́дня ве́чером.	Where is Tanya? She promised **to come see us** this evening.
Я не зна́ю. Она́ та́кже обеща́ла **принести́ нам** пе́пси-ко́лу и лимона́д.	I don't know. She also promised **to bring us** some Pepsi and juice.

Note the conjugation patterns of each of these perfective verbs.

прийти́ to come/arrive	принести́ to bring
приду́	принесу́
придёшь	принесёшь
приду́т	принесу́т
(пршёл, пришла́,	(принёс, принесла́,
пришло́, пришли́)	принесло́, принесли́)

Expressions with and without the preposition к

1) To go/arrive to someone's: **прийти́ к + кому́**

Сего́дня Мари́я **прийдёт к нам** на ве́чер.	Maria is coming over **to our house** (*lit.,* to us) today for a party.
Ты **придёшь** в суббо́ту **к Ка́те**?	Are you going **to Katya's** on Saturday?
Она́ придёт **к Бори́су**.	She's going **to Boris's.**

2) To bring something to someone: **принести́ что, кому́**

Я **принесу́ дру́гу** пода́рок.	I'll bring **my friend** a present.
Мы **принесём сестре́** кни́гу.	We'll bring our **sister** the book.
Они́ **принесу́т учи́телю** альбо́м.	They'll bring **the teacher** the album.

7.42 THE PERFECTIVE VERB ПОНРА́ВИТЬСЯ
Function: Relating impressions and activities

Face to Face L 2
Chapter 11 B, D
Pages 234-236, 242

The perfective понра́виться (to like) is used in the past tense to convey the meaning of a good or bad lasting impression. Impersonal constructions with понра́виться place the logical subject in the dative case and express the person who *likes*. The object or person liked is in the nominative case.

Dative of person (subject)	+ понрáвиться (agrees in number and gender with object/person that is liked)	+ Nominative of object/ person liked

Sample sentences

У вас óчень хорóшая шкóла. **Онá мне понрáвилась.**

You have a very nice school. **I like it.** (*lit.*, I liked it, and I still do.)

Вам не **понрáвился нóвый учи́тель?**   Don't **you like the new teacher?**

Sometimes the neuter form is used in the past tense to denote the fact that something was good, but no definite object is referred to:

Вчерá мы бы́ли в гостя́х и там **нам óчень понрáвилось.**

Yesterday we were invited to someone's house and **we had a good time.** (*lit.*, It was pleasing to us.)

In the past tense, **понрáвиться** is conjugated like other reflexive verbs ending in the particle -**ся**.

Мне ...   понрáви**лся** учи́тель (masculine, singular)

понрáви**лась** шкóла (feminine, singular)

понрáви**лось** Чéрное мóре (neuter, singular)

понрáви**лись** твои́ друзья́ (plural)

7.43 THE VERB ВЗЯТЬ *Function:* Choosing and purchasing items in a store (taking)	Face to Face L 2 Chapter 19 A, B, D Pages 408-415, 423-424

The perfective verb **взять** (to take) takes an accusative case complement (когó/что):

	взять	когó/что
я	возьмý	э́ти мáрки.
ты	возьмёшь	э́ту кни́гу.
он/á	возьмёт	э́тот журнáл.
мы	возьмём	э́ту матрёшку.
вы	возьмёте	э́ти сéрьги.
они́	возьмýт	э́тот сувени́р.

Past: взял; взялá; взя́ли

Imperatives Возьми́(те)!

Sample sentences

— Каки́е мáрки **возьмёшь?**   Which stamps will you **take** (buy)?

— Я **возьмý** вот э́ти стáрые мáрки.   **I'll take** these old stamps here.

In this sense, **взять** carries the same meaning as its English counterpart *to take*—instead of saying *I'll buy...* one would say *I'll take...*

7.44 THE VERBS БРАТЬ/ВЗЯТЬ (ЧТО? У КОГО?)
Function: Interviewing someone

Faces and Voices
Chapter 1 A
Page 5

The verbs **брать/взять** (to take) are used in two contexts:

	1) take something:	2) take from someone:
	что?	**у кого?**
брать (impf.) (беру́, берёшь, беру́т)	интервью́ interview	у ро́к-музыка́нта from the rock musician
взять (pf.) (возьму́, возьмёшь, возьму́т)	кни́гу book	у учи́тельницы from the teacher

Sample sentences

Я всегда́ **беру́** магнитофо́н **у** бра́та.

I always **take** (get, borrow) the tape player **from** my brother.

Ири́на **взяла́** интервью́ **у** балери́ны.

Irina interviewed the ballerina (*She **took** it **from** her*).

Ната́ша **взяла́** интервью́ **у** врача́, **у** секретаря́, **у** крестья́нки, **у** манеке́нщицы.

Natasha interviewed the doctor, the secretary, the [female] farmer, and the model.

7.45 THE USE OF THE VERB ПЕРЕВОДИ́ТЬ/ПЕРЕВЕСТИ́ (TO TRANSLATE/INTERPRET)
Function: Translating/interpreting a language

Faces and Voices
Chapter 1 Б
Pages 12-15

The Russian verbs **переводи́ть/перевести́** correspond to two English verbs—*to translate* and *to interpret*. In Russian, a **перево́дчик** can be a person who translates books or a person who interprets oral communication, while a **перево́д** is the product of his or her work—a translation.

Переводи́ть (impf.) перевожу́, перево́дишь, перево́дят
Перевести́ (pf.) переведу́, переведёшь, переведу́т
past tense: перевёл, перевела́, перевели́

To express translation from one language to another use the following formula:

Переводи́ть/перевести́

с + genitive of the original language	**на + accusative of the new language**
с ру́сского from Russian	на англи́йский to English
с англи́йского from English	на ру́сский to Russian
с францу́зского from French	на испа́нский to Spanish

Sample sentences

Ната́ша **перевела́** интервью́ с ру́сского на англи́йский язы́к.	Natasha **translated** the interview **from Russian into English**.
Он **перево́дит** э́тот рома́н с англи́йского на ру́сский язы́к.	He **is translating** this novel **from English into Russian**.
На дома́шнее зада́ние мы **перевели́** предложе́ния **на ру́сский**.	For homework we **translated** the sentences **into Russian**.

7.46 REVIEW OF IMPERFECTIVE/PERFECTIVE VERB PAIRS
Function: Review

Faces and Voices
Chapter 5 Г
Page 140

The review list of imperfective/perfective verb pairs below includes the conjugation pattern, Type I or II, for each verb.

Imperfective	Perfective		
чита́ть (I)	прочита́ть (I)	(что?)	to read
печа́тать (I)	напеча́тать (I)	(что? на чём?)	to type, print
учи́ть (II)	вы́учить (II)	(что?)	to study, memorize
зараба́тывать (I)	зарабо́тать (I)	(что?)	to earn
дава́ть (I)	дать (irr.)	(что? кому́?)	to give
спо́рить (II)	поспо́рить (II)	(о чём? с кем?)	to argue
гото́вить (II)	пригото́вить (II)	(что?)	to prepare
рисова́ть (I)	нарисова́ть (I)	(что? на чём?)	to draw
расска́зывать (I)	рассказа́ть (I)	(о чём? кому́?)	to tell, relate
реша́ть (I)	реши́ть (II)	(что?)	to decide, solve
приглаша́ть (I)	пригласи́ть (II)	(кого́? куда́?)	to invite
покупа́ть (I)	купи́ть (II)	(что? кому́?)	to buy
поздравля́ть (I)	поздра́вить (II)	(кого́? с чем?)	to congratulate
отвеча́ть (I)	отве́тить (II)	(на что? кому́?)	to answer
проси́ть (II)	попроси́ть (II)	(что? у кого́?)	to request
получа́ть (I)	получи́ть (II)	(что? от кого́?)	to receive, get

Sample sentences

Изобрета́тель ксе́рокса Че́стер Ка́рлсон на́чал **зараба́тывать** де́ньги, когда́ ему́ бы́ло 12 лет.	The inventor of the photocopier, Chester Carlson, began **earning money** when he was 12 years old.
Илю́ша в кани́кулы **зарабо́тал** мно́го де́нег.	Ilyusha **earned** a lot of money for the holidays.
Ната́ша **напеча́тала** интервью́ со шко́льником, а пото́м начала́ **печа́тать** интервью́ с учи́телем.	Natasha **typed** the interview with the student and then began **typing** the interview with the teacher.
— Когда́ ты ко́нчишь **гото́вить** обе́д? — спроси́л муж.	"When will you finish **preparing** lunch?" asked the husband.
Когда́ ты **пригото́вила**, мы пойдём гуля́ть?	When you have **prepared** it, will we go on a walk?

Ты уже́ ко́нчила **учи́ть** стихотворе́ние?	Have you already finished **studying** the poem?
Когда́ **вы́учила** , посмотри́ вот э́тот журна́л: там интере́сная статья́ «Челове́к и компью́тер».	When you have **memorized** it, look at this magazine. There is an interesting article, "Man and Computer."
Ты не по́мнишь, когда́ Пу́шкин на́чал **писа́ть** рома́н «Евге́ний Оне́гин»?	Do you remember when Pushkin began **writing** the novel "Eugene Onegin?"
— Ната́ша уже́ **написа́ла** статью́ в газе́ту «Моско́вские но́вости».	Natasha already **wrote** the article for the newspaper "Moscow News."

7.47 USE OF VERBAL ASPECTS IN THE INFINITIVE FORM

Function: Expressing the infinitive form of an action (to do, to make, etc.) in conjunction with another verb

Мир ру́сских Lesson 5 Pages 158-159

Only the perfective infinitive is used after the verbs **успе́ть** (to manage, succeed), **забы́ть** (to forget), and **удало́сь** (to be lucky/fortunate).

Sample sentences

Мы **не успе́ли посмотре́ть** переда́чу по телеви́зору.	We **didn't have time to watch** the television show.
Я **забы́ла посла́ть** письмо́.	I **forgot to send** the letter.
Мне **удало́сь написа́ть** сочине́ние до конца́ уро́ка.	I **was fortunate to have finished** the composition before the end of class.

Only the imperfective infinitive is used after the following verbs:

полюби́ть	(to come to like)
привы́кнуть	(to get used {to})
научи́ться	(to learn)
продолжа́ть	(to continue)
надое́сть	(to bore, to bother, to get sick of)

Sample sentences

Когда́ я была́ в Росси́и—	When I was in Russia:
Я **полюби́ла гуля́ть** по краси́вым па́ркам.	I **came to like walking** in the beautiful parks.
Я **привы́кнула пить** чай по́сле за́втрака, обе́да и у́жина.	I **got used to drinking** tea after breakfast, lunch, and dinner.
Я **научи́лась игра́ть** на гита́ре.	I **learned how to play** the guitar.
Я **продолжа́ла писа́ть** в дневнике́ ка́ждый ве́чер.	I **continued to write** in my diary every evening.
Мне **надо́ело писа́ть** пи́сьма.	I **got bored with writing** letters.

7.48 THE PERFECTIVE ASPECT OF VERBS: SPECIFIC, FACTUAL STATEMENTS

Function: Expressing a specific or single occurring action

| Мир русских |
| Lesson 8 |
| Pages 269-274 |

The perfective aspect of verbs is used for a specific or a single, one-time action. This meaning may convey different kinds of information about the result of the action, depending upon the actual verb used.

1)   The verb may name a specific action in the past with *a result that is preserved until the moment of speech.*

Sample sentences

Кандинский **родился** в Москве в 1866 г.   Kandinsky **was born** in Moscow in 1866.

Всем нам **понравилась** Третьяковка.   We all **liked** the Tretyakov Gallery.

2)   The verb may name an action that *represents a change or a shift of direction.* The following words are often used in this context:

неожиданно	unexpectedly
вдруг	suddenly
наконец	finally
и вот …	and here is…

The perfective verb is often prefixed (often with **у-** or **по-**) and conveys the idea of initiation of or beginning an action.

Sample sentences

Однажды вечером, когда было почти темно, художник вошёл в комнату и **вдруг увидел** прекрасную картину.

One evening, when it was almost dark, the artist entered the room and **caught sight of** a marvelous painting.

Мы **увидели** в Третьяковке много картин, **узнали** имена русских художников.

We **saw** many paintings in the Tretyakov (Gallery) and **learned** the names of Russian painters.

Сначала он сказал, что не пойдёт на экскурсию в галерею, но потом **неожиданно согласился**.

At first he said that he wouldn't go on the excursion to the gallery, but then **unexpectedly agreed** (to it).

Мы долго ждали его, и **наконец** он приехал.

We waited for him for a long time, and **finally he arrived**.

7.49 THE IMPERFECTIVE ASPECT OF VERBS IN GENERAL FACTUAL STATEMENTS

Function: Establishing that an action took place

| Мир русских |
| Lesson 8 |
| Pages 269-274 |

The imperfective aspect may be used to establish *the simple fact that an action occurred.* In this usage the action is not characterized as in progress, instantaneous, or complete (these meanings are not excluded, they are simply irrelevant to the speaker at the moment).

Sample sentences

Третьяко́в хорошо́ **знал** иску́сство, **люби́л** ру́сскую жи́вопись.	Tretyakov **knew** art well and **loved** Russian painting.
Экскурсово́д **расска́зывал** нам о том, что Третьяко́в одни́м из пе́рвых на́чал коллекциони́ровать ико́ны.	The tour guide **told** us that Tretyakov was one of the first to begin collecting icons.
Нам **расска́зывали**, что в 1892 г. Третьяко́в подари́л свои́ карти́ны го́роду Москве́.	We **were told** that in 1892 Tretyakov gave his paintings to the city of Moscow.
Он **увлека́лся** в жи́вописи пейза́жем.	He **was fascinated** by landscape paintings.

7.50 USAGE OF IMPERFECTIVE AND PERFECTIVE INFINITIVE VERB FORMS

Function: Expressing infinitive verb forms (to do, to make, etc.) with specific connotations

Мир русских	
Lesson 9	
Pages 301-305	

The infinitive forms of imperfective and perfective verbs are used in various constructions to denote specific connotations. The following summary chart outlines these basic rules and constructions. Note that their usage often reflects opposing ideas (the opposite connotation is expressed using the other aspect).

Imperfective infinitives express:	**Perfective infinitives express:**
1) **Action without a limit or deadline**	1) **The result of the action is stressed**
Сего́дня мне **на́до писа́ть** сочине́ние на те́му «Ру́сская душа́». Today I **need to write (work on)** a composition on the theme, "The Russian Soul."	Сего́дня мне **на́до написа́ть** сочине́ние на те́му «Ру́сская душа́». Today I **need to write** a composition on the theme, "The Russian Soul."
О ру́сском **мо́жно писа́ть** и **говори́ть** о́чень мно́го. **It is possible to write** and **to talk** a lot about the Russians.	О ру́сском **мо́жно написа́ть** и **сказа́ть** о́чень мно́го. **It is possible to write** and **to say** a lot about the Russians (*lit., about the Russian*).
Я хочу́ **изуча́ть** ру́сский язы́к. **I want to study** Russian.	Я хочу́ **изучи́ть** ру́сский язы́к. **I want to learn Russian** (fully, as well as possible).

Imperfective infinitives express:	Perfective infinitives express:
2) **Repeated or habitual action**	2) **Completion of a single, one-time action**
Мой родители **хотят ездить** на дачу как можно чаще.	Мой родители **хотят поехать** в эту субботу на дачу.
My parents **want to go** to the dacha as often as possible.	My parents **want to go** to the dacha this Saturday.
Ветераны войны **решили встречаться** каждый год 9 мая около Большого театра.	Ветераны войны **решили встретиться** в этом году 9 мая около Большого театра.
The war veterans **decided to meet** every year on May 9 near the Bolshoi Theater.	The war veterans **decided to meet** this year on May 9 near the Bolshoi Theater.
3) **Indication of an action in process**	
Мы **стали вспоминать** сколько в русском языке слов с корнем «род».	
We **began to recall** so many words in Russian that have the root «род».	
4) **With the verbs:** надоесть, устать, начать, кончить, продолжить, перестать, любить	4) **With the perfective verbs:** забыть, успеть, удасться
Мы **продолжали работать** в саду до вечера.	Мне **удалось сходить** на выставку картин Кандинского.
We **continued to work** in the garden until evening.	I **managed to go** to the exhibition of Kandinsky paintings.
Мы **начали заниматься** в школе 1-ого сентября.	Папа **успел приготовить** ужин до прихода мамы с работы.
We **began to study** at school on September 1st.	Dad **managed to prepare** supper by the time Mom returned from work.
5) **To denote the *beginning* of an action with the meaning *it is time***	5) **To denote necessity of an action with the meaning *it is necessary to***
Совсем тепло! **Пора ехать** на дачу.	Ребята! **Пора кончить** работу!
It's quite warm! **It is time to go to** the dacha.	Kids! We **need to finish up** our work!

Obligation, Possibility, Potential, Necessity, and Permission

7.51 Summary of common expressions. The reference table below provides an overview of the variety of constructions used in Russian to convey meanings of obligation, possibility, potential, necessity, and permission.

REFERENCE TABLE 7J : BASIC CONSTRUCTIONS OF OBLIGATION, POSSIBILITY, POTENTIAL, NECESSITY, AND PERMISSION

Construction	Usage - Example
To express obligation, the Russian equivalent of the English word *must* or *have to* is often used. This construction is the short-form adjective **до́лжен/должна́/ должны́ + the infinitive form of the verb** whose action is required.	Masculine: Я/Ты/Он...**до́лжен**... сде́лать дома́шнее зада́ние. I/you/he...has to...do the assignment. Feminine: Я/Ты/Она́...**должна́**... сде́лать дома́шнее зада́ние. I/you/she...has to...do the assignment. Plural: Мы/Вы/Они́...**должны́**... сде́лать дома́шнее зада́ние. We/you/they...have to...do the assignment.
To express possibility, the word **мо́жно + the infinitive of the verb** can be used. It is also possible to use the verb **мочь** (могу́, мо́жешь, мо́гут), which means *to be able*.	Здесь **мо́жно игра́ть** в бейсбо́л. It's possible (allowed, permitted) to play baseball here. Тепе́рь **мы мо́жем** пойти́ в парк. Now we can go to the park (not only are we physically able to do so, but we also now have the time, chance, or option to do so).
To express possibility in the future, the conversational form **мо́жет быть** (maybe) is used.	Совсе́м **мо́жет быть**, что она́ придёт на репети́ции. It's entirely likely that she'll show up for the rehearsals.
To express potential, the verb **мочь/смочь** can be used. If it is a question of time, the verb **успева́ть/успе́ть** (to manage) **+ a perfective infinitive** can be used.	Если **я смогу́**, я позвоню́ тебе́ сего́дня ве́чером. If I can, I'll call you this evening. Я наде́юсь, что мы ещё **успе́ем пообе́дать**. I hope that we'll still be able to (find time to) eat lunch.

REFERENCE TABLE 7J : BASIC CONSTRUCTIONS OF OBLIGATION, POSSIBILITY, POTENTIAL, NECESSITY, AND PERMISSION (cont.)

To express necessity, the modals **на́до/ну́жно + the infinitive form of the verb** whose action is required is used. With these words, the logical subject is in the dative case. **На́до** and **ну́жно** are interchangeable, though **на́до** expresses a slightly higher degree of necessity.	Мне на́до написа́ть письмо́. I need to write a letter. Ей ну́жно позвони́ть ма́ме. She needs to call her mom.
To express a recommended action or its worth, use the construction **сто́ит + the verb infinitive.**	Это хоро́шая кни́га. (Тебе́) **Сто́ит чита́ть** её. This is a good book. I **recommend** you **read** it. (**It's worth reading**.)
To express a recommended action, **сле́дует + the verb infinitive** is sometimes used. (**Сле́дует** is more characteristic of higher, literary style and carries the meaning *one should/shouldn't*).	Сле́дует до́лго **жева́ть** пищу. You should (always) chew your food for a long time (before swallowing). Тебе́ **сле́дует** пойти́ к врачу́. You should go to a doctor. (It would be in your best interest if you saw a doctor.)
To express permission, the words **мо́жно** (possible, permitted) and **нельзя́** (not allowed or permitted) are used, along **with the infinitive of the verb.**	**Мо́жно есть** конфе́ты на уро́ке? Is (one) allowed to eat candy in class? Нет, **нельзя́**. No, it isn't allowed.

7.52 VERBS ВИДЕТЬ, СМОТРЕТЬ: ASKING FOR PERMISSION (МОЖНО; НЕЛЬЗЯ)
Function: Asking for permission

Face to Face L 1
Chapter 11 A
Pages 228-230

The verbs **ви́деть** (to see) and **смотре́ть** (to watch) are second conjugation verbs. Note the consonant mutation in the first person singular form of **ви́деть** (д > ж).

	ви́деть (II) to see		**смотре́ть** (II) to watch
я	ви́жу	я	смотрю́
ты	ви́дишь	ты	смо́тришь
он/а́	ви́дит	он/а́	смо́трит
мы	ви́дим	мы	смо́трим
вы	ви́дите	вы	смо́трите
они	ви́дят	они	смо́трят

Asking permission— **мо́жно** and **нельзя́**. **Мо́жно** means *May I?/Is it possible?*. **Нельзя́** is the negative answer to this question and means *It is not allowed/You may not*. Both **мо́жно** and **нельзя́** can be used by themselves or with infinitive verbs in asking for and granting permission.

Sample sentences

Мо́жно здесь **игра́ть** в бейсбо́л?	**Can (one) play** baseball here?
Нет, **нельзя́**.	No, **it's not allowed**.
А где **мо́жно**?	Where **is it allowed**?
Мо́жно игра́ть в па́рке и́ли на стадио́не.	In the park or at the stadium.

7.53 USING THE MODAL НА́ДО	Face to Face L 1
Function: Telling what needs to be done	Chapter 19 C Pages 396-397

To express that *someone needs to do something*, the construction **на́до + the dative case (person) + the infinitive of a verb** is used. Note the examples expressing needs below.

Sample sentences

Мне сего́дня **на́до купи́ть** ма́рки, тетра́ди и ру́чки.	**I need to buy** stamps, notebooks, and pens today.
Сестре́ **на́до занима́ться** те́ннисом по́сле шко́лы, **а бра́ту на́до вы́учить** слова́.	**My sister needs to play** tennis after school, and **my brother needs to learn** the words.
Али́се и Ка́те **на́до сде́лать** дома́шнее зада́ние и пото́м пойти́ домо́й.	**Alisa and Katya need to do** the homework assignment and then go home.

The word **ну́жно** may be used interchangeably with **на́до**:

Кому́ **ну́жно** (**на́до**) **идти́** в магази́н сего́дня, **Бори́су** и́ли **Лари́се**?	**Who needs to go** to the store today, **Boris or Larisa**?

7.54 THE VERB МОЧЬ	Face to Face L 2
Function: Expressing ability or permission	Chapter 14 B, D Pages 302-303, 311-312

Depending on context, the verb **мочь** (to be able) can express the **possibility** or impossibility of performing an action for physical reasons, or the **permission** to perform certain actions:

Я не **могу́** сфотографи́ровать тебя́ — у меня́ нет фотоаппара́та.	**I can't** take your picture: I don't have a camera. (action deemed **impossible** due to lack of the necessary item)
Я **могу́** сфотографи́ровать тебя́? (Мо́жно я сфотографи́рую тебя́?)	**Can I** take your picture? (asking for **permission** to perform an action)

The verb мочь has shifting stress and consonant change (г>ж):

Conjugation +infinitive verb

я	могу́	прийти́ на встре́чу	to come to the meeting
ты	мо́жешь	принести́ цветы́	to bring flowers
он/а́	мо́жет	купи́ть пода́рок	to buy a present
мы	мо́жем	съе́здить в центр	to go downtown
вы	мо́жете	сходи́ть в магази́н	to go to the store
они́	мо́гут	заказа́ть биле́ты	to order tickets
Past tense	мог, могла́, могли́		

7.55 THE VERB УСПЕВАТЬ, УСПЕТЬ
Function: Managing time to do something, succeeding in doing something

<table><tr><td>Face to Face L 2
Chapter 17 A, D
Pages 366-369,
379</td></tr></table>

The verb pair **успева́ть/успе́ть** (imperfective/perfective) means *to have time (to do something), succeed, manage (to do something)* and is often used with a **perfective verb**:

Я не **успе́ю сде́лать** упражне́ние.	I **won't be able to do** the exercise.
Мы **успе́ем прочита́ть** газе́ту?	Will **we be able (find time) to read** the newspaper?

A noun preceded by the preposition **в** or **на + the accusative case** can be used to express *to a destination or event*:

Ты ещё **успе́ешь на уро́к**, но они́ не **успе́ют в шко́лу**.	You still **have time to get to class**, but they **won't make it to school on time**.

успева́ть	успе́ть
я успева́ю	успе́ю
ты успева́ешь	успе́ешь
они́ успева́ют	успе́ют

7.56 ДОЛЖЕН WITH THE INFINITIVE
Function: Expressing an obligation

<table><tr><td>Faces and Voices
Chapter 5 A
Page 121</td></tr></table>

The construction **до́лжен/должна́/должны́ + an infinitive verb form** expresses an *obligation to do something*. This conveys a stronger connotation than the **на́до** or **ну́жно** constructions. **До́лжен** expresses that *one must, and is obligated to, perform the action*. Note below that the masculine, feminine, or plural forms of **до́лжен** agree with the gender and number of the subject. The future and the past tense of this construction are formed by the conjugated verb **быть** following **до́лжен** and reflect the gender and number of the subject.

Sample sentences

Он **до́лжен** (**был, бу́дет**) рабо́тать на компью́тере.	He **must (had to, will have to)** work on the computer.
Она́ **должна́** (**была́, бу́дет**) изуча́ть англи́йский язы́к.	She **must (had to, will have to)** study English.
Они́ **должны́** (**бы́ли, бу́дут**) учи́ться печа́тать на маши́нке.	They **must (had to, will have to)** learn to use the typewriter.
— Что вы **должны́** де́лать на рабо́те в музе́е?	What do you **have to** do at work in the museum?
— Я **должна́** отвеча́ть на телефо́нные звонки́, **должна́** принима́ть посети́телей, отвеча́ть на пи́сьма.	I **have to/must** answer phone calls, receive visitors and answer letters.

7.57 THE VERBS УМЕ́ТЬ/МОЧЬ COMBINED WITH THE INFINITIVE

Function: Talking about ability. Talking about the equipment people use at work.

Faces and Voices
Chapter 5 Б
Pages 128-129

The contruction with the verb **уме́ть** (I) (to know how, be able [to]) **+ the infinitive form of a verb** indicates *an ability which is due to an acquired knowledge or skill, something one has learned to do* (**научи́ться де́лать**).

Что вы **уме́ете** де́лать? What **can** you do?
(What **have you learned** to do?)

	уме́ть	**что де́лать**	
Я	уме́ю	говори́ть по-ру́сски	speak Russian
Ты	уме́ешь	танцева́ть	dance
Они́	уме́ют	рисова́ть	draw
		рабо́тать на компью́тере	work on a computer

Note the differences between the verbs **уме́ть** (to know how, be able [to]), **мочь** (to be physically or mentally able to), and **знать** (to know something or someone):

уме́ть + infinitive	expresses an ability which is due to an acquired knowledge or skill.	Мла́дшая сестра́ Илю́ши **не уме́ет чита́ть**: она́ ещё ма́ленькая, ей 3 го́да. Ilyusha's younger sister **can't read**. She's still small; only 3 years old.
мочь + infinitive	expresses a physical or mental ability to do something.	Сейча́с 11 часо́в ве́чера, и Илю́ша **не мо́жет чита́ть** эконо́мику: он о́чень хо́чет спать. It's 11 p.m. now and Ilyusha **can't** read his economics. He really wants to sleep.

знать кого? что?	is the basic verb for *to know*. 1) It requires a direct object or a clause; 2) is never used with an infinitive.	1) Илюша не о́чень хорошо́ **зна́ет** англи́йский язы́к. Ilyusha **doesn't know** English well. 2) Мы **зна́ем**, кем хо́чет стать Илюша. We **know** what Ilyusha wants to become.

Sample sentences

Ты **уме́ешь** игра́ть на скри́пке?
— Нет, но я хорошо́ игра́ю на гита́ре.
Ольга рабо́тала в Инди́и перево́дчиком. Она́ хорошо́ **зна́ет** англи́йский язы́к. Она́ **уме́ет** чита́ть кни́ги на англи́йском языке́ без словаря́.

Do you **(know how to)** play the violin?
No, but I play the guitar well.
Olga worked in India as a translator. She **knows** English well. She **can** read books in English without a dictionary.

— Илюша, почему́ ты не́ был вчера́ в шко́ле?
— Я не **мог** прийти́, потому́ что встреча́л америка́нских шко́льников в аэропорту́.

Ilyusha, why weren't you at school yesterday?
I **couldn't** go because I was meeting the American students at the airport.

7.58 THE USE OF IMPERFECTIVE AND PERFECTIVE INFINITIVES WITH THE MODAL EXPRESSIONS: НЕЛЬЗЯ, МОЖНО, НАДО НУЖНО, СЛЕДУЕТ

Function: Expressing various connotations of permission, possibility, necessity and obligation

Мир ру́сских Lesson 3 Pages 84-89

Perfective and imperfective infinitives are used with the modal words: **нельзя́**, **мо́жно**, **на́до (ну́жно)**, and **сле́дует**.

<u>Нельзя́</u> **Нельзя́** is used with an imperfective infinitive *to state a prohibition* or with a perfective infinitive *to state the impossibility* (often physical, conceived as a one-time action) of performing some action.

A prohibition (imperfective):

Нельзя́ **есть** проду́кты, в кото́рых мно́го жи́ра.

Don't eat foods that contain a lot of fat.

Идёт экза́мен: **нельзя́ открыва́ть** дверь.

An exam is in session; **you can't open** the door.

An impossibility (perfective):

Нельзя́ сра́зу **съесть** тако́е большо́е коли́чество шокола́да.

It's not possible to eat such a large amount of chocolate at one time.

Замо́к не рабо́тает: **нельзя́ откры́ть** дверь.

You can't open the door; the lock doesn't work.

Мóжно, нáдо, and слéдует with imperfective verbs Мóжно or нáдо is used with an imperfective infinitive *to name an action, the accomplishment of which is permitted, necessary, or possible.* Мóжно is also used with an imperfective infinitive *to name an action which is usual or repeated.*

Слéдует, used with an imperfective infinitive, conveys the same meaning as does the modal нáдо but is *more characteristic of literary style.*

Sample sentences

Все собралйсь, **мóжно** начинáть собрáние.	Everyone has gathered; **we can** begin the meeting.
Ужé пóздно, **нáдо** ложúться спать.	It's already late; **you have** to go to bed.
Недалекó от нáшего дóма есть óзеро, там **мóжно** купáться.	There's a lake not far from our house; **you may** swim there.
Чтобы сидéть на диéте, **нáдо** имéть сúлу вóли и терпéние.	In order to diet **one must** have willpower and patience.
От нáшего гóрода до Красноя́рска **мóжно** плыть на парохóде.	**You can** travel from our town to Krasnoyarsk by steamship.
Слéдует дóлго жевáть пúщу.	**You should** chew your food for a long time.

Мóжно, нáдо, and слéдует with perfective verbs Мóжно or нáдо is used with a perfective infinitive to state the necessity or possibility of accomplishing an action. In questions, мóжно is used with perfective infinitives. In responses, it is followed by an imperfective verb.

Showing that a requested action is not necessary is expressed by не нáдо. Слéдует is usually used with a perfective infinitive to convey advice to perform (and complete) an action. Нáдо is used in all styles of speech.

Sample sentences

— Мóжно **откры́ть** окнó?	**May I open** the window?
— Открывáйте.	Please do.
— Мóжно **закры́ть** дверь?	**May I close** the door?
— Не нáдо.	**It's not necessary.**
Мне **нáдо купúть** рýсско-англúйский словáрь, чтóбы перевестú эту статью́.	I **need to buy** a Russian-English dictionary in order to translate this article.
Тебé **слéдует пойтú** к врачý.	You **should go** to the doctor.

The **dative case** is used to name the person or persons for whom the action is **possible or necessary:**

Ей **нáдо сказáть** Рúку, что онá не хóчет поéхать с нáми.	**She should tell** Rick that she doesn't want to go with us.
Емý **нáдо занимáться.**	**He has to study.**

An **imperfective infinitive** is normally used in sentences where the modal is **negated**:

— На́до включи́ть свет.	We should turn on the light.
—Не на́до (не сле́дует) включа́ть, ещё светло́.	**Don't turn it on**, it's still light.
— На́до посмотре́ть э́тот фильм.	I should see that film.
—Не на́до (не сле́дует) смотре́ть э́тот фильм, он неинтере́сный.	**Don't see** that film; it's not interesting.

Additional constructions expressing obligation or recommended action

1)   The word **сто́ит** (it is worth), like the word **сле́дует**, also refers to a recommended action:

Сто́ит пойти́ в э́тот рестора́н: там о́чень вку́сно гото́вят.	**It's worth** going (you should go) to this restaurant; they have good food there.

2)   The verb **прийти́сь** (had/obliged/forced to) usually implies that something is extremely important, and/or that the speaker will do the action no matter what, however **reluctantly**. Because **прийти́сь** is perfective, it can be used only in the past and future tenses, and is conjugated like the verb **прийти́** + the reflexive particle **-ся (-сь)** in the third person neuter singular (**оно́**) form: **пришло́сь, придётся**. Like with the modals **на́до/ну́жно/мо́жно**, the person who needs to perform the action is in the dative case:

До́ма не́ было маши́ны, поэ́тому **мне пришло́сь** идти́ сюда́ пешко́м.	The car wasn't around at home, so therefore **I had** to walk here.
Зна́чит, потеря́ли паспорта́. Тепе́рь **нам придётся** заказа́ть но́вые.	So you lost your passports. Well now **we'll have** to order new ones.

3)   The words **вы́нужден** (forced) and **обя́зан** (obliged) are short form adjectives (like **до́лжен**) and decline for gender and number. Like many other words denoting obligation, necessity, permission or recommended action, these words are used with the **infinitive** form of the action to be done:

Он был вы́нужден (она́ была́ вы́нуждена, они́ бы́ли вы́нуждены) держа́ться пра́вой стороны́ доро́ги из-за ава́рии.	**He was (she was, they were) forced** to stay on the right side of the road, due to the accident.
Адвока́ты обя́заны не злоупотребля́ть дове́рием свои́х клие́нтов.	**Lawyers are obliged** not to abuse the trust (confidence) of their clients.

Verbs of Motion

The following topics are covered extensively in this chapter on Verbs of Motion:

	Grammar points:
Overview of Verbs of Motion	7.59
Basic Verbs of Motion	7.60-7.62
Transitive Verbs of Motion	7.63-7.64
Prefixed Verbs of Motion and Verbal Aspect	7.65-7.72

7.59 What are verbs of motion? These are verbs which indicate *motion to or around a place, either on foot or by some form of transportation (cars, buses, trains, planes, etc.).* Important characteristics of Russian verbs of motion are:
• Some motion verbs are transitive in nature; that is, they indicate common motions like carrying or delivering.
• Verbs of motion commonly indicate some sort of direction, and normally take an accusative case complement: **Я иду́ в шко́лу.** (I'm going to *school.*) The direction in this case functions as a destination.
• Each verb of motion has a specific meaning to a Russian speaker. Motion is expressed not simply by "going", but by doing a particular type of activity: driving/riding, walking, running, carrying, bringing, etc.
• Each type of motion verb is represented by two **imperfective** verbs, one indicating motion in one direction (**determinate or unidirectional**) and the other indicating motion in two directions or general, repeated motion (**indeterminate or multidirectional**).
• When used with a prefix (**по-, у-, до-, про-, вы-, в-, при-,** etc.) determinate/unidirectional verbs become **perfective** in aspect.

REFERENCE TABLE 7K: VERBS OF MOTION—DETERMINATE AND INDETERMINATE

	Determinate or Unidirectional/(perfective)	Indeterminate or Multidirectional
to go (on foot)	идти́/(пойти́)	ходи́ть
to go (by vehicle)	е́хать/(пое́хать)	е́здить
to run	бежа́ть/(побежа́ть)	бе́гать
to fly	лете́ть/(полете́ть)	лета́ть
to swim	плыть/(поплы́ть)	пла́вать
to carry (on foot)*	нести́/(понести́)	носи́ть
to lead, drive*	вести́/(повести́)	води́ть
to convey, carry, transport (by vehicle)*	везти́/(повезти́)	вози́ть

***Note:** These three verbs are sometimes called **transitive** motion verbs, as something or someone is brought or carried. Transitive verbs of motion are explained in more detail below.

Differences in meaning between English and Russian Motion verbs in Russian have very specific meanings. Below are some examples of how English and Russian differ in this respect:

English	Russian (infinitive)
I go/am going to the store. (don't have to specify whether riding, walking, bicycling, etc., and action could be one-way or two-way/repeated, depending solely upon context)	Я идý (идти) в магазин. (walking, one-way) Я хожý (ходить) в магазин. (walking, two-way—there and back—or action that occurs repeatedly) Я éду (éхать) в магазин. (riding/driving in a vehicle, on a bicycle, etc., one-way) Я éзжу (éздить) в магазин. (riding/driving in a vehicle, on a bicycle, etc., two-way—there and back—or action that occurs repeatedly)
I swim. (action could be one-time or many times, depending on context)	Я плывý (плыть). (one-way, from one side of a pool, river, lake, etc., to the other) Я плáваю (плáвать). (two-way, or general action; swimming every day or on a regular basis)
I bring/am bringing bread. (no mention of whether the bread is being carried while walking, or is being transported by means of a vehicle; action could be either one-way or two-way, depending on context)	Я несý (нести) хлеб. (carrying while walking, one-way, doing it now) Я ношý (носить) хлеб. (carrying while walking, two-way or general, repeated action) Я везý (везти) хлеб. (bringing by vehicle, one-way, doing it now) Я вожý (возить) хлеб. (bringing by vehicle, two-way or general, repeated action)

Basic Unprefixed Verbs of Motion: Grammar Points 7.60-7.62

Verbs of motions are generally listed in indeterminate/determinate verb pairs.

Indeterminate (multidirectional) verbs of motion Indeterminate verbs of motion are also referred to as *multidirectional: two-way (round-trip)* or *general motion* about a place. They are always imperfective, even when prefixed, because the action either occurs more than once or is a process. For this reason indeterminate verbs are often used with frequency words like **чáсто** (often), **иногдá** (sometimes), **рéдко** (rarely), **никогдá не** (never), **кáждый день** (every day), **обычно** (usually), **всегдá** (always). Below are some indeterminate verbs with their determinate "partners":

REFERENCE TABLE 7L: COMMON INDETERMINATE VERBS (LISTED WITH THEIR DETERMINATE PARTNER)

Indeterminate verb/ [determinate partner]	Example usage
ходи́ть/[идти́] (хожу́, хо́дишь, хо́дят) Past: я/ты/он...ходи́л я/ты/она́...ходи́ла мы/вы/они́...ходи́ли	Они́ ча́сто **хо́дят** в апте́ку. They often **go** to the pharmacy. В понеде́льник я **ходи́л** на спекта́кль. On Monday I **went** to see a play.
е́здить/[е́хать] (е́зжу, е́здишь, е́здят) Past: я/ты/он...е́здил я/ты/она́...е́здила мы/вы/они́...е́здили	Ка́ждый год мы **е́здим** в Москву́. Every year we **go** to Moscow. (we go and come back) Вчера́ мы **е́здили** в кино́. Yesterday we **went** to the movies.
бе́гать/[бежа́ть] (бе́гаю, бе́гаешь, бе́гают) Past: я/ты/он...бе́гал я/ты/она́...бе́гала мы/вы/они́...бе́гали	Ка́тя о́чень лю́бит **бе́гать**. Katya really likes **to run**. (general action, like a sport or activity) В суббо́ту Аня **бе́гала** по го́роду. On Saturday Anya **went running** around town.
лета́ть/[лете́ть] (лета́ю, лета́ешь, лета́ют) Past: я/ты/он...лета́л я/ты/она́...лета́ла мы/вы/они́...лета́ли	Вы иногда́ **лета́ете** в Балтимо́р? You sometimes **fly** to Baltimore? Джон ра́ньше **лета́л** в Нью-Йо́рк; а сейча́с он е́здит туда́ на по́езде. John used **to fly** to New York, but now he goes there by train.
пла́вать/[плыть] (пла́ваю, пла́ваешь, пла́вают) Past: я/ты/он...пла́вал я/ты/она́...пла́вала мы/вы/они́...пла́вали	Зи́та **пла́вает** ка́ждый день. Zita **swims** every day. В пя́тницу Джордж и Том мно́го **пла́вали**. On Friday George and Tom **swam** a lot.

When used in the future, these verbs operate like other imperfective verbs by using the conjugated forms of the verb быть + **the infinitive form of the indeterminate motion verb**:

Я бу́ду/Ты бу́дешь/Они́ бу́дут	ходи́ть е́здить бе́гать лета́ть	I/you/they will	go (on foot) go (by vehicle) run fly

Determinate (Unidirectional) verbs of motion Determinate verbs of motion are often referred to as *unidirectional*: motion towards *one* specific or determined destination. When used without a prefix, these verbs are always imperfective in aspect. When the verb is one that requires movement by vehicle, the form of transport is conveyed by using the preposition на + **the prepositional case**: Мы е́дем в Чика́го на авто́бусе (на маши́не, на по́езде, на мотоци́кле). (We are going to Chicago by bus/by car/by train/by motorcycle.)

REFERENCE TABLE 7M: COMMON DETERMINATE VERBS OF MOTION

Unidirectional verb	Example usage
идти́ (to go by foot; to walk) (иду́, идёшь, иду́т) Past: я/ты/он...шёл я/ты/она́...шла мы/вы/они́...шли	Куда́ ты **идёшь**? — Я **иду́** на стадио́н. Where are you **going**? -- I'm **going** to the stadium. Когда́ я ви́дел её, она́ **шла** домо́й. When I saw her, she **was walking** home.
е́хать (to go by vehicle) (е́ду, е́дешь, е́дут) Past: я/ты/он...е́хал я/ты/она́...е́хала мы/вы/они́...е́хали	Мы сейча́с **е́дем** в Чика́го. We're now **going** to Chicago. Они́ **е́хали** в магази́н, пото́м в кафе́. They **were going** to the store, then to a cafe.
бежа́ть (to run) (бегу́, бежи́шь, бегу́т) Past: я/ты/он...бежа́л я/ты/она́...бежа́ла мы/вы/они́...бежа́ли	Ребя́та, вы куда́ **бежи́те**? Where are you guys **running** off to? Марк **бежа́л** пять киломе́тров в 15 мину́т. Mark **ran** five kilometers in 15 minutes.
лете́ть (to fly) (лечу́, лети́шь, летя́т) Past: я/ты/он...лете́л я/ты/она́...лете́ла мы/вы/они́...лете́ли	На́ши друзья́ **летя́т** в Лос-Анжелес. Our friends **are flying** to Los Angeles. Мой брат уже́ **лете́л** в Са́нта-Ба́рбару. My brother already **flew** to Santa Barbara.
плыть (to swim, float) (плыву́, плывёшь, плыву́т) Past: я/ты/он...плыл я/ты/она́...плыла́ мы/вы/они́...плы́ли	Ребя́та сейча́с **плыву́т** че́рез ре́ку. The kids are now **swimming** across the river. Мы ви́дели, как Аня **плыла́** на бе́рег. We saw how Anya **swam** to the bank (of a river or lake).

In future tense, determinate verbs normally become **perfective** in aspect by adding a prefix. (See the section below on prefixed verbs of motion.) If the speaker wishes to stress **the process** of the one-way action (e.g., *while I will be flying to Chicago*), then the conjugated forms of the verb быть + **the infinitive forms of the determinate verb** may be used, as with other imperfective verbs in the future tense:

Я бу́ду/Ты бу́дешь/Они́ бу́дут	идти́ е́хать бежа́ть лете́ть	I/you/they will be	walking riding running flying

7.60 VERBS OF MOTION ИДТИ-ЕХАТЬ
  Function: Going places

Face to Face L 1 Chapter 12 A Pages 243-247

The verbs of motion идти́ (to go by foot) and е́хать (to go by vehicle) generally describe one-way motion towards a specific destination (unidirectional or determinate). Both verbs are of the first conjugation pattern. They include a consonant stem change (the consonant -д- is added to the stem, and the endings -у/-ут are used with the я and они́ forms).

	идти́ (to go by foot)		е́хать (to go by vehicle)
я	иду́	я	е́ду
ты	идёшь	ты	е́дешь
он/а́	идёт	он/а́	е́дет
мы	идём	мы	е́дем
вы	идёте	вы	е́дете
они́	иду́т	они́	е́дут

Sample sentences

— Куда́ ты идёшь?*   **Where** are you **going**?

— Я иду́ в шко́лу.   I am **going** to school. (on foot)

— Они́ е́дут домо́й.   They are **going/driving** home.

— Вы е́дете в шко́лу?   Are you **going/driving** to school?

*Note: Куда́ (where) is used to ask the destination toward which someone is going. Где (where) is used to describe the location of objects.

Куда́ она́ идёт? В шко́лу.   (To) Where is she going? To school.

Где она́? В шко́ле.   Where is she? At school.

7.61 **THE VERBS OF MOTION** ХОДИ́ТЬ/Е́ЗДИТЬ, СХОДИ́ТЬ/СЪЕ́ЗДИТЬ ***Function:*** Relating activities and impressions	Face to Face L 2 Chapter 11 B, D Pages 233-235, 240-241

Just as the determinate verbs **идти́** and **е́хать** mean *to go by foot* and *to go by vehicle*, respectively, so do the two-way/indeterminate verbs **ходи́ть** and **е́здить** mean the same things. These indeterminate, or multidirectional, verbs can be used without a prefix, depending on the type of action one would like to specify. For many general, everyday actions, these verbs are used without a prefix:

Ма́ше всего́ шесть лет и уже́ **хо́дит** в   Masha is only six years old and already
шко́лу.   **goes** to school.

Ка́ждый год мы **е́здим** в Калифо́рнию   Every year we **go** to California or to New
или Нью-Йо́рк.   York.

Indeterminate—*two-way*   Determinate—*one-way*

ходи́ть (хожу́, хо́дишь, хо́дят)   идти́ (иду, идёшь, иду́т)

е́здить (е́зжу, е́здишь, е́здят)   е́хать (е́ду, е́дешь, е́дут)

All these verbs have regular past tense endings except for **идти́**:

Masculine:	я/ты/он	шёл
Neuter:	оно́	шло
Feminine:	я/ты/она́	шла
Plural:	мы/вы/они́	шли

The verb **е́здить** corresponds to **ходи́ть** (two-way) the same way **е́хать** corresponds to **идти́** (one-way). Note the difference between **determinate** and **indeterminate** verbs:

Determinate (unidirectional) идти, ехать

1)   Action happening now, in a definite direction.

Куда́ ты **идёшь/е́дешь**? Where are you **going**?

2)   One-way motion to a particular destination on a specific occasion:

Я **иду́/е́ду** в музе́й.   I am **going** to the museum.

Indeterminate (multidirectional) ходить, ездить

1)   Motion somewhere and back (a round-trip):

Вчера́ я **ходи́ла/е́здила** в теа́тр.   Yesterday I went to the theater.

2)   Motion without any particular destination; walking or driving for its own sake:

Я люблю́ **ходи́ть/е́здить** по го́роду. I like **to walk/drive** around town.

3)   Simple indication of motion or merely the ability to move:

Ребёнок уже́ хорошо́ **хо́дит**.   The child already **walks** well.
Я ещё пло́хо **е́зжу** на маши́не.   I still **drive** badly.

The verbs **ходи́ть** and **е́здить** are often used with words denoting frequency of action, such as **ча́сто, всегда́, никогда́, ре́дко, иногда́**, and other such words.

Sample sentences

А́нна **ча́сто хо́дит** в магази́н, но она́   Anna **often goes** to the store, but she
  ре́дко хо́дит в теа́тр.   **rarely goes** to the theatre.
На́ша семья́ **иногда́ е́здит** в Виско́нсин Our family **sometimes goes** to Wisconsin
  или Мичига́н на выходны́е дни.   or Michigan for the weekend.

7.62 **THE VERBS OF MOTION** ЛЕТА́ТЬ/ЛЕТЕ́ТЬ **IN THE PAST TENSE** *Function:* Talking about flying	Faces and Voices Chapter 3 A Pages 61-62

The verbs of motion **лета́ть/лете́ть** (to fly, to be flying) are used in the same way as **ходи́ть/идти́** and **е́здить/е́хать**. Usage of these verbs in the past and present tense denote connotations specific to indeterminate and determinate verbs.

REFERENCE TABLE 7N: PRESENT AND PAST TENSE USAGE OF UNPREFIXED VERBS OF MOTION

Indeterminate (multidirectional) летáть (I) (impf. летáю, летáешь, летáют)	Determinate (unidirectional) летéть (II) (impf. лечý, летúшь, летя́т)
Present tense	**Present tense**
1) **Movement in various directions.** В нéбе **летáют** птúцы. Birds **are flying about** in the sky.	1) **Movement in one direction.** Смотрú: птúцы **летя́т** на юг. Look! The birds **are flying** south.
2) **Repeated movement in one direction. A round-trip is assumed.** Самолёты из Балтимóра в Сан-Франци́ско **летáют** кáждый день. Planes **fly** from Baltimore to San Francisco everyday.	2) **Movement in one direction.** Самолёт в Сан-Франци́ско **летúт** ýтром. The plane to San Francisco **is flying** in the morning.
Past tense	**Past tense**
3) **Movement there and back (round-trip). Habitual or repeated motion.** — В прóшлом годý я **летáла** в Москвý (= былá в Москвé). Last year **I flew** to Moscow. (I am back home now.). — Лéтом я чáсто **летáл** в Москвý. During the summer I often **flew** to Moscow.	3) **Movement in one direction, viewed while in progress.** — Когдá я **летéла** в Москвý, я всё врéмя смотрéла в окнó. While/When I **was flying** to Moscow, I looked out the window the whole time.
4) **Naming an action. (Birds fly, people walk, fish swim.)** Волóдя хотéл **летáть** как птúца. Volodya wanted **to fly** like a bird.	

Transitive Verbs of Motion: 7.63-7.64

7.63 What are transitive verbs of motion? These verbs are also considered motion verbs, only *with the intention of bringing, carrying, or leading someone or something to a specific place.* Note the following:

- All of these verbs, like other motion verbs, have the destination in the accusative case. **Я несу́ портфе́ль в магази́н.** (I'm carrying the briefcase *into the store.*) If something is being carried or brought to a person, that person is in the dative case: **Я несу́ торт Алику и Ма́ше.** (I'm bringing the cake over *to Alik and Masha's.*)
- They use the accusative case for the object being carried or brought (the direct object): **Я несу́ *торт, кни́гу.***
- They also take the same prefixes as the other motion verbs.
- The future tense is formed by using either the conjugated form of **быть + the infinitive verb form**, or, in the case of determinate transitive verbs, the perfective future when adding a prefix to the conjugated verb.

REFERENCE TABLE 70: COMMON TRANSITIVE VERBS OF MOTION

Action	Unidirectional verb	Multidirectional verb
to carry, take, bring (on foot)	**нести** (кого́, что) (несу́, несёшь, несу́т) Past: нёс, несла́, несли́	**носить** (кого́, что) (ношу́; но́сишь, но́сят) Past: носи́л/а/и
to carry, take, bring (by vehicle)	**везти** (кого́; что) (везу́, везёшь, везу́т) Past: вёз, везла́, везли́	**возить** (кого́, что) (вожу́, во́зишь, во́зят) Past: вози́л/а/и
to lead (on foot) to drive (a vehicle)	**вести** (кого́) (веду́, ведёшь, веду́т) Past: вёл, вела́, вели́	**водить** (что) вожу́, во́дишь, во́дят Past: води́л/а/и

7.64 TRANSITIVE VERBS OF MOTION: НОСИТЬ-НЕСТИ, ВОДИТЬ-ВЕСТИ, ВОЗИТЬ-ВЕЗТИ, ЛЕТАТЬ-ЛЕТЕТЬ, ПЛАВАТЬ-ПЛЫТЬ
Function: Moving, transporting, carrying, and leading objects and people

Мир русских
Lesson 4
Pages 120-126

Transitive verbs of motion denote the movement of both object and subject in space. Not only is the subject *going*, but it is *transporting, carrying,* or *leading* another person or thing. Compare transitive verbs of motion with intransitive:

Transitive Verbs of Motion: denote carrying, leading, transporting something or somone	**(Intransitive) Verbs of Motion:** denote motion, going
Она́ всегда́ **но́сит** с собо́й зонт. She always **carries** an umbrella with her.	Она́ **хо́дит** в кино́ ка́ждую суббо́ту. She **goes** to the movies every Saturday.
Мужчи́на **несёт** рюкза́к на спине́, а чемода́н в руке́. The man **is carrying** a backpack on his back and a suitcase in his hand.	Он **идёт** на вокза́л. He **is walking** to the train station.

Transitive verbs of motion form indeterminate (multidirectional) and determinate (unidirectional) pairs with the same usage as regular verbs of motion: **ходить** (indet.)/**идти** (det.) and **ездить** (indet.)/**ехать** (det.). The table below provides an overview of these verb pairs and expressions related to their usage.

REFERENCE TABLE 7P: TRANSITIVE VERBS OF MOTION AND RELATED EXPRESSIONS

Type	Transitive Verb		Related Expressions	
multidirectional (like **ходить**) unidirectional (like **идти**)	**носить** (ношу́, но́сишь, но́сят) **нести** (несу́, несёшь, несу́т)	to carry, transport while holding	**в руке́** in one's hand **в (пра́вой, ле́вой) руке́** in one's (right, left) hand	
	что? **кого́?**	what? whom?	**в рука́х** in one's hands	
	куда́? **по чему́?**	(to) where? along where?	**на руке́** on one's hand	
			на рука́х on/in one's arms	
			на спине́ on one's back	
			в зуба́х in one's teeth	
multidirectional (like **ездить**) unidirectional (like **ехать**)	**возить** (вожу́, во́зишь, во́зят) **везти** (везу́, везёшь, везу́т)	to carry by vehicle, transport	**в коля́ске** in a/by stroller **на маши́не** by car	
			на велосипе́де by bike	
	что? **кого́?**	what? whom?		
	куда́? **по чему́?**	(to) where? along where?		
multidirectional unidirectional	**водить** (вожу́, во́дишь, во́дят) **вести** (веду́, ведёшь, веду́т)	to lead by the hand, take	**за́ руку** by the hand **за́ руки** by the hands	
			по́д руку (руки) by the arm, supporting some- one's arm	
	что? **кого́?**	what? whom?		
	куда́? **по чему́?**	(to) where? along where?	**маши́ну** (drive) a car	

Verbs with both intransitive and transitive usage:

multidirectional unidirectional	**лета́ть** (лета́ю, лета́ешь, лета́ют) **лети́ть** (лечу́, лети́шь, летя́т)	to fly or to be transported by air		
multidirectional unidirectional	**пла́вать** (пла́ваю, пла́ваешь, пла́вают) **плыть** (плыву́, плывёшь, плыву́т)	to swim or to be transported by ship or boat		

	Additional transitive verbs of motion which are encountered less frequently:	
multidirectional	катить (качу́, ка́тишь, ка́тят)	to take for a drive, roll, push (as on a swing)
unidirectional	ката́ть (ката́ю, ката́ешь, ката́ют)	
multidirectional	гоня́ть (гоня́ю, гоня́ешь, гоня́ют)	to herd, drive, chase, urge on
unidirectional	гнать (гоню́, го́нишь, го́нят)	
multidirectional	таска́ть (таска́ю, таска́ешь, таска́ют)	to drag, pull, haul
unidirectional	тащи́ть (тащу́, та́щишь, та́щат)	

Sample sentences

носи́ть/нести́

Он всегда́ **но́сит** с собо́й зонт.	He always **carries** an umbrella with him.
Оте́ц несёт ребёнка **на рука́х**.	The father **is carrying** the child **in his arms**.
Мужчи́на **несёт** рюкза́к на спине́, а чемода́н в руке́.	The man **is carrying** a backpack on his back and a suitcase in his hand.
Соба́ка **несёт** кость **в зуба́х**.	The dog **is carrying** a bone **between his teeth (in his mouth)**.

во́зит/везти́

Ма́ма ча́сто **во́зит** дочь в парк в коля́ске.	The mother often **takes** her daughter to the park in a stroller.
Ма́ма **везёт** дочь в парк **в коля́ске**.	The mother **is taking** her daughter to the park **in the stroller**.
Роди́тели **во́зят** сы́на в шко́лу **на маши́не**.	The parents **take** their son to school **by car**.
Я **везу́** бра́та домо́й **на мотоци́кле**.	I'm **taking** my brother home **by motorcycle**.

води́ть/вести́

Молодо́й оте́ц **во́дит** дочь в де́тский сад ка́ждый день.	The young father **takes** his daughter to kindergarten every day.
Ма́ма **ведёт** дочь в де́тский сад.	The mother **is taking** her daughter to kindergarten.
Же́нщина **вела́** ребёнка **за́ руку**.	The woman **was leading** the child **by the hand**.
Ты уме́ешь **води́ть** маши́ну?	Do you know how **to drive** a car?

летáть/летéть

Я **летáю** на юг два рáза в год.

Турúсты сейчáс **летя́т** в Москвý.

I **fly** to the South twice a year.

The tourists are now **flying** to Moscow.

плáвать/плыть

Пассажúры **плáвают на парахóде** от Санкт-Петербýрга до Хельсúнки кáждую недéлю.

Тётя **плывёт** в Волгогрáд на теплохóде.

The passengers **travel (by boat)** from St. Petersburg to Helsinki every week.

My aunt is **going** to Volgograd by ship.

Prefixed Verbs of Motion: Grammar Points 7.65-7.72

7.65 What are prefixed verbs of motions? By adding a prefix to a verb of motion, the movement gains additional meaning. The verb's conjugation stays the same, whether in the past, present or future tense. When a prefix is added to a determinate verb, that verb becomes **perfective**, and can only be used in the past or future tenses. One prefix may also have different meanings, depending on whether it is used with a determinate or indeterminate verb. A prefixed determinate verb is perfective and therefore indicates only a one-time action; a prefixed indeterminate verb remains imperfective and refers to actions that occur more than once.

REFERENCE TABLE 7Q: COMMON PREFIXES AND MEANINGS WHEN USED WITH VERBS OF MOTION (INDETERMINATE/DETERMINATE)

Prefix	ходúть/идтú	éздить/éхать	бéгать/бежáть	летáть/летéть
по- to set off (uni); to do s.t. a little (multi)	похoдúть to walk around a little bit пойтú to set off	поéздить to drive, ride around a little поéхать to set off (by vehicle)	побéгать to run around a little побежáть to take off running	полетáть to fly around a little bit полетéть to set off flying
при- to arrive	приходúть/ прийтú to arrive on foot	приезжáть/ приéхать to arrive (by vehicle)	прибéгать/ прибежáть to arrive running	прилетáть/ прилетéть to arrive flying
у- to leave	уходúть/уйтú to leave, go away on foot	уезжáть/ уéхать to leave by vehicle, go far away, emigrate	убéгать/убежáть to run away	улетáть/улетéть to fly away
до- to go as far as	доходúть/ дойтú to get to, as far as	доезжáть/ доéхать to go as far as (by vehicle)	добéгать/ добежáть to get to, as far as, by running	долетáть/ долетéть to get to, as far as, by flying
в(о,ъ)- to enter (into enclosed space); to go into	входúть/ войтú to enter, come into (a room, building, etc.)	въезжáть/ въéхать to drive, ride, go into (a garage, etc.) by vehicle; hit s.t. with a vehicle	вбéгать/вбежáть to run into; to go into by running	влетáть/влетéть to fly into; to into by flying

REFERENCE TABLE 7Q: COMMON PREFIXES AND MEANINGS WHEN USED WITH VERBS OF MOTION (INDETERMINATE/DETERMINATE) (cont.)

вы- to exit; to leave (an enclosed space)	выходи́ть/ вы́йти to exit, leave (a room, building, etc.)	выезжа́ть/ вы́ехать to drive, ride, go out of (garage, etc.)	выбега́ть/ вы́бежать to run out; go out by running	вылета́ть/ вы́лететь to fly out; go out by flying; take off (by plane)
про- to go through, across	проходи́ть/ пройти́ to walk through; to undergo s.t.; to walk by s.t.	проезжа́ть/ прое́хать to drive, ride through or by s.t.	пробега́ть/ пробежа́ть to run through, by, across	пролета́ть/ пролете́ть to pass through or by while flying

7.66 VERBS OF MOTION WITH THE PREFIXES В-, ВЫ-, ПРИ-, У-

Function: Expressing motion in, out, arriving, and away

Мир русских
Lesson 4
Pages 126-131

The addition of prefixes to verbs of motion adds additional connotations to their meaning and creates verbal aspectual pairs from these verbs. Four basic prefixes, their connotations, and the resultant verbal aspect is outlined below.

When using prefixed verbs of motion, observe the following:

- **new meanings and connotations are created**
- **verbal aspectual pairs are formed (imperfective/perfective)**
- **spelling and stress changes occur**

Basic Russian prefixes and their meanings

в- motion into

e.g. входи́ть — to enter (on foot)
въезжа́ть — to drive into
вноси́ть — to carry into

вы- motion out of, out from

e.g. вы́йти — to exit (on foot)
вы́ехать — to drive out of
вы́нести — to carry out of

при- arriving, bringing

e.g. приходи́ть — to arrive (on foot)
приезжа́ть — to arrive
приноси́ть — to bring (by hand)

у- leaving, motion away

e.g. уйти́ — to leave (on foot)
уе́хать — to leave
унести́ — to take/carry away

Она́ **вошла́** в ко́мнату. — She **entered** the room.
Он **вы́шел** на пять мину́т. — He **left (stepped out)** for five minutes.
Ба́бушка **принесла́** мой обе́д. — My Grandmother **brought** my lunch.
Они́ **уе́хали** на ле́то. — They **left** for the summer.

Basic formation of verbal aspect pairs with prefixes

Indeterminate verbs of motion are also called *multidirectional verbs* (movement there and back, round-trip, wandering, many directions)	Determinate verbs of motion are also called *unidirectional verbs* (one-way, toward one direction, single destination, result still in effect)
prefix + indeterminate verb **Imperfective**	**prefix + determinate verb** **Perfective**
ходи́ть е́здить бе́гать лета́ть + *prefix remain imperfective:*	идти́ е́хать бежа́ть лете́ть + *prefix become perfective:*
входи́ть to walk/go into выезжа́ть to leave by vehicle убега́ть to run away прилета́ть to arrive by plane	войти́ to walk/go into вы́ехать to leave by vehicle убежа́ть to run away прилете́ть to arrive by plane

Spelling and stress changes

1) When adding a prefix to the verb of motion **е́здить**, a *stress shift* and a *consonant change* occur: -езжа́ть **(д>ж)**:

    въезжа́ть
    выезжа́ть
    приезжа́ть
    уезжа́ть

2) The stem of the verb **идти́** changes in two ways:
- with prefixes ending in a *consonant*, the stem is **-ойти́**:

      войти́
      обойти́ (to walk around/avoid something)

- with prefixes ending in a *vowel*, the stem is **-йти́**:

      вы́йти
      прийти́
      уйти́

3) Before the verb **е́хать**, if a prefix ends in a *consonant*, a hard sign (**ъ**) is placed before the verb:

    въе́хать
    объе́хать (to drive around/avoid something)

4) The prefix **вы-** in *perfective verbs* is always stressed:

    выноси́ть/**вы́**нести
    вылета́ть/**вы́**лететь
    выезжа́ть/**вы́**ехать

Prefixed Verbs of Motion and their use with prepositions

The prefix в- The prefix **в-** with verbs of motion denotes movement *into*. It is commonly used with the preposition **в + accusative case** *to name a destination.*

| Он **вхо́дит в** шко́лу. | He **is entering** the school. *(imperfective verb)* |
| Он **вошёл в** шко́лу. | He **went into** the school. *(perfective verb)* |

The prefix вы- The prefix **вы-** is the exact opposite of the prefix **в-**. It denotes motion *from within* or *out of*. Вы- also denotes departure/exiting *for a short time with an expected return*. It is frequently used with the preposition **из + genitive case** *to name the place from which* a person exited or left. It may be used with the prepositions **в** and **на + accusative case** *to name the destination to which one exited*.

Ка́ждое у́тро он **выхо́дит** из до́ма в 8 часо́в.	Every morning he **leaves** the house at 8 o'clock. *(imperfective verb)*
Я **вы́шел** из ко́мнаты в коридо́р.	I **went out** of the room **into** the hall. *(perfective verb)*

The prefix при- The prefix **при-** with verbs of motion denotes the accomplishment of movement *towards* (e.g., arrival, approach). Prepositions commonly used with these prefixed verbs include the prepositions **в** and **на + accusative case** *to name the destination of motion towards* and **к + dative case** *to name a person to which one goes*.

Он **прихо́дит** к нам ка́ждый день.	He **comes** to see us every day. *(imperfective verb)*
Я **пришёл** в шко́лу во́время (**на** конце́рт, **к** дру́гу).	I **arrived** at school on time (at the concert, at a friend's). *(perfective verb)*

The prefix у- The prefix **у-** is the opposite of **при-** and denotes movement *away from, leaving*. У- denotes *departure for a long time*. It is most frequently used with the following prepositions:

из + genitive case *to denote motion away from a destination*
Use **из** with destinations that require the preposition **в** when expressing motion to:

> *remember:*
> # В ИЗ

Я **ушла́** из шко́лы в два часа́. I **left school** at two o'clock.	Я **вошла́** в шко́лу в во́семь часо́в. I **entered school** at eight o'clock.
Она́ ча́сто **ухо́дит из до́ма** и до́лго гуля́ет по у́лицам го́рода. She frequently **leaves home** and walks the streets of the town for a long time.	Она́ обы́чно **вхо́дит в дом** в пять. She usually **enters the house** at five.

с + genitive case *to denote motion away from a destination*
Use **с** with destinations that require the preposition **на** when expressing motion to:

> *remember:*
> # на с

Она́ **ушла́ с конце́рта** и пошла́ домо́й. She **left the concert** and went home.	Она́ **пошла́ на конце́рт**. She went to the concert.
Уходя́ с вы́ставки, она́ ду́мала о карти́нах. As she **was leaving the exhibition**, she thought about the pictures.	Она́ ча́сто **хо́дит на вы́ставки**. She often **goes to** exhibitions.

от + genitive case *to denote motion way from a destination or person*

Use **от** with nouns that require the preposition **к** when expressing motion to:

remember:

К ОТ

Она́ **ушла́ от дру́га** и пошла́
    в магази́н.
She **left her friend** and went to
    the store.

Она́ обы́чно **уезжа́ет от роди́телей**
    по воскресе́ньям верну́ться домо́й.
She usually **leaves her parents** on
    Sunday to return home.

Она́ **зашла́ к дру́гу**.
She **dropped in at her friend's.**

Она́ обы́чно **уезжа́ет к роди́телям**
    по суббо́там.
She usually **leaves for her parents'**
    on Saturdays.

All of the above prefixes can be used with transitive verbs of motion. For example:

Стол **внесли́ в** ко́мнату.

They **carried** the table **into** the room.

Стол **вы́несли из** ко́мнаты.

They carried the table out of the room.

Па́па **приво́дит** дочь **в** шко́лу ка́ждый день.

Dad **takes** his daughter **to** school every day.

Па́па **приво́зит** дочь **в** шко́лу на маши́не.

Dad **takes** his daughter **to** school in the car.

Па́па всегда́ **уно́сит** кни́ги домо́й.

The father always **takes** books home.

Начало́сь ле́то, и всех дете́й **увезли́ на** мо́ре.

The summer began and all the children were **taken to** the sea.

Sample sentences

в-/вы-

Уро́к ко́нчился, и шко́льники **вы́шли** из кла́сса.	The lesson ended, and the students **left** the classroom.
Когда́ нас не́ было, кто́-то **входи́л** в ко́мнату.	When we weren't here, someone **entered** the room (but he's gone now).
Откры́лась дверь и **вбежа́л** брат.	The door opened, and my brother **ran in**.
Самолёт **вы́летел** с аэродро́ма в семь часо́в.	The plane **left** the airport at seven o'clock.
Мы **въе́хали** в лес и сра́зу уви́дели большо́го медве́дя.	We **drove into** the forest and immediately saw a large bear.
Она́ вы́ключила ра́дио и **вышла́** из ко́мнаты.	She turned off the radio and **left** the room.
Маши́на **въе́хала** во двор и останови́лась.	The car **drove into** the yard and came to a stop.
Когда́ ты звони́л мне, меня́ не́ было в ко́мнате: я **вы́шла** в коридо́р.	When you phoned me, I wasn't in the room. I had **stepped out** into the hall.
Окна́ откры́ли, и пти́ца **вы́летела** на у́лицу.	They opened the windows, and the bird **flew** outside.

при-/у-

Когда́ я позвони́л, друг уже́ **ушёл** из до́ма.	When I called, my friend had already **left** home.
За́втра у нас на уро́к **приду́т** шко́льники из Росси́и.	Tomorrow students from Russia **will visit** us in class.
Ле́том меня́ не́ было в Москве́: я **уезжа́л** в дере́вню.	I was not in Moscow during the summer. I **went** to the countryside.
Во вре́мя кани́кул ко мне в го́сти **приезжа́ла** сестра́.	During the holidays my sister **came** to visit me (but she's gone now).
Зимо́й э́ти пти́цы не быва́ют у нас: они́ **улета́ют** в жа́ркие стра́ны.	During the winter we don't have birds. They **fly off** to warm countries.
Дру́га не́ было до́ма: он **ушёл** в шко́лу.	My friend wasn't home. He **had left** for school.
Мы не поговори́ли с Са́шей, потому́ что он **уходи́л** в шко́лу.	We didn't speak with Sasha because he **was leaving** for school (he was in the process of heading off).
Ле́том я **уе́ду** на мо́ре отдыха́ть.	During the summer **I'll go** to the sea to relax.
Иногда́ дельфи́ны **припла́вают** на бе́рег и мо́жно их уви́деть .	Sometimes dolphins **swim** to the shore, and it is possible to catch a glimpse of them.

7.67 VERBS OF MOTION WITH THE PREFIX ПРИ-
Function: Asking and telling where one is from

> Face to Face L 2
> Chapter 1 A, D
> Pages 21-22, 31

The prefix **при-** added to a verb of motion denotes the meaning *reaching a final goal* or *arrival at a desination*. This can also change the **aspect** of the verb. When a prefix is added to a determinate verb, the verb becomes **perfective**. The perfective verbs can be used only in the past and future tenses. When this occurs, a result or completed action is emphasized.

Unprefixed determinate verb **IMPERFECTIVE** éхать	Prefixed determinate verb **PERFECTIVE** при- + ехать = приéхать
Present tense--Imperfective Лариса сейчáс **идёт** в шкóлу. Larisa is now **walking** to school.	**Future--Perfective** Лариса **придёт** в шкóлу в 8 часóв. Larisa **will arrive** at school at eight o'clock.
Past tense--Imperfective Я видел, как Лариса **шла** в шкóлу. I saw Larisa walking to school.	**Past tense--Perfective** Лариса **пришлá** в шкóлу. Larisa arrived at/is at school.

The prefix -при is also used to talk about *direction from a place*.

Sample sentences

Откýда вы **приéхали**?	Where did you **come** from?
Мы **приéхали** из Вашингтóна.	We **came** from Washington.
Откýда вы?	Where are you from?
Я **из** Амéрики.	I'm **from** America.

7.68 THE VERBAL PREFIX ПО- *Function:* Discussing an activity of short duration	Face to Face L 2 Chapter 12 A, D Pages 249-250, 268

The prefix по- + **indeterminate verbs** (ходúть, éздить, etc.) implies that *an activity or action will be of short duration*. This prefixed verb often utilizes the preposition **по + the dative case** to indicate *the location where the activity or motion takes place*.

Sample sentences

| Вúтя и Кáтя бы́ли в Вашингтóне и немнóго **походúли по** цéнтру гóрода. | Vitya and Katya were in Washington and **walked around the center of town (downtown)** a little bit. |
| Марúя и Джéннифер **поéздили по** Лос-Анжелесу и мнóго вúдели. | Maria and Jennifer **drove around Los Angeles** a little and saw a lot (of things). |

It is also possible to combine indeterminate and determinate verbs in the same sentence:

| Вúтя и Кáтя немнóго **походúли по** цéнтру и потóм **пошлú** в музéй.* | Vitya and Katya **walked around downtown a little bit** and then **went** to the museum. |

*Note: Strolling around (indeterminate—походúть) and then having an intention to go somewhere on purpose (determinate—пойтú).

When the verbal prefix по- is used with regular verbs, other than verbs of motion, it adds the connotation *to perform some action for a short period of time*.

Sample sentences

Мне о́чень нра́вится э́то ме́сто. Я хоте́л бы здесь ещё **погуля́ть**.	I really like this place. I'd like **to walk around** here a little bit more.
Дава́й **поигра́ем** в ша́хматы.	**Let's play a little** chess.

7.69 VERBS OF MOTION WITH THE PREFIXES ДО-, ПРО-
(ДОЙТИ/ДОЕХАТЬ, ПРОЙТИ/ПРОЕХАТЬ)
Function: Asking and giving directions

> Face to Face L 2
> Chapter 6 B
> Pages 119-123,
> 135-136

Prefixed verbs of motion with the prefixes **до-** and **про-** express the ideas *to reach, get to, go as far as* when used in questions of location and direction. Each prefixed verb of motion takes a specific preposition and case when a place or location is named.

доéхать/дойти́ до + genitive case of destination
Sample sentences

Извини́те, как **дойти́/доéхать до**	Excuse me, **how do (I) get to**
Кра́сной пло́щади?	Red Square (from here)?
гости́ницы «Росси́я»?	the Hotel "Russia"?
Пу́шкинского музе́я?	the Pushkin Museum?
шко́лы № 156?	School #156?
Тве́рской у́лицы?	Tverskaya Street?

проéхать/пройти́ в/на + accusative case of destination
Sample sentences

Извини́те, как **пройти́/проéхать**	Excuse me, **how do (I) get to**
на Кра́сную пло́щадь?	Red Square (from here)?
в гости́ницу «Росси́я»?	hotel "Russia"?
в Пу́шкинский музе́й?	Pushkin museum?
в шко́лу № 156?	School #156?
на Тве́рскую у́лицу?	Tverskaya Street?

The conjugations of the unidirectional verbs of motion **идти́** and **éхать** with the prefixes **до-** and **про-** are presented. Note that these prefixed verbs are perfective and conjugate the same way as their unprefixed equivalents.

Prefective future

	Motion verb	до-	про-
я	иду́/éду	дойду́/доéду	пройду́/проéду
ты	идёшь/éдешь	дойдёшь/доéдешь	пройдёшь/проéдешь
он/а́	идёт/éдет	дойдёт/доéдет	пройдёт/проéдет
мы	идём/éдем	дойдём/доéдем	пройдём/проéдем
вы	идёте/éдете	дойдёте/доéдете	пройдёте/проéдете
они́	иду́т/éдут	дойду́т/доéдут	пройду́т/проéдут

Past

я, ты, он	шёл/éхал	дошёл/доéхал	прошёл/проéхал
я, ты, она́	шла/éхала	дошла́/доéхала	прошла́/проéхала
мы, вы, они́	шли/éхали	дошли́/доéхали	прошли́/проéхали

7.70 THE VERBS OF MOTION ХОДИ́ТЬ/ЕЗДИТЬ,
СХОДИ́ТЬ/СЪЕ́ЗДИТЬ
Function: Relating activities and impressions

Face to Face L 2
Chapter 11 B, D
Pages 233-235,
240-241

There are several specific cases in which adding a prefix to an indeterminate verb creates a perfective verb*. When the prefix **с(ъ)-** is added to either the indeterminate verb **ходи́ть** or **е́здить**, these verbs become perfective. The meaning of the verbs **сходи́ть** and **съе́здить** is *to make a quick round trip.*

Perfectives сходи́ть and съе́здить
Sample sentences

Е́сли ты здесь ещё бу́дешь, я тогда́ бы́стро **схожу́** в э́тот магази́н.	If you will still be here, **I will run** to the store. (very quick round-trip, not an habitual action)
Я хочу́ сего́дня днём **съе́здить** на Арба́т: там есть, что посмотре́ть.	I want **to take a quick trip** to the Arbat this afternoon: there's something worth seeing there.
Сходи́ в магази́н и купи́ хле́ба.	**Run down** to the store and buy some bread.

*****Note:** The prefixe **за-** when used to convey the meaning *to begin an action*, forms perfective verbs from indeterminate verbs of motion: **Он заходи́л по ко́мнате.** He **began walking** about the room.

7.71 THE PREFIX ЗА- WITH VERBS OF MOTION
Function: Expressing "to drop in", "along the way," motion behind

Мир ру́сских
Lesson 5
Pages 157-159

The prefix **за-** with verbs of motion denotes several meanings:

1) Motion into or dropping in along the way (usually short term):

Sample sentences

По доро́ге в институ́т я **зашёл** в магази́н. (Шёл в институ́т и по доро́ге **зашёл** в магази́н).	On the way to the institute I **dropped by** a store. (I was on my way to the institute and on the way **went into** a store.)
Я ча́сто **захожу́** на по́чту (к дру́гу).	I often **drop by** the post office (by my friend's).
По доро́ге домо́й я **зашла́** за* хле́бом.	On the way home I **stopped** for bread.

*****Note:** The preposition **за** has the meaning "for" (to get or fetch) when used with a verb of motion and followed by a noun in the instrumental case.

Like other prefixed indeterminate verbs, **заходи́ть** (to stop by) is used to describe a side trip completed in both directions, while the prefixed determinate verb, **зайти́**, is used for a side trip still in effect.

Вади́м **зашёл** к И́нне.	Vadim stopped by Inna's. (He is still there.)
Вади́м **заходи́л** к И́нне.	Vadim stopped by Inna's. (He was there, but left.)

2)   Motion behind an object:

Sample sentences: зайти за + accusative

Со́лнце **зашло́ за ту́чу**.	The sun **went behind a cloud**.
Со́лнце **захо́дит за ту́чи**.	The sun **is going behind the clouds**.

3)   The beginning of an action, when combined with a multidirectional verb (resulting verb then becomes perfective):

Sample sentences

В попы́тке найти́ вку́сное моро́женое он **зае́здил** по го́роду на па́пиной маши́не.	In an attempt to find some good ice cream, **he began** driving all around town in his dad's car.

Other (idiomatic) meanings of motion verbs with the prefix за-
Sample sentences

заводи́ть/завести́ часы́	to wind up a watch
заводи́ть/завести́...семью́, де́ло, ссо́ру, разгово́р, знако́мство	to start up a...family, business, quarrel, conversation, acquaintance
заводи́ть/завести́ привы́чку	to start a habit (of doing something)
завози́ть/завезти́ (что, кого́) (куда́)	to drop off (something/someone) somewhere along the way
заноси́ть/занести́	to record, register
заходи́ть/зайти́ сли́шком далеко́	to go too far

7.72 THE PREFIXES ОТ- AND ПОД- WITH VERBS OF MOTION *Function:* Expressing motion away and toward	Мир ру́сских Lesson 7 Pages 225-227

The prefix **от-** with verbs of motion denotes *movement away from something or someone, frequently only a short distance away.*

отходи́ть/отойти́	**от + genitive**	to walk away (from)
отбега́ть/отбежа́ть		to run away (from)
отплыва́ть/отплы́ть		to swim, sail away

Sample sentences

Она́ **отошла́ от карти́ны** и посмотре́ла на неё ещё раз.	She **stepped away from the picture** and looked at it once more.
По́езд «Кра́сная стрела́» всегда́ **отхо́дит** в 23.55.	The "Red Arrow" train always **leaves** (the station) at 11:55 p.m.

The prefix **под-** has a meaning opposite to that of **от-**, such as *to approach or move towards*:

подходи́ть/подойти́	**к + dative**	to walk up (to)
подбега́ть/подбежа́ть		to run up (to)
подплыва́ть/подплы́ть		to swim, sail up (to)

Sample sentences

Николай попрощался и отошёл от меня. Через минуту он **подошёл к какой-то девушке**.	Nicholas said goodbye and walked away from me. A minute later **he had approached some girl**.
Как только отплыл один корабль, **подплыл** другой.	Just as soon as one ship left, **another approached**.

Note the following points on usage with these prefixed verbs:

1)   The prepositions usually used with these prefixes are:

подойти к окну (**к + dative**)	to walk up to the window
отойти от окна (**от + genitive**)	to walk away from the window

2)   Transitive verbs of motion are also used with these prefixes. These verbs require both a direct object and the stated destination or place to which someone or something is taken.

относить/отнести	to take/carry away (to)
отвозить/отвезти	to drive away (to)
отводить/отвести	to lead away (to)

Sample sentences

Мальчик прочитал книгу и **отнёс её в библиотеку**.	The boy read the book and **returned it to the library**.
Фермер уже **отвёз стадо от пастбища и на другое ранчо**.	The farmer already **drove the herd away from the pasture and to another ranch**.

3)   Prefixed indeterminate verbs of motion (like **подходить**) are imperfective and denote motion to something or someone and then away from it (or them).

Sample sentences

— Кто это **подходил** к тебе?	"Who **walked up** to you?"
— Это был мой друг. (motion up to a person and then away from him)	"That was my friend."

Other (idiomatic) uses of going verbs with от-, под-
Sample phrases

отводить/отвести глаза	take one's eyes off (something/one)
отводить/отвести обвинение	to reject an accusation
отводить/отвести душу	to unburden one's heart, soul
отходить/отойти...от...темы, оригинала, обычая	to deviate/digress...from...the topic, original, tradition
подводить/подвести (кого)	to undermine, let someone down
подводить/подвести часы	to change one's watch
подводить баланс	to balance (financial) accounts
подвести баланс	to strike a balance
подходить/подойти	to be suitable
подходить/подойти к концу, вопросу	to approach...the end, a question

Impersonal Constructions

7.73 What are impersonal constructions? Impersonal constructions generally take a logical subject in the dative case to describe a mental or physical state of being, or when speaking about clothing, or to state how something fits. The logical subject is in the dative case, rather than the nominative.

Regular construction (logical subject in nominative case):	**Impersonal construction** (logical subject in dative case)
Я люблю́ те́ннис и борьбу́. I like/love tennis and wrestling.	**Мне нра́вится** те́ннис и борьба́. **I like** tennis and wrestling.
Я ду́маю, что э́то краси́вый сви́тер. I think that's a beautiful sweater.	**Мне ка́жется**, что э́то краси́вый сви́тер. **It seems to me** that that's a beautiful sweater.
Я сего́дня до́лжен (должна́) занима́ться аэро́бикой. I have to do aerobics today.	Мне сего́дня **прихо́дится/ придётся** занима́ться аэро́бикой. **I absolutely have to** do aerobics today. (no choice involved)
Я хочу́ есть пи́ццу и спаге́тти. I want to eat pizza and spaghetti.	**Мне хо́чется** есть пи́ццу и спаге́тти. **I would like** to eat pizza and spaghetti.

Physical or mental state When describing a mental or physical state, the impersonal construction can be used without a verb, since the verb is understood. Often the logical subject in the dative is used with an adverb, as in the second example:

| Ну, как вам Аме́рика? | Well, what do you think of America? (lit., *How for you is America?*) |
| Мне здесь о́чень хо́лодно. | I'm very cold here. (lit., *To me here is very cold.*) |

Speaking about fit or clothing When speaking about clothing, the third person forms of the verb **идти́** are used with the logical subject in the dative:

| Тебе́ идёт э́тот сви́тер. | That sweater looks good on you. |
| Мне́ не иду́т э́ти джи́нсы. | These jeans don't look good on me. |

Use with reflexive verbs Often impersonal constructions are used with reflexive -ся verbs to indicate a desire or that the speaker likes something:

| Ему́ хо́чется есть. | He would like to eat. (*instead of* Он хо́чет есть.) |
| Им нра́вится э́то ме́сто. | They like this place. |

REFERENCE TABLE 7R: COMMON IMPERSONAL CONSTRUCTIONS

Logical subject in dative		+ impersonal construction:	
Мне	I am...	хóлодно.	cold.
Тебé	You are...	теплó.	warm.
Емý/Ей	He/She is...	хорошó.	good (doing well).
Нам	We are...	плóхо.	bad (doing badly).
Вам	You are...	скýчно.	bored.
Им...	They are...	интерéсно.	interested.
Ивáну	Ivan is...	любопы́тно.	curious.
Мáше	Masha...	хóчется.	would like, want(s).
Ли́нде	To Linda...	кáжется...	it seems...
Учи́телю...	The teacher...	нрáвится...	likes...; finds pleasing...

7.74 IMPERSONAL CONSTRUCTIONS (THE LOGICAL SUBJECT IN THE DATIVE).
Function: Review

Faces and Voices
Chapter 9 Г
Pages 249-250

Some verbs require that the logical subject appear in the dative case. The same is true of the verb **идти́** when it is used to tell whether clothing fits well or is flattering or suitable. The short-form adjectives **вели́к**, **мал**, **дли́нен**, and **кóроток** are also commonly used with the dative case, as are constructions which decribe a mental or physical state.

Sample sentences (logical subjects in dative)

Эта шля́па **мне нрáвится**, но, по-мóему, **мне не идёт**.	**I like** this hat, but I think **it doesn't suit me.**
Этот плащ **вели́к Антóну**, **мал Макси́му**, но **как раз Ви́ктору**.	This raincoat is **too big for Anton, too small for Maxim**, but **just right for Victor.**
Антóн болéл, у негó былá высóкая температýра, **емý бы́ло плóхо**.	Anton was sick, he had a high temperature, and **he felt bad.**
На ýлице морóз, пургá, **мне** óчень **хóлодно**.	Outside it's freezing, there's a blizzard, and **I am cold.**
Хорошó, когдá мы мóжем сказáть себé: «**Мне хорошó!** У меня́ всё хорошó в жи́зни!»	It's good when we can say to ourselves, **"I'm great!** Everything in my life is good!"
Ири́на сегóдня óчень счастли́вая, **ей хóчется** улыбáться всем лю́дям.	Irina is very happy today. **She feels like** smiling at everyone.

Subjunctive and Conditional Moods

7.75 What are the conditional and subjunctive moods? The conditional mood is a construction which *states an unreal condition*. The speaker indicates his/her desire for an action to occur, but also indicates that it is *a condition that is wished for, but not necessarily possible*. These constructions are similar to those in English (e.g., "If I had the time/money/ clothes, etc., I *would...*").

The conditional mood is formed with **the past tense form of the verb + бы**. This rule applies to both imperfective and perfective verbs:

I would...	Imperfective verb	Perfective verb
...take a shower.	принимáл/а бы душ.	принял/á бы...
...take the money.	брал/á бы дéньги.	взял/á бы...
...eat spaghetti.	éл/а бы спагéтти.	съéл/а бы...
...drink milk.	пил/á бы молокó.	вы́пил/а бы...
...fly to London.	летéл/а бы в Лóндон.	полетéл/а бы...
...buy a cake.	покупáл/а бы торт.	купи́л/а бы...
...see the stars.	ви́дел/а бы звёзды.	уви́дел/а бы...
...paint the house.	крáсил/а бы дом.	покрáсил/а бы...
...go to the movies.	шёл/шла бы в кинó.	пошёл/пошлá бы..
...play chess.	игрáл/а бы в шáхматы.	сыгрáл/а бы...

Russian expresses the subjunctive mood by the construction **чтóбы + the past tense of a verb**. Compare the following two sentences:

Я хочý бéгать.	I want to run.
Я хочý, **чтóбы вы бéгали**.	I want **you to run**.

Чтóбы is used only with verbs in the past tense, never with verbs in the present or future tenses. However, it can be used with the **infinitive** form if the action to be completed will be performed by the main subject/speaker. In this sense it is no longer a subjunctive, but a **purpose** clause; that is, it describes an action taken with the aim of achieving some desired result:

Я встал рáно, **чтóбы бéгать**.   I got up early so I could run.

7.76 **THE CONJUNCTION ЧТОБЫ AND THE PAST TENSE AFTER THE VERB ХОТЕТЬ. SUBJUNCTIVE MOOD**
Function: Saying what is desired of another person

Faces and Voices
Chapter 3 A
Pages 63-64

Use the following constructions to express *wanting to perform an action or wanting someone else to perform an action.*

If the subject of the sentence desires something for himself/herself/ themselves, the following construction is used:	If the subject of the sentence wishes that **someone else** perform an action, the following construction is used:

хотéть + infinitive

Я хочý стать лётчиком.
(Я хочý, и я стáну.)
I want to become a pilot.
(I want and I will become.)

Я хочý прочитáть этот ромáн.
(Я хочý и я прочитáю.)
I want to finish (reading) the novel.
(I want and I will read.)

Sample sentences

— Владúмир Николáевич, **мы хотúм, чтóбы вы рассказáли** нам о сéвере.
— **Я хочý рассказáть** вам о сéвере.
— Михаúл, **я хочý, чтóбы ты помóг** мне с домáшним задáнием.
— Онá хóчет, чтóбы вы познакóмили её с трéнером клýба «моржéй».
— Я хочý, чтóбы ты сфотографúровала меня с дрýгом.

хотéть, чтóбы . . .
+the verb in the past tense

Я хочý, чтóбы мой брат стал лётчиком.
(Я хочý, но брат стáнет.)
I want my brother **to become** a pilot.
(I want, but my brother will become.)

Учúтель хóчет, чтóбы мы прочитáли этот ромáн.
(Учúтель хóчет, но мы прочитáем.)
The teacher wants us **to finish** (reading) the novel.
(The teacher wants, but we will read.)

Vladimir Nikolaevich, **we want you to tell** us about the North.

I want to tell you about the North.
Mikhail, **I want you to help** me with my homework.
She wants you to introduce her to the coach of the "Walrus" club.

I want you to photograph me with my friend.

7.77 CONDITIONAL MOOD: THE CONSTRUCTION ЕСЛИ БЫ + THE PAST TENSE OF THE CONJUGATED VERB
Function: Indicating conditions. Indicating a planned or desire action.

Faces and Voices Chapter 11 A Pages 295-297

To designate an action which can take place only under certain conditions, Russian uses the conditional mood. The **past tense** of the verb and the particle **бы** are used to form the conditional mood.

Although **бы** is often used directly after the verb, it can occupy various places in a sentence. However, **бы** can never begin a sentence.

Я с удовóльствием **пошёл бы** в теáтр.
Я **бы** с удовóльствием **пошёл** в теáтр.
Я с удовóльствием **бы пошёл** в теáтр.

I would very much **like to go** (with you) to the theater.

In **compound sentences**, the particle **бы** is used in both the main and subordinate clauses. **Если бы** is used in the first clause to set the condition: *If this were the case, then...*

Sample sentences

Если бы у меня нé было лишнего вéса, я пошлá бы в балéтный кружóк.	**If** I didn't have the extra weight, **I would go** to the ballet club.
Если бы я не боялась хóлода, я началá бы занимáться в клýбе «моржéй».	**If** I wasn't afraid of the cold, **I would join** the "Walrus" club.
Если бы я моглá купить билéты, я пошлá бы в суббóту на балéт «Лебеди́ное óзеро».	**If** I could buy the tickets, **I would go** on Saturday to the ballet "Swan Lake."
Если бы кáждый день нé было урóка, бы́ло бы скýчно.	**If** there was not class every day, **it would be** boring.

The conditional mood is also used to designate an **action which is being planned or desired.**

Sample sentences

Если бы у меня бы́ло свобóдное врéмя, я пошёл бы в теáтр на балéт «Щелкýнчик».	**If** I had the free time, **I would go** to the theater to the ballet "The Nutcracker."
Если бы у меня бы́ло свобóдное врéмя, я бы поéхала отдыхáть на океáн.	**If** I had the free time, **I would go** on vacation by the ocean.
Если бы у меня бы́ло свобóдное врéмя, я бы всё врéмя игрáл в настóльный тéннис.	**If** I had the free time, **I would play** table tennis (ping-pong) all the time.
Если бы у меня бы́ло мнóго дéнег, я бы купи́ла нóвую маши́ну.	**If** I had the money, **I would buy** a new car.

7.78 THE CONSTRUCTION ХОТЕЛ(А) БЫ
   Function: Expressing wishes

Face to Face L 2
Chapter 4 A, D
Pages 78-79, 89

To express a simple wish, the conditional phrase **хотéл бы** is often used:

Sample sentences

Он хотéл бы встрéтиться с вáми.	**He would like** to meet with you.
Онá хотéла бы познакóмиться с тобóй.	**She would like** to get acquainted with you.
Они́ хотéли бы сфотографи́роваться с нáми.	**They would like** to have their picture taken with us.

Note that with each of these constructions, the **past tense** of the verb **хотéть** (to want) has been used, plus the conditional particle **бы**. If a second verb is used, as in expressing a desire to do something, **хотéл бы** is followed by the infinitive form of the verb.

Мы хотéли бы уви́деть Кремль и Крáсную плóщадь.	We **would like to see** the Kremlin and Red Square.

Participles

7.79 What are participles? Participles, or **verbal adjectives**, replace the relative adjective кото́рый (which, who) in a subordinate clause. They reflect the action of the subordinate clause onto the subject or direct object of the main clause and in doing so, further describe it.

Я зна́ю ученика́, **чита́ющего** кни́гу.   I know the student **reading** a book.
Я зна́ю ученика́, кото́рый чита́ет кни́гу.   I know the boy who is reading a book.

Participles are formed from verbs, can be either transitive or intransitive, and can be reflexive (with the particle **-ся**). They can be used in either aspect, in both present and past tense, can be active or passive, and govern nouns like other verbs. Like an adjective, participles are declined and agree with nouns in gender, number and case. It should be noted that the general usage of participles is confined to literary and formal written texts.

7.80 PARTICIPLES: PRESENT ACTIVE, PRESENT PASSIVE, PAST ACTIVE, PAST PASSIVE

Function: Expressing and reading formal written clauses and replacing кото́рый (which..., who...) clauses with participles

| Мир ру́сских |
| Lesson 2 |
| Pages 50-55 |

Participles are formed from verbs. They have characteristics of both verbs and adjectives and decline in gender, number, and case.

Characteristics of Verbs	Characteristics of Adjectives
1) Time present: Я зна́ю ма́льчика, чита́ющего кни́гу. past: Ма́льчик, прочита́вший кни́гу, оста́вил её на столе́ и пошёл домо́й.	**1) Gender** masculine: чита́ющий feminine: чита́ющая neuter: чита́ющее·
2) Aspect imperfective: чита́вший perfective: прочита́вший	**2) Number** singular: чита́ющий plural: чита́ющие
3) Voice active: чита́ющий passive: чита́емый	**3) Case** (depends upon the case of the noun with which it agrees) nominative: Ма́льчик, чита́ющий accusative/genitive: Ма́льчика, чита́ющего dative: Ма́льчику, чита́ющему

There are four types of participles in Russian:

Present active	чита́ющий	who is reading
Past active (impf.)	чита́вший	who was reading
Past active (pf.)	прочита́вший	who read
Present passive (impf.)	чита́емый	which is read
Past passive (pf.) -short	прочи́тан	has been read
-long	прочи́танный	which has been read

Participles, like the **кото́рый** clauses they replace, generally form their own (subordinate) clause which refers back to the main noun or subject of the sentence. Participle clauses follow a comma. Because participles can replace **кото́рый** clauses, their meaning is similar:

REFERENCE TABLE 7S: COMPARISON OF PARTICIPLE AND КОТО́РЫЙ CLAUSES

Present Active Participle Я зна́ю ма́льчика, **чита́ющего** кни́гу. Я зна́ю ма́льчика, кото́рый чита́ет кни́гу.	I know the boy **reading** a book. I know the boy who is reading a book.
Past Active Participle Писа́тель, **написа́вший** э́ту кни́гу, изве́стен всему́ ми́ру. Писа́тель, кото́рый написа́л э́ту кни́гу, изве́стен всему́ ми́ру.	The author **who wrote** this book is famous throughout the world. The author who wrote this book is famous throughout the world.
Present Passive Participle Письмо́, **чита́емое** Ни́ной, пришло́ то́лько сего́дня. Письмо́, кото́рое чита́ет Ни́на, пришло́ то́лько сего́дня.	The letter **being read** by Nina came only today. The letter that Nina is reading came only today.
Past Passive Participle Мне нра́вится кни́га, **напи́санная** э́тим писа́телем. Мне нра́вится кни́га, кото́рую написа́л э́тот писа́тель. Он чита́ет кни́гу, **пода́ренную** ему́ дру́гом. Он чита́ет кни́гу, кото́рую подари́л ему́ друг.	I like the book **written** by this writer. I like the book which this author wrote. He is reading a book **given** to him by his friend. He is reading a book which a friend gave to him.

Formation of the present active participle The present active participle is formed from imperfective verbs by replacing the -т of the third person plural (**они́**) ending with -щ- and adding adjectival endings:

	3rd person pl.	**Present active participle**
(чита́ть)	чита́ют	чита́**ющий**, чита́**ющая**, чита́**ющее**, чита́**ющие** *who is/are reading*
(бежа́ть)	бегу́т	бегу́**щий**, бегу́**щая**, бегу́**щее**, бегу́**щие** *who is/are running*

| (крича́ть) | крича́т | крича́щий, крича́щая, крича́щее, крича́щие *who is/are shouting* |
| (учи́ться) | у́чатся | у́чащийся, у́чащаяся, у́чащееся, у́чащиеся *who studies/study* |

All participles, except for short past passive forms, decline according to case in agreement with the noun they modify.

Sample sentences

Вот ма́льчик, **чита́ющий** кни́гу. (nominative case—regular adjective ending)	Here is the boy **who is reading** the book.
Я зна́ю ма́льчика, **чита́ющего** кни́гу. (accusative case—**чита́ющий** changes to **чита́ющего** to agree with **ма́льчика**)	I know the boy **who is reading** the book.
Ма́льчику, **чита́ющему** кни́гу, всего́ пять лет. (dative case—**чита́ющему** agrees with **ма́льчику**)	The boy **who is reading** the book is only five years old.

Formation of the past active participles (imperfective/perfective) Past active participles are formed by adding -вш- and adjectival endings to the past tense (or infinitive) stem. This stem is obtained by dropping the -ть, -чь, -ти of the infinitive or the -л of the masculine singular past tense form. If the past tense stem ends in a consonant (**принёс, спас**), -ший is added to the consonant:

Past tense stem	Imperfective	Past tense stem	Perfective
чита́л	чита́вший, -ая, -ее, -ие *who was/were reading*	прочита́л	прочита́вший, ... *who read*
бежа́л	бежа́вший, -ая, -ее, -ие *who was/were running*	побежа́л	побежа́вший, ... *who ran*
крича́л	крича́вший, -ая, -ее, -ие *who was/were shouting*	кри́кнул	кри́кнувший, ... *who shouted*
учи́лся	учи́вшийся,-аяся,-ееся,-иеся *who was/were studying*	научи́лся	научи́вшийся, ... *who learned to*
приноси́л	приноси́вший, -ая, -ее, -ие *who was/were bringing*	принёс	принёсший, ... *who brought*

Sample sentences

Писа́тель, **написа́вший** э́ту кни́гу, изве́стен всему́ ми́ру.	The author **who wrote** this book is famous throughout the world.
Де́вушку, **учи́вшуюся** в на́шей шко́ле, зову́т Элла.	The girl **who used to go** to our school is named Ella.
Я хорошо́ знако́м с архите́ктором, **постро́ившим** наш дом.	I'm well acquainted with the architect **who built** our house.

Formation of the present passive participle The present passive participle is formed from transitive imperfective verbs by adding adjectival endings to the first person plural (**мы**) form of the verb. Infinitives with -ав- (**дава́ть, узнава́ть**, etc.) retain that suffix:

	1st person pl.	Present passive participle
(читáть)	читáем	читáемый, -ая, -ое, -ые *which is/are read*
(любúть)	любим	любúмый, -ая, -ое, -ые *which is/are loved*
(давáть)	даём	давáемый, -ая, -ое, -ые *which is/are given*

Sample sentences

Письмó, **читáемое** Нúной, пришлó тóлько сегóдня.	The letter **being read** by Nina arrived only today.
Оркéстр игрáл гимн, **любúмый** мнóгими людьмú.	The orchestra played a hymn **beloved** by many.

Formation of the past passive participles (long, short) Past passive participles are normally formed from transitive perfective verbs by adding -нн- or -т- to the past tense stem:

	Past tense stem	Past passive participle
прочитáть	прочитá-л	прочúтанный *which was read*
взять	взя-л	взя́тый *which was taken*

If the stem ends in the vowel **и** or a consonant, add -енн- (-ённ-). If a consonant mutation occurs in the present or future, it also occurs in the past passive participle:

встрéтить	встрéти-л (встрéчу)	встрéченный *which was met*

If the first person singular (**я**) form of the conjugated verb has an -**м**- or -**н**-, the past passive participle is formed by adding the suffix -**т**-:

взять	взя-л (возьмý)	взя́тый *which was taken*
начáть	нáчал (начнý)	нáчатый *which was begun*

Past passive participles also can have **short forms** that agree with the noun in gender and number but which **are not declined for case**:

Что?		Long form	Short form
masc.	ромáн	прочúтанный	прочúтан
fem.	кнúга	прочúтанная	прочúтана
neut.	письмó	прочúтанное	прочúтано
pl.	газéты	прочúтанные	прочúтаны

Sample sentences

Мне нра́вится кни́га, **напи́санная** э́тим писа́телем. Кни́га была́ **напи́сана** в 1878.

I like the book **written** by this writer. The book **was written** in 1878.

В венге́рском языке́ есть не́сколько слов, **взя́тых** от славя́нских языко́в.

The Hungarian language has several words **taken (borrowed)** from Slavic languages.

7.81 THE FORMATION AND USE OF SHORT PASSIVE PARTICIPLES IN THE PAST TENSE
Function: Saying something is done, built, or opened by someone

Faces and Voices Chapter 10 A Pages 264-265

Compare the sentences below:

(Кто сде́лал что?)
Худо́жник написа́л ико́ну.

(Who did what?)
The artist painted the icon.

(Что сде́лано кем?)
Ико́на **была́ напи́сана худо́жником.**

(What was done by whom?)
The icon **was painted by the artist.**

In the first sentence, **худо́жник** (in the nominative case) is the subject, **написа́л** (the verb in the past tense) is the predicate, and **ико́ну** (in the accusative case) is the direct object.

In the second sentence, what was originally the direct object has become the subject **ико́на** (in the nominative case); the predicate is expressed by the short form **past passive participle**, **напи́сана**, and the noun which names the logical subject is in the instrumental case — **худо́жником.**

Formation and usage of the short form past passive participle When stating *the person who performed the action (done by whom)*, the noun is declined in **the instrumental case**.

Past passive participles are usually formed from perfective verbs. Most short form participles simply add **-н-** to the past stem. However, verbs that end in **-ить** change the **-и** to **-ен-**. Whenever this ending is stressed, the **-е** becomes **-ён-**. Note the examples below.

Past stem	add	short-form endings	By whom?—instrumental
написа́-л	-н	напи́сан, -а, -о, -ы *written by*	Кем?
нарисова́-л	-н	нарисо́ван, -а, -о, -ы *drawn by*	Кем?
сде́ла-л	-н	сде́лан, -а, -о, -ы *done by*	Кем?
постро́-и-л	-ен	постро́ен, -а, -о, -ы *built by*	Кем?
зако́нч-и-л	-ен	зако́нчен, -а, -о, -ы *finished by*	Кем?
реш-и́-л	-ён	решён, -а́, -о́, -ы́ *solved by*	Кем?

*откры́-л	-т	откры́т, -а, -о, -ы	Кем?
		opened by	
*закры́-л	-т	закры́т, -а, -о, -ы	Кем?
		closed by	

*****Note**: A few verbs (which must be memorized) take the ending -т.

The future and past tenses are formed by placing the conjugated verb **быть** before the participle:

Sample sentences

Этот рома́н **был (бу́дет) напи́сан** Че́ховым.

Эта кни́га **была́ (бу́дет) напи́сана** Че́ховым.

Это сочине́ние **бы́ло (бу́дет) напи́сано** Ма́шей.

Эти пи́сьма́ **бы́ли (бу́дут) напи́саны** Анной.

That novel **was (will be) written by Chekhov.**

This book **was (will be) written by Chekhov.**

This composition **was (will be) written by Masha.**

These letters **were (will be) written by Anna.**

Verbal Adverbs
(Gerunds)

7.82 What are Verbal Adverbs? Verbal adverbs, also referred to as **gerunds**, are indeclinable verb forms that substitute for adverbial clauses. They are formed from verbs and share characteristics of both verbs and adverbs. Verbal adverbs can be transitive (take a direct object) or intransitive. Their general function is to describe the action performed by the subject of the sentence:

Чита́я газе́ту, она́ за́втракала.

Как она́ за́втракала? **Чита́я** газе́ту...

While reading the newspaper, she ate breakfast.

How did she eat? (While) **Reading** the newspaper.

Прочита́в газе́ту, она́ пошла́ в шко́лу.

Когда́ она́ пошла́ в шко́лу? **Прочита́в** газе́ту...

Having read the newspaper, she set off for school.

When did she set off for school? (After) **Having read** the newspaper.

REFERENCE TABLE 7T: FORMATION OF VERBAL ADVERBS (GERUNDS)

Imperfective verbs	Perfective verbs
1) Take present tense **они** form: **читáют, говорят, спешáт**	1) Take the past tense stem: **открыл, сказáл, взял, привык**
2) Drop the ending to the stem: **читá-, говор-, спеш-,**	2) Drop the -л if present: **открý-, сказá-, взя-, привык-**
3) Add **-я** after vowels and most consonants or **-а** (after consonants **ш, щ, ж, ч**): **читáя, говоря, спешá**	3) Add **-в** after a vowel and **-ши** after a consonant: **открыв, сказáв, взяв, привыкши**

4) Exceptions:
  a. Imperfective infinitives with suffix **-ва-** retain the **-ва-** in the gerund:
**давáть — даю́т — *давáя*
узнавáть — узнаю́т — *узнавáя***
	4) Exceptions:
	  a. Perfective gerunds, especially for prefixed verbs of motion, sometimes add **-я** to the *future tense stem*:
	**придýт — *придя*
	принесýт — *принеся***

b. Reflexive particles always end in **-сь:** **улыбáясь, встречáясь, занимáясь**	b. Reflexive particles always end in **-вшись:** **улыбнýвшись, встрéтившись, занявшись**
Sample sentences **Читáя** свою́ кни́гу, Пéтя сидéл, кури́л. **While reading** his book, Petya sat and smoked. **Узнавáя** стáрого дрýга, Али́са встáла со стýла. **Recognizing an old friend**, Alisa got up from the chair.	**Sample sentences** **Прочитáв** свою́ кни́гу, Пéтя реши́л бóльше не кури́ть. **Having read** (finished reading) his book, Petya decided not to smoke any more. **Узнáв** стáрого дрýга, Али́са вы́бежала из кóмнаты. **Having recognized/spotted** an old friend, Alisa ran out of the room.

7.83 PAST (PERFECTIVE) AND PRESENT (IMPERFECTIVE)
VERBAL ADVERBS (GERUNDS)
    Function: Expressing simultaneous and consecutive completed actions

> Мир рýсских
> Lesson 5
> Pages 153-156

If a subject performs two actions simultaneously, one of them may be named using the **present verbal adverb** formed from the imperfective aspect.

Sample sentences

Отвечáя на комплимéнт, рýсские
   говоря́т: «Спасúбо. Я рад, что
   вам понрáвилось».

When responding to a compliment,
   Russians say: "Thank you, I'm glad
   you liked it." (*lit., I'm glad it pleased*
   you.)

(The action of **отвечáя** takes place in
   the same time frame as the action
   of **говоря́т**.)

     To name an action that is completed before the subject begins another action, a
past verbal adverb formed from the perfective aspect is used.

Sample sentences

Написáв письмó, онá положúла егó
   в конвéрт.

Having written the letter, she put it
   into an envelope.

(The action of **написáв** takes place
   before the action of **положúла**.)

Сдéлав урóки, он пошёл в кинó.

Having done his lessons, he went to
   the movies.

(The action of **сдéлав** takes place
   before the action of **пошёл**.)

     Verbal adverbs retain the same aspect as the verb from which they are
formed. Unlike verbs, they **do not** change according to **person, gender, or number.**
     Note the difference in meaning between the present (imperfective) and past
(perfective) verbal adverbs:

Present—Imperfective verbs		Past—Perfective verbs	
читáя	reading	прочитáв	having read
говоря́	speaking	сказáв	having spoken, said
кричá	shouting	крúкнув	having shouted
отвечáя	answering	отвéтив	having answered
спрáшивая	asking	спросúв	having asked
принося́	bringing	принеся́	having brought
возвращáясь	returning	вернýвшись	having returned
проходя́	passing (foot)	пройдя́	having passed (foot)
слы́ша	hearing	услы́шав	having heard

Special Verb Groups

7.84 **THE PHRASES** ВЫЙТИ ЗАМУЖ ЗА КОГО, ЖЕНИТЬСЯ НА КОМ, **AND THE VERB** ПОЖЕНИТЬСЯ *Function:* Talking about people getting married	Faces and Voices Chapter 5 Б Page 130

To express *getting married* in Russian, different verbs are used depending on whether the person getting married is a man, woman, or a couple. Note the different constructions below.

For women: **Выйти за́муж за** + **the accusative case of the man** (кого́?)

Ольга **вышла за́муж за Алекса́ндра**.   Olga **married Alexander**.

For men: **Жени́ться на** + **the prepositional case of the woman** (ком)?

Алекса́ндр **жени́лся на Ольге**.   Alexander **married Olga**.

For couples: **пожени́ться**

Ольга и Алекса́ндр **пожени́лись**.   Olga and Alexander **got/were married**.
(*lit., married each other*)

Sample sentences

— **За како́го челове́ка** ты хо́чешь **выйти за́муж**?

— Я хочу́ **выйти за́муж за у́много и си́льного чело́ле́ка**.

Ива́н хо́чет **жени́ться на до́брой, весёлой де́вушке**.

Мои́ роди́тели **пожени́лись** в 1965-ом году́.

What kind of person do you want **to marry**?

I want **to marry an intelligent and strong man**.

Ivan wants **to marry an honest, happy girl**.

My parents **got married** in 1965.

7.85 **THE VERBS** ОШИБА́ТЬСЯ/ОШИБИ́ТЬСЯ, ПОПАДА́ТЬ/ПОПА́СТЬ, ЗВОНИ́ТЬ/ПОЗВОНИ́ТЬ (КОМУ, КУДА) *Function:* Talking on the telephone	Faces and Voices Chapter 5 Б Pages 132-135

The following verbs are commonly used in phone conversations and talking about phone calls.

звони́ть (impf. II: звоню́, -йшь, -я́т; past: звони́л/а/и) позвони́ть (pf. II: as above) (кому́? куда́?)	To call, phone (кому́/куда́— to someone/to a place) Я **звоню́** Ива́ну. I **am calling** Ivan. Мы позвони́ли в о́фис АСПРЯЛ. We phoned the ACTR office.
ошиба́ться (impf. I: ошиба́юсь, -ешься, -ются) ошиби́ться (pf. II: ошиблю́сь, -йшься, -я́тся; past: оши́бся, оши́блась, оши́блись) (чем?)	To make a mistake, be mistaken (чем— with/in something) Я **оши́бся/оши́блась** но́мером. I **have the wrong** number.
попада́ть (impf. I: попада́ю, -ешь, -ют) попа́сть (pf. I: попаду́, -ёшь, -у́т; past: попа́л/а/и) (туда́)	To reach, (lit., to fall to) (туда́—to there) Я **не** туда́ **попа́л**. Вы **не** туда́ **попа́ли**! I **didn't reach** the right number. You don't have the right number!

Note the use of these verbs in the phone dialogues below.

Sample sentences

— Здра́вствуйте! Мо́жно Макси́ма к
    телефо́ну?

— Его́ нет до́ма. Кто его́ спра́шивает?

— Ка́тя.

— Что ему́ переда́ть?

— Спаси́бо, ничего́. Я пото́м **позвоню́**.

Hello! Can Maxim come to the phone?

He's not home. Who is asking for him?

Katya.

Is there a message (lit., relay)?

No, thanks. **I'll call** later.

— Алло́! Э́то магази́н?

— Нет. Вы **не** туда́ **попа́ли**. Э́то
    кварти́ра.

— Э́то 281-46-05?

— Нет. Вы **оши́блись**.

Hello! Is this the store?

No. You've **reached** the wrong place.
    This is an apartment.

Is this 281-46-05?

No. You **have the wrong** number (lit., You
    made a mistake).

— Извини́те.

Excuse me.

— Мо́жно Макси́ма?

— Его́ нет до́ма. Кто его́ спра́шивает?
    Что ему́ переда́ть?

— Переда́йте, пожа́луйста, что **звони́ла**
    Ма́ша. А Ни́на до́ма?

— И её нет. Я и ей переда́м, что вы
    звони́ли.

Can Maxim come to the phone?

He's not home. Who is calling? Can I
    take a message?

Please tell him that Masha **called**. Is Nina
    home?

She's not home either. I'll tell her you
    called.

— Позови́те Бори́са Миха́йловича,
    пожа́луйста.

— Вы **не** туда́ **попа́ли**.

Boris Mikhailovich, please. (lit., Call Boris
    mikhailovich to the phone, please.)

You've got the wrong place.

— Здра́вствуйте! Мо́жно Игоря к телефо́ну?	Hello! Can Igor come to the phone?
— Вы **оши́блись**.	You **have the wrong** number.
— Я не туда́ попа́л? Извини́те.	I've got the wrong place? Excuse me.

7.86 IDIOMATIC USE OF THE VERBS ИДТИ, СИДЕТЬ
Function: Saying whether something looks good or bad on someone

Faces and Voices
Chapter 9 A
Page 236

The verbs **идти** and **сиде́ть** may be used to express *to suit, to become* and *to fit* when talking about objects people wear. With constructions using **идти**, the person whose clothing does or does not suit or fit is in the dative case.

Что	идёт/шёл, шла, шло, шли	кому́?
Кра́сный сви́тер The red sweater	не шёл didn't fit/suit	мне /Андре́ю. me/Andre.
Голуба́я ку́ртка The blue skirt	не идёт/шла doesn't/didn't look good on	тебе́/Ната́ше. you/Natasha.
Зелёное пла́тье The green dress	шло became/suited	ей. her.
Спорти́вные костю́мы The warm-up suits	не иду́т/шли don't/didn't look good/fit	им/ребя́там. them/the kids.

The construction using the verb **сиде́ть** may use either the **dative** or the preposition **на + the accusative case**.

Что	сиди́т/сиде́л/а/ о/и	на кого́/ кому́?
Это пла́тье The dress	сиди́т looks good	на вас /вам хорошо́. on you.
Эта чёрная руба́шка The black shirt	сиде́ла looked good	на тебя/тебе́ хорошо́. on you.
Эти ту́фли These shoes	сидя́т/сиде́ли fit/looked good	на её/ей хорошо́. on her.
Ва́ша причёска Your haircut/ hairstyle	сиди́т suits	на вас /вам хорошо́. you.

7.87 **THE VERB** ВЕРИТЬ/ПОВЕРИТЬ **WITH THE ACCUSATIVE AND DATIVE CASES**
Function: Talking about beliefs

Faces and Voices
Chapter 10 А, Г
Pages 268, 279

The verbs **вéрить (II)/повéрить** (to believe [in], have faith [in]) are used with either the accusative or the dative case depending on the connotation or meaning of the statement.

(по)вéрить в + the accusative—to believe *in* something/*in* someone:

Вся моя семья **вéрит в Бóга**.		All of my family **believes in God.**
	в когó? во что?	**in whom? in what?**
	в Бóга	in God
(по) вéрить	в счáстье	in luck
	в бýдущее	in the future
	в дрýжбу	in friendship
	в побéду	in victory

(по)вéрить + the dative case—to believe something or someone:

Я не вéрю Антóну и егó словáм.		I **don't believe Anton and his words.**
	комý? чемý?	**whom? what?**
(по) вéрить	дрýгу	a friend
	слóву	a word
	расскáзу	a story

7.88 **THE VERBS** СТАВИТЬ/ПОСТАВИТЬ **AND** КЛАСТЬ/ПОЛОЖИТЬ
Function: Expressing putting/placing in a standing position and a lying position

Мир русских
Lesson 5
Pages 160-161

Russian expresses *putting* and *placing* objects by distinguishing whether they are placed in a standing or lying position. The verbs **стáвить/постáвить** denote the placing of objects in a standing position, while **класть/положить** denote laying down or placement in a lying position. These verbs require the use of **prepositions + the accusative case** to answer the question Кудá?: (To) Where?

Стáвить/постáвить когó?/что? кудá? **To put/place in a standing position**

— Кудá постáвить лáмпу? — **Where** should I put the lamp?
— Постáвь её **на пóлку.** — Put in **on the shelf.**
— Кудá? — **Where?**
— На пóлку. — **On the shelf.**

Класть/положить когó?/что? кудá? **To put/place in a lying position**

— Кудá положить газéту? — **Where** should I put the newspaper?
— Положи её **на стол.** — Lay it **on the table.**
— Кудá? — **Where?**
— На стол. — **On the table.**

Note that both **положи́(те)**... (Put...! in a lying position) and **поста́вь(те)**... (Put...! in a standing position) are commonly encountered imperatives.

Putting and placing verbs can be used with various prepositions to describe movement or the *motion* of objects in (**в**), *behind* (**за**), *under* (**под**), etc.. This motion requires the use of the *accusative case* with a preposition in naming the destination.

ста́вить	[ста́влю, ста́вишь, ста́вят; ставь(те)!]	**Куда́?**	**+ accusative case**
поста́вить	[поста́влю, поста́вишь, поста́вят; поста́вь(те)!]	**на** стол	**on** the table
		в шкаф	**into** the wardrobe
		за дверь	**behind** the door
класть	[кладу́, кладёшь, кладу́т; кла́дь(те)!]	**пе́ред** окно́	**in front of** the window
		под стол	**under** the table
положи́ть	[положу́, поло́жишь, поло́жат; положи́(те)!]	**над** вход	**over** the entrance

These verbs must be distinguished from the verbs **стоя́ть** (to be standing) and **лежа́ть** (to be lying) which answer the question **Где?** (Where?) and describe the location of objects and people.

Sample sentences

Куда́?	**Поста́вьте** стака́ны на стол.	**Put** the glasses on the table.
Где?	Стака́ны стоя́т на столе́.	The glasses are (standing) on the table.
Куда́?	Я **поста́влю** ча́йник на плиту́.	I will **place** the teapot on the stove.
Где?	Ча́йник стои́т на плите́.	The teapot is on the stove.
Куда́?	**Положи́те** своё пальто́ туда́.	**Lay** your coat over there.
Где?	Ва́ше пальто́ лежи́т на дива́не.	Your coat is lying on the couch.
Куда́?	Я **положу́** журна́лы в у́гол.	I'll **put** these magazines in the corner.
Где?	Журна́лы лежа́т в углу́.	The magazines are lying in the corner.
Куда́?	**Положи́те** уче́бники под столы́! Контро́льная начина́ется!	**Put** your textbooks under your desks! The exam is beginning!
Где?	На́ши уче́бники лежа́т под стола́ми.	Our textbooks are (lying) under our desks.

7.89 THE VERBS ВЕШАТЬ/ПОВЕСИТЬ (ЧТО? КУДА?) AND ВЕСИТЬ (ГДЕ?)

  Function: Expressing "to hang" and "to be hanging"

> Мир ру́сских
> Lesson 11
> Pages 369-371

The verbs **ве́шать/пове́сить что/кого́? куда́?** are transitive and mean *to hang (something) up.* The intransitive verb **висе́ть где?** means *to be hanging.* Their usage is the same as that of the "putting and placing" verbs described in the grammar point above.

вéшать (вéшаю, вéшаешь, вéшают; вéшай(те)!) повéсить (повéшу, повéсишь, повéсят; повéсь(те)!) **что/кого? кудá?** *transitive*; to hang something (up)	висéть (висúт, вися́т) **где?** *intransitive*; to be hanging
Родúтели купúли нóвую картúну и **повéсили** её на стéну. My parents bought a new picture and **hung** it on the wall. Брат вошёл в квартúру, снял пальтó и **повéсил** егó на вéшалку. My brother came into the apartment, took off his coat and **hung** it on the hanger. **Повéсьте** вáшу одéжду в шкаф. **Hang** your clothes in the wardrobe.	Сейчáс картúна **висúт** в моéй кóмнате на стенé. Now the picture **is hanging** on the wall in my room. Сейчáс пальтó **висúт** на вéшалке. Now the coat **is hanging** on the hanger. Вáши джúсны **вися́т** в шкафý. Your jeans **are hanging** in the wardrobe.

Вéшать/повéсить require the use of a preposition + **the accusative case** when expressing *where something is being hung* (**кудá**).

Кудá **повéсить** э́ту картúну? Картúну нáдо **повéсить на стенý**. **Повéсь** её **над** телевúзор.	**Where** should this picture be **hung**? The picture should be **hung on the wall**. **Hang** it **above the television**.

Note: Refer to grammar point 7.88, *putting and placing verbs*, for additional examples of prepositions with the accusative case.

7.90 THE VERBS СТАРАТЬСЯ/ПОСТАРАТЬСЯ, ПЫТАТЬСЯ/ ПОПЫТАТЬСЯ AND ПРОБОВАТЬ/ПОПРОБОВАТЬ
Function: Expressing *to try* in Russian with specific connotations

Мир русских
Lesson 7
Pages 230-232

The Russian equivalent to the English *to try* is expressed by several verbs, each denoting a specific connotation:

The verbs стара́ться/постара́ться, пыта́ться/попыта́ться, and прóбовать/попрóбовать are frequently translated as *to try*. All of these verbs are used with infinitives. Прóбовать/попрóбовать can also be used with direct objects. Although these verbs are sometimes interchangeable, there are some basic differences:

Стара́ться/постара́ться are used for *a concentrated effort* or *striving to accomplish a goal*. These actions are of an intense, well-thought-out and purposeful nature. These verbs are accompanied by an infinitive verb, either stated or implied.

Онá **стара́лась написáть** диктáнт как мóжно лýчше.	She **tried to write** the dictation as well as possible.

Пыта́ться/попыта́ться are used *when achievement of the goal is difficult* or *when there is a possibility (or probability) of failure*. These verbs are accompanied by an infinitive verb, either stated or implied.

Врачи́ **пыта́лись спасти́** его́ от сме́рти.	The doctors **tried to save** him from death.

Про́бовать/попро́бовать do not specify the achievement or the failure to reach a goal, but *simply state the action of trying*. This verb pair is most often used with the idea of trying/tasting food and sampling an activity or an object. They can be used both with a direct object and an infinitive verb, either stated or implied.

Ты **попро́бовал** когда́-нибудь **писа́ть** стихи́?	Have you ever **tried to write** poems?
Ва́ня, **попро́буй борщ**, он о́чень вку́сный.	Vanya, **try the borsch**, it's very delicious.

Sample sentences

стара́ться/постара́ться

Ма́льчик **стара́лся** писа́ть аккура́тно.	The boy **tried** to write neatly.
Она́ **стара́лась** быва́ть у роди́телей ка́ждую суббо́ту.	She **tried** to be at her parents' every Saturday.
Он **стара́лся** говори́ть о́чень гро́мко, чтобы все слы́шали его́.	He **tried** to speak very loudly, so that everyone could hear him.

пыта́ться/попыта́ться

Он **пыта́лся** писа́ть стихи́, но у него́ не получа́лось.	He **tried** to write a poem, but it didn't turn out well.
Мы **пыта́лись** попа́сть в теа́тр на премье́ру, но ли́шных биле́тов не́ было.	We **tried** to make the premier, but there were no extra tickets.
Хотя́ у меня́ ма́ло свобо́дного вре́мени, я **пыта́юсь** научи́ться игра́ть на гита́ре.	Although I have little free time, I am **trying** to learn to play the guitar.
Я **попыта́лась** объясни́ть свою́ мысль на ру́сском языке́, но я не уве́рена, по́няли ли они́.	I **tried** to explain my thought in Russian, but I'm not certain they understood.

про́бовать/попро́бовать

Татья́на **попро́бовала** писа́ть но́вой авторучкой, но в ней не́ было черны́лы.	Tatyana **tried** to write with the new pen, but there was no ink in it.
Вы когда́-нибудь **попро́бовали** блины́ со смета́ной? На́до же в Росси́и!	Have you ever **tried** *bliny* (crêpes) with sour cream? You must when you're in Russia!
Попро́буй сде́лать свою́ рабо́ту в библиоте́ке. Там ти́ше.	**Try** finishing your work at the library. It's quieter there.

7.91 THE VERBS ПОСЕЩАТЬ **AND** НАВЕЩАТЬ
Function: Expressing "to visit" places and people

| Мир русских
Lesson 8
Pages 274-275 |

Two verbs in Russian express *to visit* denoting different connotations:

Посещать/посетить что? — *to visit something*: an exhibit, a town, an institute. This verb pair is usually used in the official style of speech.

Американские студенты **посетили**...	The American college students **visited**...
несколько школ города Москва.	several Moscow city schools.
выставку.	the exhibition.
город.	the city.
институт.	the institute.

Note: Посещать/посетить кого can be used to express an official visit to a person: **Делегация посетила нас в школе.** The delegation **visited us** at school.

Навещать/навестить кого? — *to visit someone*: parents, a friend. This verb pair is used in a neutral, informal style of speech.

Летом поеду домой, **навещу**...	I will go home during the summer and will **visit** my...
родителей.	parents.
друга.	friend.
друзей.	friends.
бабушку.	grandmother.

Sample sentences

Посещать/посетить что

| В городе открылась новая библиотека.
Вчера её **посетил** мэр города. | A new library opened in our city.
Yesterday the mayor of the city **visited** it. |
| В мае будущего года президент США **посетит** Москву. | In May of next year, the President of the U.S. **will visit** Moscow. |

Навещать/навестить кого

| Моя сестра лежит в больнице. Завтра я **невещу** её. | My sister is in the hospital. I'll **visit** her tomorrow. |
| Наш друг **навестил** нас на две недели. | Our friend **visited** us for two weeks. |

7.92 THE VERBS ПЕРЕЖИВАТЬ/ПЕРЕЖИТЬ
Function: Expressing *to experience, endure* and
to survive, outlive

| Мир русских
Lesson 10
Page 330 |

The verb pair **переживать/пережить что?/кого?** have two meanings:

1) **to experience, go through, endure, suffer**

| Он сильно **переживал**, когда ребёнок умер. | He **suffered** a lot when the child died. |

2) **to survive, outlive, outlast**

Он **пережи́л** всех свои́х друзе́й.   He **outlived** all his friends.

Sample sentences

По́сле сме́рти жены́ Ива́н IV си́льно **пережива́л**, не спал ноча́ми, ни с кем не разгова́ривал.

After the death of his wife, Ivan IV **suffered** a lot, didn't sleep nights, and would not speak with anyone.

Они́ **пережи́ли** войну́ и го́лод.

They **lived through** war and famine.

Его́ шко́льные друзья́ поги́бли во вре́мя войны́: то́лько он **пережи́л** всех кла́сса.

His school friends died during the war; he was the only **survivor** of all his classmates.

Он **пережи́л** рак в де́тстве и стал знамени́тым футболи́стом.

He **survived** cancer in childhood and became a famous soccer player.

Она́ **пережи́ла** землетрясе́ние в Арме́нии.

She **survived** the earthquake in Armenia.

7.93 **THE VERBS** ПОМНИТЬ, ВСПОМИНА́ТЬ/ВСПО́МНИТЬ, ЗАПОМИНА́ТЬ/ЗАПО́МНИТЬ

Function: Expressing *to remember, to recall,* and *to commit to memory*

| Мир ру́сских |
| Lesson 10 |
| Pages 331-332 |

To express *to remember* and *to recall* in Russian, specific verbs must be used depending on the connotation of the statement.

The imperfective, Type I, verb **по́мнить что?/кого́?, о ко́м?/о чём?** means: *to remember (something/someone, for a long time).*

По́мнить	Как?		что?/кого́?, о ко́м?/чём?	
	до́лго	a long time	де́тство	childhood
	всю жизнь	one's entire life	мать	mother
	хорошо́	well	о сестре́	about one's sister
	то́чно	exactly	о про́сьбе	about the request

Вспомина́ть/вспо́мнить что?/кого́?, о ко́м?/о чём? mean: *to remember, recollect, recall (something which was forgotten).*

Вспомина́ть	Как?		что?/кого́?, о ко́м?/чём?	
	ча́сто	often	де́тство	childhood
	ре́дко	rarely	роди́телей	parents
			о до́ме	about one's home
Вспо́мнить	вдруг	suddenly	сло́во	the word
	сра́зу же	at once	дру́га	friend
	с трудо́м	with difficulty	о семье́	about one's family

запомина́ть/запо́мнить что?/кого́? mean: *to memorize, to commit to memory, to remember, or to learn by heart.*

	Как?		Что?/кого?	
запомина́ть	сра́зу	immediately	лицо́ дру́га	a friend's face
	надо́лго	for a long time	а́дрес	address
запо́мнить	на всю жизнь	for the rest of one's life	слу́чай	incident
			граммати́ческое пра́вило	grammar rule

All these verbs have reflexive counterparts in which the addition of **-ся** indicates the passive voice.

Я не по́мню, что случи́лось вчера́, но хорошо́ **по́мнится** то, что бы́ло в де́тстве.	I don't remember what happened yesterday, but what happened in my childhood **is** well **remembered**.
Когда́ пережива́ешь наводне́ние у себя́ до́ма, это **запомина́ется** на всю жизнь.	When you live through the flooding of a home, it **is remembered** your whole life.
Это на́до знать на па́мять, что́бы оно́ навсегда́ **запо́мнилось**.	You have to know this by memory so that it **is remembered** forever.

Sample sentences

На уро́ке:	In class:
Я **не по́мню**.	I **don't remember**. (I may not recall this information.)
Я **не могу́ вспо́мнить**.	I **don't remember**. (I **can't recall** at the moment, but might be able to remember.)
Сейча́с **вспо́мню**.	I'll tell you in a moment. (Just a moment, **I'll recall it**. It's on the tip of my tongue.)
Я **запо́мнил** его́ а́дрес.	I **memorized** his address.
Она́ то́лько оди́н раз прочита́ла стихотворе́ние и сра́зу **запо́мнила** его́.	She read the poem only once and immediately **memorized it**.
Я **по́мню** обеща́ние.	I **remember** the promise.
Он **запо́мнил** все номера́ телефо́нов.	He **memorized** all of the phone numbers.
Его́ слова́ навсегда́ **запомина́ются** в мое́й па́мяти (мной).	I will remember his words forever (*lit., His words will always be remembered in my memory*).
Я ча́сто **вспомина́ю** слова́ Ильича́ о ру́сском наро́де и си́льных вождя́х.	I often **recall** the words of Ilych (Lenin) about the Russian people and strong leaders.
Граммати́ческие табли́цы обы́чно **запомина́ются** ученика́ми.	Grammar tables **are** usually **remembered** by students.

7.94 **THE VERBS** ПОЛЬЗОВАТЬСЯ/ВОСПОЛЬЗОВАТЬСЯ (ЧЕМ?), ИСПОЛЬЗОВАТЬ (ЧТО?), УПОТРЕБЛЯТЬ/УПОТРЕБИТЬ (ЧТО?)

Мир русских Lesson 10 Pages 333-338

Function: Expressing the various connotations of *to use* in Russian

There are several verbs in Russian which express different connotations of the English *to use*.

Basic usage of пóльзоваться/воспóльзоваться Пóльзоваться/воспóльзоваться **чем?** **(+ instrumental case)** mean *to use something to perform a specific function.* The object named is normally used for its intended purpose (telephone to phone someone, computer to write something, etc.). This meaning is most often conveyed by the **imperfective** verb.

Когдá я читáю кнѝги на рýсском языкѐ, я обычно **пóльзуюсь** словарём.	I usually **use** a dictionary when I read books in Russian.

While the imperfective form is generally used more frequently in this meaning, the perfective can be used to denote single complete actions.

Я забыла дóма свой словáрь. Мóжно **воспóльзоваться** вáшим?	I forgot my dictionary at home. Can I **use** yours? (To look up a word quickly.)

Пóльзоваться/воспóльзоваться Чем?		(с/дѐлать что?)	
телефóном	telephone	(звонѝть)	(to phone)
космéтикой	cosmetics	(крáситься)	(to make oneself up)
словарём	dictionary	(читáть)	(to read)
учéбником	textbook	(учѝть)	(to study)
зóнтиком	umbrella	(гулять)	(to walk)
трáнспортом	public transportation	(éздить)	(to go)

The **perfective** is used most often in the meaning *to make use (of), to take advantage (of), to derive some use or gain (from).*

Онá **воспóльзовалась** возмóжностью отпрáвить посылку в Москвý.	She **took advantage** of the opportunity to send a package to Moscow.

This usage occasionally occurs in the imperfective:

Онá **пóльзуется** любóй возмóжностью, чтóбы передáть привѐт своим друзьям в Москвѐ.	She **makes use** of any opportunity to say hello to her friends in Moscow.

Пó́льзоваться/воспóльзоваться
Чем?
слу́чаем	(the incident, occasion)
ситуáцией	(the situation)
добротóй	(the kindness)
мя́гким харáктером	(one's gentle character)
хорóшим настроéнием	(one's good mood)

Use only the **imperfective** пóльзоваться to express the connotation *to have* (*for one's use*), *to enjoy*, *to experience*.

Роди́тели должны́ **имéть** авторитéт у детéй.	Parents should **have** authority over their children.
Роди́тели должны́ **пóльзоваться** авторитéтом у детéй.	Parents should **have** authority over their children.

Пóльзоваться Чем?

любóвью	love
уважéнием	respect
успéхом	success
прáвом	the right
свобóдой	the freedom, freedom

Sample sentences

— Вы читáете без очкóв?	Do you read without glasses?
— Нет, я **пóльзуюсь** очкáми.	No, I **use** glasses.
Я предпочитáю **пóльзоваться** автóбусом éздить по гóроду.	I prefer **to use** the bus to get around town.
Я **пóльзуюсь** компью́тером писáть э́ту рабóту.	I **am using** a computer to write this work.
Он **пóльзуется** кáждой свобóдной мину́той для воспитáния детéй.	He **uses** every free moment to raise his children.
Мы **воспóльзовались** прекрáсной погóдой поéхать на дáчу.	We **took advantage** of the beautiful weather to go to the dacha.
Мои́ роди́тели éдут на дачу.	My parents are going to the dacha.
Моя́ млáдшая сестрá **воспóльзуется** э́тим слу́чаем смотрéть по телеви́зору передáчу для взрóслых.	My little sister **will use** this occasion to watch television shows for adults.
Карти́ны э́того худóжника **пóльзуются** у всех популя́рностью.	This artist's pictures **enjoy** the popularity of all.
К сожалéнию, тóлько в нéкоторых стрáнах жéнщины **пóльзуются** таки́ми же правáми, как и мужчи́ны.	Unfortunately, women **enjoy** the same rights as men only in certain countries.
Ру́сские **пóльзуются** любóвью бáни.	Russians **enjoy** a love for the banya.

Usage of употребля́ть/употреби́ть что? The verbs **употребля́ть/ употреби́ть** express *to use* two ways:

1) To use in language expressions, punctuation, and in speaking about the structures of languages, etc.

Употреблять/употребить

Что?		Где?		Как?
сло́во	a word	в ре́чи	in speech	пра́вильно
выраже́ние	a phrase	в разгово́ре	in conversation	correctly
предложе́ние	a sentence	в расска́зе	in a story	непра́вильно
посло́вицу	a proverb	в упражне́нии	in a sentence	incorrectly
сино́ним	a synonym			

Врачи́ **употребля́ют** в свое́й ре́чи мно́го медици́нских те́рминов.	Doctors **use** many medical terms in their speech.

2) To use food or drink for or in a dish; in formal speech

Э́ти грибы́ мо́жно **употребля́ть** в пи́щу.	These mushrooms can be **used** in food.
Э́тому челове́ку нельзя́ **употребля́ть** мно́го солёного.	That person can't **use** much salt.
Лук на́чали **употребля́ть** в пи́щу о́чень давно́.	They began **to use** onions in foods a long time ago.

Sample sentences

В э́том уче́бнике а́вторы **употребля́ли** посло́вицу в ка́ждом уро́ке.	In this textbook the authors **used** proverbs in every lesson.
Е́сли хо́чешь быть серьёзным писа́телем, тебе́ ну́жно пра́вильно **употребля́ть** зна́ки ; [то́чка с запято́й] и ' [апостро́ф] в предложе́ниях.	If you want to be a serious writer, you need to correctly **use** the semicolon and apostrophe (signs) in sentences.
Сего́дня врачи́ говоря́т что вре́дно **употребля́ть** майоне́з, а за́втра, други́е врачи́ говоря́т, что в майоне́зе есть поле́зный витами́н Э. Кому́ ве́рить?	Today doctors say that it is unhealthy **to use** mayonnaise, and tomorrow other doctors will say that the beneficial vitamin E is in mayonnaise. Whom do you believe?
В уро́ке «Ру́сская ку́хня» вы чита́ли, что америка́нский врач сове́товал, что ну́жно **употребля́ть** нежи́рное молоко́.	In the "Russian Cooking" lesson you read that an American doctor advised that one should **use** nonfat milk.

7.95 **THE VERBS** ОСВА́ИВАТЬ/ОСВО́ИТЬ (ЧТО?), УСВА́ИВАТЬ/ УСВО́ИТЬ (ЧТО?)

Function: Expressing the process of the acquisition of knowledge, skills, and abilities as in *to master* and *to learn*

Мир русских Lesson 11 Pages 367-368

The verbs **осва́ивать/осво́ить** and **усва́ивать/усво́ить** generally translate as *to master, to learn* and indicate the acquisition of knowledge, skills, or abilities in the process of learning something.

Осва́ивать/осво́ить are usually used in a general sense. The following adverbial phrases often accompany their usage:

легко́	easily	с трудо́м	with difficulty
постепе́нно	gradually	бы́стро	quickly
хорошо́	well	по́лностью	entirely; fully
с успе́хом	successfully		

Мо́жно сказа́ть, что она́ **осво́ила** грамма́тику ру́сского языка́.	One can say that she **mastered** the grammar of the Russian language.
Пока́ я стро́ил да́чу, постепе́нно **осва́ивал** профе́ссию строи́теля.	As I built the dacha, I gradually **learned** the profession of builder.

The verbs **усва́ивать/усво́ить** are more often used for specific instances or for one part of a whole.

Экза́мен показа́л, что студе́нт пло́хо **усво́ил** не́которые граммати́ческие пра́вила.	The exam showed that the student had poorly **mastered** some grammar rules.
Я с трудо́м **усво́ил**, как рабо́тает э́тот прибо́р.	I **learned** how to operate this instrument with difficulty.

Sample sentences

Совреме́нная же́нщина с успе́хом **осво́ила** профе́ссии, кото́рые ра́ньше бы́ли мужски́ми.	The modern woman has successfully **mastered** professions which earlier were male ones.
До́лгие го́ды Канди́нский изуча́л и **осва́ивал** о́пыт живопи́сцев ра́зных школ и сти́лей.	Kandinsky studied and **learned** the methods of painters of various schools and styles.
Когда́ я впервы́е прие́хала в Росси́ю, я до́лжен была́ сра́зу же **усво́ить** не́которые пра́вила поведе́ния.	When I first arrived in Russia, I had **to learn** certain rules of behavior (ways of acting) right away.
Что́бы быть здоро́вым, поле́зно уже́ в де́тстве **усво́ить** не́которые диети́ческие пра́вила.	In order to be healthy, it is helpful **to learn** certain dietary rules even in childhood.

7.96 THE VERBS ПОДПИСЫВАТЬ/ПОДПИСАТЬ (ЧТО?)
ПОДПИСЫВАТЬСЯ/ПОДПИСАТЬСЯ (ГДЕ? ПОД ЧЕМ?)
РАСПИСЫВАТЬСЯ/РАСПИСАТЬСЯ (ГДЕ?)
Function: Expressing the various connotations of
to sign in Russian

Мир ру́сских Lesson 11 Pages 374-375

Russian utilizes several verb pairs to express connotations of the English *to sign one's name.*

<u>подпи́сывать/подписа́ть</u>   Подпи́сывать/подписа́ть что? mean:

1)   to put one's signature (on a document).

Ви́ктор Неча́ев жени́лся на америка́нке, прие́хал в Шта́ты и **подписа́л** контра́кт с кома́ндой «Лос-Анджелес Кингс».	Victor Nechaev married an American, came to the States, and **signed** a contract with the Los Angeles Kings.

2)   to sign one's name (on something to show ownership).

Мой брат часто теряет свои учебники, поэтому всегда **подписывает** их.	My brother often loses his textbooks, therefore he always **writes his name** in them.

<u>подписываться/подписа́ться</u> Подписываться/подписа́ться где? под чем? mean:

1)   to sign one's name (at the end of a letter, card, note, story, etc.).

Я написа́ла заявле́ние дире́ктору о том, что не смогу́ за́втра вы́йти на рабо́ту и **подписа́лась**.	I wrote a statement to the director that I couldn't come to work tomorrow and **signed** it.

2)   to sign a petition or document (saying you agree with the contents).

Все учёные-эко́логи **подписа́лись** под докуме́нтом «Сохрани́м приро́ду!».	All the research ecologists **signed** the petition "Let's Preserve Nature!"

<u>расписываться /расписа́ться (где?)</u> Расписываться/расписа́ться где? mean *to sign (for something).*

Получи́те ва́шу посы́лку и **распиши́тесь**, пожа́луйста.	Take your package and **sign** here, please.

Sample sentences

Вот ваш контра́кт. **Подпиши́те**, пожа́луйста.	Here's your contract. **Sign** it please.
— Когда́ мой мла́дший брат пошёл в пе́рвый класс, ма́ма **подписа́ла** все его́ учебники.	When my younger brother went to first grade, mom **wrote his name** in all his textbooks.
— А у нас в Аме́рике мама **подпи́сывает** всю оде́жду когда́ де́ти иду́т в ла́герь.	In America the mom **writes her kids' names** on all their clothes when they go to camp.
Когда́ Че́хов отдава́л свои расска́зы в журна́лы, он **подпи́сывался** под ра́зными псевдони́мами.	When Chekhov submitted his stories to magazines, he **signed** them using various pseudonyms.
Наш де́душка — фронтови́к. Мы поздра́вили его́ с пра́здником 9 Ма́я, написа́ли откры́тку и **подписа́лись**.	Our grandfather fought on the front. We congratulated him on the May 9th holiday, wrote him a card, and **signed** it.
Вам телегра́мма из Москвы́. **Распиши́тесь**, пожа́луйста.	There's a telegram for you from Moscow. **Sign** for it please.
Я получи́л в пра́чечной чи́стое бельё и **расписа́лся**.	I received clean linens from the laundry and **signed** for them.
Вы зака́зывали путёвки на Гава́йи? Вот они́. Пожа́луйста, **распиши́тесь**.	You ordered vouchers for a trip to Hawaii? Here they are. **Sign** for them please.

REFERENCE TABLE 7U: COMPREHENSIVE LIST OF VERB PAIRS: (IMPERFECTIVE/ PERFECTIVE

Imperfective verbs are listed first, followed by their perfective partner. Conjugations are given in the present (imperfective) and future (perfective) tenses for the я, ты, and они forms. All forms are conjugated for irregular verbs.

RUSSIAN FACE TO FACE, LEVEL I

быть — бу́д-у, -ешь, -ут *(impf. future)* (в, на чём) (где) (кем)	to be (in, on, at something) (somewhere) (to be someone/ profession)
ви́деть — ви́ж-у, ви́д-ишь, -ят уви́деть — уви́ж-у, уви́д-ишь, -ят (что) (кого́)	to see; to catch sight of (something/one)
выбира́ть — выбира́-ю, -ешь, -ют вы́брать — вы́бер-у, -ешь, -ут (что) (кого́)	to choose (something, someone)
выступа́ть — выступа́-ю, -ешь, -ют вы́ступить — вы́ступ-лю, -ишь,-ят (в, на чём) (где)	to appear; perform (someplace—at a meeting, concert, etc.)
говори́ть — говор-ю́, йшь, ят сказа́ть — скаж-у́, ска́ж-ешь, -ут (что) (кому́) (or) поговори́ть — поговор-ю́, йшь, ят (говори́ть (о чём, ком) (где)) (кому́) (с кем)	to speak, to say, tell; (say something to someone), to talk a little, chat (to speak about something/one; somewhere) (to someone) (with someone)
гуля́ть — гуля́-ю, -ешь, -ют погуля́ть — погуля́-ю, -ешь, -ют (в, на чём) (по чему́) (где)	to take a walk, stroll (around somewhere) (somewhere)
де́лать — де́ла-ю, -ешь, -ют сде́лать — сде́ла-ю, -ешь, -ют (что)	to do, make (something)
ду́мать — ду́ма-ю, -ешь, -ют поду́мать — поду́ма-ю, -ешь, -ют (о чём, ком)	to think (about something/one)
е́хать — е́д-у, -ешь, -ут пое́хать — пое́д-у, -ешь, -ут (на чём) (в, на что) (куда́) (чем)	to go (by vehicle); to set out (by vehicle—car, bus, etc.) (to somewhere) (by vehicle)
жить — жив-у́, -ёшь, -у́т пожи́ть — пожив-у́, -ёшь, -у́т (в, на чём) (где) (с кем)	to live (somewhere) (with someone)
занима́ться — занима́-юсь, -ешься, ются заня́ться — займ-у́сь, -ёшься, у́тся (чем, кем)	to be involved (with something/one)
зараба́тывать — зараба́тыва-ю, -ешь,-ют (что) зарабо́тать — зарабо́та-ю, -ешь, -ют	to earn (something) to begin to work
знать — зна́-ю, -ешь, -ют *(impf.)* (что) (кого́) (о чём, ком)	to know (something, someone) (about something/one)
игра́ть — игра́-ю, -ешь, -ют сыгра́ть — сыгра́-ю, -ешь, -ют (во что) (на чём)	to play (во что — a sport) (на чём — a musical instrument)
идти́ — ид-у́, -ёшь, -у́т пойти́ — пойд-у́, -ёшь, -у́т (в, на) (куда́) (к кому́)	to go (on foot) to set out (to somewhere) (to someone's)
изуча́ть — изуча́-ю, -ешь, -ют изучи́ть — изуч-у́, изу́ч-ишь, -ат (что) (кого́)	to study, learn to study (master) (something, someone)
конча́ть — конча́-ю, -ешь, -ют ко́нчить — конч-у, -ишь, -ат (что)	to finish to complete (something)
люби́ть — люб-лю́, лю́б-ишь, -ят полюби́ть — полюб-лю́, полю́б-ишь, -ят (что) (кого́)	to love, like to fall in love, grow fond of (something, someone)
находи́ться — нахожу́сь, нахо́д-ишься, -ятся найти́сь — найд-у́сь, -ёшься, -у́тся (где)	to be found, to be located (somewhere)
начина́ть — начина́-ю, -ешь, -ют нача́ть — начн-у́, -ёшь, -у́т (что)	to begin, start (something)
нра́виться — нра́в-люсь, -ишься, -ятся понра́виться — понра́в-люсь, -ишься, -ятся (что) (кому́)	to please, like; (something) is pleasing, is liked (by someone)
отвеча́ть — отвеча́-ю, -ешь, -ют отве́тить — отве́ч-у, отве́т-ишь, -ят (на что)	to answer, reply (to something, e.g., a question)
отдыха́ть — отдыха́-ю, -ешь, -ют отдохну́ть — отдохн-у́, -ёшь, -у́т (в, на чём) (где)	to rest, vacation, relax (somewhere)

писа́ть — пиш-у́, пи́ш-ешь, -ут написа́ть — напиш-у́, напи́ш-ешь, -ут (что) (на чём) (что кому)	to write, paint (something) (on something) (s.t. to someone)
побежда́ть — побежда́-ю, -ешь, -ют победи́ть — [no я form] , побед-и́шь, я́т (что, кого)	to win, conquer, defeat (something, someone)
пока́зывать — пока́зыва-ю, -ешь, -ют показа́ть — покаж-у́, пока́ж-ешь, -ут (на что, кого), (что, кого) (кому)	to show; to point (at something, someone) to show (something, someone) (to someone)
покупа́ть — покупа́-ю, -ешь, -ют купи́ть — куп-лю́, ку́п-ишь, -ят (что) (что у кого за что) (что кому)	to buy (something) (something from someone for a certain cost) (s.t. for someone)
понима́ть — понима́-ю, -ешь, -ют поня́ть — пойм-у́, -ёшь, -у́т (что, кого)	to understand, comprehend (something, someone)
поступа́ть — поступа́-ю, -ешь, -ют поступи́ть — поступ-лю́, посту́п-ишь, -ят (в, на что)	to act, enter, join (a university, etc.) (into something)
рабо́тать — рабо́та-ю, -ешь, -ют порабо́тать — порабо́та-ю, -ешь, -ют (в, на чём) (где) (кем)	to work, run, function (somewhere) (as someone—profession)
разгова́ривать—разгова́рива-ю,-ешь,-ют (impf.) (о чём, ком) (с кем)	to converse (about something/one) (with someone)
расска́зывать — расска́зыва-ю, -ешь, -ют рассказа́ть — расскаж-у́, расска́ж-ешь, -ут (что кому) (о чём, ком)	to recount, tell, narrate (something to someone) (about something/one)
реша́ть — реша́-ю, -ешь, -ют реши́ть — реш-у́, и́шь, а́т (что), (+ infinitive)	to decide, to work on, try to solve (a problem) to decide, solve (something) (to do something)
рисова́ть — рису́-ю, -ешь, -ют нарисова́ть — нарису́-ю, -ешь, -ют (что, кого) (на чём) (чем)	to paint, draw (something, someone) (on something) (with something)
слу́шать — слу́ша-ю, -ешь, -ют послу́шать — послу́ша-ю, -ешь, -ют (что, кого)	to listen to (something, someone)
смотре́ть — смотр-ю́, смо́тр-ишь, -ят посмотре́ть — посмотр-ю́, посмо́тр-ишь, -ят (что, кого), (в, на что, кого)	to look, see, watch (something, someone); look at (something, someone)
собира́ть — собира́-ю, -ешь, -ют собра́ть — собер-у́, -ёшь, -у́т (что, кого)	to collect, gather, pick (something, someone)
спо́рить — спо́р-ю, -ишь, -ят поспо́рить — поспо́р-ю, -ишь, -ят (о чём, ком)	to argue, quarrel, debate (about something, someone)
спра́шивать — спра́шива-ю, -ешь, -ют спроси́ть — спрош-у́, спро́с-ишь, -ят (что, кого) (о чём, ком)	to ask, inquire (something, someone) (about something, someone)
танцева́ть — танцу́-ю, -ешь, -ют потанцева́ть — потанцу́-ю, -ешь, -ют (что) (с кем) (в, на чём) (где)	to dance (something) (with someone) (somewhere)
уме́ть — уме́-ю, -ешь, -ют суме́ть — суме́-ю, -ешь, -ют	to be able, know how
учи́ть — уч-у́, у́ч-ишь, -ат вы́учить — вы́уч-у, вы́уч-ишь, -ат (что), (кого, что чему)	to learn, study, teach (something) teach (someone something)
учи́ться — уч-у́сь, у́ч-ишься, -атся (impf.) (в, на чём) (где)	to study, be enrolled as a student (somewhere)
хоте́ть — хочу́, хо́чешь, хо́чет, хоти́м, хоти́те, хотя́т захоте́ть — захочу́, захо́чешь, захо́чет, захоти́м, захоти́те, захотя́т (что, кого)	to want (something, someone)
чита́ть — чита́-ю, -ешь, -ют (что) (кому) прочита́ть — прочита́-ю, -ешь,-ют (or) почита́ть — почита́-ю, -ешь, -ют	to read (something) (to someone) to read a little

RUSSIAN FACE TO FACE, LEVEL 2

боле́ть — боле́-ю, -ешь, -ют заболе́ть — заболе́-ю, -ешь, -ют (за кого, что) (чем)	to be ill, support (a team) to become ill to cheer (for someone/thing); be sick (with something—illness)
брать — бер-у́, -ёшь, -у́т взять — возьм-у́, -ёшь, -у́т (что, кого) (что у кого)	to take (something, someone) (something from someone)
быва́ть — быва́-ю, -ешь, -ют	to occur, happen

волнова́ться — волну́-юсь, -ешься, -ются взволнова́ться — взволну́-юсь, -ешься, -ются	to be worried
встреча́ть(ся) — встреча́-ю(сь), -ешь(ся), -ют(ся) (с чем, кем) встре́тить(ся) — встре́ч-у(сь), встре́т-ишь(ся), -ят(ся)	to meet, encounter (something/ one)
гото́вить — гото́в-лю, -ишь, -ят пригото́вить — пригото́в-лю, -ишь, -ят (что, кого́) (к чему́)	to prepare, cook (something, someone) (for something, e.g., an event)
дава́ть — да-ю́, -ёшь, -ю́т дать — дам, дашь, даст, дади́м, дади́те, даду́т (что) (кому́)	to give, let, allow (something) (to someone)
дари́ть — дар-ю́, да́р-ишь, -ят подари́ть — подар-ю́, пода́р-ишь, -ят (что) (кому́)	to give (as a gift) (something) (to someone)
доезжа́ть — доезжа́-ю, -ешь, -ют дое́хать — дое́д-у, -ешь, -ут (до чего́, кого́)	to reach by vehicle, ride as far as (something/one)
долета́ть — долета́-ю, -ешь, -ют долете́ть — долеч-у́, долет-и́шь, -я́т (до чего́, кого́)	to reach by plane, fly as far as (something/one)
доходи́ть — дохож-у́, дохо́д-ишь, -ят дойти́ — дойд-у́, -ёшь, -у́т (до чего́, кого́)	to reach (on foot), go as far as (something/one)
е́здить — е́зж-у, е́зд-ишь, -ят *(multidirectional)* е́хать/пое́хать *(unidirectional)* (в, на) (куда́) (на чём) *or* (чем)	to go (by vehicle) (to somewhere) (by...car/bus, etc.)
есть — ем, ешь, ест, еди́м, еди́те, едя́т (что) съесть — съем, съешь, съест, съеди́м, съеди́те, съедя́т (or) пое́сть — пое́м, пое́шь, пое́ст, поеди́м, поеди́те, поедя́т	to eat (something) to eat a little (something)
жела́ть — жела́-ю, -ешь, -ют пожела́ть — пожела́-ю, -ешь, -ют (кому́ чего́, кого́)	to wish for, desire (wish someone something/one)
звони́ть — звон-ю́, -и́шь, -я́т позвони́ть — позвон-ю́, -и́шь, -я́т (кому́)	to telephone, call (someone)
знако́миться — знако́м-люсь, -ишься, -ятся познако́миться — познако́м-люсь, -ишься, -ятся (с кем)	to get acquainted, meet (with someone)

конча́ться — *(3rd person only)* конча́-ется, -ются
ко́нчиться — *(3rd person only)* конч-ится, -атся (чем, кем)
   (both verbs are intransitive/reflexive)
	to finish, be completed (with
	   something/one—as a result)
	to finish (transitive—without -ся

мочь — могу́, мо́жешь, мо́жет, мо́жем, мо́жете, мо́гут смочь — смогу́, смо́жешь, смо́жет, смо́жем, смо́жете, смо́гут	to be able (to), (one) can
надева́ть — надева́-ю, -ешь, -ют наде́ть — наде́н-у, -ешь, -ут (что) (что на кого́)	to put on (something: clothes, etc.) (something on someone)
начина́ться — *(3rd person only)* начина́-ется, -ются нача́ться — *(3rd person only)* начн-ётся, у́тся	to begin, start (intransitive/reflexive) to begin (transitive—without -ся)
обеща́ть — обеща́-ю, -ешь, -ют пообеща́ть — пообеща́-ю, -ешь, -ют (что кому́, чему́)	to promise (something to someone, something)

одева́ть(ся) — одева́-ю(сь), -ешь(ся), -ют(ся)
оде́ть(ся) — оде́н-у(сь), -ешь(ся), -ут(ся)
одева́ть (что, кого́ во что); одева́ться (во что), (кем, чем)
	to dress oneself, get dressed
	   одева́ть...—(dress something/one in
	   something) ; одева́ться...—(into
	   something) (as someone/thing)

опа́здывать — опа́здыва-ю, -ешь, -ют опозда́ть — опозда́-ю, -ешь, -ют (в, на что) (куда́)	to be late (to something—place, event) (somewhere)
отстава́ть — отста-ю́, -ёшь, -ют отста́ть — отста́н-у, -ешь, -ут (от чего́, кого́ в чём)	to lag behind, be behind, be slow, fall behind (something/one in s.t.)
петь — по-ю́, -ёшь, -ю́т (что) (кому́) спеть — спо-ю́, -ёшь, -ю́т	to sing (something) (to someone)
пить — пь-ю, -ёшь, -ют (что, чего́) вы́пить — вы́пь-ю, -ешь, -ют (or) попи́ть — попь-ю́, -ёшь, -ю́т	to drink (something, a little of something) to drink a little
поздравля́ть — поздравля́-ю, -ешь, -ют поздра́вить — поздра́в-лю, -ишь, -ят (что, кого́ с чем)	to congratulate, to wish (on an event) (something/one with something)
познако́мить — познако́м-лю, -ишь, -ят *(pf.)* (кого́ с кем)	to introduce (someone to someone)
приглаша́ть — приглаша́-ю, -ешь, -ют пригласи́ть — приглаш-у́, приглас-и́шь, -я́т (что, кого́ на что)	to invite (something/one to something)
приезжа́ть — приезжа́-ю, -ешь, -ют прие́хать — прие́д-у, -ешь, -ут (в, на) (куда́) (к кому́)	to arrive (by vehicle) (to somewhere) (to someone's)

прилета́ть — прилета́-ю, -ешь, -ют прилете́ть — прилеч-у́, прилет-и́шь, -я́т (в, на) (куда́) (к кому́)	to arrive (by plane) (to somewhere) (to someone's)
приноси́ть — принош-у́, принóс-ишь, -ят принести́ — принес-у́, -ёшь, -у́т (что, когó куда́, комý)	to bring, carry to (something/one to somewhere/one)
приходи́ть — прихож-у́, прихóд-ишь, -ят прийти́ — прид-у́, -ёшь, -у́т (в, на) (куда́) (к кому́)	to arrive (on foot) (to somewhere) (to someone's)
прóбовать — прóбу-ю, -ешь, -ют попрóбовать — попрóбу-ю, -ешь, -ют (что)	to try, taste, sample (something)
проезжа́ть — проезжа́-ю, -ешь, -ют прое́хать — прое́д-у, -ешь, -ут (в, на) (куда́) (ми́мо чего́, когó)	to pass, ride by, ride through (by vehicle) (to someplace) (by something/one)
пролета́ть — пролета́-ю, -ешь, -ют пролете́ть — пролеч-у́, пролет-и́шь, -я́т (в, на) (куда́) (ми́мо чегó, когó)	to fly through (to someplace) (by something/one)
просыпа́ться — просыпа́-юсь, -ешься, -ются проснýться — просн-у́сь, -ёшься, -у́тся	to wake up, awake
проходи́ть — прохож-у́, прохóд-ишь, -ят пройти́ — пройд-у́, -ёшь, -у́т (в, на) (куда́) (ми́мо чегó, когó) (что) (где)	to pass by, walk through (on foot), (to somewhere) (by something/one) to occur, happen (s.t.) (somewhere)
сади́ться — саж-у́сь, сад-и́шься, -я́тся сесть — ся́д-у, -ешь, -ут (в, за что) (в маши́ну) (за стол)	to sit down (somewhere) (to get in the car) (to sit down at the table)
совéтовать — совéту-ю, -ешь, -ют посовéтовать — посовéту-ю, -ешь, -ют (комý что, чемý)	to advise, counsel, give advice (to someone/something, on something)
спать — сп-лю, -ишь, -ят поспа́ть — посп-лю́, -и́шь, -я́т	to sleep ` to take a nap
спеши́ть — спеш-у́, -и́шь, -а́т поспеши́ть — поспеш-у́, -и́шь, -а́т (в, на) (куда́)	to hurry, rush (to somewhere)
стоя́ть — сто-ю́, йшь, -я́т постоя́ть — посто-ю́, йшь, -я́т (где) (за когó, что)	to stand, be situated, stop (somewhere) (behind someone, for something—as in giving support to)
сходи́ть — схож-у́, схóд-ишь, -ят * сойти́ — сойд-у́, -ёшь, -у́т (с чего на что) *as a perfective verb, сходи́ть means "to go somewhere and return, to stop by somewhere" (в, на) (куда́)	to come down, go down, get off; come down (from one place onto another) (to somewhere—stopping by)
съéздить — съéзж-у, съéзд-ишь, -ят (pf.) (в, на) (куда́)	to go somewhere and return, stop by somewhere (vehicle) (to somewhere)
успева́ть — успева́-ю, -ешь, -ют успéть — успé-ю, -ешь, -ют (на что) (к чемý) (в чём)	to have time, succeed, manage (to get somewhere) (to get something done) (in something)
фотографи́ровать(ся) — фотографи́ру-ю(сь), -ешь(ся), -ют(ся сфотографи́ровать(ся) —сфотографи́ру-ю(сь), -ешь(ся), -ют(ся) (с чем, кем) фотографи́ровать (что, когó)	to photograph; be photographed (with something/one) to photograph (something/one)
ходи́ть — хож-у́, хóд-ишь, -ят (multidirectional) идти́/пойти́ (unidirectional) (в, на) (куда́) (к кому́)	to go (on foot) (to somewhere) (to someone's)

RUSSIAN FACES AND VOICES

болéть — (3rd person form) боли́т, боля́т заболéть — заболи́т, заболя́т	to ache to begin to ache
болта́ть — болта́-ю, -ешь, -ют поболта́-ю, -ешь, -ют	to talk (chit-chat)
боя́ться — бо-ю́сь, -и́шься, -я́тся побоя́ться — побо-ю́сь, -и́шься, -я́тся (чегó, когó)	to be afraid (of something/one)
вéрить — вéр-ю, -ишь, -ят повéрить — повéр-ю, -ишь, -ят (во что, когó) (чемý, комý)	to believe, trust (in something/one) (something/one)
взлета́ть — взлета́-ю, -ешь, -ют взлетéть — взлеч-у́, взлет-и́шь, -я́т (на что— вóздух)	to take off (flying) (to blow up—into the air)
вкла́дывать — вкла́дыва-ю, -ешь, -ют вложи́ть — влож-у́, влóж-ишь, -ат (во что) (дýшу в когó/во что)	to put , insert (into something) (to put one's heart or soul into someone/thing)

водѝть — вож-ý, вóд-ишь, -ят (*multidirectional*) вестѝ/повестѝ — (по)вед-ý, -ёшь, -ýт (*unidirect.*) (что, когó)	to lead, conduct, drive (drive, lead, conduct something, lead someone)
вспоминáть — вспоминá-ю, -ешь, -ют вспóмнить — вспóмн-ю, -ишь, -ят (что, когó)	to remember, recall, recollect (something, someone)
вылетáть — вылетá-ю, -ешь, -ют вы́лететь — вы́леч-у, вы́лет-ишь, -ят (во что) (из, от чегó)	to fly out, take off (into something) (from someplace)
выполня́ть — выполня́-ю, -ешь, -ют вы́полнить — вы́полн-ю, -ишь, -ят (что)	to carry out, fulfill (something—order, requirement)
выра́щивать — выра́щива-ю, -ешь, -ют вы́растить — вы́ращ-у, вы́раст-ишь, -ят (что, когó)	to bring up, rear, cultivate, raise (something—crop) (someone—child)
выходѝть — выхож-ý, выхóд-ишь, -ят вы́йти — вы́йд-у, -ешь, -ут(зáмуж за когó) (из, от, с чегó) (в, на что, кудá)	to go out, exit (*to get married—woman to a man*) (from something to something, somewhere)
вязáть — вяж-ý, вя́ж-ешь, -ут связáть — свяж-ý, свя́ж-ешь, -ут (что)	to knit (something)
гордѝться — горж-ýсь, гóрд-ишься, -ятся (чем, кем) возгордѝться — возгорж-ýсь, возгóрд-ишься, -ятся	to be proud of (something/one)
дойть — до-ю́, -йшь, -я́т (когó) подойть — подо-ю́, -йшь, -я́т	to milk (an animal)
жалéть — жалé-ю, -ешь, -ют пожалéть — пожалé-ю, -ешь, -ют (что, когó) (о чём, ком)	to pity, feel sorry for, regret (something, someone) (about something, someone)
жáловаться — жáлу-юсь, -ешься, -ются пожáловаться — пожáлу-юсь, -ешься, -ются (комý на что, когó)	to complain (to someone about something/one)
ждать — жд-у, -ёшь, -ут подождáть — подожд-ý, -ёшь, -ут (что, когó) (чегó, когó)	to wait (for something, someone)
женѝться — жен-ю́сь, жéн-ишься, -ятся (на ком) поженѝться — (*по я, ты, он/а forms*) поже́нятся	to marry (*for a man*) (to someone) to marry (*for a couple*)
зáвтракать — зáвтрака-ю, -ешь, -ют позáвтракать — позáвтрака-ю, -ешь, -ют	to eat breakfast
задавáть — задá-ю, -ёшь, -ют (что—вопрóс) задáть — задáм, задáшь, задáст, зададѝм, зададѝте, зададýт (что комý)	to assign, give (to ask a question) (pose something—a question, etc., to someone)
закáнчивать — закáнчива-ю, -ешь, -ют закóнчить — закóнч-у, -ишь, -ат (что)	to finish (something)
катáться — катá-юсь, -ешься, -ются (*multidirectional*) катѝться/покатѝться — (по)кач-ýсь, (по)кáт-ишься, -ятся (*unidirectional*) (на чём)	to roll (skates), ride (bike/skis), go fast, go for a drive (in something)
кáшлять — кáшля-ю, -ешь, -ют покáшлять — покáшля-ю, -ешь, -ют	to cough, have a cough
курѝть — кур-ю́, кýр-ишь, -ят (что) покурѝть — покур-ю́, покýр-ишь, -ят	to smoke (something)
летáть — летá-ю, -ешь, -ют (*multidirectional*) летéть/(по)летéть — (по)леч-ý, (по)лет-йшь, -ят (*unidirectional*) (в, на) (кудá) (на чём) *or* (чем)	to fly (to somewhere) (by means of something)
лечѝть(ся) — леч-ý(сь), лéч-ишь(ся), -ат(ся) вы́лечить(ся) — вы́леч-у(сь), -ишь(ся), -ат(ся) (чем)	to treat, cure (to be cured, or under medical care) (by means of s.t.)
ложѝться — лож-ýсь, -йшься, -áтся лечь — ля́гу, ля́жешь, ля́жет, ля́жем, ля́жете, ля́гут	to lie down, go to bed
мéрить — мéр-ю, -ишь, -ят помéрить — помéр-ю, -ишь, -ят (что, когó)	to measure, try on (measure something/one, try on something)
мечтáть — мечтá-ю, -ешь, -ют помечтáть — помечтá-ю, -ешь, -ют (о чём, ком)	to dream, daydream (about something/one)
молѝться — мол-ю́сь, мóл-ешься, -ются помолѝться — помол-ю́сь, помóл-ешься, -ются	to pray
мы́ться — мó-юсь, -ешься, -ются помы́ться — помó-юсь, -ешься, -ются	to wash oneself, get washed up
нарабáтываться — нарабáтыва-юсь, -ешься, -ются нарабóтаться — нарабóта-юсь, -ешься, -ются	to work too much, to overwork

обéдать — обéда-ю, -ешь, -ют пообéдать — пообéда-ю, -ешь, -ют	to eat lunch
одевáть(ся) — одевá-ю(сь), -ешь(ся), -ют(ся) одéть(ся) — одéн-у(сь), -ешь(ся), -ут(ся)	to dress someone (to get dressed, dress oneself)
оснóвывать — оснóвыва-ю, -ешь, -ют основáть — осну-ю́, -ёшь, -ю́т (что на чём)	to found, establish, base (something on something)
открывáть — открывá-ю, -ешь, -ют откры́ть — открó-ю, -ешь, -ют (что, когó)	to open (something, someone)
относи́ться — отнош-у́сь, отнóс-ишься, -ятся (к чему́, кому́) отнести́сь — отнес-у́сь, -ёшься, -у́тся	to treat, regard, relate to, think about (something, someone)
общáться — общá-юсь, -ешься, -ются пообщáться — пообщá-юсь, -ешься, -ются (с кем)	to communicate, get together (with someone)
ошибáться — ошибá-юсь, -ешься, -ются ошиби́ться — ошиб-у́сь, -ёшься, -у́тся	to be mistaken
пáдать — пáда-ю, -ешь, -ют упáсть — упад-у́, -ешь, -у́т (на что)	to fall, drop down (on something)
печáтать — печáта-ю, -ешь, -ют (что на чём) напечáтать — напечáта-ю, -ешь, -ют	to print, type (something on s.t.—on a keyboard, computer, typewriter)
плáвать — плáва-ю, -ешь, -ют (multidirectional) плыть/поплы́ть — (по) плыв-у́, -ёшь, -у́т (unidirectional)	to swim
погибáть — погибá-ю, -ешь, -ют поги́бнуть — поги́бн-у, -ешь, -ут (от чего)	to perish, be killed, lost (due to something)
подскáзывать — подскáзыва-ю, -ешь, -ют подсказáть — подскаж-у́, подскáж-ешь, -ут (что кому́)	to prompt, hint (something to someone)
получáть — получá-ю, -ешь, -ют (что) получи́ть — получ-у́, полу́ч-ишь, -ат	to receive (something)
помогáть — помогá-ю, -ешь, -ют помóчь — помогу́, помóжешь, помóжет, помóжем, помóжете, помогу́т (чему́, кому́)	to help, give aid (to something/one)
попадáть — попадá-ю, -ешь, -ют попáсть — попад-у́, -ёшь, -у́т (в, на что, когó)	to hit, get (to), find oneself (at), end up (at) (into, on something, someone) (чем)—(by means of something)
появля́ться — появля́-юсь, -ешься, -ются появи́ться — появ-лю́сь, поя́в-ишься, -ятся	to appear
преподавáть — препода-ю́, -ёшь, -ю́т (no pf.) (что кому́)	to teach (something to someone)
принимáть — принимá-ю, -ешь, -ют приня́ть — прим-у́, при́м-ешь, -ут (что, когó) (во что)	to take, accept, receive, admit (something/one)(into something)
причёсываться — причёсыва-юсь, -ешься, -ются причесáться — причеш-у́сь, причéш-ешься, причеш-у́тся	to comb, brush one's hair
продавáть — прода-ю́, -ёшь, -ю́т продáть — продáм, продáшь, продáст, продади́м, продади́те, продаду́т (что, когó)(кому́)	to sell (something/one) (to someone)
продолжáть — продолжá-ю, -ешь, -ют продóлжить — продолж-у́, продóлж-ишь, -ат (что)	to continue, extend (something)
пряcть — пряд-у́, -ёшь, -у́т (что) напря́сть — напряд-у́, -ёшь, -у́т	to spin (something—like wool, yarn)
развивáть — развивá-ю, -ешь, -ют разви́ть — разовь-ю́, -ёшь, -ю́т (что)	to develop (something)
реставри́ровать — реставри́ру-ю, -ешь, -ют (impf./pf.) отреставри́ровать — отреставри́ру-ю, -ешь, -ют (pf.) (что)	to restore, remodel (something)
рождáться — рождá-юсь, -ешься, -ются роди́ться — рож-у́сь, род-и́шься, -я́тся	to be born, spring up
сажáть — сажá-ю, -ешь, -ют посади́ть — посаж-у́, посáд-ишь, -ят (что, когó в/на что)	to plant, seat, imprison (something/one in something, somewhere)
свя́зывать — свя́зыва-ю, -ешь, -ют связáть — свяж-у́, свя́ж-ешь, -ут (что, когó с чем, кем)	to connect, tie together, bind, knit (something/one to, with something/one)
сдавáть — сда-ю́, -ёшь, -ю́т сдать — сдам, сдашь, сдаст, сдади́м, сдади́те, сдаду́т (что)	to hand over, rent, to pass (exam), turn in, take (s.t.)

сиде́ть — сиж-у́, сид-и́шь, -я́т посиде́ть — посиж-у́, посид-и́шь, -я́т (на чём) (где)	to sit, fit (clothes on someone) (to sit somewhere)
собира́ться — собира́-юсь, -ешься, -ются собра́ться — собер-у́сь, -ёшься, -у́тся (где)	to gather, assemble, get ready to, get prepared for s.t. (gather, assemble somewhere)
создава́ть — созда-ю́, -ёшь, -ют созда́ть — созда́м, сода́шь, созда́ст, создади́м, создади́те, создаду́т (что, кого́)	to create, found, build [from the beginning] (something, someone)
спаса́ть — спаса́-ю, -ешь, -ют спасти́ — спас-у́, -ёшь, -у́т (что, кого́)	to save, rescue (something, someone)
счита́ть — счита́-ю, -ешь, -ют посчита́ть — посчита́-ю, -ешь, -ют (что, кого́ чем, кем)	to think, consider (something/one as something/one)
теря́ть — теря́-ю, -ешь, -ют потеря́ть — потеря́-ю, -ешь, -ют (что, кого́)	to lose (something, someone)
убира́ть — убира́-ю, -ешь, -ют убра́ть — убер-у́, -ёшь, -у́т (что)	to clean up, tidy up (house, living area) to remove (something)
увлека́ться — увлека́-юсь, -ешься, -ются увле́чься — увлек-у́сь, увлеч-ёшься, увлек-у́тся	to be involved (in), interested (in), captivated (by)
удивля́ть — удивля́-ю, -ешь, -ют удиви́ть — удив-лю́, -и́шь, -я́т (что, кого́)	to surprise, amaze (something, someone)
у́жинать — у́жина-ю, -ешь, -ют поу́жинать — поу́жина-ю, -ешь, -ют	to eat supper, dinner
улыба́ться — улыба́-юсь, -ешься, -ются улыбну́ться — улыбн-у́сь, -ёшься, у́тся	to smile
уме́ть — уме́-ю, -ешь, -ют суме́ть — суме́-ю, -ешь, -ют	to be able, know how to know how, succeed (at)
умира́ть — умира́-ю, -ешь, -ют (с, от чего́) умере́ть — умр-у́, -ёшь, -у́т	to die (from something)
учи́ть — уч-у́, у́ч-ишь, -ат научи́ть — науч-у́, нау́ч-ишь, -ат (кого́/чему́/что де́лать)	to teach (someone something/how to do something)
хвата́ть — (3rd person only): хвата́ет, хвата́ют хвати́ть (3rd person only): хва́тит, хва́тят (чего́)	to be enough, suffice (of something)
чу́вствовать — чу́вству-ю, -ешь, -ют (себя́) почу́вствовать — почу́вству-ю, -ешь, -ют (что)	to feel (when speaking of how a person feels, referring to health)

МИР РУССКИХ

бала́кать — бала́ка-ю, -ешь, -ют (impf. only) (dialectical variant of болта́ть)	to chat
баю́кать — баю́ка-ю, -ешь, -ют] (impf. only) (кого́)	to lull to sleep, sing lullabies (to s.o.)
бере́чь — берегу́, береж-ёшь, берегу́т] (impf.) (что, кого́) (как зени́цу о́ка)	to take care of; to cherish (something/one) ; to cherish (something) as the apple of one's eye
бесе́довать — бесе́ду-ю, -ешь, -ут (impf. (с кем)	to converse (with someone)
бить — бь-ю, -ёшь, -ют поби́ть — побь-ю́, -ёшь, -ют (что, кого́ по чему́, во что)	to hit, beat (something/someone on something, into something)
боро́ться — борю́сь, бо́р-ешься, -ются (impf.) (с чем, кем) (за что, кого́) (про́тив чего́, кого́)	to fight, to struggle (with something/one) (for something/one) (against something/one)
броса́ться — броса́-юсь, -ешься, -ются бро́ситься — бро́шусь, бро́с-ишься, -ятся (на что, кого́) (во что)	to hurl oneself at, to rush (on something/one) (into something)
буди́ть — бужу́, бу́д-ишь, -ят разбуди́ть — разбужу́, разбу́д-ишь, -ят (что, кого́)	to awaken (something/one)
вари́ть — вар-ю́, ва́р-ишь, -ят (что) свари́ть — свар-ю́, сва́р-ишь, -ят	to cook by boiling (something)
везти́ (кому́) (impersonal construction + dative) повезти́ — (мне/ему́ везёт)	to be lucky (someone) is lucky (I/he is lucky)
венча́ться — венча́-юсь, -ешься, -ются повенча́ться — повенча́-юсь, -ешься, -ются обвенча́ться — обвенча́-юсь, -ешься, -ются	to marry, be married
вести́ (себя́) — вед-у́, -ёшь, -у́т (impf.)	to behave, conduct (oneself)

владе́ть — владе́-ю, -ешь, -ют *(impf.)* (чем, кем) (владе́ть се́рдцем)	to own, possess (something/one) *(to rule the heart)*
возвраща́ть — возвраща́-ю, -ешь, -ют возврати́ть — возвращу́, возврат-и́шь, -я́т верну́ть — верн-у́, -ёшь, -у́т (что, кого́) (чему́, кому́)	to return (something, someone) (to something, someone)
возвраща́ться — возвраща́-юсь, -ешься, -ются верну́ться — верн-у́сь, -ёшься, -у́ться (куда́) (к кому́)	to return (somewhere) (to someone)
вози́ться — вожу́сь, во́з-ишься, -ятся *(impf. only)* (чем, кем)	to spend time, bother, take pains (with something/one)
возобновля́ться — возобновля́-юсь, -ешься, -ются возобнови́ться — возобновлю́сь, возобнов-и́шься, -я́тся	to resume
воспи́тывать — воспи́тыва-ю, ешь, -ют воспита́ть — воспита́-ю, ешь, -ют (что, кого́)	to bring up, raise (something/one)
воспринима́ться — воспринима́-юсь, -ешься, -ются восприня́ться — восприму́сь, восприм-ишься, -утся	to be perceived
впада́ть — впада́-ю, -ешь, -ют впасть — впад-у́, -ёшь, -у́т	to fall into
врать — вр-у, -ёшь, -ут *(impf.)*	to lie (not tell the truth)
вспомина́ться — вспомина́-юсь, -ешься, -ются (кому́) вспо́мниться — вспо́мн-юсь, -ишься, -ятся *(impers.+ dat.)*	to remember, call to mind
встреча́ть(ся) — встреча́-ю(сь), -ешь(ся), -ют(ся) встре́тить(ся) — встре́ч-у(сь), встре́т-ишь(ся),-ят(ся) встреча́ть/встре́тить (что, кого́) встреча́ться/встре́титься (с чем, кем)	to meet, encounter (something, someone) to meet (with something, someone)
втя́гивать — втя́гива-ю, -ешь, -ют втяну́ть — втяну́, втян-ешь, -ут (что, кого́)	to draw into, pull in, tug at (something, someone)
вы́глядеть — вы́гляжу, вы́гляд-ишь, -ят *(impf. only)*	to look (younger, beautiful, etc.)
выжива́ть — выжива́-ю, -ешь, -ют вы́жить — вы́живу, вы́жив-ешь, -ут	to survive
вызыва́ть — вызыва́-ю, -ешь, -ют вы́звать — вы́зов-у, -ешь, -ут (что, кого́) (что у кого́)	to call or send for (something/one) to provoke, evoke (something in s.o.)
вылива́ться — вылива́-юсь, -ешься, -ются вы́литься — вы́ль-юсь, -ешься, -ются (во что)	to take the form (of); to express (as something)
вымира́ть — *(3rd person only)* вымира́-ет, -ют вы́м(е)реть — вы́мр-ет, -ут	to die out
вы́мыться — вы́мо-юсь, -ешься, -ются *(pf. only)*	to wash oneself fully
выража́ть — выража́-ю, -ешь, -ют вы́разить — вы́ражу, вы́разишь, вы́ражат (что)	to express (something)
выража́ться — выража́-юсь, -ешься, -ются вы́разиться — вы́ражусь, вы́разишься, вы́ражатся	to be expressed
выруба́ть — выруба́-ю, -ешь, -ют вы́рубить — вы́руб-лю, -ишь, -ят (что)	to cut down (something)
выска́зывать — выска́зыва-ю, -ешь, -ют вы́сказать — вы́скажу, -ешь, -ут (что кому́)	to state (something to someone)
выска́кивать — выска́кива-ю, -ешь, -ют вы́скочить — вы́скоч-у, -ишь, -ат (из чего́)	to jump out (from something)
выта́скивать — выта́скива-ю, -ешь, -ют вы́тащить — вы́тащ-у, -ишь, -ат (что, кого́) (из чего́)	to drag out (something, someone) (from something)
выхва́тывать — выхва́тыва-ю, -ешь, -ют вы́хватить — вы́хвачу, вы́хватишь, -ят (из чего́) (что из рук у кого́)	to pull quickly, snatch out (from something) (something from the hands of someone)
выходи́ть — выхожу́, выхо́д-ишь, -ят (из, от чего́) вы́йти — вы́йд-у, -ешь, -ут *(не выходи́ть из головы́)*	to leave, go out, exit (from someplace) *(to stick in one's mind)*
гла́дить — гла́жу, -ишь, -ят погла́дить — (что, кого́) (по чему́) (чем)	to iron, press, stroke (something/one) (on something—head, face) (with something, e.g., an iron)
гляде́ть — гляжу́, гляди́шь, -я́т *(impf.)* (на что, кого́)	to look (at something, someone)
гнать — гон-ю́, го́н-ишь, -я́т погна́ть — погон-ю́, пого́н-ишь, -я́т (что, кого́)	to chase, to drive (something, e.g., a herd of animals)
горе́ть — гор-ю́, -и́шь, -я́т *(impf.)*	to burn

губи́ть — гу́б-лю, гу́б-ишь, -ят погуби́ть — погублю́, погу́бишь, погу́бят (что, кого́)	to kill, destroy (something, someone)
дискути́ровать — дискути́ру-ю, -ешь, -ют *(impf. only)* (что, о чём)	to discuss (something, about something)
добавля́ть — добавля́-ю, -ешь, -ют доба́вить — доба́влю, доба́в-ишь, -ят (что, чего́) (что к чему́)	to add (something, part of something) (something to something)
доверя́ть — доверя́-ю, -ешь, -ют дове́рить — дове́р-ю, -ишь, -ят (что кому́) (кому́) (чему́)	to trust; to confide (in) (something to someone); to take (someone) into one's confidence
догова́риваться — догова́рива-юсь, -ешься, -ются договори́ться — договор-ю́сь, -и́шься, -я́тся (с кем о чём)	to make arrangements, negotiate (with someone about something)
дока́зывать — дока́зыва-ю, -ешь, -ют доказа́ть — докажу́, дока́ж-ешь, -ут (что)	to prove (something)
достава́ться — доста-ю́сь, -ёшься, -ю́тся доста́ться — доста́н-усь, -ешься, -утся (кому́)	to have problems; *(colloq.)* to bear, to endure (for someone)
достига́ть — достига́-ю, -ешь, -ют дости́чь, дости́гнуть — дости́гн-у, -ешь, -ут	to achieve
дрема́ть — дремл-ю́, дрёмл-ешь, -ют *(impf. only)*	to doze off
забира́ть — забира́-ю, -ешь, -ют забра́ть — забер-у́, -ёшь, -у́т (что, кого́)	to take (away) (something/one)
забыва́ться — забыва́-юсь, -ешься, -ются забы́ться — забу́д-усь -ешься, -утся	to be forgotten
зави́сеть — зави́шу, зави́с-ишь, -ят *(impf. only)* (от чего́/кого́)	to depend (on something/one)
заводи́ть — завожу́, заво́д-ишь, -ят завести́ — завед-у́, -ёшь, -у́т (что, кого́)	to set up, to start, to acquire (something, someone)
завоёвывать — завоёвыва-ю, -ешь, -ют завоева́ть — заво-ю́ю, -ю́ешь, -ю́ют (что, кого́)	to conquer; to gain (something, someone)
загля́дывать — загля́дыва-ю, -ешь, -ют загляну́ть — загляну́, -ёшь, -у́т (кому́ во что) (к кому́)	to look, take a peek (at s.t.) (someone in something—e.g., in the eyes, face, etc.) (drop by and see s.o.)
загора́ться — загора́-юсь, -ешься, -ются загоре́ться — загор-ю́сь, -и́шься, -я́тся	to catch fire
заду́мываться — заду́мыва-юсь, -ешься, -ются заду́маться — заду́ма-юсь, -ешься, -ются (о чём)	to become lost in thought (about something)
заключа́ть — заключа́-ю, -ешь, -ют заключи́ть — заключ-у́, -ишь, -ат (что чем) (кого́, что во что)	to conclude (something by/with s.t.); to deduce (s.t. on the basis of something); to convict (someone)
заключа́ться — заключа́-юсь, -ешься, -ются заключи́ться — заключ-у́сь, -и́шься, -а́тся (в чём) (чем)	to consist (of), to lie, to be (contained in); to end, conclude (in, with s.t.)
заменя́ть — заменя́-ю, -ешь, -ют замени́ть — заменю́, заме́н-ишь, -ят (что, кого́ чем, кем) (что, кого́ чему́, кому́)	to take the place (of) (something/one is replaced by something/one) (something/one replaces something/one else)
замеча́ть — замеча́-ю, ешь, -ют заме́тить — заме́чу, заме́тишь, -ят (что, кого́)	to notice, observe (something, someone)
замеча́ться — замеча́-юсь, -ешься, -ются заме́титься — заме́чусь, заме́т-ишься, -ятся	to be noticed
запе́ть — запою́, -ёшь, -ю́т (pf.) (что)	to start singing (something)
зараба́тывать — зарабатыва́-ю, -ешь, -ют (что) зарабо́тать — зарабо́та-ю, -ешь, -ют	to earn (something) to begin to work
заставля́ть — заставля́-ю, -ешь, -ют заста́вить — заста́влю, -ишь, -ят (что, кого́)	to force (something, someone)
засыпа́ть — засыпа́-ю, -ешь, -ют засну́ть — засну́-ю, -ешь, -ют	to fall asleep
затиха́ть — затиха́-ю, -ешь, -ют зати́хнуть — зати́хн-у, -ешь, -ют	to subside, abate, to become silent, die away
захлёбываться — захлёбыва-юсь, -ешься, -ются захлебну́ться — захлебн-у́сь, -ёшься, -ну́тся	to choke, drown
защища́ть — защища́-ю, -ешь, -ют защити́ть — защищу́, защит-и́шь, -я́т (что, кого́ от чего́, кого́)	to defend, protect (something/one from something/one)

звать — зов-ý, -ёшь, -ýт *(impf.)* (что, кого чем, кем)	to call (something, someone by something, someone)
звенéть — *(3rd person only)* звен-úт, -я́т прозвенéть — *(3rd person only)* прозвен-úт, -я́т	to ring, resound
изменя́ть — изменя́-ю, -ешь, -ют (что, кого) изменúть — измен-ю́, -и́шь, -я́т (чему́, кому́)	to change (something, someone) to betray (something, someone)
изменя́ться — изменя́-юсь, -ешься, -ются *(intrans.)* (к чему́) изменúться — измен-ю́сь, -и́шься, -я́тся *(intrans.)*	to change (to, for something)
изобража́ть — изобража́-ю, -ешь, -ют изобразúть — изображу́, изобраз-и́шь, -я́т (что, кого́)	to depict; to express (something, someone)
имéть — имé-ю, -ешь, -ют *(impf. only)* дéло (с чем, кем) (значéние)	to deal (with something/one) *(to matter, have importance)*
имитúровать — имитúру-ю, -ешь, -ют *(impf. only)* (что, кого́)	to imitate (something, someone)
исполня́ть — исполня́-ю, -ешь, -ют испóлнить — испóлн-ю, -ишь, -ят (что, кого́)	to perform, play, use (something, someone)
испóльзовать — испóльзу-ю, -ешь,-ют *(impf./pf.)* (что, кого́)	to use (something, someone)
испóльзоваться — испóльзу-юсь, -ешься, -ются *(impf. only)* (чем, кем)	to be used (by something/one)
исправля́ть — исправля́-ю, -ешь, -ют испрáвить — исправлю, испрáв-ишь, -ят (что, кого́)	to correct (something, someone)
иссуша́ть — иссуша́-ю, -ешь, -ют иссушúть — иссушу́, иссýш-ишь, -ат (что)	to dry up (something)
истребля́ть — истребля́-ю, -ешь, -ют истребúть — истреблю́, истреб-úшь, -я́т (что, кого́)	to devour, annihilate (something, someone)
исчéрпывать — исчéрпыва-ю, -ешь, -ют исчерпáть — исчерпá-ю, -ешь, -ют (что)	to exhaust (something)
казáться — кажу́сь, кáжешься, кáжутся показáться — покажу́сь, покáжешься, покáжутся (кому́ чем, кем)	to seem, to appear (to someone as something/one)
казнúть — казн-ю́, -úшь, -я́т *(impf. and pf.)* (кого́)	to execute (someone)
коллекционúровать — коллекционúру-ю, -ешь, -ют *(impf.)* (что)	to collect (something)
консервúровать — консервúру-ю, -ешь, -ют законсервúровать — законсервúру-ю, -ешь, -ют (что)	to can, to preserve (food)
красть — крад-ý, -ёшь, -ýт украсть — украд-ý, -ёшь, -ýт (что) (у кого́)	to steal (something) (from someone)
критиковáть — критику́-ю, -ешь, -ют *(impf. only)* (что, кого́)	to criticize (something, someone)
купáться — купá-юсь, -ешься, -ются *(impf. only)* (где)	to swim (somewhere)
лéзть — лéз-у, -ешь, -ут *(impf.)*	to crawl
меня́ться — меня́-юсь, -ешься,- ются поменя́ться — поменя́-юсь, -ешься,- ются (чем с чем, кем)	to exchange, change (something for, with something/one)
мстить — мщу, мст-úшь, -я́т *(impf.)* (кому́ за что)	to avenge; to take revenge on (someone for something done)
мчáться — мч-ýсь, -úшься, -áтся *(impf.)*	to speed by, to rush
мыть — мó-ю, -ешь, -ют помы́ть — помó-ю, -ешь, -ют *(pf.)* вы́мыть — вы́мо-ю, -ешь, -ют *(pf.)* (что, кого́)	to wash (something, someone)
наблюдáть — наблюдá-ю, -ешь, -ют *(impf.)* (что, кого́) (как кто что дéлает)	to observe (something, someone) (how someone does something)
накрывáть — накрывá-ю, -ешь, -ют (что) (на что) накры́ть — накрóю, -óешь, -óют [(на) стол]	to set, to cover (something) *[to set the table]*
наливáть — наливá-ю, -ешь, -ют налúть — нал-ью́, -ьёшь, -ью́т (что кому́)	to pour (something for someone)
напоминáть — напоминá-ю, -ешь, -ют (кому́ о чём, ком) напóмнить — напóмн-ю, -ишь, -ят (что, кого́)	to remind (someone of something) to resemble (something, someone)
направля́ть — направля́-ю, -ешь, -ют напрáвить — напрáвлю, напрáв-ишь, -ят (что на что)	to direct, send (something to/toward something)
наступáть — наступá-ю, -ешь, -ют наступúть — наступлю́, настýп-ишь, -ят (на кого́)	to begin; to advance (on someone), as in an armed attack

натыка́ться — натыка́-юсь, -ешься, -ются наткну́ться — наткн-у́сь, -ёшся, -у́тся (на что, кого)	to come across, to run into (something, someone)
находи́ть — нахожу́, нахо́д-ишь, -ят найти́ — найд-у́, -ёшь, -у́т (что, кого)	to find, locate (something, someone)
находи́ться — нахожу́сь, нахо́д-ишься, -ятся найти́сь — найд-у́сь, -ёшься, -у́тся (в, на чём) (где)	to be found, to be located (somewhere)
нужда́ться — нужда́-юсь, -ешься, -ются (в чём, ком)	to need, have need (of something/one)
обижа́ться — обижа́-юсь, -ешься, -ются оби́деться — обижусь, оби́ди-шься, -ятся (на что, кого)	to be offended (by something, someone)
обнима́ть — обнима́-ю, -ешь, -ют обня́ть — обним-у́, -ешь, -у́т (что, кого)	to embrace, hug (something, someone)
образо́вываться — образо́быва-юсь, -ешься, -ются образова́ться — образу́-юсь, -ешься, -ются	to be created, to form, to arise
обраща́ться — обраща́-юсь, -ешься, -ются обрати́ться — обращу́сь, обрат-и́шься, -я́тся (к кому)	to address (someone, when speaking), to turn (to someone—when needing s.t.)
обрета́ть — обрета́-ю, -ешь, -ют обрести́ — обрет-у́, -ёшь, -у́т (что, кого)	to find (something, someone)
объединя́ть — объединя́-ю, -ешь, -ют объедини́ть — объедин-ю́, -и́шь, -я́т (что, кого)	to unite (something, someone)
объявля́ть — объявля́-ю, -ешь, -ют объяви́ть — объявлю, объя́в-ишь, -ят (что/о чём кому) (что, кого чем, кем)	to announce, declare, proclaim (something to someone); to declare (something/one as something/one)
огля́дывать — огля́дыва-ю, -ешь, -ют огляде́ть — огляжу́, огляд-и́шь, -я́т (что, кого)	to look around, glance at (something, someone)
одобря́ть — одобря́-ю, -ешь, -ют одо́брить — одо́бр-ю, -ишь, -ят (что, кого)	to approve (of), to support (something, someone)
ока́зываться — ока́зыва-юсь -ешься, -ются оказа́ться — окаж-у́сь, ока́ж-ешься, -утся (чем, кем)	to turn out (to be) (something/one)
ока́нчивать — ока́нчива-ю, -ешь, -ют око́нчить — око́нч-у, -ишь, -ат (что)	to finish (something)
определя́ть — определя́-ю, -ешь, -ют определи́ть — определ-ю́, -и́шь, -я́т (что, кого)	to determine (something, someone)
осва́ивать — осва́ива-ю, -ешь, -ют осво́ить — осво́-ю, -ишь, -ят (что)	to assimilate, master, cope (with something)
оседа́ть — оседа́-ю, -ешь, -ют осе́сть — ося́д-у, -ешь, -ут	to establish residence
осно́вывать — осно́выва-ю, -ешь, -ют основа́ть — осну-ю́, -ёшь, ю́т (что на чём)	to found, establish, base (something on something)
остава́ться — оста-ю́сь, -ёшься,- ю́тся оста́ться — остан-у́сь, -ешся, -утся (где)	to remain, stay (somewhere)
оставля́ть — оставля́-ю, -ешь, -ют оста́вить — оставлю, оста́в-ишь, -ят (что, кого)	to leave, leave behind (something, someone)
осужда́ть — осужда́-ю, -ешь, -ют осуди́ть — осужу́, осу́д-ишь, -ят (что, кого за что)	to condemn; denounce (something/one for something done)
отбега́ть — отбега́-ю, -ешь, -ют отбежа́ть — отбе-гу́, -жи́шь, -гу́т (от чего, кого)	to run off, away (from something/one)
отдаля́ть — отдаля́-ю, -ешь, -ют отдали́ть — отдал-ю́, -и́шь, -я́т (что, кого от чего, кого)	to remove, separate, isolate (something/one from something/one)
откла́дывать — откла́дыва-ю, -ешь, -ют отложи́ть — отлож-у́, отло́ж-ишь, -ат (в, на что)	to put off (procrastinate), to set aside (something)
отлича́ть — отлича́-ю, -ешь, -ют отличи́ть — отлич-у́, -и́шь, -а́т (что, кого)	to distinguish between, differentiate, single out (something, someone)
отлича́ться — отлича́-юсь, -ешься, -ются отличи́ться — отлич-у́сь, -и́шься, -а́тся (от чего, кого чем)	to be notable (for); to distinguish oneself; to differ (from something/one in something)
отправля́ть — отправля́-ю, -ешь, -ют (что, кого) (куда) отпра́вить — отпра́в-лю, -ишь, -ят (что, кого кому) (что, кого куда чем)	to send (something/one to somewhere) (something/one to s.o.) *(something/one somewhere by some means, e.g., mail)*

отпуска́ть — отпуска́-ю, -ешь, -ют отпусти́ть — отпущу́, отпу́ст-ишь, -ят (что, кого́)	to allow, let go, release (something, someone)
отстава́ть — отста-ю́, -ёшь, ю́т отста́ть — отста́н-у, -ешь, -ут (от чего́, кого́ в чём)	to fall behind, be behind, be slow (fall behind something/one in something)
охо́титься — охо́чусь, охо́т-ишься, -ятся (impf.) (на кого́, за кем)	to hunt (for animals)
очаро́вывать — очаро́выва-ю, -ешь, -ют (кого́) очарова́ть — очару́-ю, -ешь, -ют	to charm (someone)
очища́ть — очища́-ю, -ешь, -ют (что) очи́стить — очи́щу, очи́ст-ишь -ят	to clean, purify (something)
па́риться — па́р-юсь, ишься, -ятся попа́риться — попа́р-юсь, -ишься, -ятся (где—в ба́не, са́уне)	to steam, sweat (somewhere—in a banya, sauna)
пасти́сь — (usually 3rd person only) пасётся, пасу́тся (impf.) (где)	to graze (somewhere)
перевози́ть — перевожу́, перево́з-ишь, -ят (indet.,) перевезти́ — перевез-у́, -ёшь, -у́т (что, кого́)	to bring (something, someone) by vehicle
передава́ть — переда-ю́, -ёшь, -ю́т переда́ть — переда́м, переда́шь, переда́ст, передад-и́м, -и́те, -у́т (кому́ что, кого́)	to give, convey, pass (on), hand (something, someone over to someone)
передава́ться — (3rd pers. only) переда-ётся, -ю́тся переда́ться — переда́стся, передаду́тся	to be inherited, to be handed down (to something/one)
переезжа́ть — переезжа́-ю, -ешь, -ют (в, на) (куда́) перее́хать — перее́д-у, -ешь, -ут (отку́да - туда́) (из го́рода в го́род)	to move (to another place), (from one place to another), (from city to city)
пережива́ть — пережива́-ю, -ешь, -ют пережи́ть — пережив-у́. -ёшь, -у́т (что)	to suffer, endure, outlive (something)
переу́чиваться — переучива́-юсь, -ешься, -ются переучи́ться — переучу́сь, переу́ч-ишься, -атся	to relearn, undergo retraining
пла́кать — пла́ч-у, -ешь, -ат (impf.)	to weep, cry
плати́ть — плачу́, пла́-тишь, -тят заплати́ть — заплачу́, запла́т -ишь, -ят (что за что, чем)	to pay (for something with something—e.g., money)
повествова́ть — повеству́-ю, -ешь, -ют (impf.) (о чём)	to recount, narrate (something)
повторя́ться — повторя́-юсь, -ешься, -ются повтори́ться — повтор-ю́сь, -и́шься, -я́тся	to be repeated
подава́ть — пода-ю́, -ёшь -ю́т (что) (кому́) пода́ть — пода́м, пода́шь, пода́ст, подад-и́м, -и́те, -у́т	to serve, to give out (something—e.g., food) (to someone)
подбега́ть — подбега́-ю, -ешь, -ют (indet..) (к чему́, кому́) подбежа́ть — подбегу́, подбеж-и́шь, подбегу́т (det.)	to run up (to) (something/one)
подверга́ться — подверга́-юсь, -ешься, -ются (чему́) подве́ргнуться — подве́ргн-усь, -ешься, -утся	to be subjected (to something)
поджида́ть — поджида́-ю, -ешь, -ют (impf.) (что/чего́, кого́)	to wait (for something, someone)
подкупа́ть — подкупа́-ю, -ешь, -ют подкупи́ть — подкуплю́, подку́п-ишь, -ят (что, кого́)	to win over (something, someone)
поднима́ть — поднима́-ю, -ешь, -ют подня́ть — подним-у́, подни́м-ешь, -ут (что, кого́)	to raise, lift up (something, someone)
поднима́ться — поднима́-юсь, -ешься, -ются подня́ться — поднимусь, подни́м-ешься, -утся	to develop, rise, surge
подозрева́ть — подозрева́-ю, -ешь, -ют (impf.) (что, кого́ в чём)	to suspect (something/one in s.t.)
подпи́сывать — подписыва-ю, -ешь, -ют подписа́ть — подпиш-у́, -ешь, -ут (что)	to sign (something)
подража́ть — подража́-ю, -ешь, -ют (impf.) (что, кого́)	to imitate (something, someone)
подразумева́ть — подразумева́-ю, -ешь, -ют (impf.) (что)	to imply (something)
подраста́ть — подраста́-ю, -ешь, -ют подрасти́ — подраст-у́, -ёшь, -у́т (что)	to grow up, raise (something)
подсчи́тывать — подсчи́тыва-ю, -ешь, -ют подсчита́ть — подсчита́-ю, -ешь, -ют (что)	to count up, calculate (something)
подходи́ть — подхожу́, подхо́д-ишь, -ят подойти́ — подойд-у́, -ёшь, -у́т	to come up (to); to approach

показываться — показыва-юсь, -ешься, -ются показаться — покажусь, покажешься, покажутся (кому)	to seem, to appear, to come into view (to someone)
поливать — полива-ю, -ешь, -ют полить — поль-ю -ёшь, -ют (что, кого чем)	to pour; to water (something/one with something)
получаться — получа-юсь, -ешься, -ются получиться — получ-усь, получ-ишься, -атся	to turn out
поменяться — поменя-юсь, -ешься, -ются (impf.) (с чем, кем)	to change, exchange (with something/one)
помещаться — помеща-юсь, -ешься, -ются (где) поместиться — помещусь, помест-ишься, -ятся (в, на чём)	to be located, situated, to fit (somewhere, in/at someplace)
помирать — помира-ю, -ешь, -ют помереть — помр-у, -ёшь, -ут	to die
помнить — помн-ю, -ишь, -ят (impf.) (что, кого)	to remember (something, someone)
попадать — попада-ю, -ешь, -ют попасть — попад-у, -ёшь, -ут (в, на что, кого чем)	to get (to something/one by means of s.t.)
попадаться — попада-юсь, -ешься, -ются попасться — попад-усь, -ёшься, -утся	to come across, to turn up
поражать — поража-ю, -ешь, -ют поразить — поражу, пораз-ишь, -ят (кого)	to affect, strike, make an impression (on someone)
поселяться — поселя- юсь, -ешься, -ются поселиться — посел-юсь, -ишься, -ятся (где)	to settle in, take up residence (somewhere)
посещать — посеща-ю, -ешь, -ют посетить — посещу, посет-ишь, -ят (что, кого)	to visit (something, someone)
постигать — постига-ю, -ешь, -ют постичь (or) постигнуть — постигн-у, -ешь, -ут (что, кого)	to comprehend (something, someone)
праздновать — праздн-ую, -уешь, -уют отпраздновать — отпраздн-ую, -уешь, -уют (что)	to celebrate (something)
превращать — превраща-ю, -ешь, -ют (что, кого в что, кого) превратить — превращу, преврат-ишь, -ят	to change, turn, transform (something, someone into something, someone)
предлагать — предлага-ю, -ешь, -ют (что, кого чему, кому) предложить — предлож-у, предлож-ишь, -ат	to propose (something/one to something/one)
предпочитать — предпочита-ю, -ешь, -ют предпочесть — предпочт-у, -ёшь, -ут (что, кого чему, кому)	to prefer (something/one to something/one)
представлять — представля-ю, -ешь, -ют представить — представлю, представ-ишь, -ят (что, кого чему, кому) (себе)	to present (something/one to something/one) (to imagine)
предчувствовать — предчувств-ую, -уешь, -уют (pf.)	to have a feeling, premonition (about)
преобладать — преоблада-ю, -ешь, -ют (impf.) (над чем)	to predominate (over something)
приближать — приближа-ю, -ешь, -ют (что, кого) приблизить — приближу, приблиз-ишь, -ят (к чему, кому)	to move closer (something/one) closer (to something/one)
приближаться — приближа-юсь, -ешься, -ются приблизиться — приближусь, приблизишься, -ятся (к чему, кому)	to approach, to come near (something/one)
привозить — привожу, привоз-ишь, -ят привезти — привез-у, -ёшь, -ут (что)	to bring (something) by vehicle
приговаривать — приговарива-ю, -ешь, -ют приговорить — приговор-ю, -ишь, -ят (что, кого к чему)	to keep saying, repeating; to sentence, condemn (something/one to s.t.)
придумывать — придумыва-ю, -ешь, -ют придумать — придума-ю, -ешь, -ют (что)	to think up, to devise (something)
придуриваться — придурива-юсь, -ешься, -ются(impf.)	to play the fool
признаваться — призна-юсь, -ёшься, -ются признаться — призна-юсь, -ешься, -ются (чему, кому в чём)	to admit (to something/one concerning something)
приказывать — приказыва-ю, -ешь, -ют приказать — прикаж-у, прикаж-ешь, -ут	to order, give an order
приласкать — приласка-ю, -ешь, -ют (pf.) (кого)	to be nice to (someone)
приниматся — примина-юсь, -ешся, -ются (за + acc.) приняться — примусь, прим-ешься, -утся (за дела)	to set (to), to get (to) (to get down to business)
принуждать — принужда-ю, -ешь, -ют принудить — принужу, принуд-ишь, -ят (что, кого)	to force, compel (something, someone)

приходи́ться — прихожу́сь, прихо́д-ишься, -ятся (кому́) прийти́сь — приду́сь, прид-ёшься, -у́тся (кому́ по чему́) *(по душе́)*	to have to; to fit, suit (someone in some regard, e.g., clothing, qualities) *[to be in harmony with (one's) soul]*
проверя́ть — проверя́-ю, -ешь, -ют прове́рить — прове́р-ю, -ишь, -ят (что, кого́)	to check (something, someone)
проводи́ть — провожу́, прово́дишь, -ят провести́ — проведу́, ёшь, -у́т (что, кого́ ми́мо чего́, кого́)	to conduct, guide, lead (something/one by something/one); to spend time (doing something)
проводи́ться — *(3rd person only)* прово́дится, -ятся провести́сь— *(3rd person only)* проведётся -у́тся (где)	to take place, occur (somewhere)
провожа́ть — провожа́-ю, -ешь, -ют проводи́ть — провожу́, прово́д-ишь, -ят (что, кого́)	to accompany (home) (something, someone)
прожива́ть — прожива́-ю, -ешь, -ют прожи́ть — прожив-у́, -ёшь, -у́т (что)	to live; to endure (something)
производи́ть — произвожу́, производ-ишь, -ят произвести́ — произвед-у́, -ёшь,-у́т (что, кого́) *(впечатле́ние)*	to produce (something/one) *(to make an impression on)*
происходи́ть — происхожу́, происхо́д-ишь, -ят произойти́ — произойд-у, -ёшь, -у́т (от чего́, кого́)	to derive, to occur (from something/one)
проплыва́ть — проплыва́-ю, -ешь, -ют проплы́ть — проплыв-у́, -ёшь, -у́т (ми́мо чего́, кого́)	to float (by something/one); to sail
пропуска́ть — пропуска́-ю, -ешь, -ют пропусти́ть — пропущу́, пропу́ст-ишь, -ят (что, кого́)	to pass, to miss (something, someone)
проруба́ть — проруба́-ю, -ешь, -ют проруби́ть — прорублю́, прору́б-ишь, -ят (что)	to cut through (something)
просыпа́ться — просыпа́-юсь, -ешся, -ются просну́ться — просн-у́сь, -ёшся, -утся	to awaken
протека́ть — *(1st and 2nd person not used)* протека́-ет, -ют проте́чь — протечёт, протеку́т	to run, to flow, to pass
протя́гивать — протя́гива-ю, -ешь, -ют протяну́ть — протяну́, протя́н-ешь, -ут (что)	to stretch out, extend (something)
проща́ть — проща́-ю, -ешь, -ют прости́ть — прощу́, прост-и́шь, -я́т (что, кого́)	to forgive (something, someone)
пры́гать — пры́га-ю, -ешь, -ут пры́гнуть — пры́гн-у, -ешь, -ут	to jump
пыта́ться — пыта́-юсь, -ешься, -ются попыта́ться — попыта́-юсь, -ешься, -ются	to try
разводи́ться — развожу́сь, развод-ишься,-ятся развести́сь — разведу́сь, -ёшься, -у́тся (с кем)	to divorce, get divorced (from someone)
развора́чиваться — развора́чива-юсь, -ешся, -ются разверну́ться — разверн-у́сь, -ёшься, -у́тся *(с + instr.)*	to turn (to)
разреша́ть — разреша́-ю, -ешь, -ют разреши́ть — разреш-у́, -и́шь, -а́т (что) (кому́ + *inf.*)	to allow, permit (something) (someone to do something)
разруша́ть — разруша́-ю, -ешь, -ют разру́шить — разру́ш-у, -ишь, -ат (что)	to destroy (something)
раскрыва́ть — раскрыва́-ю, -ешь, -ют раскры́ть — раскро́-ю, -ешь, -ют (что)	to open, expose (something)
распи́сываться — расписыва́-юсь, -ешься, -ются расписа́ться — распиш-у́сь, распиш-ешься, -утся (в чём)	to sign (for something)
рассекре́чивать — рассекре́чива-ю, -ешь, -ют рассекре́тить — рассекре́чу, рассекре́т-ишь, -ят (что)	to disclose a secret; to declassify (something)
расска́зываться — *(3rd person only)* расска́зыва-ется, -ются рассказа́ться — *(3rd person only)* расска́ж-ется, -утся (о чём)	to tell (of something)
рассма́триваться — рассма́трива-юсь, -ешься, -ются рассмотре́ться — рассмотрю́сь, рассмо́тр-ишься, -ятся	to be considered
рассмея́ться — рассме-ю́сь, -ёшься, -ю́тся *(pf.)*	to burst out laughing
расти́ть — ращу́, раст-ишь, -ят вы́растить — выращу́, выраст-ишь, -ят (что, кого́)	to cultivate, grow, raise (something, someone)
реве́ть — рев-у́, -ёшь, -у́т *(impf.)*	to roar, howl

садиться — сажу́сь, сад-и́шься, -я́тся (куда́) (за стол) сесть — ся́д-у, -ешь, -ут (в маши́ну)	to sit down (somewhere) *(at the table)* *(to get in the car)*
сбра́сывать — сбра́сыва-ю, -ешь, -ют сбро́сить — сброшу́, сбро́с-ишь, -ят (что, кого́ с чего́)	to dump, throw (off, down) (something/one from something)
сги́нуть — сги́н-у, -ешь, -ут *(colloq.) (pf.)*	to disappear
сдвига́ться — сдвига́-юсь, -ешься, -ются (с чего́) (отку́да) сдви́нуться — сдви́н-усь, -ешься, -утся (с места́)	to move; to progress (from someplace) *(to move from one's spot)*
се́ять — се́-ю, -ешь, -ют посе́ять — посе́-ю, -ешь, -ют (что)	to sow (something)
сла́виться — сла́в-люсь, -ишься, -ятся *(impf.)* (чем, кем)	to be famous (for something/one)
слага́ться — слага́-юсь, -ешься, -ются сложи́ться — сложу́сь, сло́ж-ишься, -атся	to take shape; to be made up (of)
сле́довать — сле́дует *(3rd pers. only) (impf., dat. + infin.)* (кому́)	ought, should (someone ought to...)
следи́ть — слежу́, след-и́шь, -я́т *(impf.)* (за кем чем) *(за ней взгля́дом)*	to follow (someone, something) *[to follow her with (one's) eyes]*
слы́шиться — слы́ш-усь, -ишься, -атся послы́шиться — послы́ш-усь, -ишься, -атся	to hear, be heard
снима́ть — снима́-ю, -ешь, -ют снять — сниму́, сним-ешь, -ут (что, кого́ с чего́, кого́)	to rent, take off, remove (something/ one from something/one)
сни́ться — сн-юсь, -и́шся, -я́тся присни́ться — присн-ю́сь, -и́шся, -я́тся	to dream
соверша́ть — соверша́-ю, -ешь, -ют (что) соверши́ть — соверш-у́, -и́шь, -а́т	to commit, carry out, accomplish, draft (something)
сове́товаться — сове́ту-юсь, -ешься, -ются посове́товаться — посове́ту-юсь, -ешься, -ются (с кем)	to consult (with someone)
совмеща́ться — совмеща́-юсь, -ешься, -ются (с чем, кем) совмести́ться — совмещу́сь, совмест-и́шься, -я́тся	to be combined (with something/one)
соглаша́ться — соглаша́-юсь, -ешься, -ются согласи́ться — соглашу́сь, соглас-и́шься, -я́тся (с чем, кем)	to agree (with something/one)
соединя́ться — соединя́-юсь, -ешься, -ются соедини́ться — соедин-ю́сь, -и́шься, -я́тся (с чем, кем)	to be united, combined, joined together (with something/one)
сообща́ть — сообща́-ю, -ешь, -ют сообщи́ть — сообщ-у́, -и́шь, -а́т (что о чём) (кому́)	to announce, inform, communicate (an announcement about something) (to someone)
соотноси́ть — соотношу́, соотно́с-ишь, -ят соотнести́ — соотнес-у́, -ёшь, -у́т (что, кого́ с чем, кем)	to relate, connect (something/one with something, someone)
соску́читься — соску́ч-усь, -ишься, -атся *(impf.)* (по кому́, чему́)	to feel lonely (without somebody), to miss (someone, something)
состоя́ть — состо-ю́, -и́шь, -я́т *(impf.)*	to consist (of)
сохраня́ться — сохраня́-юсь, -ешься, -ются сохрани́ться — сохран-ю́сь, -и́шься, -я́тся	to remain, to be preserved
спаса́ться — спаса́-юсь, -ешься, -ются спасти́сь — спас-у́сь, -ёшься, -у́тся (чем)	to save oneself (by means of something)
сруба́ть — сруба́-ю, -ешь, -ют сруби́ть — срублю́, сру́б-ишь, -ят (что)	to chop, fell (timber)
ста́вить — ста́влю, ста́в-ишь, -ят *(impf.)* (что, кого́) (куда́) *(вари́ть суп)*	to put (something, someone) (somewhere); *(to put the soup on)*
станови́ться — становл-ю́сь, стано́в-ишься, -ятся (кем) стать — ста́н-у, -ешь, -ут	to become (someone) to begin, start (perf. only)
ста́риться — ста́р-юсь, -ишься, -ятся соста́риться — соста́р-юсь, -ишься, -ятся	to grow old, to age
стира́ть — стира́-ю, -ешь, -ют постира́ть — постира́-ю, -ешь, -ют (что)	to wash (clothes)
стоя́ть — сто-ю́, йшь, -я́т постоя́ть — посто-ю́, йшь, -я́т (где)	to stand, be situated, stop (somewhere)
тащи́ть — тащу́, та́щ-ишь, -ат *(unidirect. impf.)* (что, кого́) потащи́ть — потащу́, пота́щ-ишь, -ат	to drag (something, someone) around
тверди́ть — твер-жу́, -ди́шь, -дя́т *(impf.)* (что)	to repeat; say (something) over and over

теплéть — (3rd pers. only) теплé-ет, -ют (impf.)	to get warm
торговáть — торгý-ю, -ешь, -ют (impf.) (чем)	to trade (in, with something)
трáтить — трáчу, трáт-ишь, -ят потрáтить — потрáчу, потрáт-ишь, -ят(pf.) истрáтить — истрáчу, истрáт-ишь, -ят(pf.)　(что)	to spend, use up (something)
убивáть — убивá-ю, -ешь, -ют убить — убь-ю, -ёшь, - ют (что, когó)	to kill (something, someone)
убирáть — убирá-ю, -ешь, -ют (что) убрáть — убер-ý, -ёшь, -ýт　(со столá)	to clear, clean (something) (to clear the table)
увелúчивать — увелúчива-ю, -ешь, -ют увелúчить — увелúч-у, -ишь, -ат (что)	to increase, enlarge (something)
уверять — уверя-ю, -ешь, -ют увéрить — увéр-ю, -ишь, -ят (что, когó в чём)	to assure (something, someone of something)
удавáться — удá-юсь, -ёшься, -ются удáться — (3rd person only) удáстся, удадýтся (комý)	to be a success; to manage to make things work out well (for oneself)
удивляться — удивля-юсь, -ешься, -ются удивúться — удивлюсь, удив-úшься, -ятся (чемý)	to be surprised (by something)
уезжáть— уезжá-ю, -ешь, -ют (откýда—кудá) уéхать — уéд-у, -ешь, -ут　(из, от, с чегó в, на что)	to leave (from somewhere to/for somewhere)
уклáдывать — уклáдыва-ю, -ешь, -ют уложúть — уложý, улóж-ишь, -ат (что)	to lay (something) down
уменьшáть — уменьшá-ю, -ешь, -ют уменьшúть — уменьш-ý, -úшь, -áт (что)	to decrease, reduce (something)
уничтожáть — уничтожá-ю, -ешь, -ют уничтóжить — уничтóж-у, -ишь, -ат (что, когó)	to annihilate (something, someone)
усúливаться — усúлива-юсь, -ешься, -ются усúлиться — усúл-юсь, -ишься, -ятся	to become stronger; to increase
успокáиваться — успокáива-юсь, -ешься, -ются успокóиться — успокó-юсь, -ешься, -ются	to calm down, compose oneself
устрáивать — устрáива-ю, -ешь, -ют устрóить — устрó-ю, -ишь, -ят (что, когó на что)	to make; to organize (something/one for something)
устрáиваться — устрáива-юсь, -ешься, -ются (где) устрóиться — устрó-юсь, -ишься, -ятся	to get settled, to manage (somewhere)
уступáть — уступá-ю, -ешь, -ют уступúть — уступлю, устýп-ишь, -ят (что, когó чемý, комý в чём)	to yield, give in, be inferior (something/one, to something/one else in something)
утверждáть — утверждá-ю, -ешь, -ют (impf.) (что, когó)	to assert, to claim (something) to confirm (someone)
утешáть — утешá-ю, -ешь, -ют утéшить — -ý, -úшь, -áт (когó)	to console (someone)
утрáчивать — утрáчива-ю, -ешь, -ют утрáтить — утрáчу, утрáт-ишь, -ят (что)	to lose (something)
уходúть — ухожý, ухóд-ишь, -ят уйтú — уйд-ý, -ёшь, -ýт (из, от, с чегó в, на что) (кудá) (в прóшлое)	to leave (from one place to go somewhere else); (to disappear with time, to become a thing of the past)
учáствовать — учáству-ю, -ешь, -ют (impf.) (в чём)	to participate, take part (in something)
хлынуть — хлын-ý, -ёшь, -ýт (pf.)	to surge, to rush
хранúть — хран-ю, -úшь, -ят (impf.) (что)	to keep, safeguard (something)
хранúться — (3rd pers. only) хран-úтся, -ятся (impf.)	to be kept, preserved
целовáться — целý-юсь, -ешься, -ются поцеловáться — поцелý-юсь, -ешься, -ются (с кем)	to kiss (one another) (someone)
ценúть — цен-ю, цéн-ишь, -ят (impf.) (что, когó)	to value, appreciate (something/one)
шúриться — (3rd pers. only) шúр-ится, -ятся (impf.)	to spread, expand
являть — явля-ю, -ешь, -ют (что, когó) явúть — явлю, яв-ишь, -ят	to show, to display (something/one)
являться — явля-юсь, -ешься, -ются (чем, кем) явúться — явлюсь, яв-úшься, -ятся	to appear, to be (something/one)

Chapter 8

ADVERBS
Наречия

8.1 Overview: What are adverbs? Adverbs generally answer the following questions:

question		**adverb**	
Как?	How?	быстро	quickly
Когда?	When?	сейчас	now
Как часто?	How often?	редко	rarely
Почему?	Why?	Потому что,...	Because...
Зачем?	For what reason?	чтобы...	in order to...

Adverbs can modify a verb, an adjective, or another adverb. In English, adverbs often end with the letters **-ly**: *costly, cheaply, pleasantly, badly,* etc.

In Russian, a great number of adverbs end with the letter **-o**:

дорого	costly
дёшево	cheaply
приятно	pleasantly
плохо	poorly

Most adverbs ending in -**o** can be made to express the opposite quality by adding the prefix **не-**:

недорого	not expensive/costly
недёшево	not cheaply
неприятно	unpleasantly
неплохо	not badly

A number of other adverbs in Russian are formed as "with..." phrases, using the preposition **с** (with) plus a noun in **the instrumental case**:

с интересом	with interest
со стилем	with style
с удовольствием	with pleasure

Other common Russian adverbs use the hyphenated **по-** construction to indicate how something is done: **по-русски** ("in Russian", or "in the Russian fashion"). Below are some examples of usage:

Adverbs modifying verbs

Максим о́чень **пло́хо** игра́ет в футбо́л.

Maxim plays soccer **very badly**.

Они́ **ре́дко** хо́дят в кино́.

They **rarely** go to the movies.

Мы **с интере́сом** слу́шали его́ расска́з.

We listened to his story **with great interest**.

Adverbs modifying adjectives

Ната́ша сего́дня **осо́бенно** краси́вая.

Natasha looks **especially** pretty today.

Эти блю́да **прия́тно** о́стрые.

These dishes are **pleasantly** spicy.

Ми́ша **о́чень** тала́нтливый.

Misha is **very** talented.

Adverbs modifying other adverbs

Вы **о́чень хорошо́** говори́те по-ру́сски.

You speak Russian **very well**.

Брэ́нда **всегда́** одева́ется **со вку́сом**.

Brenda **always** dresses **tastefully**.

Пле́еры **обы́чно де́шево** продаю́тся.

Walkmans are **usually** sold **at a low price**.

REFERENCE TABLE 8A: COMMON ADVERBS

хорошо́	well	сме́ло	bravely
пло́хо	badly	трусли́во	cowardly
отли́чно	excellently	гро́мко	loudly
ужа́сно	terribly	ти́хо	quietly
норма́льно	normally/okay	замеча́тельно	wonderfully
удовлетвори́тельно	satisfactorily	прекра́сно	fantastically/great
мо́дно	stylishly	здо́рово	great (interjection)
сти́льно, со сти́лем	stylishly, with style	кла́ссно, кру́то	great/cool (slang)
со вку́сом	tastefully/with taste	всегда́	always
с удово́льствием	with pleasure	никогда́	never
до́рого	expensively	иногда́	sometimes
де́шево	cheaply	ре́дко	rarely
мно́го	a lot	ча́сто	often
ма́ло	little	обы́чно	usually
краси́во	beautifully	ве́село	happily, fun
некраси́во	not beautifully	прия́тно	pleasantly
интере́сно	interestingly	неприя́тно	not pleasantly
неинтере́сно	not interestingly	у́мно	intelligently
ску́чно	boring	глу́по	stupidly
си́льно	strongly	коне́чно	of course/certainly
сла́бо	weakly	осо́бенно	especially
по-ру́сски, по-англи́йски...	Russian, English, etc.	специа́льно	specifically/on purpose

8.2   ADJECTIVE-ADVERB RELATIONSHIPS
Function: Expressing activities and impressions

Face to Face L2
Chapter 11 B, D
Pages 235-236;
242

Many adverbs are derived from adjectives. In such cases, the adjectival ending is replaced with the adverb ending **-о**:

Adverb	*formed from the*	**Adjective:**	
хорошо́	good, well	хоро́ш-ий	good,
ве́село	happi(-ly)	весёл-ый	happy
интере́сно	interesting(-ly)	интере́сн-ый	interesting
прия́тно	pleasant(-ly)	прия́тн-ый	pleasant
ску́чно	boring(-ly)	ску́чн-ый	boring

Recall that while an adjective modifies a noun, an adverb generally modifies a verb, an adjective, or another adverb.

Sample Sentences

Ми́ша хоро́ший учени́к.   Misha is a good student.
Он **хорошо́** у́чится в шко́ле.   He does **well** in school.

In the above example **хоро́ший** modifies the noun **учени́к**, while the adverb **хорошо́** modifies the verb **у́чится**.

8.3   ADVERB ПО-РУ́ССКИ , ETC.
Function: Saying that you understand or do not
            understand

Face to Face L1
Chapter 6 B
Pages 138-139

<u>**Expressing "in Russian" versus "Russian language"**</u> The adverb **по-ру́сски** is used when expressing that something is done *in Russian*. When adverbs use the hyphenated **по-**, the indicated meaning is *in the...fashion* :

говори́ть по-ру́сски
to speak in Russian (in the Russian fashion)

This can be done for most foreign languages and cultures:

по-англи́йски	in English, in the English fashion, etc.
по-францу́зски	in French, "
по-неме́цки	in German, "
по-италья́нски	in Italian, "
по-япо́нски	in Japanese, "

This form is also used with different common actions that are associated with proficiency in another language (writing, reading, etc.). Some specific actions, however, take a form ending in ...язык (...language) as in **Он знáет рýсский язык** (He knows Russian). Even though the English meaning for these two forms would be the same, Russian makes a distinction. The hyphenated по- form is an adverb, while the ...язык form is a noun and functions as a direct object:

verb		adverb	verb		direct object
читáть	to read	по-рýсски	знать	to know	рýсский язык
писáть	to write	по-англúйски	учúть	study	англúйский язык
дýмать	to think		изучáть	study	
говорúть	to speak		понимáть	*understand	

*Note: The verb **понимáть** may be modified by an adverb to indicate the thinking process *by which* one understands: **Онá понимáет по-рýсски.** She understands in Russian.

8.4 **THE ADVERBS** ВСЕГДА, ЧАСТО, ОБЫЧНО, ИНОГДА, РЕДКО, НИКОГДА *Function:* Discussing the frequency of actions	Face to Face L2 Chapter 12 A, D Pages 248-254, 265

The adverbs **всегдá** (always), **обы́чно** (usually), **иногдá** (sometimes), **рéдко** (rarely), and **никогдá** (never) indicate the frequency with which actions take place. As a rule, they are used with imperfective verbs:

Sample Sentences

Джек и Эми **обы́чно** хóдят в магазúн пешкóм, но **иногдá** они éздят на машúне.

Jack and Amy **usually** walk to the store, but **sometimes** they go by car.

When the word **никогдá** (never) is used, the verb must always be preceded by the particle **не** (Russian principle of "double-negation"):

Мы **никогдá не** éздим на машúне по гóроду.

We **never** drive the car around town.

8.5 **USING ADVERBS TO EVALUATE ACTIONS** *Function:* Expressing opinions about actions	Face to Face L1 Chapter 7 B Pages 154-155

Adverbs may be used to express how (**как**) something is done. Adverbs in this case modify the verb. Below are several examples. (Note that adverbs can be used with almost any verb, not just the ones listed below!)

Verb	**Adverb—How? Как?**	
одеваться/одеться (to dress)	стильно	stylishly
	модно	in fashion, stylishly
	красиво	beautifully
	со вкусом	tastefully
	классно	great
учиться (to study; be enrolled as a student)	хорошо	well
	отлично	excellently
	плохо	badly
	удовлетворительно	satisfactorily
говорить (to speak, say)	с акцентом	with an accent
	красноречиво	eloquently
	хорошо/плохо	well/badly
работать (to work)	мало	little
	много	a lot

Sample sentences

— Как он одевается?
— Он одевается **стильно**.
— А она?
— Она одевается **модно**.

How does he dress?
He dresses **stylishly**.
And her?
She dresses **fashionably**.

Они **хорошо** учатся.

They are good students. (*lit.*, They study **well**.)

— Как она говорит **по-русски**? **С акцентом**?
— Нет, она говорит **хорошо**.

How does she speak **Russian**? **With an accent**?
No, she speaks **well**.

Он **мало** работает на компьютере.

He doesn't work on the computer much. (*lit.*, He works **little** on the computer.)

8.6	**THE ADVERBS** СНАЧАЛА, ПОТОМ	Face to Face L1
	Function: Discussing a sequence of events	Chapter 14 C Pages 292-293

The adverbs **сначала** (at first, in the beginning) and **потом** (then, later) are used when describing a sequence of events or consecutive actions. Because they describe events in consecutive fashion, they are used most often with perfective verbs:

Sample Sentences

Сначала мы пойдём в цирк, а **потом** пойдём в кафе.
Лёва **сначала** пошёл в музей, а **потом** к Грише домой.

First we'll go to the circus, and **then** we'll go to a café.
Lyova **first** went to the museum, and **then** over to Grisha's house.

If the consecutive actions involve a round-trip motion or a process, **снача́ла** and **пото́м** may also be used with imperfective verbs, though this usage is much less common:

Лёва **снача́ла** ходи́л в музе́й, а **пото́м** ходи́л к Гри́ше домо́й.	Lyova **first** went to the museum (and returned), and **then** went over to Grisha's house (and returned).

8.7 THE USE OF THE ADVERB ОСОБЕННО ***Function:*** Emphasizing something	Faces and Voices Chapter 1 A Pages 3, 6

The adverb **особенно** (especially) most commonly modifies other adverbs, like the adverb "especially" does in English:

Sample sentences

Та́ня говори́т по-англи́йски **особенно хорошо́**. (**особенно** modifies the adverb **хорошо́**)	Tanya speaks English **especially well**.

Like other adverbs, **особенно** can modify verbs and adjectives:

Ва́ня **лю́бит** де́вушек, **особенно** Та́ню. (**особенно** modifies the verb **лю́бит**)	Vanya **likes** girls, **especially** Tanya.
Макси́м всегда́ одева́ется хорошо́, но он почему́-то сего́дня **особенно краси́вый**. (**особенно** modifies the adjective **краси́вый**)	Maxim always dresses well, but today for some reason he looks **especially handsome**.

When something is done "on purpose" (i.e., specifically, specially for...) Russians use the word **специа́льно**:

Ба́бушка пригото́вит торт **специа́льно** для тебя́.	Grandma will bake a cake **specially** for you.

8.8 ADVERBS WITH THE PREFIX ПО- ***Function:*** Describing characteristics of actions	Faces and Voices Chapter 10 Б Pages 269, 273

Adverbs using the prefix **по-** describe actions and characterize, in a conversational sense, how an action is performed. This type of adverb is formed with **по- + the dative singular form of a masculine adjective**:

Sample Sentences

по-дру́гому differently, in a different way	В Аме́рике мы живём совсе́м **по-дру́гому**. In America we live altogether **differently** (than here).
по-настоя́щему in a real way; in a genuine fashion	Она́ лю́бит его́ **по-настоя́щему**. She has a **genuine** love for him (*lit.*, in a real way, the way one should).
по-ра́зному in various (a variety of) ways; it depends	Лю́ди отно́сятся к мо́де **по-ра́зному**. People have **different** attitudes about fashion.
по-но́вому in a new way; begin over again	Ты не хо́чешь нача́ть рабо́ту **по-но́вому**? Don't you want to start your work **over again**? (*lit.*, *anew*)
по-ста́рому as always; as of old; the same way (as before)	Ну как тебе́ сказа́ть? Живём **по-ста́рому**. Всё как всегда́. Well what can I tell you? Life's **the same** as always.

	Face to Face L1 Chapter 7 B, Page154 Chapter 17 B, Page 347

8.9   THE ADVERBS УЖЕ; ЕЩЁ
Function: The concept of "still" vs. "already"

The adverbs **уже́** (already) and **ещё** (still/yet) are easily confused by English speakers.

Макси́м **ещё** ма́ленький, но он **уже́** хорошо́ чита́ет.	Maxim is **still** little, but he **already** reads well.

Note the meanings and sample sentences below.

The Adverb Уже́

1)   **Уже́** is more commonly used in Russian than its English equivalent *already*. Russian utilizes this adverb to emphasize early completion of an action, particularly with perfective verbs:

Лари́са пришла́ **уже́** вчера́.	Larisa arrived yesterday/**as early as** yesterday. (She '**already**' arrived yesterday.)

2)   **Уже́ не** (or **бо́льше не**) means "no longer" or "not any more":

Он **уже́ не**/**бо́льше не** рабо́тает здесь.	He doesn't work here **any more**.

The Adverb Ещё

1)   **Ещё** or **ещё не** (not yet) can indicate a temporal (time) meaning:

Лари́са **ещё не** пришла́. Джон **ещё** рабо́тает.	Larisa hasn't arrived **yet**. John is **still** working.

2) Ещё can also be used to mean "additional":

Дай **ещё** одну ручку.

Give (me) **another** (**an additional**) pen.

3) Ещё is commonly used with other adverbs, particularly with those of the comparative degree: **ещё лучше**—still/even better.

Он хорошо играет в баскетбол, но она играет **ещё лучше**.

He plays basketball well, but she plays **even better**.

8.10 THE ADVERB ТОЛЬКО AND THE ADJECTIVE ЕДИНСТВЕННЫЙ
Function: The difference between "only" and "the only one"

Мир русских
Lesson 1
Pages 28-30

Только (only) is an adverb and should not be confused with the adjective **единственный** (the only one, single). Note the contrasting adverbial and adjectival usage in the sample sentences below.

Только—Adverb; **Только** is also often used to strengthen the meaning of or emphasize other adverbs:

Sample Sentences

Только Джереми может решить эту проблему.

Only Jeremy can/is able to solve this problem.

Эмили не купила блузку **только** потому, что блузка ей не шла.

The **only** reason Emily didn't buy the blouse was because it didn't look good on her. (*lit.,* Emily didn't buy the blouse **only** because the blouse didn't look good on her.)

Единственный—Adjective; **Единственный** can be used only to modify a noun or an assumed noun:

Sample Sentences

Джереми **единственный** человек, который может решить эту проблему.

Jeremy is the **only (single)** person who can solve this problem.

Джейсон **единственный** у нас в группе, который отлично говорит по-русски.

Jason is the **only** one in our group who speaks Russian excellently.

8.11 COMPARATIVES OF ADJECTIVES AND ADVERBS
Function: Making comparisons

Face to Face L2
Chapter 18 B,D
Pages 394-396,
399-400

The comparative degree of adjectives and adverbs is used whenever qualities, traits, amounts, or actions are compared, either within the same sentence or in a broader context. Comparative forms are the same for both adverbs and their corresponding adjectives. Below are some of the most frequently used comparatives:

comparative		adverb	adjective
бо́льше	more; larger	мно́го	большо́й
ме́ньше	less; smaller	ма́ло	ма́ленький
лу́чше	better	хорошо́	хоро́ший
ху́же	worse	пло́хо	плохо́й
доро́же	more expensive	до́рого	дорого́й
дешёвле	cheaper	дёшево	дешёвый
краси́вее	prettier	краси́во	краси́вый
интере́снее	more interesting	интере́сно	интере́сный

A basic construction for forming comparative statements uses the comparative adjective or adverb in the first clause of a sentence, followed by the second clause beginning with the word **чем** (than). Grammar points 3.14-18 in Chapter 3, Adjectives, present a thorough overview of comparative constructions using **чем**.

Sample sentences

Она́ **бо́льше** чита́ет, чем он.

She reads **more** than he does.

Ива́н **лу́чше** у́чится, чем брат.

Ivan is a **better** student than his brother. (*lit.,* Ivan studies **better**)

Мари́я зна́ет англи́йский язы́к **ху́же**, чем сестра́.

Maria's English is **worse** than her sister's. (*lit.,* Maria knows English **worse** than her sister.)

8.12 THE ADVERB лу́чше + A VERB
Function: Stating a preference

Face to Face 2
Chapter 6 A, D
Pages 115-118,
137

The comparative degree of the adverb **хорошо́** is **лу́чше** (better). It is often used with **the infinitive form of a verb** to express a preference

Sample sentences

До Большо́го теа́тра **лу́чше** е́хать на метро́.

The **best** way to get to the Bolshoi Theater is by subway. (*lit.,* The **better** way)

Наве́рное, мне **лу́чше** пое́хать на такси́.

It's probably **best/better** for me to go by taxi.

Chapter 9

PREPOSITIONS
Предло́ги

9.1 Overview: What is a preposition? A preposition expresses the relationship of one word to another:

ребёнок **под столо́м**	a child **under the table**
пое́хать **за грани́цу**	to travel **to another country**, **abroad**
разгово́р **о нас**	a conversation **about us**

Russian prepositions govern nouns, pronouns and modifying adjectives in a grammatical case. Some prepositions are used with two or three different cases to denote different meanings. Russian prepositions are formed in several ways. As in English, a single word in Russian may be used **в** *in*, **для** *for*, **на** *on/at*, etc.). However, other Russian prepositions are formed from nouns (**во вре́мя** *during*, **по сравне́нию с** *by comparison with*, etc.) and from verbs (**включа́я** *including*, **несмотря́ на** *despite*, etc.).

REFERENCE TABLE 9A: COMMON PREPOSITIONS AND THEIR MEANINGS WITH CASES

Preposition	*Accusative*	*Genitive*	*Dative*	*Instr.*	*Prep.*
без	——	without	——	——	——
в	into	——	——	——	in
для	——	for	——	——	——
до	——	as far as	——	——	——
за	(to) behind	——	——	behind	——
из	——	out of, from	——	——	——
из-за	——	from behind	——	——	——
из-под	——	from under	——	——	——
к	——	——	towards	——	——
кро́ме	——	except for	——	——	——
ме́жду	——	——	——	between	——
на	onto	——	——	——	on
над	——	——	——	above	——
о	against	——	——	——	about
от	——	from	——	——	——
пе́ред	——	——	——	in front of	——
по	up to	——	along	——	after
под	(to) under	——	——	under	——
по́сле	——	after	——	——	——
при	——	——	——	——	in the presence of, during
про	about	——	——	——	——
ра́ди	——	for the sake of	——	——	——
с	approx.	down from	——	with	——
у	——	at	——	——	——
че́рез	across, over	——	——	——	——

The use of prepositions with specific cases is covered extensively in Chapter 4, Declension of Nouns and Adjectives.

9.2 ПО + THE NOUN IN THE DATIVE CASE *Function:* Expressing the meaning *along, on, according to*	Мир русских Lesson 11 Pages 371-373

The preposition **по** is used in several ways:

1)   The preposition **по** + **the dative case** most frequently means *along, on,* or *according to*.

Sample sentences

Ребя́та погуля́ли **по у́лице**.	The kids wandered **along the street**.
Обы́чно мы е́здим на да́чу **по суббо́там**.	Usually we go to the dacha **on Saturdays**.
Мы с подру́гой говори́ли **по телефо́ну**.	My friend and I spoke **on the telephone**.
Вчера́ я ви́дела переда́чу о спо́рте **по телеви́зору**.	Yesterday I saw a program about sports **on television**.

2)   The preposition **по** + **the dative case** is also frequently used idiomatically in set phrases:

Sample sentences

Ча́сто челове́к приезжа́ет в страну́ без зна́ния языка́, **по су́ти** без профе́ссии.	Often a person arrives in this country without a knowledge of the language, **in essence** without a profession.
Ру́сская равни́на пришла́сь славя́нам **по душе́**.	The Russian plain came into harmony with the Russian **soul**.
Ба́бушка расска́зывала мне, что ра́ньше лю́ди ча́сто жени́лись не по любви́, а **по расчёту**.	Grandmother told me that earlier people often married not for love but **for personal gain**.
— Па́па ещё не пришёл с рабо́ты?	Is Dad still at work?
— Он приходи́л и опя́ть ушёл **по дела́м**. Бу́дет че́рез час.	He came home but left again **on business**. He'll be back in an hour.
По вопро́сам воспита́ния дете́й обраща́йтесь в консульта́цию «Семья́ и брак».	**Regarding the question** of child– rearing, you should consult "Family and Marriage."
Джек и Билл бы́ли **това́рищи по кла́ссу** и **по ко́мнате**.	Jack and Bill were **classmates** and **roommates**.

3)   Several proverbs also use **по** + **the dative case**:

Sample sentences

По волне́ и мо́ре знать.	A sea is known **by its waves**.
По года́м и ра́зум.	Reason comes **with age (years)**.
По кры́льям полёт, по дела́м почёт.	Flight is **by one's wings**, honor by one's work.
По рабо́те де́ньги.	One is paid **according to his work**.
По рабо́те и ма́стера знать.	You know a craftsman **by his work**.
По се́мени и плод.	You reap **what you sow**.
По това́ру цена́ и **по цене́** това́р.	You get what you pay for.

По ученику́ и об учи́теле су́дят.   A teacher is judged **by his students**.

9.3 INSTRUMENTAL VS. ACCUSATIVE CASES WITH ПОД, ЗА
Function: Expressing location and direction

Мир ру́сских
Lesson 3
Pages 93-94

The prepositions **под** (under) and **за** (behind) express *motion to* when followed by phrases in **the accusative case**. These prepositions answer the question **куда́** and are used with verbs of motion to name a destination.

The prepositions **над** (above) and **пе́ред** (in front of) answer the question **где** and **always take the instrumental case**. Similarly, the prepositions **под** (under) and **за** (behind) also denote location when used with **the instrumental case**.

Sample sentences

Ма́льчик положи́л та́почки **под свою́ крова́ть**. (куда́?)

The boy laid his slippers **under his bed**. (destination)

Я положи́ла газе́ту **за дива́н**. (куда́?)

I put the newspaper **behind the couch**. (destination)

Ма́льчик сиди́т **за столо́м**, за́втракает. (где?)

A boy is sitting **at the table** eating breakfast. (location)

Мать говори́т сы́ну: «За́втрак гото́в! Сади́сь **за стол**». (куда́?)

A mother says to her son, "Breakfast is ready! Sit down **at the table**." (destination)

Каранда́ш упа́л **под стол**. (куда́?)

The pencil fell **under the table**. (destination)

Каранда́ш лежи́т **за словарём**. (где?)

The pencil is (lying) **behind the dictionary**. (location)

Самолёт лете́л **над мо́рем**. (где?)

The airplane was flying **over the sea**. (location)

Chapter 10

PARTICLES AND INTERJECTIONS
Частицы и междометия

10.1 Overview: What are particles? Particles are words that add nuances of meaning to either to individual words or to whole sentences. They express a variety of emotions, attitudes, and general assessments, especially when used with intensified intonation in spoken speech. They are most commonly used in the following ways:

1) To point out or define something:

Вот наша машина!   **Here's** our car!

Это платье ей **как раз**.   This dress is **exactly** what she needs.
(or—the right size for her)

2) To show restriction:

У нас в группе **только** Джон знает испанский язык.   In our group **only** John knows Spanish.

3) To talk about a desired action, or confirming such action:

Поехать **бы** в Италию!   **If only** we could go to Italy! (Wouldn't it be great to go to Italy?!)

—Хочешь поехать в Италию?   —Would you like to go to Italy?
—Ещё бы!   —**Of course!** (Why are you bothering to ask? You know I'd go!)

4) To show negation:

Оля **не** занимается музыкой.   Olya **isn't** involved in music.

У них дома **не** было **ни** масла, **ни** хлеба.   They had **neither** butter **nor** bread at home.

5) As an interrogative (question):

Мама хотела знать, знала **ли** Валя, где ложки и вилки.   Mom wanted to know **whether** Valya knew where the spoons and forks were.

10.2 THE USE OF THE PARTICLE -ЛИ WHEN ASKING A QUESTION
Function: How to restate someone's question; asking a question using indirect speech

| Faces and Voices |
| Lesson 10 Б |
| Pages 272-273 |

Direct speech refers to when one asks a question **directly**, that is, in quotes. Indirect speech is retelling the question:

Direct speech	**Indirect speech**
Наташа спросила: — В вашей семье верили в Бога? Natasha asked: —Did your family believe in God?	Наташа спросила, **верили ли** в Бога в семье отца Ивана. Natasha asked **whether** Father Ivan's family **believed** in God.
Наташа спросила: — В армии знали, что вы верующий? Natasha asked: —Did they know you were a believer when you served in the army?	Наташа спросила, **знали ли** в армии, что отец Иван — верующий. Natasha asked **whether** people in the army **knew** that Father Ivan was a believer.

Note the position of the particle **ли** in the following sentences. As a rule, it *follows* the information being asked about, that is, the most important new information in the sentence:

Samples sentences

Журналист спросил: «Вы хотели стать священником»? (Хотели или не хотели?)	The journalist asked, "Did you want to become a priest?" (Did you want or did you not want?)
Журналист спросил, **хотел ли** отец Иван стать священником.	The journalist asked **whether (or not)** Father Ivan wanted to become a priest.
Журналист спросил: «Вы хорошо знаете древние языки?» (Хорошо или не очень хорошо?)	The journalist asked, "Do you know classical (ancient) languages well?" (Well or not very well?)
Журналист спросил, **хорошо ли** он знает древние языки.	The journalist asked **whether** he knows ancient languages well.
Журналист спросил: «Все семинаристы хорошо учатся»? (Все или не все?)	The journalist asked, "Are all the seminarians good students?" (All or not all?)
Журналист спросил, **все ли** семинаристы хорошо учатся.	The journalist asked **whether (or not)** all the seminarians were good students.

10.3 THE PARTICLE НИ IN EXPRESSIONS
Function: Expressing "neither...nor"

Мир русских
Lesson 7
Page 230

The negative particle **ни** is used as a coordinating conjunction in the expresion **ни...ни...** ("neither...nor").

Sample sentences

Диоксины — очень опасные вещества, которые не имеют **ни** запаха, **ни** вкуса.	Dioxins are very dangerous substances that have **neither** odor **nor** taste.
Для тебя нет **ни** письма, **ни** телеграммы.	There is **neither** a letter **nor** a telegram for you.

10.4 Overview: What are interjections?
Interjections are words which express emotions, but do not actually name them. Examples in English are words such as

Wow!, Ouch, Oh! and other exclamations. Note that a variety of emotions or feelings can be expressed in Russian, just like in English:

REFERENCE TABLE 10A: COMMON INTERJECTIONS

oh	ох, эх, ой, ай, ба, ах	Эх, ты! Как ты мо́жешь так говори́ть?! **Oh, you!** How can you talk like that?! (reproach) Ах, как хорошо́, что за́втра нет уро́ков! **Oh,** how good it is that there's no class tomorrow! (joy) Ой, я бою́сь ти́гров! **Oh,** I'm afraid of tigers. (fear) Ох, здесь так ску́чно! Мне всё надое́ло! **Oh,** it's so boring here! I'm sick of everything! (boredom, annoyance)
ouch, ow	ух, ой, ай	Ой! Я поре́зал па́лец! **Ow!** I cut my finger!
uh-huh	ого́	Ого́! То́лько сейча́с прихо́дит Матве́й. **Uh-huh**...Matt's arriving only now. (annoyance, as Matt is probably late)
aha	ага́	Ага́! Тепе́рь я зна́ю отве́т! **Aha!** Now I know the answer! (joy, surprise)
ugh, ecch	фу	Фу! Что за вонь?! **Ugh!** What's that smell?!
hooray, alright, yippee, yea	ура́	Ура́! Прие́дет мой лу́чший друг! **Yea!** My best friend is coming here!

REFERENCE TABLE 10B: INTERJECTIONS WITH LIMITED USAGE

Алло́! Аллё!	Hello! (on the phone)
На (тебе́)! (На́те!)	Here (you go)! (when giving something to someone directly)
Ау́!	Yo! Hey! Over here! (response to person trying to get your attention)
Тс! Чш! Шш! Цыц!	Sshh! Hush! (Be quiet!)
Вон (отсю́да)! Брысы! *	Aahh! Shoo! (Get out of here!) (*often said to animals)
бац! хлоп! трах! бух!	Bang! Plonk!
Динь-дины!	Ding-ding!
Мя́у!	Meow!
Кукареку́!	Cock-a-doodle-doo!
Гав-гав!	Bow-wow! Arf-arf!
Ха-ха-ха!	Ha-ha-ha!
Апчхи́!	Atchoo!
Го́споди!	Jesus! Good heavens! Lord!
Бо́же мой!	My God!
Ба́тюшки! (Ма́тушки!)	Good gracious! Oh my!
Чёрт возьми́!	Darn it! Damn it!

Chapter 11

SENTENCE STRUCTURE, CONJUNCTIONS, and PUNCTUATION
Структу́ра предложе́ний, сою́зы и зна́ки препина́ния

11.1 A word about capitalization. In Russian **capitalization** of letters in words is very similar to that of English. As in English, most *common nouns* (book—кни́га, tree—де́рево, car—маши́на) are left uncapitalized, while most *proper nouns* (names of people and places) are capitalized. However, there are areas where Russian and English differ:

1)   Names of institutions, organizations, books, newspapers, wars, festivals, etc., have only the **first** word capitalized:

Но́вый год	New Year's
Моско́вский госуда́рственный университе́т	Moscow State University
«Лос Анжелес таймс»	*Los Angeles Times*
Министе́рство образова́ния	Ministry of Education
Большо́й теа́тр	Bolshoi Theater

2)   Nouns of nationality and city origin are **not capitalized**, though **countries and cities are capitalized**:

ру́сский — Росси́я	Russian — Russia
америка́нский — Аме́рика	American — America
чика́гский — Чика́го	Chicago (adj.) — Chicago
петербу́ргский — (Санкт) Петербу́рг	Petersburg (adj.) — (St.) Petersburg

If the nationality or city name is part of a title, then the word will be capitalized:

Моско́вский цирк	Moscow Circus
Америка́нское посо́льство	American (U.S.) Embassy

3)   Names of months and days of the week are also **not capitalized**:

апре́ль	April
среда́	Wednesday

4)   With *geographical names* and other points of interest, the place is **not capitalized** (e.g., ocean, mountain, street), but the **place name** (Pacific, Carpathian, Kazan) **is capitalized**:

Ти́хий *океа́н*	Pacific Ocean
Карпа́тские *го́ры*	Carpathian Mountains
Каза́нская *у́лица*	Kazan Street

11.2 A word about punctuation. Punctuation in Russian is usually similar to English punctuation, though Russian rules are slightly more fixed and depend less on context than English does. The differences between the two languages can be seen in the use of **commas** (especially before subordinate clauses), **dashes**, and **direct speech**.

Use of commas Russian always uses commas:

1) Between clauses linked by **coordinating conjunctions**. An example of this would be before the word **но**, *but*:

Хéнри говорит по-рýсски óчень хорошó, **но** пишет плóхо.	Henry speaks Russian very well, **but** he writes poorly. (English also uses comma before *but*)
Хéнри тóлстый, **но** красúвый.	Henry is heavy **but** handsome. (English doesn't require a comma here)

2) Between clauses linked by the conjunctions **и...и** *both...and*, **ни...ни** *neither...nor*, **или...или** *either...or*, **то...то** *now...now*:

У Алика мы пúли **и** Пéпси-кóлу, **и** Кóка-кóлу.	At Alec's we drank **both** Pepsi **and** Coca-Cola.
Мэри занимáется **или** тéннисом, **или** гóльфом.	Mary is playing **either** tennis **or** golf.

3) Between the main and **subordinate clauses**:

Мы понимáем, **что** онá говорúт.	We understand **what** she is saying.
Я пришёл, **потомý что** хотéл тебя увúдеть.	I came (here) **because** I wanted to see you.
Гáля стáла врачóм, **чтóбы** зарабáтывать большúе дéньги.	Galya became a doctor **in order to** make a lot of money.

4) To separate the main and **relative clauses**:

Вот учúтель, **котóрого** мы вúдели на Арбáте.	There's the teacher **(who)** we saw on the Arbat.

5) In **comparisons**:

Нáша Сáша молчалúвая, **как** рыба.	Our Sasha is as silent **as** a fish.
Марúя ужé выше, **чем** Нáдя.	Maria is already taller **than** Nadya.

Use of dashes Russian often uses dashes, especially when defining things or separating parts of a sentence to indicate a longer pause. As such, the dash often substitutes for commas (,), colons(:) and parentheses ( ). A dash can:

1)   Separate the subject from the predicate, giving the meaning *to be*:

На́ши друзья́ — бизнесме́ны в Сиби́ри.	Our friends **are** businessmen/women in Siberia.

2)   Substitute for a comma (and thus indicate a longer pause):

С на́ми пое́дет Та́ня — на́ша лу́чшая подру́га.	With us will travel Tanya, our best friend. (English uses a comma.)

3)   Substitute for a colon:

В магази́не мы ви́дели всех на́ших ребя́т — Ва́нку, Мари́ю, Са́шу, Ди́му.	In the store we saw all of the (our) guys: Vanka, Maria, Sasha, Dima. (English prefers the colon or comma.)

4)   Substitute for parentheses:

На бульва́ре — где мно́го краси́вых дере́вьев — уже́ идёт большо́й ремо́нт.	On the boulevard (where there are many beautiful trees) there is already a lot of repair work under way.

Direct speech   Direct speech—dialogue, or quoting the speaker directly—has a punctuation style somewhat different from that of English.   If the verb indicating the action comes **before** the direct speech, the verb is followed by a colon: **Юлия говори́т:**, and then the direct speech follows on a new line after a dash **—Это я**.

Юлия сказа́ла: —Это я.	Julia said, "It's me."

Or the direct speech continues right after the colon and is enclosed by « »

Юлия сказа́ла: «Это я.»	Julia said, "It's me."

If a verb **follows** the direct speech, the direct speech is enclosed in dashes:

—Это я, — сказа́ла Джу́лия.	"It's me," said Julia.

11.3   THE VERB ПОНИМА́ТЬ IN SIMPLE AND COMPLEX SENTENCES

Function: Saying that you understand or do not understand

Face to Face L 1 Chapter 6 B Pages 138-139

Sentences in Russian can be simple or complex. A simple sentence stands alone as one complete idea and does not contain other clauses providing additional information.

Sample sentences

— Я понима́ю. Я не понима́ю.   I understand. I don't understand.

— Я понима́ю ру́сский язы́к.   I understand Russian.

Complex sentences can be formed using the explanatory conjuction **что** (that, what) and **когда́** (when) with verbs of understanding, thinking, and saying.

Sample sentences

— Я не понима́ю, **что** ты чита́ешь.   I don't understand **what** you are reading.

— Я не понима́ю, **что** она говори́т.   I don't understand **what** she is saying.

— Как э́то бу́дет по-англи́йски? Я не понима́ю, **когда́** он говори́т по-ру́сски.   How is that (will it be) in English? I don't understand **when** he speaks Russian.

11.4 **COMPOUND SENTENCES WITH THE VERB** СЧИТА́ТЬ *Function:* Expressing an opinion	Faces and Voices Chapter 2 B Pages 37-40

The verb **счита́ть** (I) expresses a carefully-thought-out opinion. It is used in the construction **счита́ть, что...** *to consider that..., to think that....* Questions are formed by the construction **Как вы счита́ете...?** Compare the use of **счита́ть** below with other expressions of opinion.

— Моя́ ма́ма **счита́ет, что**.... А как твоя́ ма́ма **счита́ет**?   My mom **thinks that**.... What does your mom **think**?

— Я ду́маю, что ... А что (как) ты ду́маешь?   I **think** that... What do you **think**?

— Мне ка́жется, что ... А тебе́ что (как) ка́жется?   **It seems to me** that... How does it **seem to you**?

Sample sentences

Я не счита́ю, что тру́дно вы́брать профе́ссию.   **I don't think** it is difficult to choose a profession.

Я счита́ю, что лю́дям на́до учи́ть иностра́нные языки́.   **I think** that people should study foreign languages.

Я счита́ю, что хоро́ший чита́тель — э́то челове́к, кото́рый мно́го ду́мает, а не мно́го чита́ет.   **I consider** a good reader to be a person who thinks a lot, but doesn't necessarily read all that much.

11.5 **THE CONJUNCTION** ЧТО́БЫ **AND THE PAST TENSE** **AFTER THE VERB** ХОТЕ́ТЬ *Function:* Saying what is desired (to do) of another person	Faces and Voices Chapter 3 A Pages 63-64

The verb **хоте́ть** (and **жела́ть**—to wish) used with **что́бы + the perfective past tense** are used to express *a wish that someone else perform an action.* While this is not a true imperative form, it is used as a form of **indirect command.** Compare the direct command (imperative) and an indirect command:

Direct command (imperative) form:
—Амáя, **послýшай** этот компáкт-диск.   Amaya, **listen** to this CD.

Indirect command (чтóбы + perfective past tense) form:
—Амáя, **я хочý, чтóбы ты послýшала**   — Amaya, **I want you to listen** to this
этот компáкт-диск.   CD.

If the subject of the sentence desires something for himself/herself/themselves, the following construction is used:	If the subject of the sentence wishes that **someone else** perform an action, the following construction is used:
хотéть + infinitive	**хотéть, чтóбы . . .+ the perfective verb in the past tense**

Я хочý стáть лётчиком. (Я хочý, и я стáну.) **I want to become** a pilot. (I want, and I will become.)

Я хочý, чтóбы мой брат **стал** лётчиком. (Я хочý, но брат стáнет.) **I want my brother to become** a pilot. (I want, but my brother will become.)

Я хочý прочитáть этот ромáн. (Я хочý, и я прочитáю.) **I want to finish** (reading) the novel. (I want, and I will read.)

Учúтель **хóчет, чтóбы мы прочитáли** этот ромáн. (Учúтель хóчет, но мы прочитáем.) The teacher **wants us to finish** (reading) the novel. (The teacher wants, but we will read.)

Sample sentences

— Владúмир Николáевич, **мы хотúм, чтóбы вы рассказáли** нам о сéвере.
Vladimir Nikolaevich, **we want you to tell** us about the North.

— Я хочý рассказáть вам о сéвере.
I want to tell you about the North.

— Михаúл, **я хочý, чтóбы ты помóг мне** с домáшним задáнием.
Mikhail, **I want you to help me** with my homework.

— Онá хóчет, чтóбы вы познакóмили её с трéнером клýба «моржéй».
She wants you to acquaint her with the coach of the "Walrus" club.

— Я хочý, чтóбы ты сфотографúровала меня с дрýгом.
I want you to take a picture of me with my friend.

11.6 THE INTERROGATIVE WORD ПОЧЕМУ AND SUBORDINATE CLAUSES WITH ПОТОМУ ЧТО
Function: Giving reasons

| Face to Face 1 |
| Chapter 17 C |
| Pages 350-353 |

The adverb почемý (Why?) and its answer потомý что (because) are used frequently in Russian, as in English. However, потомý что can not only begin a subordinate clause (as in English), but can also stand alone to begin its own sentence, which is not grammatically possible in English:

In subordinate clause:

Почему́ тебе́ нра́вится гимна́стика?
— Мне́ нра́вится гимна́стика, **потому́ что** э́то краси́вый вид спо́рта.

Why do you like gymnastics?
I like gymnastics **because** it's a beautiful sport. (**потому́ что** begins a subordinate clause within a larger sentence.)

In its own sentence:

Почему́ тебе́ нра́вится гимна́стика?
— **Потому́ что** э́то краси́вый вид спо́рта.

Why do you like gymnastics? -- Because it's a beautiful sport.*
(**потому́ что** begins its own sentence.)

*****Note:** The English translation, while making sense in conversation, cannot have "because" stand alone as the beginning of its own sentence in grammatically proper written form.

11.7 THE INTERROGATIVE WORD ЗАЧЕМ
Function: Asking about the purpose of an action

Faces and Voices
Chapter 9 A
Pages 235-236

The adverb **заче́м** (Why? For what reason?) is used to ask about the purpose or goal of an action (as opposed to **почему́**, which is used to ask about the reason behind, or cause for, an action). Often questions formed with **заче́м** are answered with **что́бы** (in order to; so that...) clauses, as in the example below:

Заче́м ты идёшь в магази́н?

— **Что́бы** купи́ть хлеб.

Почему́ ты идёшь в магази́н?
— **Потому́ что** у нас нет хле́ба.

Why (for what reason) are you going to the store?
—To buy some bread.

Why are you going to the store? —
Because we have no bread.

11.8 USING THE CONJUNCTION ПОКА
Function: Discussing simultaneous actions ("while", "when")

Face to Face L2
Chapter 12 A,D
Pages 248-253,
268

Пока́ is often translated as *while..., when..., for the present time ...* and *for now...* in sentences. It is used to combine two parts of a sentence describing actions taking place at the same time.

Sample sentences

Пока́ шёл дождь, я сде́лал все уро́ки и написа́л пять пи́сем.

Пока́ ты бу́дешь есть, я пригото́влю чай и ко́фе.

While it rained, I did all of the lessons and wrote five letters.

While you eat, I'll make the tea and coffee.

11.9 CONSTRUCTIONS WITH THE WORDS ТОЛЬКО, ЕДИНСТВЕННЫЙ
Function: Expressing *only* vs. *the only one*

Мир русских
Lesson 1
Pages 28-30

The adverb **то́лько** and the adjective **еди́нственный** are frequently translated as *only*. This should cause few difficulties, if one remembers to use **то́лько** in situations where an adverb is appropriate and to form conjunctions, and **еди́нственный** to modify nouns.

Constructions with the word то́лько

1)   Не то́лько..., но и — **not only..., but also**

Он **не то́лько** слы́шал об э́том, **но и** ви́дел э́то.	He **not only** heard about it, **but also** saw it.
Он **не то́лько** музыка́нт, **но и** худо́жник.	He is **not only** a musician, **but also** a painter.

2)   То́лько что — **only just, just**

Где Пе́тя? Он **то́лько что** был здесь!	Where is Peter? He was **just** here!
Я ещё ничего́ не зна́ю, я **то́лько что** прие́хал.	I don't know anything yet, I've only **just** arrived.

3)   Как то́лько — **as soon as**

Как то́лько я вошёл в ко́мнату, зазвони́л телефо́н.	**As soon as** I entered the room, the telephone rang.

The word Еди́нственный

1)   Еди́нственный— **the only, the only one**

Он **еди́нственный** челове́к, кото́рый зна́ет об э́том.	He is **the only** person who knows about it.
Еди́нственный иностра́нный язы́к, кото́рый он зна́ет, это францу́зский.	**The only** foreign language he knows is French.
Еди́нственная вещь, кото́рая мне сейча́с нужна́, это хоро́шая кни́га.	**The only** thing that I need now is a good book.

2)   When used without a noun **еди́нственный/еди́нственная** means the *only person*, while **еди́нственное** means the *only thing*.

Он **еди́нственный**, кто зна́ет об э́том.*	He's **the only person** who knows about this.
Еди́нственное, что мне сейча́с ну́жно, это хоро́шая кни́га.*	**The only thing** that I need now is a good book.

*****Note:** Кто and что are used instead of кото́рый in sentences when the main clause is without nouns. In the above sentences, the subjects in the main clauses are expressed by a pronoun and an adjective standing for a noun.

3)   The adjective **единственный** is usually not used with the word *one*; just as in English, Russian uses **только один** to mean *only one*.

У них **только один** ребёнок.	They have **only one** child.

Один-единственный is used as a synonym for **только один** to emphasize the soleness of someone or something, or to emphasize how small the number of something is.

У них **один-единственный** ребёнок.	They have **but one** child.
У меня **одна-единственная** неделя отпуска.	I have **only one** week off from work.

11.10 TEMPORAL PHRASES USED AS SUBORDINATE CONJUNCTIONS IN COMPLEX SENTENCES: ПЕРЕД ТЕМ, КАК; ПРЕЖДЕ ЧЕМ; ДО ТОГО, КАК; ПОСЛЕ ТОГО, КАК

Function: Actions taking place before and after

> Мир русских
> Lesson 7
> Pages 228-229

Time relationships in complex sentences can be expressed with the help of conjunctive phrases—conjunctions which express a time frame for a given action or verb: *before I leave...*, *after I finish...*, etc. Note the use of these phrases with verbs below:

1)   **Перед тем, как**—before

Перед тем, как *срубить* берёзку, Эвенк долго просил прощения у неё.	**Before** *chopping down* the birch, the Evenk asked it for forgiveness for a long time. (The action of the main clause of the sentence occurs prior to that of the subordinate clause.)

2)   **Прежде чем**—before

Прежде чем *писать* статью, надо составить её план.	**Before** *writing* an article, one should create an outline of it.

3)   **До того, как**—until, before

До того как *начнётся* урок, надо повторить стихотворение.	**Before** the lesson *begins*, it's necessary to review the poem.

4)   **После того, как**—after

После того, как он это *сделал*, я ему больше не поверю.	**After** he *did* (that), I won't believe him anymore.

Chapter 12

WORD-BUILDING
Словообразова́ние

12.1 How are words formed in Russian? As in English, Russian has many cognates (words related to one another based on a common root or stem). If we know some roots, we can guess at the meanings of unknown words having these roots. Consider words formed with the root **-уч/-ук** *learning*:

nouns	adjectives	verbs
уче́ние — learning	уче́бный (-ая, -ое, -ые) — (pertaining to education): academic	учи́ться / научи́ться — to study, learn, be a student
уче́бник — textbook		учи́ть/вы́учить — to learn, study something/ learn by heart
учени́к, учени́ца — male, female student	нау́чный (-ая, -ое, -ые) —(pertaining to science); scientific	
учи́тель(ница) — male/ (female) teacher		учи́ть/научи́ть — to teach
учёный — scientist, scholar, researcher	учи́тельский (-ая, -ое, -ие) — (pertaining to teachers); teacher's...	изуча́ть/изучи́ть — to study something/master a subject
нау́ка — science		

Some Russian words, especially those connected with certain types of occupational fields and professions, have a connection with their English counterparts:

Russian -ика, -ия	English -ics, -istry	Russian -ик	English -ician, -ist
матема́тика	mathematics	матема́тик	mathematician
фи́зика	physics	фи́зик	physicist
хи́мия	chemistry	хи́мик	chemist

Russian -ология	English -ology	Russian -олог	English -ologist
биоло́гия	biology	био́лог	biologist
психоло́гия	psychology	психо́лог	psychologist
зооло́гия	zoology	зоо́лог	zoologist

Many Russian words contain prefixes and/or suffixes to cognate roots. By adding prefixes to verbs, the verbs may change their meaning. For example, verbs with the root **-пис-** *writing, script,* may take on various meanings according to their prefixes:

в-	in, into	впи́сывать/вписа́ть	to write in
вы-	out, out of	выпи́сывать/вы́писать	to write out, subscribe
за-	begin, do a little	запи́сывать/записа́ть	to take notes
на-	on, onto	писа́ть/написа́ть	to write
о-	about, concerning	опи́сывать/описа́ть	to describe
пере-	re(do), do over, across	перепи́сывать/ перепиcа́ть	to rewrite, transcribe
под-	under	подпи́сывать/ подписа́ть	to sign (something)
про-	about, concerning	пропи́сывать/ прописа́ть	to prescribe
с-	from	спи́сывать/списа́ть	to copy

12.2 WORDS WHICH NAME DOMESTIC ANIMALS AND THEIR OFFSPRING: (-ОНОК/-ЁНОК, -АТА, -ЯТА)
Function: Talking about farm animals

> Faces and Voices
> Chapter 6 A
> Pages 153, 159-160

In Russian, baby animals are designated by the suffixes **-онок (-ёнок)** in the singular and **-áта (-я́та)** in the plural.

Sample word formations

кот	cat	котёнок	kitten	котя́та	kittens
тигр	tiger	тигрёнок	little tiger	тигря́та	tiger cubs
гусь	goose	гусёнок	gosling	гуся́та	goslings
ку́рица	chicken	цыплёнок	chick	цыпля́та	chicks
у́тка	duck	утёнок	duckling	утя́та	ducklings
волк	wolf	волчóнок	wolf cub	волчáта	wolf cubs
медвéдь	bear	медвежóнок	cub	медвежáта	bear cubs

12.3 THE DIMINUTIVE SUFFIX -KA
Function: Talking about common household objects

> Мир ру́сских
> Lesson 2
> Page 60

Note the use of the words **ру́чка**, **нóжка**, **спи́нка**, and **кровáтка**. In these words the suffix **-ка** is used to form a diminutive of the nouns **рукá** (hand), **ногá** (leg), **спинá** (back), and **кровáть** (bed) — all feminine nouns denoting objects. The diminutive in Russian seems to make the object seem smaller and more endearing to the speaker. For example, the word **ру́чка**, *pen*, from the word **рукá**, literally means *little arm*. The diminutive meaning thus usually conveys a cherishing, tender attitude toward the object. This is a very important feature of Russian.

The suffix **-ка** not only forms diminutives, it also forms new, related words. Thus, the words **ру́чка**, **нóжка**, **спи́нка** may name *a handle of a door* (**ру́чка двéри**), *the leg of a chair* (**нóжка сту́ла**), *the back of a sofa* (**спи́нка дивáна**).

12.4 NAMING THINGS WITH THE DIMINUTIVE SUFFIX -KA
Function: Naming objects in a different way

> Мир ру́сских
> Lesson 8
> Page 275

The suffix **-ка** is also used to form nouns that name things. The nouns formed are semantically linked with an adjective-noun word group.

Третьякóвская галерéя	**Третьякóвка**	Tretyakov Gallery
пятилéтный план	**пятилéтка**	five-year plan
дом в дéсять этажéй	**десятиэтáжка**	ten-story building

This is a productive suffix used in conversational style. Note some other words with this suffix that name common places or things:

| «Вечéрняя Москвá» (газéта) | *"Evening Moscow"* (newspaper) | **«Вечéрка»** |

Тага́нская пло́щадь	Taganskaya Square (Moscow)	**Тага́нка**
Библиоте́ка иностра́нной литерату́ры	Library of Foreign Literature	**иностра́нка**
трёхэта́жный дом	three-story building	**трёхэта́жка**

12.5 THE SUFFIXES -НИК/-НИЦА, -АНИН/-ЯНИН, -СК/-ОВСК; THE PREFIXES НЕДО- AND ПЕРЕ-

Function: Naming types, professions and personalities of people; expressing the connotations *over-*, *mis-*, and *under-*

Мир русских
Lesson 6
Pages 196-198

The suffix -ник/-ница The suffix **-ник** is used to form a noun that names a male person: **да́чник** (a person who owns a country home), **помо́щник** (a helper), **зави́стник** (an envious person), **защи́тник** (a defender).

The suffix **-ница** is used to form an equivalent feminine noun **да́чница, помо́щница, зави́стница, защи́тница.**

Note the names for different types of people, based on their involvement:

noun		male	person	female
рабо́та	work	рабо́тник	worker	рабо́тница
о́тпуск	vacation	отпускни́к	vacationer	отпускни́ца
любо́вь	love	любо́вник	lover	любо́вница
по́мощь	help	помо́щник	helper	помо́щница
шко́ла	school	шко́льник	schoolkid	шко́льница
чертёж	drawing	чертёжник	draftsperson	чертёжница
колхо́з	collective farm	колхо́зник	farm worker	колхо́зница
пожа́р	fire	пожа́рник	fireman	пожа́рница

The suffix -а́нин/-я́нин The suffix **-анин (-янин)** is used with the names of cities or other nouns to form masculine nouns that refer to male persons: **горожа́нин** (a city-dweller), **крестья́нин** (a peasant), **северя́нин** (a person who lives in the north), **киевля́нин** (a Kievan).

The **-ин** of the suffix is dropped in the formation of the plural and a **-е** is added: **крестья́не, северя́не,** and **киевля́не.**

The suffix **-ка** is used to form equivalent feminine nouns: **горожа́нка, крестья́нка, северя́нка, киевля́нка.**

The **-ин** of the masculine noun is dropped and an **-е** added to form the plural of these nouns: **горожа́не, крестья́не, северя́не, киевля́не.**

main noun		masculine	feminine	plural
А́нглия	England	англича́нин	англича́нка	англича́не
Росси́я	Russia	россия́нин	россия́нка	россия́не
крестья́нин	peasant	крестья́нин	крестья́нка	крестья́не
го́род	town	горожа́нин	горожа́нка	горожа́не
о́стров	island	островитя́нин	островитя́нка	островитя́не
юг	south	южа́нин	южа́нка	южа́не

христиа́нство	Christianity	христиа́нин	христиа́нка	христиа́не
мусульма́нство	Islam	мусульма́нин	мусульма́нка	мусульма́не
иудаи́зм	Judaism	иуде́й	иуде́йка	иуде́и*
Болга́рия	Bulgaria	болга́рин	болга́рка	болга́ры*

*Note: The plural ending here is different from the other examples.

The suffix -ск/-овск

The suffix **-ск (-овск)** is one of the suffixes used to form adjectives: **го́род-ск-о́й**, (urban, city...), **толст-о́вск-ий** (Tolstoy's, of Tolstoy), **моско́в-ск-ий** (Muscovite, of Moscow), **де́т-ск-ий** (kid's...).

Sample sentences

Мари́я и Кэн хотя́т поступи́ть в **Моско́вский** госуда́рственный университе́т.	Maria and Ken want to enter **Moscow** State University.
Су́сан и Ли́нда не о́чень лю́бят **городско́й** тра́нспорт.	Susan and Linda don't like **city** (public) transportation all that much.
Моя́ сестра́ хо́дит в **де́тский** сад.	My sister goes to **kinder**garten.

The prefixes недо- and пере-

The prefix **недо-** denotes **incompleteness** of an action, or **insufficiency** by comparison with the norm:

недое́сть	to not finish eating
недоспа́ть	to not get enough sleep
недоплати́ть	to not pay enough
недопоня́ть	to misunderstand

The prefix **пере-** has an opposite meaning, that of **exceeding the norm:**

перее́сть	to overeat
переспа́ть	to oversleep
переплати́ть	to overpay

12.6	**THE FORMATION OF COMPOUND ADJECTIVES AND NOUNS** *Function:* Expressing more than one quality or concept in one word	Мир ру́сских Lesson 7 Page 232

Compounds are formed by combining the stems of words.

Compound adjectives Compound adjectives are formed by combining the stems of:

1) **two adjectives** — drop the adjectival stem from the first adjective and add **-о-** (or **-е-** for soft stems) as a connecting suffix:

перворождённый (first-born)—(пе́рвый, рождённый)

---

2)   *an adjective and a noun* — drop the adjectival stem from the adjective and add -o- (or -e- for soft stems) as a connecting suffix:

синеглáзый (blue-eyed)—(синий, глаз)

Compound nouns Compound nouns are formed in the following ways:

1)   *two nouns* are joined by the vowels -o- or -e- :

ядохимикáты (poisonous chemicals)—(яд, химикáты),

2)   *a noun and a verb stem* are combined by the vowels -o- or -e- :

мясорýбка (meat grinder)—(мясо, рýбка)
водопровóд (plumbing) —(водá, проводить)

combined words				compound adjective or noun	
книга	book	любить	to love	книголюб	book-lover
хлеб	bread	завóд	factory	хлебозавóд	bread factory
крéсло	armchair	кровáть	bed	крéсло-кровáть	futon, roll-out couch
сýхо (сухóй)	dry	фрýкты	fruit	сухофрýкты	dried fruit
дóлго (дóлгий)	long	жить	to live	долгожитель	one who lives many years
слáдо (слáдкий)	sweet	есть	to eat	сладоéжка	sweet tooth
прóшло (прóшлый)	past, last	год	year	прошлогóдний	last year's
стáро (стáрый)	old	москóвский	Moscow	старомоскóвский	old Moscow
мясо	meat	молокó	milk	мясо-молóчный	meat-and-milk
áнгло (английский)	English	рýсский	Russian	áнгло-рýсский	English-Russian

12.7 ADJECTIVES WITH AUGMENTATIVE SUFFIXES
Function: Making a quality stronger

Мир русских
Lesson 7
Page 233

Adjectives with the suffix -**ющий** or -**ущий** are intensified in meaning, and are more common in informal speech.

| длинный | длинн-ющий | (очень длинный) | very long |
| большой | больш-ущий | (очень большой) | very big |

very...

		masc.	**fem.**	**neut.**	**pl.**
толстый	fat	толстущий	толстущая	толстущее	толстущие
худой	thin	худющий	худющая	худющее	худющие
злой	evil	злющий	злющая	злющее	злющие
синий	blue	синющий	синющая	синющее	синющие
хитрый	sly, crafty	хитрющий	хитрющая	хитрющее	хитрющие
жадный	greedy	жаднющий	жаднющая	жаднющее	жаднющие
кислый	sour	кислющий	кислющая	кислющее	кислющие
скучный	boring	скучнющий	скучнющая	скучнющее	скучнющие

12.8 DIMINUTIVE SUFFIXES -ОК, -ЕНЬК, -ЮШК : TERMS OF ENDEARMENT

Function: Using conversational forms to talk about people you are close to, or to make a person or quality more endearing

Мир русских
Lesson 9
Pages 305-307

The suffixes -**ок**, -**еньк**, -**юшк** attach a diminutive or affectionate meaning to nouns and adjectives. -**Ок** is added to masculine nouns only: **сын — сынок** (little son), **старик — старичок** (little old man).

друг	friend	дружок	little friend
лист	leaf (from tree)	листок	sheet (of paper)
снег	snow	снежок	light snow
орех	nut	орёшек	little nut
гриб	mushroom	грибок	little mushroom
город	city	городок	small city, town

-**Еньк /а** is added to feminine nouns and masculine nouns with feminine roots: **дочь — доченька** (little daughter), **Маша — Машенька** (little Masha), **дядя — дяденька** (little uncle, man), **нога — ноженька** (little leg). -**Еньк** is also added to adjectives: **родной — родненький** (little 'related' one—*sometimes said to someone in the same family*), **молодой — молоденький** (youngish).

рука	arm	рученька	little arm
старый	old	старенький	little old...
красный	red	красненький	little red...
умный	smart	умненький	smart little...
худой	thin, skinny	худенький	skinny little...
простой	simple	простенький	plain little...

The suffix -юшк may be added to feminine, neuter, or masculine nouns: по́ле — по́люшко (small field), Воло́дя — Воло́дюшка (little Volodya).

го́ре	grief	го́рюшко	little bit of grief
хозя́йка	owner, boss	хозя́юшка	little boss
Ва́ня	Vanya	Ва́нюшка	little Vanya

<table>
<tr><td>12.9 THE PREFIX БЕЗ- (БЕС-)
Function: Talking about things that are missing</td><td>Мир русских
Lesson 9
Page 307</td></tr>
</table>

The prefix **без-** (as well as its orthographical variant **бес-**) indicates a condition or occurrence in which something is missing or absent. This is true for both nouns and adjectives. For example:

ве́тер	безве́трие (нет ве́тра)	no wind; calm
коне́чный	бесконе́чный (нет конца́)	endless
вку́сный	безвку́сный (нет вку́са)	tasteless
ве́ра	безве́рие	disbelief
грани́ца	безграни́чность	infinity; endlessness
споко́йный	беспоко́йный	restive; anxious

Below are additional examples. Note that nouns denoting a concept or abstract idea often end with the suffix **-ность**. Both nouns and adjectives are included:

опа́сность	danger	безопа́сность	safety
духо́вность	spirituality	бездухо́вность	without spirituality
страх	fear	бесстра́шие	fearlessness
коне́ц	end	бесконе́чность	endlessness
душа́	soul	безду́шие	heartlessness
жа́лость	pity	безжа́лостность	ruthlessness
Бог	God	безбо́жие	godlessness
ра́достный	joyful	безра́достный	joyless
челове́чный	humane	безчелове́чный	inhumane
я́дерный	nuclear	безя́дерный	non-nuclear
кла́ссовой	class	бескла́ссовой	classless
у́мный	clever	безу́мный	senseless

Index of Functions

Common functional and topical uses for Russian have been grouped and alphabetized below. Grammar points from the text related to the constructions, vocabulary and grammar rules necessary to express each function are written in the corresponding right-hand column. The list of functions below, while not exhaustive, provides a listing of topical language usage covered in current textbooks and foreign language learning frameworks.

Index of Russian Grammatical System

The index below presents a more formal, or traditional, outline of the Russian grammatical system. Grammar points in the right-hand column correspond to the location of each topic within the text. The List of Reference Tables and Comprehensive Table of Contents provide additional reference to grammar topics.